William Oxford

Oxford's senior speaker: A collection of exercises in declamation, recitation and representation

For advanced classes

William Oxford

Oxford's senior speaker: A collection of exercises in declamation, recitation and representation
For advanced classes

ISBN/EAN: 9783337274757

Printed in Europe, USA, Canada, Australia, Japan

Cover: Foto ©Paul-Georg Meister /pixelio.de

More available books at **www.hansebooks.com**

THE NEW AMERICAN SERIES.

OXFORD'S

SENIOR SPEAKER.

A COLLECTION OF

EXERCISES IN DECLAMATION, RECITATION AND REPRESENTATION.

For Advanced Classes.

BY

WILLIAM OXFORD,

AUTHOR OF "THE JUNIOR SPEAKER," ETC.

WITH NINETY PORTRAITS AND ILLUSTRATIONS.

PHILADELPHIA:
J. H. BUTLER & COMPANY.

PREFACE.

IN a book bearing the title of "Speaker" the student of elocution looks for a class of pieces somewhat different from the majority of those he finds in a "Reader." The distinction, however, does not seem to be very carefully observed by compilers. Consequently, a good deal of unavailable matter is found in books promising by their title such pieces as may be suitable for declamation or recitation from memory. These pieces are comparatively rare in literature, and so, in order to make a bulky volume, much matter is generally admitted that is not wanted in a "Speaker," however appropriate in a "Reader."

In the present collection the endeavor has been to have *all* the pieces of such a character that this objection may not apply, and that the book may justify its title. The various exercises, declamatory, hortatory, pathetic, humorous, descriptive, and dramatic, are unusually numerous, and have been carefully selected and tested with a view to their elocutionary fitness and dramatic unity of purpose. Several of these are protected by copyright, and are indicated in the table of Contents by an asterisk, while many others are now for the first time presented in an elocutionary collection. Should some old favorites be missed, they may perhaps be found in "Oxford's Junior Speaker," the smaller illustrated book of the series.

To quicken and enlarge the interest of the student, likenesses of the most celebrated orators are freely introduced in this higher book; nor are the poets and moralists, from whom contributions have been culled, forgotten. This feature, now for the first time appearing in a "Speaker," will, it is believed, be readily appreciated. To form some idea of the face and figure of a Chatham, a Mirabeau, a Burke, a Webster, a Calhoun, must enhance in no slight degree the satisfaction with which extracts from their speeches are studied and declaimed. As will be seen from the " List of Illustrations," page 15, pains have been taken to have the likenesses authentic. The larger number of them are here for the first time published on wood.

W. O.

CONTENTS.

I.—PIECES IN PROSE.

MORAL, DESCRIPTIVE, AND OCCASIONAL.

POLITICAL AND SENATORIAL.

CONTENTS.

II.—PIECES IN VERSE.

LYRICAL, DESCRIPTIVE, COMMEMORATIVE, ETC.

Alphabetical List of Authors.

LIST OF ILLUSTRATIONS.*

* All the engravings in this work were executed by John Andrew & Son, Boston.

ATTITUDES OF REPOSE.

ELOCUTION AS AN ART.

ARTICULATION AND PRONUNCIATION.

THE first step to success as an elocutionist is the attainment of a distinct, audible and engaging delivery. Words uttered clearly and distinctly—dropped, as Austin expresses it, "like beautiful coins newly issued from the mint, perfectly finished, neatly struck by the proper organ"—do not require half the vocal effort to make them audible that the same words would if precipitately and indistinctly emitted.

To acquire this clear, distinct utterance, begin with exercises limited to the one act of proper articulation. Practice the vowel and consonant sounds first in their elements, then united in syllables, in words, in sentences; and do this, *at first*, with exclusive reference to accuracy, clearness and audibility. Words thus uttered may be said to be uttered *mechanically*.

To make reading *significant* will be the next step; and now not only must the words be nicely articulated, and those meant to join in sense be completely joined in pronunciation, but the various relations of clause to clause and of sentence to sentence must be made manifest by

17

the inflections of the voice. *We must know these relations beforehand, or as we proceed in reading, in order to convey their full significance to the hearer.*

To become an *expressive* reader, the student must cease to think himself a reader, and be a speaker; for the principles of *reading* and *speaking* are the same, though the latter may allow more action and emotion than the former.

If it be asked, In what does *expression* consist, over and above the modulation which conveys the sense? the answer is that it consists in the quality of the tone imparted by passion or emotion, and that it cannot be genuine unless the passion or emotion is real. Expression, therefore, cannot be taught like articulation and modulation, but it may be drawn out, where nature has furnished the material, by the force of example and the exercise of the imagination.

With a voice flexible, capable of transition, resonant and sympathetic, the facile speaker finds that words serve him as colors do the painter. His voice, charged with the execution of the picture he would present, will by turns be sweet, harsh, lively, severe, insinuating, cold, fervent, humble, arrogant, majestic, simple, wrathful, affectionate, expressing all the various sentiments of the human heart, and illustrating all ages and conditions.

To attempt to teach this highest order of elocution, the *expressive*, by any system of rule, sign or notation, is unphilosophical and hopeless, likely to defeat the very object it would aid. We cannot supply the imaginative and emotional faculties which are needed in the work.

By *pronunciation*, in its restricted sense, we understand the exact employment in utterance of the proper vowel and consonant sounds and accents which custom has established. As leading authorities differ in their mode of expressing these sounds, and in the degree of importance they attach to nice shades of difference, great care should be taken in training the voice to follow those modes which the best usage has sanctioned.

A not uncommon fault is the attempt to give certain letters or combinations their regular sound, although usage has introduced a modification to which all intelligent teachers conform. Thus we hear the *ai* in *again* pronounced as long *a* instead of short *e*, as it ought to be; the *ee* in *been* pronounced as long *e* instead of short *i;* the unaccented vowel sounded in *even, heaven, evil*, etc.; the *u* in *minute* (the noun) pronounced with its regular long sound instead of the sound of short *i; apron* pronounced as written, instead of *a'purn*. These faults, as they exhibit either affectation or ignorance, ought to be shunned.

The power of articulation constitutes a marked difference between men and brutes. The latter, being unable to articulate, can only utter indistinct sounds. There can be no good elocution without a pure, accurate articulation. Be careful to give to every word its proper sound, however rapid your utterance. Do not say *an* for *and*, *spere* for *sphere*, *prmote* for *promote*. Do not add to a word a sound that does not belong to it. Do not say *helum* for *helm*, *chasum* for *chasm*, *acrost* for *across*, *lawr* for *law*, *git* for *get*, *kittle* for *kettle*, *kindniss* for *kindness*.

Distinguish between *r* trilled as in *rage*, and untrilled as in *more*. The practice of running words together, so as to make two or more sounds like one, is not proper in English. Do not say *beforeher* instead of *before her;* *acrosser*, instead of *across her*, etc. Let every word be enunciated separately and clearly. When a word ends with *s* and the next begins with *s*, the first must be pronounced distinctly and unmingled with the second; as, *the hosts still fought, the mists seem gathering*, etc. Do not pervert the sound of *aw* into *or;* do not say *droring* for *drawing, sorring* for *sawing*.

Too much precision in utterance is almost as offensive as its opposite. There are some speakers so over-precise as to fall into the error of sounding the vowel in the last syllable of such words as *evil, even, heaven, shovel*, etc. Let them consult their dictionaries, and they will see their error.

INFLECTION, EMPHASIS, PAUSE.

The *rising* inflection is that upward turn of the voice which we generally use at the comma, or in asking a question which begins with a verb; as, "Did he say no′ ?"

The *falling* inflection is generally, though not always, heard at the colon and semicolon, and must necessarily be heard in answer to the last question: "He did‵; he said no‵." Both these inflections are found in the following passage: "Does Cæsar deserve fame‵ or blame‵?" The slide upward, primarily, signifies suspension or incompleteness, and the downward slide completion. The rising inflection is the tone of doubt and entreaty. In every conversation the upward or downward slide of the voice suggests either that the speaker has not finished the sentence or that he has entirely concluded the period.

The peculiar emotion with which a question is put is the true guide to the inflection. Rules, therefore, for inflecting the voice, are likely to mislead. Direct questions, or those commencing with a verb, and which can be grammatically answered by a simple *Yes* or *No*, generally take the rising inflection; as, "Will you ride′ ?" "Can he read′ ?" But a direct question, to which the answer is anticipated, takes the falling inflection, as, "Is not that a beautiful sunset‵ ?" A direct question, made emphatic by passion, may also take the falling inflection.

Emphasis is the mode of drawing attention to one or more words in a sentence, by pronouncing them with a greater volume and duration of sound and in a higher or lower note than the adjoining words. In the sentence, "I do not *ask*, I *demand*, your attention," the italicised words are the emphatic. That emphasis which is suggested by the sense is the most proper. Let a speaker be sure of the sense of what he is uttering, and his emphasis will be natural and varied. In comparison with this general rule, all minor rules are worse than useless.

"*Pauses*," says Knowles, "are essential only where the omission would obscure the sense. The orator who, in the act of delivering himself, is studiously solicitous about parceling his words, is sure to leave the best part of his work undone. He delivers words, not thoughts. Deliver thoughts, and words will take care of themselves. *Mind* is the thing."

GESTURE AND ACTION.

Modulation, inflection and vocal expression, however perfect, would fail to give delivery its full impressiveness, if the *face* and *whole body* did not sympathetically manifest the feeling which vibrates in the tones. Nothing can be more spiritless and unnatural than rigid stillness on the part of the orator. Unaided by language, a person may by gesture alone convey his meaning to another; whereas, without it, the most powerful language will often be tame and ineffective. "With the hand alone," says Sheridan, "we can demand a promise, call, dismiss, threaten, supplicate, ask, deny, manifest joy, sorrow, detestation, fear, admiration," etc.

But the tendency to gesticulate is so natural that instruction will generally be needed rather to subdue and chasten than to produce gesticulation. To a speaker of any animation, the greatest difficulty is to stand still. The judicious employment of moderate gesture is more effective than any possible amplification of spasmodic attitudes or redundancy of grimace. No one can recite with propriety what he does not feel, and the key to gesture, as well as to moderation, is earnestness. No actor can portray character unless he can realize it, and he can only realize it by making it for the time his own.

As the head gives the chief grace to the person, so does it principally contribute to the expression of grace in delivery. It must be held in an erect and natural position, for when drooped, it is expressive of humility; when turned upward, of arrogance; when inclined to one side, it expresses languor; and when stiff and rigid, it indicates a lack of ease and self-possession. Its movements should be suited to the character of the delivery; they should accord with the gesture, and fall in with the action of the hand and the motion of the body.

The eyes, which are of the utmost consequence in aiding the expression of the orator, are generally to be directed as the gesture points, except when we have occasion to condemn or refuse, or to require an object to be removed; on which occasion we should at the same moment express aversion in our countenance and reject by our gesture. A listless, inanimate expression of countenance will always detract from the effect of the most eloquent sentiments and the most appropriate utterance.

In the natural order of passionate expression, looks are first, gestures second, and words last. Inexpressive motions should always be avoided. No gesture should be made without a reason for it; and when any position has been assumed, there should be no change from it without a reason. The habit of allowing the hands to fall to the side immediately after every gesture produces an ungracefully restless effect. A gesture that illustrates nothing is worse than useless. It destroys the effect of really appropriate movements. Perhaps the most difficult part of delivery is gracefully to stand still. Let the speaker study this. It was happily said by Churchill, in describing Garrick's acting, " Each start is Nature, and each pause is Thought."

DELIVERY OF DIALOGUES.

In a dialogue between two, each speaker should, as a general rule, stand obliquely, except in passages not directly addressed to the other, or where inattention is to be expressed. The party to the dialogue who is listening should, for the most part, let his arms hang naturally by his side, or with hands approaching, unless what is said by the other is of a character to excite agitation or surprise; or he may, with propriety, occasionally stand with arms folded, or with the right hand in the left breast, or the left in the right.

In dialogues having more than two characters for representation, the persons should be arranged in a picturesque manner, agreeably to the laws of perspective.

Before being adopted for representation, the *business*, as it is technically called, of the dialogue should be fully marked in; all the action, even to walking across the stage and the change of position by one or more of the characters, should be clearly noted. The directions of exit and entrance, whether on the right or left, should be all prearranged and marked. In marking the relative positions, etc., let R. stand for right; L. for left; C. for Centre; R. C. for Right of Centre; L. C. for Left of Centre, etc. To indicate a crossing of the stage from right to left, the following abbreviation may be used, namely, X to L.

Passages marked for *aside* utterance should be so delivered as to be fully intelligible to the audience, though they are supposed to be un-heard by the other person or persons on the stage.

Bowing to the audience, on entering to take part in a dialogue, should, as a general rule, be avoided, inasmuch as it may interfere greatly with the effect upon the imagination which it may be desirable to produce. When Brutus and Cassius enter quarreling, it detracts from the abrupt-ness and naturalness of the scene to preface it with a formal bow to an audience. Still, there may be occasions at the close of a dialogue where a bow is not inappropriate.

We need not urge the importance of being perfect in the language of a part. Nothing so destroys the illusion of a representation as to hear the prompter's voice breaking in, or to see any one of the *dramatis per-sonæ* under the embarrassment of not knowing what to say.

EXERCISES IN INFLECTION.

1. For I am persuaded that neither death', nor life'—nor angels', nor principalities', nor powers'—nor things present', nor things to come'— nor height', nor depth', nor any other' creature—shall be able to sepa-rate us from the love of God'.

2. They, through faith, subdued kingdoms', wrought righteousness', obtained promises', stopped the mouths of lions', quenched the violence of fire', escaped the edge of the sword'—out of weakness were made strong', waxed valiant in fight', and turned to flight the armies of the aliens'.

3. Can such things be',
   And overcome us like a summer cloud',
   Without our special wonder'?

4. Who can look down upon the grave, even of an enemy', and not feel a compunctious throb that he should ever have warred with the poor handful of earth that lies mouldering before him'?

5. O my son Absalom'! my son', my son Absalom! Would God I had died for thee, Absalom', my son', my son'!   .

6. If I were an American', as I am an Englishman', while a foreign troop was landed in my country', I never' would lay down my arms'— never', never', never'!

7. Could you come back to me, Douglas', Douglas',
   In the old likeness that I knew',
   I would be so faithful', so loving', Douglas',
   Douglas', Douglas', tender and true'.

Stretch out your hand to me', Douglas', Douglas',
  Drop forgiveness from heaven' like dew';
As I lay my hand on your dead heart, Douglas',
  Douglas', Douglas', tender and true'.

8. How shall I curse' whom God hath not cursed'? or how shall I defy' whom the Lord' hath not' defied'?

9. Abhor the sword'? Stigmatize the sword'? No! for at its blow a giant nation started from the waters of the Atlantic', and by the redeeming magic of the sword', and in the quivering of its crimson light', the crippled colony sprang into the attitude of a proud republic'—prosperous', limitless' and invincible'!

10. "Knowledge is power'." Yes', power'!—power to do what'? Power to employ the senses and faculties which God has given us' in examining the works which he has made', and thus to acknowledge, in all creation, "These are thy glorious works'!"

11. Flag of the heroes who left us their glory',
      Borne through our battle-fields' thunder and flame',
    Blazoned in song and illumined in story',
      Wave o'er us all who inherit thy fame';
        Up with our banner bright',
        Sprinkled with starry light';
    Spread its fair emblems from mountain to shore';
        While through the sounding sky',
        Loud rings the nation's cry',
      Union and Liberty'! one evermore'!

12. Swear', sir'?—I', a man', an American citizen', a Christian', swear to submit myself to the guidance and direction of other men', surrendering my *own* judgment to *their* judgment, and my own *conscience* to *their keeping'?* No', sir, no'!

13. Secession'? Peaceable secession'? Sir, your eyes and mine are never destined to see that miracle'. The dismemberment of this vast country without convulsion'! The breaking up of the fountains of the great deep without ruffling the surface'! Who is so foolish'—I beg everybody's pardon'—as to expect to see any such thing'?

14. What is a man',
    If his chief good and market of his time'
    Be but to sleep and feed'?—a beast', no more'!
    Sure, He that made us with such large discourse',
    Looking before and after, gave us not
    That capability and godlike reason'
    To rust in us unused'!

15. And what is death′, my friends, that I should fear it‵?
    To die′! why, 'tis to triumph‵! 'tis to join
    The great assembly of the good and just‵;
    Immortal worthies′, heroes′, prophets′, saints‵!
    'Tis to behold′ (oh, rapture to conceive′!)
    Those we have known and loved and lost below‵!
    To join in blest hosannas to their King‵!
    This is to die′!   Who would not die for this?
    Who would not *die′?*   Who would not live for ever‵!

16. Show me what thou'lt do‵!
    Wilt weep′? wilt fight′? wilt fast′? wilt tear′ thyself?
    Wilt drink up Esill′? eat a crocodile′?
    I'll‸ do't‵!   Dost thou come here to whine′?
    To outface me with leaping in her grave′?
    Be‵ buried quick with her, and so will I‵:
    And, if thou prate of mountains′, let them throw
    Millions of acres on us‵; till our ground,
    Singeing his pate against the burning zone,
    Make Ossa like a wart‵!   Nay, an thou'lt mou‸th,
    I'll rant as well as thou‸.

SENIOR SPEAKER.

1.—THE ENTERPRISE OF COLUMBUS.

ABOUT half a league from the little seaport of Palos, in the province of Andalusia, in Spain, stands a convent dedicated to St. Mary. Some time in the year 1486 a poor wayfaring

COLUMBUS.

stranger, accompanied by a small boy, makes his appearance on foot at the gate of this convent, and begs of the porters a little bread and water for his child. This friendless stranger is Columbus. Brought up in the hardy occupation of a mariner, occasionally serving in the fleets of his native country, with the burden of fifty years upon his frame, the unprotected foreigner makes his suit to the sovereigns of Portugal and Spain.

He tells them that the broad flat earth on which we tread is round, and he proposes, with what seems a sacrilegious hand, to lift the veil which had hung, from the creation of the world, over the bounds of the ocean. He promises by a western cours᠎ to reach the eastern shore of Asia—the region of gold, and diamonds, and spices; to extend the sovereignty of Christian kings over realms and nations hitherto unapproached and unknown; and ultimately to perform a new crusade to the Holy Land, and with the new-found gold of the East to ransom the sepulchre of our Saviour.

Who shall believe the chimerical pretension? The learned men examine it, and pronounce it futile. The royal pilots have ascertained, by their own experience, that it is a groundless scheme. The common sense and popular feeling of men have been kindled into disdain and indignation toward a project which represented one half of mankind as walking with their feet toward the other half.

Such is the reception which his proposal meets. For a long time the great cause of humanity, depending on the discovery of this fair continent, is involved in the fortitude, perseverance and spirit of the solitary stranger, already past the time of life when the pulse of adventure beats full and high. If, sinking beneath the indifference of the great, the sneers of the wise, the enmity of the masses and the persecution of a host of adversaries, high and low, he give up the thankless pursuit of his noble vision, what a hope for mankind is blasted! But he does not sink.

At length, after years of expectation, importunity and hope deferred, he launches forth upon the unknown deep to discover a new world under the patronage of Ferdinand and Isabella. From his ancient resort of Palos, which he first visited as a mendicant, in three frail barks, of which two were without decks, the great discoverer of America sails forth on the first voyage across the unexplored ocean. Such is the patronage of kings.

A few years pass by; he discovers a new hemisphere; the wildest of his visions fade into insignificance before the reality of their fulfillment; he finds a new world for Castile and Leon, and comes back to Spain loaded with chains. Republics, it is said, are ungrateful; such are the rewards of monarchies!

EDWARD EVERETT.

2.—THE ATLANTIC TELEGRAPH.

LET me offer you two feebly outlined word-pictures of events which were transacted on the same arena at the interval of nearly four centuries. The epoch of the first is the autumn of 1492. The scene is the mid-Atlantic, and on its bosom floats the frail caravel of Columbus. It is midnight, and the astonished pilots are gazing with awe on the compass needle, which has ceased to point to the north star, and has veered round to the west, and they ask the great admiral what this unheard-of variation may mean. To him it is a mystery as well as to them, but he has an explanation which contents them ; and for himself, however mysterious it may be, it is anew the finger of God bidding him sail westward still, and he follows its new pointing, till it lands him on the shore he has so often seen in his dreams. The time of the second picture is 1858. The scene, as before, is the mid-Atlantic, and on its bosom a great English steamship is silently gliding with every sail furled. It is midnight again, and the sailors, as in the caravel four centuries ago, are gazing with intent eyes upon a quivering needle. It is not now, however, a mere compass needle; but armed with a tiny mirror, it lies in the centre of a coil of wire looped to the great cable which, as electric signals pass along it, is every moment bringing the Old and the New Worlds nearer each other in time.

Every quiver to east and west that the needle makes, as the voltaic current sweeps round the coil, flashes from the mirror a spot of light on a screen, and marks a step in progress ; and all watch the face of the electrician, the Columbus of this voyage, to whom alone these spots of light are intelligible and eloquent of success. And so the mirrored, flashing galvanometer sways about till the voyage ends ; and then *Gloria in Excelsis* is literally quivered in light, as it was by its first singers the angels, and in unconscious repetition of its chant by the kneeling crews of Columbus four centuries ago. Let us wish all success to the telegraph everywhere. The best interests of the world are bound up in its progress, and its mission is em-

phatically one of peace.   It does not merely speak swiftly, but
softly; and it offers men a common speech in which all man-
kind can converse together.

"Men have spoken, men have dreamed, of a universal tongue;
  Universal speech can be only when the words are sung.
  When our harp has all its strings, and its music fills the air,
  In a universal tongue all the world shall share."

3.—A TRUE HERO.

At a great fire in London, June 22, 1861, James Braidwood lost his life
while venturing into a burning warehouse to encourage his men. He was
killed by a falling wall. Similar deaths took place at the great fire in
Boston, November, 1872.

Not at the battle front, writ of in story,
Not on the blazing wreck, steering to glory,
Not while in mortal pangs soul and flesh sever,
Died he, this hero new—hero for ever!

No pomp poetic crowned, no forms enchained him,
No friends applauding watched, no foes arraigned him;
Death found him there without grandeur or beauty—
Only an honest man doing his duty!

Just a God-fearing man, simple and lowly,
Constant at kirk and hearth, kindly and lowly;
Death found and touched him with finger in flying,
So he rose up complete—hero undying.

All now lament for him—lovingly raise him
Up from his life obscure, chronicle, praise him;
Tell his last act, done midst peril appalling,
And the last words of cheer from his lips falling.

So many a hero walks daily beside us
Till comes the hour supreme sent to divide us.
Then the Lord calls his own, like this man even,
Carried, Elijah-like, fire-winged, to heaven!

                                    MRS. MULOCK CRAIK.

4.—REGULUS TO THE ROMAN SENATE.

ILL does it become *me*, O Senators of Rome!—ill does it become Reg'ulus, after having so often stood in this venerable assembly, clothed with the supreme dignity of the republic— to stand before you now a captive—the captive of Carthage! For though outwardly I am free, the heaviest of chains, the pledge of a Roman consul, makes me the bondsman of the Carthaginians. They have my promise to return to them in the event of the failure of this their embassy. My life is at their mercy. My honor is at no man's mercy. It is my own— my own even in death.

Ambassadors of Carthage! ye have brought me here, expecting that I would argue your cause, and that my very presence would secure your object. Listen, then, to what I now say, in your presence, to the Senate. Conscript Fathers, there is but one course to be pursued. Abandon all thought of peace. Reject the overtures of Carthage. What! Give back to her a thousand able-bodied men, and receive in return this one attenuated, war-worn, fever-wasted frame, this weed whitened in a dungeon's darkness, pale and sapless, which no kindness of the sun, no softness of the summer breeze, can ever restore to health and vigor? It must not, it shall not, be!

Were Regulus what he once was, he might pause, and proudly think he were well worth a thousand of the foe. But *now*— his very armor would be a burthen now! But if he cannot live, he can at least die, for his country. Do not deny him this

3 *

supreme consolation. Every indignity, every torture, which Carthage shall heap on his dying hours, will be better than a trumpet's call to your armies. Romans will remember only Regulus, their fellow-soldier and their leader. They will forget his defeats and think only of his triumphs—of his many services to the republic. Tunis, Sardinia, Sicily—every well-fought field won by his blood and theirs—will flash on their remembrance and kindle their avenging wrath. And so shall Regulus, in the *spirit*, fight better against the foe than he ever fought in the *flesh*.

To you, Conscript Fathers, to you and to Rome, I confide my family. I leave them no legacy but my name, no estate but my example.

Ambassadors of Carthage, I have spoken, though not as you desired. I am your captive. Lead me back to whatever fate your disappointment and your wrath may prepare for me. Doubt not that you shall find, to Roman hearts country is dearer than life, and integrity more precious than freedom.

SARGENT.

5.—THE DIGNITY OF LABOR.

THERE is dignity in toil—in toil of the hand as well as toil of the head—in toil to provide for the bodily wants of an individual life, as well as in toil to promote some enterprise of world-wide fame. All labor that tends to supply man's wants, to increase man's happiness, to elevate man's nature—in a word, all labor that is honest—is honorable too. Labor clears the forest, and drains the morass, and makes "the wilderness rejoice and blossom as the rose." Labor drives the plow, and scatters the seeds, and reaps the harvest, and grinds the corn, and converts it into bread, the staff of life. Labor, tending the pastures and sweeping the waters as well as cultivating the soil, provides with daily sustenance the nine hundred millions of the family of man. Labor gathers the gossamer web of the caterpillar, the cotton from the field and the fleece from the flock, and weaves it into raiment soft and warm and beautiful, the purple robe of the prince and the gray gown of the peasant being alike its handiwork. Labor moulds the brick, and splits the slate, and quarries the stone, and shapes the column, and rears not only the humble cottage, but the gorgeous palace, and the tapering spire, and the stately dome. Labor, diving deep into the solid earth, brings up its long-hidden stores of coal to feed ten thousand furnaces, and in millions of homes to defy the winter's cold.

Labor explores the rich veins of deeply-buried rocks, extracting the gold and silver, the copper and tin. Labor smelts the iron, and moulds it into a thousand shapes for use and ornament, from the massive pillar to the tiniest needle, from the ponderous anchor to the wire gauze, from the mighty fly-wheel of the steam-engine to the polished purse-ring or the glittering bead. Labor hews down the gnarled oak, and shapes the timber, and builds the ship, and guides it over the deep, plunging through the billows, and wrestling with the tempest, to bear to our shores the produce of every clime.

Labor, laughing at difficulties, spans majestic rivers, carries viaducts over marshy swamps, suspends bridges over deep ravines, pierces the solid mountain with its dark tunnel, blasting rocks and filling hollows, and while linking together with its iron but loving grasp all nations of the earth, verifying, in a literal sense, the ancient prophecy, "Every valley shall be exalted, and every mountain and hill shall be brought low;" labor draws forth its delicate iron thread, and stretching it from city to city, from province to province, through mountains and beneath the sea, realizes more than fancy ever fabled, while it constructs a chariot on which speech may outstrip the wind, and compete with the lightning, for the telegraph flies as rapidly as thought itself.

Labor, a mighty magician, walks forth into a region uninhabited and waste; he looks earnestly at the scene, so quiet in its desolation; then waving his wonder-working wand, those dreary valleys smile with golden harvests; those barren mountain-slopes are clothed with foliage; the furnace blazes; the anvil rings; the busy wheel whirls round; the town appears; the mart of commerce, the hall of science, the temple of religion, rear high their lofty fronts; a forest of masts gay with varied pennons rises from the harbor; representatives of far-off regions make it their resort; Science enlists the elements of earth and heaven in its service; Art, awakening, clothes its strength with beauty; Civilization smiles; Liberty is glad; Humanity rejoices; Piety exults, for the voice of industry and gladness is heard on every side.

Working men, walk worthy of your vocation! You have a noble escutcheon; disgrace it not. There is nothing really mean and low but sin. Stoop not from your lofty throne to defile yourselves by contamination with intemperance, licentiousness or any form of evil. Labor, allied with virtue, may look up to Heaven and not blush, while all worldly dignities, prostituted to vice, will leave their owner without a corner of the universe in which to hide his shame. You will most successfully prove the honor of toil by illustrating in your own persons its alliance with a sober, righteous and godly life. Be ye sure of this, that the man of toil, who works in a spirit of obedient, loving homage to God, does no less than cherubim and seraphim in their loftiest flights and holiest songs.

NEWMAN HALL.

6.—A CHINESE STORY.

NONE are so wise as they who make pretense
To know what fate conceals from mortal sense.
This moral from a tale of Ho-hang-ho
Might have been drawn a thousand years ago,
When men were left to their unaided senses,
Long ere the days of spectacles and lenses.

Two young short-sighted fellows, Chang and Ching,
Over their chopsticks idly chattering,
Fell to disputing which could see the best;
At last they agreed to put it to the test.

Said Chang, "A marble tablet, so I hear,
Is placed upon the Bo-hee temple near,
  With an inscription on it.   Let us go
  And read it (since you boast your optics so),
Standing together at a certain place
In front, where we the letters just may trace;
  Then he who quickest reads the inscription there
  The palm for keenest eyes henceforth shall bear."
"Agreed," said Ching, "but let us try it soon:
Suppose we say to-morrow afternoon."

"Nay, not so soon," said Chang; "I'm bound to go
To-morrow a day's ride from Ho-hang-ho,
  And sha'n't be ready till the following day:
  At ten A. M. on Thursday, let us say."

So 'twas arranged; but Ching was wide awake:
Time by the forelock he resolved to take;
  And to the temple went at once, and read
  Upon the tablet: "To the illustrious dead,
The chief of mandarins, the great Goh-Bang."
Scarce had he gone when stealthily came Chang,
  Who read the same; but peering closer, he
  Spied in a corner what Ching failed to see—
The words, "This tablet is erected here
By those to whom the great Goh-Bang was dear."

So on the appointed day—both innocent
As babes, of course—these honest fellows went,
  And took their distant station; and Ching said,
  "I can read plainly, 'To the illustrious dead,
The chief of mandarins, the great Goh-Bang.'"
"And is that all that you can spell?" said Chang;
  "I see what you have read, but furthermore,
  In smaller letters, toward the temple door,
Quite plain, 'This tablet is erected here
By those to whom the great Goh-Bang was dear.'"

" My sharp-eyed friend, there are no such words ! " said Ching.
" They're there," said Chang, " if I see anything,
  As clear as daylight." " Patent eyes, indeed,
  You have ! " cried Ching ; " do you think I cannot read ? "
" Not at this distance as I can," Chang said,
" If what you say you saw is all you read."

In fine, they quarreled, and their wrath increased,
Till Chang said, " Let us leave it to the priest ;
Lo ! here he comes to meet us." " It is well,"
Said honest Ching ; " no falsehood *he* will tell."

The good man heard their artless story through,
And said, " I think, dear sirs, there must be few
Blest with such wondrous eyes as those you wear :
There's no such tablet or inscription there !
There *was* one, it is true ; 'twas moved away
And placed *within* the temple yesterday."

C. P. CRANCH.

7.—COMPULSORY EDUCATION.

THE public safety demands that a huge mass of ignorance
and imbecility be not allowed to accumulate, generating untold
damage to the commonwealth. It is therefore just and proper
that Society should take measures to guard herself against
dangers thus foreseen. Compulsory education is logically
desirable and highly philosophic. But is it practicable ?

If compulsory education, after a period of discussion and
agitation, at last take its place among our laws, it will be
needful to pass another law compelling the policemen, super-
intendents and other executives to compel the parents. If this
do not make the wheels move smoothly, it will be needful, after
a proper period of waiting, to pass another law, compelling the
official compellers to do *their* duty. Continue this process far
enough, and it becomes mathematically certain that at last

every member of the community will become *officially respon-sible* to compel somebody to do something. And when every man is thus armed and made responsible for his neighbor's fidelity, the happy days have come.

Of all this we have a beautiful prophecy in the old English nursery ballad which sets forth the trials of the old woman that went to the fair and bought a kid, which was to be driven home. But the kid wouldn't go. Whereupon she appealed to the dog: "Dog, dog, bite kid. Kid won't go." The dog being easy-tempered, she appealed to the stick: "Stick, stick, beat dog; dog won't bite kid; kid won't go." The stick needed compulsion, and she called to the fire: "Fire, fire, burn stick; stick won't beat dog; dog won't bite kid; kid won't go." But the fire was slow. "Water, water, quench fire," cried the compulsory old lady. And when the water hesitated, "Ox, ox, drink water; water won't quench fire," etc. To compel the ox she found the butcher: "Butcher, butcher, kill ox." And when he was slack she appealed to the rope: "Rope, rope, hang butcher."

At last she had found the *primum mob'i-le,* and like a vision of the millennium, the whole concatenation of compulsion be-gan to go, driving and driven. I remember—I can never for-get—the delight with which I viewed it. The rope began to hang the butcher. The butcher began to kill the ox. The ox began to drink the water. The water began to quench the fire. The fire began to burn the stick. The stick began to beat the dog. The dog began to bite the kid. The kid began to go.

And so in these days, when earnest-minded patriots, viewing great evils, think out an admirable future—"If we could only get a compulsory law"—my mind makes a short question of it. Where is the rope that will begin to hang somebody? In Prussia we have no difficulty in finding the rope; compulsion works admirably there. But in this land of the free and home of the brave, I look in vain for the man or class of men to originate compulsions. "Drive on," all cry. But where is the driver?   THOS. K. BEECHER.

8.—NAPOLEON.

Out of the sanguinary chaos of the French revolution there rose a soldier whose immense ability, joined with his absolute unscrupulousness, made him now general, now consul, now autocrat. He was untruthful in an extreme degree, lying in his despatches day by day, never writing a page without bad faith—nay, even giving to others lessons in telling falsehoods. He professed friendship while plotting to betray, and quite early in his career made the wolf-and-lamb fable his guide. He got antagonists into his power by promises of clemency, and then executed them. To strike terror, he descended to barbarities like those of the bloodthirsty conquerors of old, of whom his career reminds us; as in Egypt, when, to avenge fifty of his soldiers, he beheaded two thousand fellahs, throwing their headless corpses into the Nile; or as at Jaffa, when twenty-five hundred of the garrison, who finally surrendered, were at his order deliberately massacred. Even his own officers, not over-scrupulous, as we may suppose, were shocked by his brutality, sometimes refusing to execute his sanguinary decrees.

Year after year he went on sacrificing, by tens of thousands and hundreds of thousands, the French people and the people of Europe at large, to gratify his lust of power and his hatred of opponents. To feed his insatiable ambition, and to crush those who resisted his efforts after universal dominion, he went on seizing the young men of France, forming army after army that were destroyed in destroying like armies raised by neighboring nations.

In the Russian campaign alone, out of 552,000 French left dead or prisoners, but a small portion returned to France; while the Russian force of more than 200,000 was reduced to 30,000 or 40,000; implying a total sacrifice of considerably more than half a million lives. And when the mortality on both sides by death in battle, by wounds and by disease, throughout all the Napoleonic campaigns, is summed up, it exceeds, at the lowest computation, two millions. And all this slaughter, all this suffering, all this devastation, was gone through because one man had a restless desire to be despot over all men. And now what has been thought and felt in England about the two sets of events above contrasted, and about the actors in them? For the bloodshed of the Revolution there has been utter detestation, and for those who wrought it, unqualified hate; for the immeasurably greater bloodshed which these wars of the consulate and the empire entailed, little or no horror is expressed; while the feeling toward the modern Attila, who was guilty of this bloodshed, is shown by decorating rooms with portraits and busts of him.

HERBERT SPENCER.

9.—KILLED AT THE FORD.

He is dead, the beautiful youth,
The heart of honor, the tongue of truth—
He, the life and light of us all,
Whose voice was blithe as a bugle call.

Whom all eyes followed with one consent,
The cheer of whose laugh, and whose pleasant word,
Hushed all murmurs of discontent.

Only last night, as we rode along,
Down the dark of the mountain gap,
To visit the picket-guard at the ford,
Little dreaming of any mishap,
He was humming the words of some old song:
"Two red roses he had on his cap,
And another he bore at the point of his sword."

Sudden and swift a whistling ball
Came out of a wood, and the voice was still:
Something I heard in the darkness fall,
And for a moment my blood grew chill;
I spake in a whisper, as he who speaks
In a room where some one is lying dead;
But he made no answer to what I said.

We lifted him up to his saddle again,
And through the mire and the mist and the rain
Carried him back to the silent camp,
And laid him as if asleep on his bed;
And I saw by the light of the surgeon's lamp
Two white roses upon his cheeks,
And one just over his heart, blood-red.

And I saw in a vision how far and fleet
That fatal bullet went speeding forth,
Till it reached a town in the distant North,
Till it reached a house in a sunny street,
Till it reached a heart that ceased to beat
Without a murmur, without a cry;
And a bell was tolled in that far-off town,
For one that had passed from cross to crown,
And the neighbors wondered that she should die.

                    H. W. LONGFELLOW, b. 1807.

10.—BRUTUS OVER THE DEAD LUCRETIA.

You are amazed, O Romans! even amid the general horror at Lucretia's death, that Brutus, whom you have known hitherto only as the fool, should all at once assume the language and bearing of a man! Did not the sibyl say a fool should set Rome free? I am that fool! Brutus bids Rome be free! If he has played the fool, it was to seize the wise man's opportunity. Here he throws off the mask of madness. 'Tis Lucius Junius now, your countryman, who calls upon you, by this innocent blood, to swear eternal vengeance against kings!

Look, Romans! turn your eyes on this sad spectacle—the daughter of Lucretius, Collatinus' wife! By her own hand she died. See there a noble lady, whom the ruffian lust of a Tarquin reduced to the necessity of being her own executioner to attest her innocence. Hospitably entertained by her as her husband's kinsman, Sextus, the perfidious guest, inflicted an outrage which the chaste, the generous Lucretia could not survive. Heroic matron! But once only treated as a slave, life was no longer endurable!

And if she, with her soft woman's nature, disdained a life that depended on a tyrant's will, shall we—shall *men*, with such an example before their eyes, and after five-and-twenty years of ignominious servitude—shall we, through a fear of death, delay one moment to assert our freedom? No, Romans! The favorable moment is come. The time is—now! Fear not that the army will take the part of their generals, rather than of the people. The love of liberty is natural to all, and your fellow-citizens in the camp feel the weight of oppression as sensibly as you. Doubt not they will as eagerly seize the opportunity of throwing off their yoke. Courage, Romans! The gods are for us—those gods whose temples and altars the impious Tarquin has profaned. By the blood of the wronged Lucretia, I swear—hear me, ye powers supreme—by this blood, which was once so pure and which nothing but royal villainy could have polluted, I swear that I will pursue, with fire and sword, these Tarquins to the death; nor will I ever

suffer any one of that family, or of any other family what-
soever, to be king in Rome! On to the Forum! Bear the
body hence high in the public view through all the streets!
On, Romans, on! The *fool* shall set you free.

11.—HARD WORKERS.

THERE is, in the present day, an overplus of raving about
genius and its prescriptive rights of vagabondage, its irrespon-
sibility, and its insubordination to all the laws of common
sense. Common sense is so prosaic! Yet it appears from the
history of art that the real men of genius did not rave about
anything of the kind. They were resolute workers, not idle
dreamers. They knew that their genius was not a frenzy, not
a supernatural thing, at all, but simply the colossal proportions
of faculties which, in a lesser degree, the meanest of mankind
shared with them. They knew that, whatever it was, it would
not enable them to accomplish with success the things they
undertook, unless they devoted their whole energies to the task.

" Use the pen," says a thoughtful and subtle author; "there
is no magic in it, *but it keeps the mind from staggering about.*"
This is an aphorism which should be printed in letters of gold
over the studio door of every artist. Use the pen or the brush;
do not pause, do not trifle, have no misgivings, but keep your
mind from staggering about by fixing it resolutely upon the
matter before you, and then all that you *can* do you *will* do;
inspiration will not enable you to do more. Write or paint;
act, do not hesitate. If what you have written or painted
should turn out imperfect, you can correct it, and the correc-
tion will be more efficient than that correction which takes
place in the shifting thoughts of hesitation.

You will learn from your failures infinitely more than from
the vague wandering reflections of a mind loosened from its
moorings, because the failure is absolute, it is precise, it stands
bodily before you; your eyes and judgment cannot be juggled
with; you know whether a certain verse is harmonious, whether

the rhyme is there or not there; but in the other case you not only *can* juggle with yourself, but *do* so—the very indeterminateness of your thoughts makes you do so; as long as the idea is not positively clothed in its artistic form, it is impossible accurately to say what it will be. The magic of the pen lies in the concentration of your thoughts upon an object.

Let your pen fall, begin to trifle with the blotting-paper, look at the ceiling, bite your nails, and otherwise dally with your purpose, and you waste your time, scatter your thoughts, and repress the nervous energy necessary for your task. Some men dally, hesitate and trifle until the last possible moment, and when the printer's boy is knocking at the door, they begin; necessity goading them, they write with singular success; they are astonished at themselves. What is the secret? Simply this, they have had no time to hesitate. Concentrating their powers upon the one object before them, they have done what they *could*.   G. H. LEWES.

———◦———

12.—THE BRIDAL OF GALTRIM.

THE priest's at the altar; the bride and the groom,
The bridesmaids—and gallants, with doff'd cap and plume,
Are kneeling around till the word forth is gone
That blesses the union of two into one.
But while the devout were responding "Amen,"
The blast of a war-trumpet rang through the glen,
And each man, as he sprang to his feet, gripp'd his sword,
While the fresh-plighted hand of the bride held her lord.

"Oh, hold me not, dearest!—you would not detain?
It is honor to go—'twere disgrace to remain.
The foe's at the gate; we must drive him away:
A joust is befitting a chief's wedding-day!"
He buckled his mail o'er his gay wedding garb;
He call'd for his lance, and he sprang on his barb,
And waved back a graceful adieu as he cried,
"A victor I soon will be back with my bride!"

4 *

And soon *was* he back, and a victor beside,
But 'twas to his widow, and not to his bride;
For foremost in danger the foe to repel,
In the moment of conquest the conqueror fell.
Slowly the victors return from the field,
Lamenting the knight whom they bore on his shield;
And the Lady of Galtrim, as chronicles say,
Was maid, wife and widow, and all in one day.

SAMUEL LOVER.

13.—OF REVENGE.

REVENGE is a kind of wild justice which the more man's nature runs to, the more ought law to weed it out; for as for the first wrong, it doth but offend law, but the revenge of that wrong putteth law out of office. Certainly, in taking revenge a man is but even with his enemy, but in passing it over he is superior, for it is a prince's part to pardon; and Solomon, I am sure,

LORD BACON.

saith, "It is the glory of a man to pass by an offense."

That which is past is gone and irrevocable, and wise men have enough to do with things present and to come; therefore those do but trifle with themselves who labor in past matters. There is no man doth a wrong for the wrong's sake, but thereby to purchase himself profit, or pleasure, or honor, or the like; therefore why should I be angry with a man for loving himself better than me? And if any man should do wrong merely out of ill-nature, why, yet it is but like the thorn or brier, which prick and scratch because they can do no other.

The most tolerable sort of revenge is for those wrongs which there is no law to remedy; but then let a man take heed the revenge be such as there is no law to punish, else a man's enemy is still beforehand, and it is two for one. Some, when they take revenge, are desirous the party should know when it cometh. This is the more generous, for the delight seemeth to be not so much in doing the hurt as in making the party repent. But base and crafty cowards are like the arrow that flieth in the dark. Cosmus, duke of Florence, had a desperate saying against perfidious or neglecting friends, as if those wrongs were unpardonable. "You shall read," said he, "that we are commanded to forgive our enemies, but you never read that we are commanded to forgive our friends."

But yet the spirit of Job was in a better tune. "Shall we," saith he, "take good at God's hands, and not be content to take evil also?" And so of friends in a proportion. This is certain, that a man that studieth revenge keeps his own wounds green which otherwise would heal and do well. Public revenges are for the most part fortunate, as that for the death of Cæsar, for the death of Pertinax, for the death of Henry the Third of France, and many more. But in private revenges it is not so; nay, rather vindictive persons live the life of witches, who as they are mischievous, so end they unfortunate.

LORD BACON, 1561–1626.

14.—THE DINNER AT FAYAL.

THE Portuguese pennies or *reis* (pronounced *rays*) are prodigious. It takes one thousand reis to make a dollar, and all financial estimates are made in reis. We did not know this until after we had found it out through Blucher.

Blucher said he was so happy and so grateful to be on solid land once more that he wanted to give a feast—said he had heard it was a cheap land, and he was bound to have a grand banquet. He invited nine of us, and we ate an excellent dinner at the principal hotel of Fayal.

In the midst of the jollity produced by good cigars, good wine and passable anecdotes, the landlord presented his bill.

Blucher glanced at it, and his countenance fell. He took another look, to assure himself that his senses had not deceived him, and then read the items aloud, in a faltering voice, while the roses in his cheeks turned to ashes:

"'Ten dinners, at 600 reis, 6000 reis'! Ruin and desolation! 'Twenty-five cigars, at 100 reis, 2500 reis'! O my sainted mother! 'Eleven bottles of wine, at 1200 reis, 13,200 reis'! Be with us all! 'Total, *twenty-one thousand seven hundred reis*'! The suffering Moses! There isn't money enough in the ship to pay that bill! Go! leave me to my misery, boys; I am a ruined community."

I think it was the blankest-looking party I ever saw. Nobody could say a word. It was as if every soul had been stricken dumb. Wine-glasses descended slowly to the table, their contents untasted. Cigars dropped unnoticed from nerveless fingers. Each man sought his neighbor's eye, but found in it no ray of hope, no encouragement.

At last the fearful silence was broken. The shadow of a desperate resolve settled upon Blucher's countenance like a cloud, and he rose up and said, "Landlord, this is a low, mean swindle, and I'll never stand it. Here's a hundred and fifty dollars, sir, and it's all you'll get; I'll swim in blood before I'll pay a cent more."

Our spirits rose, and the landlord's fell—at least we thought so; he was confused, at any rate, notwithstanding he had not understood a word that was said. He glanced from the little pile of gold pieces to Blucher several times, and then went out.

He must have visited an American; for when he returned, he brought back his bill translated into a language that a Christian could understand, thus:

10 dinners, 6000 reis, or	$6.00
25 cigars, 2500 reis, or	2.50
11 bottles wine, 13,200 reis, or . . .	13.20
Total, 21,700 reis, or	$21.70

Happiness reigned once more in Blucher's dinner-party. More refreshments were ordered. MARK TWAIN.

15.—PLATONIC PARADOXES.

I.

In how many strange ways human nature displays
    The caprices that enter her pate, O!
To which view you'll be led if some pages you've read
    In the Oxford translation of Plato.
    What a wonderful writer is Plato!
    And how well Jowett's pen can translate, O!
But I clearly discover, in reading him over,
    Some rather odd notions in Plato,
    Yes, *very* odd notions in Plato.

II.

The fears of the brave make us always look grave,
    And the mean little tricks of the great, O!
So the foolish things, too, that the wise say and do,
    Are ridiculous, even in Plato.
    On *some* points I quite go with Plato,
    In the same way as Addison's Cato,
But some marvelous flaws as to justice and laws
    Mark the model Republic of Plato,
    The Republic according to Plato.

III.

Every honest man grieves at the number of thieves
    That our social temptations create, O!
And our hearts are all sore for the wretchedly poor,
    And I'm sure the same feelings had Plato.
    But the system propounded by Plato
    These deplorable ills to abate, O!
Was to break off with Mammon, have all things in common!
    "Private property's gammon," said Plato;
    "It all should be public," said Plato.

IV.

There of course is no theft, when no property's left
    To give Meum and Tuum their weight, O!

And when all's a dead level, starvation and revel
    Alike are excluded by Plato.
    These Communist doctrines of Plato
    Have again come in fashion of late, O!
But the makers of money, the hoarders of honey,
    Won't be pleased with these projects of Plato,
    These leveling projects of Plato.

V.

Then the struggles and strife that attend married life,
    And that often turn love into hate, O!
Its quarrelsome courses, desertions, divorces,
    Must have hurt the fine feelings of Plato.
    But a very bad cure proposed Plato
    (For I don't think him here the *potato*)—
The family tether Plato broke altogether.
    "The child is the State's," argued Plato,
    "It belongs to the public," said Plato.

VI.

No folks were to wed that were not thoroughbred,
    A very hard case to relate, O!
And if children appeared not quite fit to be reared,
    They were never acknowledged by Plato.
    'Twas a delicate question with Plato,
    Upon which he disliked to dilate, O!
But we all of us know where the puppy-dogs go
    When the litter's too many for Plato.
    "Let the fittest survive," counsels Plato.

VII.

On this question that vexes us as to the sexes
    Not long does our sage hesitate, O!
Women's duties and rights, whether beauties or frights,
    Are completely conceded by Plato.
    But the pace here adopted by Plato
    Seems to move at too rapid a rate, O!

All must go to the wars, and be servants of Mars,
    Both the women and men, under Plato,
    Yes, the women must fight, under Plato.

VIII.

On another small point he appears out of joint,
    For perhaps it admits of debate, O!
If philosophers solely should govern us wholly,
    Or our rulers be pupils of Plato.
    Suppose them as clever as Plato,
    How would Darwin or Mill rule the State, O!
Should you think Epicurus a good Palinurus,
    Or would Yankees be governed by Plato?
    Imagine them, governed by Plato!

IX.

A philosopher's schemes are made up of fond dreams
    And of idle Utopian prate, O!
For while Theory preaches, 'tis Practice that teaches,
    And corrects the wild crotchets of Plato.
    So the model Republic of Plato
    Must submit to the general fate, O!
Lay the book on the shelf, and each man make himself
    What a Christian would wish for in Plato.
    Good-bye to the crotchets of Plato!

16.—MAN EVEN NOW A SPIRIT.

Sweep away the illusions of time, compress the threescore years into three minutes, and what are we ourselves but ghosts? Are we not *spirits* that are shaped into a body, into an appearance? This is no metaphor; it is a simple scientific fact. We start out of nothingness, take figure, and are apparitions. Round us, as round the veriest spectre, is—eternity! And to eternity minutes are as years and æons. O Heaven! It is mysterious, it is awful, to consider that we not only carry each a future ghost within him, but are in very deed ghosts. These limbs, whence had we them? this stormy force, this life-blood, with its burning passion? They are dust and shadow —a shadow-system gathered around our ME, wherein through some moments or years the divine essence is to be revealed in the flesh.

That warrior on his strong war-horse: fire flashes through his eyes, force dwells in his arms and heart; but warrior and war-horse are a vision, a revealed force, nothing more. Stately they tread the earth as if it were a firm substance. Fools! the earth is but a film; it cracks in twain, and warrior and war-horse sink beyond plummet's sounding. Plummet's! Fantasy herself will not follow them. A little while ago, and they were not; a little while, and they are not; their very ashes are not. So has it been from the beginning, so will it be to the end. Generation after generation takes to itself the form of a body, and forth issuing from Cimmerian night on Heaven's mission APPEARS. What force and fire is in each he expends: one grinding in the mill of industry, one, hunter-like, climbing the giddy Alpine heights of science, one madly dashed in pieces on the rocks of strife in war with his fellow, and then the Heaven-sent is recalled, his earthly vesture falls away, and soon even to sense becomes a vanished shadow.

Thus like wild-flaming, wild-thundering trains of Heaven's artillery does this mysterious mankind thunder and flame in long-drawn, quick-succeeding grandeur through the unknown deep. Earth's mountains are leveled and her seas filled up in our passage; can the earth, which is but dead and a vision, resist spirits which have reality and are alive? On the hardest adamant some footprint of us is stamped in; the last rear of the host will read traces of the earliest van. But whence? O Heaven, whither? Sense knows not, faith knows not— only that it is through mystery to mystery, from God to God.

THOMAS CARLYLE, b. 1798.

17.—CHATHAM'S LAST SPEECH.

THE most splendid passage in Chatham's public life was
certainly the closing one, when, on the 7th of April, 1778,
wasted by disease, but impelled by an overruling sense of duty,
he repaired for the last time to the House of Lords. Totter-
ing from weakness, he was supported on one side by his son-in-
law, and on the other by his second son, William Pitt, soon to
become, at the age of twenty-four, prime minister of England.

Lord Chatham looked, as he was, a dying man; yet never
was seen a figure of more dignity. The lords stood up and
made a lane for him to pass to his seat, whilst with that grace
for which he was distinguished he bowed as he moved along.
Taking his seat, he listened to Lord Weymouth's speech in
defense of the American war; and when his lordship had con-
cluded, Chatham rose slowly and with difficulty, leaning on
his crutches and supported by his two relatives.

Taking one arm from its crutch, he raised his hand, and

5 D

looking toward heaven, said :* " I thank God that I have been
enabled to come here this day to perform a duty and to speak
on a subject which has so deeply impressed my mind. I am
old and infirm, have one foot—more than one foot—in the
grave ; I have risen from my bed to stand up in the cause of
my country—perhaps never again to speak in this House.

"My lords, I contend that we have not procured, nor can
we procure, any force sufficient to subdue America ; it is mon-
strous to think of it. The mode in which the war has been
carried on has been the most bloody, barbarous and ferocious
in the annals of mankind. We have sullied and tarnished
the arms of Britain for ever by employing savages in our ser-
vice, by drawing them up in a British line, and mingling the
scalping-knife and tomahawk with the sword and firelock.
Had it fallen to my lot to serve in an army where such cruelty
was practiced, I believe in my conscience that sooner than sub-
mit to it I would have mutinied.

" Withdraw the German bayonet and the Indian scalping-
knife from America. The colonies must consider us as friends
before they will ever consent to treat with us. A formal
acknowledgment of our errors and a renunciation of our unjust,
ill-founded and oppressive claims must precede every, the least
attempt to conciliate. You cannot conciliate America by your
present measures ; you cannot *subdue* her by your present or
by any measures.

" Ministers have been in error—experience has proved it ;
and what is worse, in that error they persist. Instead of
meanly truckling to every insult of French caprice and Span-
ish punctilio, let us be reconciled with America. I rejoice
that I am still alive to lift up my voice against the dismem-
berment of this ancient monarchy. Shall *we* now fall pros-
trate before the House of Bourbon? Shall a people so lately
the terror of the world now stoop so low as to tell its ancient,

---

*To these remarks the duke of Richmond replied. Eager to answer
him, Chatham tried to stand ; then, pressing his heart, he fell back in con-
vulsions. The House, in great agitation, at once adjourned. The wood-
cut we give is from the painting by Copley, commemorative of the scene.
Chatham died May 11, 1778, aged 70.

inveterate enemy, 'Take all we have, only give us peace'?
Impossible! Where is the man who will dare to advise such
a measure? I am not, I confess, well informed as to the
resources of this kingdom; but I trust it has still sufficient
to maintain its just rights. Any state is better than despair.
Let us at least make one effort; and if we must fall, let us
fall like men."

18.—THE KING OF BRENTFORD'S TESTAMENT.

THE noble king of Brentford was old and very sick:
He summoned his physicians to wait upon him quick;
They stepped into their coaches and brought their best phy-*sick'*.
They crammed their gracious master with potion and with pill,
They drenched him and they bled him; they could not cure
    his ill.
"Go fetch," says he, "my lawyer; I'd better make my will."

The monarch's royal mandate the lawyer did obey;
The thought of six-and-eightpence did make his heart full gay.
"What is't," says he, "your Majesty would wish of me to-day?"
"The doctors have belabored me with potion and with pill:
My hours of life are counted, O man of tape and quill!
Sit down and mend a pen or two—I want to make my will.

"O'er all the land of Brentford I'm lord, and eke of Kew:
I've three per cents. and five per cents., my debts are but a few;
And to inherit after me I have but children two.
Prince Thomas is my eldest son, a sober prince is he,
And from the day we breechĕd him till now (he's twenty-three)
He never caused disquiet to his poor mamma or me.

"He never owed a shilling, went never drunk to bed,
He has not two ideas within his honest head;
In all respects he differs from my second son, Prince Ned.
When Tom has half his income laid by at the year's end,
Poor Ned has ne'er a stiver that rightly he may spend,
But sponges on a tradesman or borrows from a friend.

"While Tom his legal studies most soberly pursues,
Poor Ned must pass his mornings a-dawdling with the Muse;
While Tom frequents his banker, young Ned frequents the
    Jews.
Ned drives about in buggies, Tom sometimes takes a 'bus.
Ah, cruel Fate, why made you my children differ thus?
Why make Tom a *dullard*, and Ned a *ge-ni-us?*"

"You'll cut him with a shilling," exclaimed the man of wits.
"I'll leave my wealth," said Brentford, "Sir Lawyer, as befits;
And portion both their fortunes unto their several wits."
"Your Grace knows best," the lawyer said, "on your commands
    I wait."
"Be silent, sir," says Brentford; "a plague upon your prate!
Come, take your pen and paper, and write as I dictate."

The will as Brentford spoke it was writ and signed and closed;
He bade the lawyer leave him, and turned him round and
    dozed;
And next week in the churchyard the good old king reposed.
Tom, dressed in crape and hatband, of mourners was the chief;
In bitter self-upbraidings poor Edward showed his grief;
Tom hid his fat white countenance in his pocket-handkerchief.

Ned's eyes were full of weeping, he faltered in his walk;
Tom never shed a tear, but onward he did stalk,
As pompous, black and solemn as any catafalque.
And when the bones of Brentford—that gentle king and just—
With bell and book and candle, were duly laid in dust,
"Now, gentlemen," says Thomas, "let business be discussed.

"When late our sire beloved was taken deadly ill,
Sir Lawyer, you attended him (I mean to tax your bill);
And as you signed and wrote it, I pr'ythee read the will."
The lawyer wiped his spectacles, and drew the parchment out,
And all the Brentford family sate eager round about;
Poor Ned was somewhat anxious, but Tom had ne'er a doubt.

"My son, as I make ready to seek my last long home,
Some cares I had for Neddy, but none for thee, my Tom:
Sobriety and order you ne'er departed from.
Though small was your allowance, you saved a little store;
And those who save a little shall get a plenty more."
As the lawyer read this compliment, Tom's eyes were running
    o'er.

"The tortoise and the hare, Tom, set out, at each his pace;
The hare it was the fleeter—the tortoise won the race;
And since the world's beginning this ever was the case.
Thank Heaven, then, for the blinkers it placed before your eyes;
The stupidest are strongest, the witty are not wise;
Oh, bless your good stupidity—it is your dearest prize!

"And though my lands are wide, and plenty is my gold,
Still better gifts from Nature, my Thomas, do you hold:
A brain that's thick and heavy, a heart that's dull and cold—
Too dull to feel depression, too hard to heed distress,
Too cold to yield to passion or silly tenderness.
March on—your road is open to wealth, Tom, and success.

"Ned sinneth in extravagance, and you in greedy lust"
("I' faith," says Ned, "our father is less polite than just");
"In you, son Tom, I've confidence, but Ned I cannot trust.
Wherefore my lease and copyholds, my lands and tenements,
My parks, my farms and orchards, my houses and my rents,
My Dutch stock and my Spanish stock, my five and three per
    cents.,—

I leave to you, my Thomas" ("What, all?" poor Edward said;
"Well, well, I should have spent them, and Tom's a prudent
    head ")—
"I leave to you, my Thomas—to you IN TRUST for Ned."
The wrath and consternation what poet e'er could trace
That at this fatal passage came o'er Prince Tom his face—
The wonder of the company, and honest Ned's amaze!

"'Tis surely some mistake," good-naturedly cries Ned;
The lawyer answered gravely, "'Tis even as I said;
'Twas thus his gracious Majesty ordained on his death-bed.
See, here the will is witnessed, and here's his autograph!"
"In truth, our father's writing," says Edward with a laugh;
"But thou shalt not be loser, Tom, we'll share it half and half."

"Alas! my kind young gentleman, this sharing cannot be;
'Tis written in the testament that Brentford spoke to me,
'I do forbid Prince Ned to give Prince Tom a halfpenny.
He hath a store of money, but ne'er was known to lend it;
He never helped his brother; the poor he ne'er befriended;
He hath no need of property who knows not how to spend it.

"'Poor Edward knows but how to spend, and thrifty Tom to
        hoard;
Let Thomas be the steward, then, and Edward be the lord;
And as the honest laborer is worthy his reward,
I pray Prince Ned, my second son, and my successor dear,
To pay to his intendant five hundred pounds a year,
And to think of his old father, and live and make good cheer.'"

Such was old Brentford's honest testament;
    He did devise his moneys for the best,
    And lies in Brentford church in peaceful rest.
Prince Edward lived, and money made and spent;
    But his good sire was wrong, it is confessed,
To say his son, young Thomas, never lent.
    He did.   Young Thomas lent at interest,
And nobly took his twenty-five per cent.

Long time the famous reign of Ned endured
    O'er Chiswick, Fulham, Brentford, Putney, Kew;
But of extravagance he ne'er was cured.
    And when both died, as mortal men will do,
'Twas commonly reported that the steward
    Was very much the richer of the two.

W. M. THACKERAY.

MIRABEAU SPEAKING FROM THE FRENCH TRIBUNE.

19.—THE PRIVILEGED CLASSES.

WHEN, during our session yesterday, those words which you have taught Frenchmen to unlearn—*orders, privileges*—fell on my ears; when a private corporation of one of the provinces of this empire spoke to you of the impossibility of consenting to the execution of your decrees, sanctioned by the king; when certain magistrates declared to you that *their conscience and their honor* forbade their obedience to your laws,—I said to myself, Are these, then, dethroned sovereigns who, in a transport of imprudent but generous pride, are addressing successful usurpers? No, these are men whose arrogant pretensions have too long been an insult to all ideas of social order—champions, even more interested than audacious, of a system which has cost France centuries of oppression, public and private, political and fiscal, feudal and judicial, and whose hope it is to make us regret and revive that system.

The people of Brittany have sent among you sixty-six representatives who assured you that the new constitution crowns all their wishes; and here come eleven judges of the province who cannot consent that you should be the benefactors of their country. They have disobeyed your laws, and they pride themselves on their disobedience and believe it will make their names honored by posterity. No, gentlemen, the remembrance of their folly will not pass to posterity. What avail their pigmy efforts to brace themselves against the progress of a revolution the grandest and most glorious in the world's history, and one that must infallibly change the face of the globe and the lot of humanity? Strange and silly presumption, that would arrest liberty in its course and roll back the destinies of a great nation!

It is not to antiquated transactions, it is not to musty treaties, wherein fraud combined with force to chain men to the car of certain haughty masters, that the National Assembly have resorted in their investigations into popular rights. The titles we offer are more imposing by far, ancient as time, sacred and imprescriptible as nature. What! Must the terms of the marriage contract of one Anne of Brittany make the people slaves to the nobles till the consummation of the ages?

These refractory magistrates speak of the statutes which "*immutably* fix our powers of legislation." *Immutably* fix! Oh how that word tears the veil from their innermost thoughts! How would they like to have abuses *immutable* upon the earth, and evil eternal? Indeed, what is lacking to their felicity but the *perpetuity* of that feudal scourge which unhappily has lasted *only six centuries?* But it is in vain that they rage. All now is changed or changing. There is nothing immutable save reason—save the sovereignty of the people—save the inviolability of its decrees!

In all countries, in all ages have aristocrats implacably pursued the friends of the people; and when, by I know not what combination of fortune, such a friend has uprisen from the very bosom of the aristocracy, it has been at him pre-eminently that they have struck, eager to inspire wider terror by the elevation of their victim. So perished the last of the Gracchi by the hands of the patricians. But mortally smitten he flung dust toward heaven, calling the avenging gods to witness; and from that dust sprang Marius—Marius, less illustrious for having exterminated the Cimbri than for having beaten down the despotism of the nobility in Rome.

But you, commons, listen to one who, unseduced by your applauses, yet cherishes them in his heart. Man is strong only by union, happy only by peace. Be firm, not obstinate; courageous, not turbulent; free, not undisciplined; prompt, not precipitate.

For myself, who, in my public career, have had no other fear but that of wrong-doing, who, girt with my conscience and armed with my principles, would brave the universe, be sure that the vain clamors, the wrathful menaces, the injurious protestations—all the convulsions, in a word, of expiring prejudices—shall not on *me* impose.

What! shall *he* now pause in his civic course who, first among all the men of France, emphatically proclaimed his opinions on national affairs at a time when circumstances were much less urgent than now, and the task one of much greater peril? Never! No measure of outrages shall bear down my patience. I *have* been, I *am*, I *shall* be even to the tomb, the man of the public liberty, the man of the constitution. If to be such be to become the man of the people rather than of the nobles, then woe to the privileged orders! For privileges shall have an end, but the people is eternal!

MIRABEAU,* 1749–1791.

* Victor Gabriel Riquette, marquis of Mirabeau, was one of the most remarkable characters of the early period of the first French revolution. In the French National Assembly members speak from a raised platform or pulpit called a *tribune*. The above translation is from Sargent's Standard Speaker.

20.—LAISSEZ ALLER.

No more words! try it with your swords—
Try it with the arms of your bravest and your best!
You are proud of your manhood, now put it to the test:
    Not another word! try it by the sword.

    No more *notes!* try it by the throats
Of the cannon that will roar till the earth and air be shaken;
For they speak what they mean, and they cannot be mistaken;
    No more doubt! come—fight it out.

No child's play! waste not a day:
Serve out the deadliest weapons that you know;
Let them pitilessly hail in the faces of the foe;
    No blind strife! waste not one life.

You that in the front bear the battle's brunt,
When the sun gleams at dawn on the bayonets abreast,
Remember 'tis for country and for freedom you contest;
    For love of all you guard, stand and strike hard.

You at home that stay, from danger far away,
Leave not a jot to chance, while you rest at quiet ease;
Quick forge the bolts of death; quick ship them o'er the seas;
    If war's feet are lame, yours will be the blame.

    You, my lads abroad, "Steady!" be your word;
You at home be the anchor of your soldiers, young and brave:
Spare no cost, none is lost, that may strengthen or may save;
    Sloth were sin and shame—now play out the game!
                    FRANKLIN LUSHINGTON.

21.—PUBLIC OPINION AND THE SWORD.

OCTOBER 10, 1831.

AT the present moment I can see only one question in the State—the question of reform; only two parties—the friends of the bill and its enemies. No observant and unprejudiced man can look forward, without great alarm, to the effects which the recent decision of the lords may possibly produce. I do not predict, I do not expect, open, armed insurrection. What I apprehend is this—that the people may engage in a silent but extensive and persevering war against the law. It is easy to say, "Be bold; be firm; defy intimidation; let the law have its course; the law is strong enough to put down the seditious." Sir, we have heard this blustering before; and we know in what it ended. It is

MACAULAY.

the blustering of little men whose lot has fallen on a great crisis. Xerxes scourging the waves, Canute commanding the waves to recede from his footstool, were but types of the folly.

The law has no eyes; the law has no hands; the law is nothing—nothing but a piece of paper printed by the king's printer, with the king's arms at the top—till public opinion breathes the breath of life into the dead letter. We found this in Ireland. The elections of 1828—the Clare election, two years later—proved the folly of those who think that nations are governed by wax and parchment; and, at length, in the close of 1828, the government had only one plain alternative before it—concession or civil war.

I know of only two ways in which societies can permanently be governed—by public opinion and by the sword. A government having at its command the armies, the fleets and the revenues of Great Britain, might possibly hold Ireland by the sword. So Oliver Cromwell held Ireland; so William the

Third held it; so Mr. Pitt held it; so the duke of Wellington might, perhaps, have held it. But to govern Great Britain by the sword! So wild a thought has never, I will venture to say, occurred to any public man of any party; and if any man were frantic enough to make the attempt, he would find, before three days had 'expired, that there is no better sword than that which is fashioned out of a plowshare!

But if not by the sword, how is the people to be governed? I understand how the peace is kept at New York. It is by the assent and support of the people. I understand, also, how the peace is kept at Milan. It is by the bayonet of the Austrian soldier. But how the peace is to be kept when you have neither the popular assent nor the military force—how the peace is to be kept in England by a government acting on the principles of the present opposition—I do not understand.

Sir, we read that in old times, when the villeins were driven to revolt by oppression—when the castles of the nobility were burned to the ground—when the warehouses of London were pillaged—when a hundred thousand insurgents appeared in arms on Blackheath—when a foul murder, perpetrated in their presence, had raised their passions to madness—when they were looking around for some captain to succeed and avenge him whom they had lost,—just then, before Hob Miller, or Tom Carter, or Jack Straw, could place himself at their head, the king rode up to them and exclaimed, "I will be your leader!" And at once the infuriated multitude laid down their arms, submitted to his guidance, dispersed at his command. Herein let us imitate him. Let us say to the people, "We are your leaders—we, your own House of Commons." This tone it is our interest and our duty to take. The circumstances admit of no delay. Even while I speak, the moments are passing away—the irrevocable moments pregnant with the destiny of a great people. The country is in danger; it may be saved: *we* can save it. This is the way—this is the time. In our hands are the issues of great good and great evil—the issues of the life and death of the State!

MACAULAY, 1800–1859.

22.—IMPRESSMENT OF AN AMERICAN SEAMAN.*

CHARACTERS—*Capt. Martinet, Lieut. Perley, Hiram Handy, Capt. Jotham Luff.*

Enter CAPT. MARTINET *and* LIEUT. PERLEY, *meeting.*

Capt. Martinet. Well, lieutenant, how does the prisoner bear his sentence?

Lieut. Perley. Stiffly and stubbornly, sir. He sticks to the assertion that he is a Yankee.

Capt. M. Yankee or Yahoo, he will have to swing at the yard-arm for mutiny in striking his commanding officer. The rascal hit me full in the face.

Lieut. P. Will it not be rather awkward, sir, if it should turn out that he is an American?

Capt. M. Of course he is an American—a regular Down-easter. You can tell it by his talking through his nose. But what do I care for that?

Lieut. P. We are on the verge of a war with the United States; this may help it on.

Capt. M. Let it come. What are we to do? We must have seamen. The law tells us we may take them by impressment. The Yankee ships are manned more than half by British seamen. We must board the Yankee ships to get the men we want. If, now and then, we impress a Yankee instead of a British subject, is that any reason why we should suffer the Yankee to break the first law of the service and strike his commander? No! Get ready the yard-arm, lieutenant. The fellow must swing for it.

Lieut. P. Ay, ay, sir. I will see that everything is ready.

Capt. M. Send the prisoner to me.

Lieut. P. Ay, ay, sir.   [*Exit.*]

Capt. M. British subject or not, he put his dirty fist in my face. He has been tried by a court-martial and convicted, and it shall not be my fault if he is not punished.

* An incident similar to that represented in the dialogue actually happened in the British Channel during the last war with Great Britain.

6

[*Enter* HIRAM, *with his arms pinioned.*]

Hiram. I was told you wished to see me.

Capt. M. Well, prisoner, what have you to say for yourself? You have had a fair trial, and been convicted of mutiny. The penalty is death by hanging at the yard-arm. The ceremony is fixed for this afternoon. Have you any objection to make?

Hiram. Objection? Yes, the objection that the murderer's victim makes to the murderer's blow. You know in your heart that it will be murder.

Capt. M. What do you mean?

Hiram. I mean that I am not a British subject, and you know it. What right had you to take me out of an American vessel?

Capt. M. The right that British law and British power give us to seize and impress a British seaman wherever we can find one, on the high seas or elsewhere.

Hiram. But I am not a British seaman. I am a native-born American. Defend your claim to touch me if you can.

Capt. M. We find we cannot distinguish between English and Americans. If we took the word of every sailor who claims to be an American, we couldn't get enough for our ships. So it is a case of necessity, you see. Your true way was to keep quiet, and not turn mutineer.

Hiram. What if you were seized by an American press-gang and placed on board an American ship, and what if, in trying to escape, you should strike an officer, and be sentenced to death? would not those who took your life for the act be rightly called murderers?

Capt. M. Prisoner, I do not choose to argue with you. If you have fallen under our laws—

Hiram. *Fallen* under your laws? I was forced—forced from my own ship on the high seas. Your plea is the pirate's plea.

Capt. M. Prisoner, the subordinate who strikes me must die either by my own hand or that of the law.

Hiram. I understand you now. You are more anxious to revenge your personal dignity than to punish a public wrong. But do not be too sure. There is many a slip between the cup and the lip. The diversion you have promised yourself for this afternoon will not come off.

Capt. M. If I live, you shall be strung up at the yard-arm this day.

Hiram. You think so, but you will be disappointed.

Capt. M. What is to prevent it, here on my own ship, with my own crew?

Hiram. As I left the deck just now I saw a little sail-boat coming this way. Jotham was at the helm.

Capt. M. And who is Jotham?

Hiram. You know him; Captain Jotham Luff, of the American brig Nancy, *my* captain, from whom your press-gang forced me.

Capt. M. I told that impudent fellow not to come near me again. What will he do?

Hiram. I don't know. I only know he'll do something. He would never dare to go back to Marblehead and say that he had left me to be strung up at the yard-arm of a British frigate. The women would tar and feather him, and drag him in a cart as they did old Floyd Ireson.

Capt. M. The execution shall take place at once.

Hiram. You are too late. I hear Captain Jotham's step on the deck. Here he comes.

[*Enter* CAPTAIN JOTHAM LUFF.]

Jotham. How are you, captain? Middling well, I hope. Well, Hiram, my boy, they have trussed you up like a turkey for the spit. [*Takes out jack-knife, cuts cords and frees* HIRAM.] There, captain; it looked so uncomfortable, I couldn't help it.

Capt. M. [*shaking his fist*]. You impudent Yankee! I'll have you keel-hauled, you—

Jotham. Come, now, don't blaze away in that style! Where's the harm? You aren't afraid, are you, of Hiram and me?

Capt. M. What's the object of this visit?

Jotham. To take Hiram back with me.

Capt. M. I told you yesterday that no power on earth could save him from being hung. So leave this ship, or I will call those who will put you into your boat by force.

Jotham. I reckon you'll do no such thing. I reckon you'll hear what I have to say, and then do what I tell you to. Sit down and make yourself at home. [*Sits.*] Sit down, Hiram. [*Hiram sits.*]

Capt. M. [*standing*]. Well, there's no impudence like that of a Yankee.

Jotham [*whittling the stick that* HIRAM *was pinioned by*]. You must know, captain, that when I left you yesterday I was almost as mad as you are now—pretty badly roiled up. When I got on board my brig, whom should I find there but two lords—Lord Pembroke and Lord Annesley—who had been out in a sail-boat, and had stopped to take a look at my vessel. Perhaps you know them?

Capt. M. Yes; one of them is my nephew.

Jotham. Well, it occurred to me at once that two lords were about a fair exchange for an American sailor; so I impressed them.

Capt. M. Impressed them! What do you mean?

Jotham [*rising*]. Don't you know what *impressment* is? When you force a man into your service against his will, that's impressment. Do you think we Americans are going to stand that? Never! War, first, to the hilt. We are ready for you; the whole country is eager to wipe out the disgrace, and war will come. Let it come.

Capt. M. What have you done to their lordships?

Jotham. Treated them precisely as you have been treating Hiram here.

Capt. M. Rascal! Scoundrel!

Jotham. Keep cool! It's a fact. I put a stick through their elbows, and trussed them up just as you had Hiram, kept them on bread and water, and this afternoon, if I don't prevent it, they will both be hung at the yard-arm of the Nancy.

Capt. M. Hung! Your proof of this?

Jotham [*producing a letter*]. There's the proof, in a letter from their lordships. Read it. You know the handwriting?

Capt. M. [*reading aloud*]. "The Yankee will do what he threatens. Be sure of that. His vessel is a fast sailer, and can not be overtaken. Grant all he asks, if you would save our lives. Yours, Annesley, Pembroke." Villain! Do you mean to say you would hang two noblemen within sight of the English coast?

Jotham. I *do* mean to say just that. Touch a hair of that lad's head, and before sundown they shall die like dogs.

Capt. M. What if I seize your person as a security for their lives? You didn't think of that—eh?

Jotham. Oh, but I did! That was my risk. I left their lordships in the hands of my mate, Persevere Peabody, who has orders to hang them, in case I don't send him a signal from your vessel before five o'clock not to do it. [*Shows his watch.*] It's after four already, captain.

Capt. M. Your mate will not dare to touch a hair of their heads!

Jotham. Oh, you don't know Persevere Peabody. Says he, as I was leaving, "Captain Jotham," says he, "I never hung a lord in all my life; but never fear, I'll do it in a style that shall be an eternal credit to the American eagle." And will you believe it?—the rogue, when he thought I wasn't looking, put the clock half an hour ahead, that he might have an excuse for finishing the job the sooner. The critter set the steward to work on some old black silk neckerchiefs. Says I, "What's all this for, Persevere?" Says he, "Their lordships will need black caps to be hung in. I mean to do everything regular, captain." Oh, he is a terrible fellow, is Persevere Peabody.

Capt. M. [*alarmed*]. Did you say he put the clock half an hour ahead? Then he may be about it now.

Jotham. That's a fact.

Capt. M. What's your signal for stopping this barbarity?

Jotham. That's my secret. I'm not such a simpleton as to tell you that before I have made all right.

Capt. M. Name your terms quickly.

Jotham. First, Hiram's release, and a safe return for him and me to our vessel.

Capt. M. Never! I'll never consent.

Jotham. Yes, you will. Second, ten guineas to Hiram, by way of damages.

Capt. M. I'll sink my ship first!

Jotham. No, you'll not. Third, and last, a hundred guineas for me, for losses by detention of my brig in waiting for Hiram.

Capt. M. Do your worst! I'll never agree to such terms.

Jotham. Yes, you will.

Capt. M. Not till I am struck idiotic.

Jotham. Yes, you will.

Hiram. Never mind the ten guineas, Captain Jotham.

Jotham. Hold your tongue, Hiram; I'll not bate a farthing.

[*Re-enter* LIEUT. PERLEY.]

Lieut. P. The Yankee ship in the offing, sir, is firing minute-guns.

Jotham. All right.

Capt. M. What does it mean?

Jotham. It means that Captain Persevere Peabody is making all ready to hang the two lords we impressed yesterday.

Capt. M. Stop him at once, or I'll have you put to the torture.

Jotham. You have my terms, captain. I can't budge, let the British lion roar ever so loud.

Capt. M. What shall I do, Perley?

Lieut. P. The Yankee has proved too clever for us. My advice to you is to knock under at once.

Capt. M. Confound the extortionate, tobacco-chewing, psalm-singing trickster!

Lieut. P. Should any harm come to their lordships, you will be severely censured.

Capt. M. Too true. [*To Jotham.*] Look you, sir, I accept your terms.

Jotham. A safe return for Hiram and me; ten guineas for Hiram; a hundred guineas for me.

Capt. M. Yes, yes, yes.

Jotham. You hear, lieutenant?

Capt. M. The pledge is given. There is no escape from it. The word of a British officer is as good as his bond.

Jotham. Then take the American flag out of my boat and run it up to your fore peak. Persevere Peabody will be disappointed, but he'll not dare to disobey.

Lieut. P. I'll have it done. [*Exit.*]

Jotham. Now, captain, you'll sleep better, and feel better all the rest of your life, to think you've been saved from putting a fellow-creature to death. What would have been your reflections—

Capt. M. Stop your palaver, and come and get your money. [*Exit.*]

Jotham. Well, Hiram, it will not turn out a bad speculation, after all.

Hiram. Better than my last whaling voyage, captain.

Jotham. Hurrah for our side! Hurrah for free trade and sailors' rights!

Hiram. Just my sentiments, captain. Hurrah!

SARGENT.

23.—ITALY.

VOICES from the mountains speak,
　　Apennines to Alps reply,
Vale to vale and peak to peak
　　Toss an old remembered cry—
　　　Italy shall be free!
　　Such the mighty shout that fills
　　All the passes of her hills.

All the old Italian lakes
　　Quiver at that wakening word;
Como with a thrill awakes,
　　Garda to her depths is stirred;
　　　'Mid the steeps where he sleeps,
　　Dreaming of the elder years,
　　Startled Thrasymenus hears.

Sweeping Arno, swelling Po,
  Murmur freedom to their meads.
Tiber swift and Liris slow
  Send strange whispers from their reeds.
      Italy shall be free!
  Sing the glittering brooks that glide
  Toward the sea from Etna's side.

Long ago was Gracchus slain,
  Brutus perished long ago,
Yet the living roots remain
  Whence the shoots of greatness grow.
      Yet again god-like men,
  Sprung from that heroic stem,
  Call the land to rise with them.

They who haunt the swarming street,
  They who chase the mountain boar,
Or where cliff and billow meet
  Prune the vine or pull the oar,
      With a stroke break their yoke;
  Slaves but yester eve were they—
  Freemen with the dawning day.

Looking in his children's eyes,
  While his own with gladness flash,
"These," the Umbrian father cries,
  "Ne'er shall crouch beneath the lash!
      These shall ne'er brook to wear
  Chains whose cruel links are twined
  Round the crushed and withering mind."

Monarchs! ye whose armies stand
  Harnessed for the battle-field,
Pause, and from the lifted hand
  Drop the bolts of war ye wield;
      Stand aloof, while the proof
  Of the people's might is given:
  Leave their kings to them and Heaven.

Stand aloof, and see the oppressed
 Chase the oppressor, pale with fear,
As the fresh winds of the west
 Blow the misty valleys clear.
  Stand and see Italy
 Cast the gyves she wears no more
To the gulfs that steep her shore.
W. C. BRYANT, b. 1798.

24.—NATIONAL ARMAMENTS (1849).

OTHER nations, be assured, gentlemen, are far too intelligent to require that we should always be armed to the teeth in order to let them know how strong we are. Take the case of the United States. America has three times within the last few years had a misunderstanding with two of the greatest powers of the world—twice with England, once with France. We had the Maine boundary and the Oregon Territory questions to settle with the United States, and America had her quarrel with France, growing out of a claim for compensation of one million pounds sterling which the French government refused to pay. What was the issue of those controversies? When the claim was refused by France, General Jackson, then the head of the American government, published his declaration that if the money was not paid forthwith, he would seize French ships and pay himself.

At that time—I have it from Americans themselves—the French had three times the force of ships-of-war the Americans had. Admiral Mackau was in the Gulf of Florida with a fleet large enough to ravage the whole coast of America and bombard her towns, but did France rush into a war with America? *She paid the money.* Why? Because she knew well, if she provoked an unjust war with the United States, their men-of-war were nothing compared with the force that would swarm out of every American port when brought into collision with another country. France knew that America had the larger mercantile marine; and though at first the battle might be to the stronger in an armed fleet, in the end it would be to that country which had the greater amount of public spirit and the greater number of mercantile ships and sailors.

What was the case with England? In 1842 there was a talk of war with America on account of the Maine boundary question. Bear in mind that America never spent more than one million two hundred thousand pounds sterling on her navy in any year of peace previous to 1842. We are spending this year seven millions or eight millions; but will anybody tell me that America fared worse in that dispute because her resources in ships-of-war were far inferior to ours? No, but we increased our navy, and we had a *squadron of evolution,* as it was called. America never mounted a gun at New York to prevent the bombardment of the city, but did she fare the worse? We sent a peer of the realm (Lord Ashburton) to Washington; it was on American soil that the quarrel was adjusted, and rumor does say the Americans made a very good bargain. It is the spirit of a people, the prosperity of a people, the growing strength, the union, the determination of a people, that command respect.

RICHARD COBDEN, 1804–1865.

———•○•———

25.—ABSOLUTISM AND REPUBLICANISM.

MR. CARLYLE holds that the great object in government is that the people should be well governed, good laws passed with good sanctions, good roads and bridges made, good schools established, good connections formed with foreign countries, good measures taken for war and for peace—in short, that things should be well done for the people, so that the people should be thoroughly and effectually *governed.* Now, this requires that the best man should be made governor; and the king, the true king, according to Carlyle's derivation, is the " canning " or able man, the " cunning " or knowing man; he it is whom the Saxons called *cyning,* or king; he is *de jure* the king, the sovereign, of his people. Gifted with faculty to discern what is best for the people, and with commanding energy to execute what he discerns to be best, it is his right to rule; it is the duty of others to obey; and the more implicit and submissive the obedience, the better.

This is the political creed of a man who deifies power, and, above all, power of will; who does not scruple to say that ever in this world *might is right* in the long run—a principle which has, however, its relation to truth.

That Carlyle should deride republicanism, and especially democracy, is a natural consequence of this way of thinking. But in his scheme there are two fatal deficiencies; he provides no answer for these two momentous questions:

First, how we are to ascertain this *canning, cunning* man who is to be our king?—if without previous trial, by what criteria? if with trial, by what system that shall afford fair field for all competitors? *Secondly*, how we are to shift in the mean time, how we are to get along, if he does not exist, until he does? or if he does exist unknown to us, how we are to get along until we know him?

But the theory of Carlyle, like all absolutist theories, has another deeper and more fatal deficiency. It assumes that the good of a government lies only in its ends, its acts, laws, measures and so on, and that when these are given it matters little by what means they come about, only the simpler and more effectual the means, the better.

An absolute government may provide as well as a republic for the material wants and interests of the people, but the absolute government holds them in tutelage, and calls them and keeps them children; the republic holds them in partnership, treats them as men, and makes them men. If I am a democrat, it is on this ground; not because a democracy is the safest, strongest, quickest government, but because it is the *manliest* —it is a gymnasium for making men, strong-minded, vigorous, active men. This gymnastic training has its dangers, its peculiar difficulties and embarrassments, but the advantages are more than worth the risks.

JAMES HADLEY, 1820–1872.

26.—THE RAVEN.

ONCE upon a midnight dreary, while I pondered, weak and weary,
Over many a quaint and curious volume of forgotten lore,
While I nodded, nearly napping, suddenly there came a tapping,
As of some one gently rapping, rapping at my chamber-door.
"'Tis some visitor," I muttered, "tapping at my chamber-door;
      Only this and nothing more."

Ah, distinctly I remember, it was in the bleak December,
And each separate dying ember wrought its ghost upon the floor.
Eagerly I wished the morrow; vainly I had sought to borrow
From my books surcease of sorrow—sorrow for the lost Lenore,
For the rare and radiant maiden whom the angels name Lenore,
      Nameless here for evermore.

And the silken, sad, uncertain rustling of each purple curtain
Thrilled me—filled me with fantastic terrors never felt before;
So that now, to still the beating of my heart, I stood repeating,
"'Tis some visitor entreating entrance at my chamber-door,
Some late visitor entreating entrance at my chamber-door;
      That it is, and nothing more."

Presently my soul grew stronger; hesitating then no longer,
"Sir," said I, "or madam, truly your forgiveness I implore;
But the fact is I was napping, and so gently you came rapping,

And so faintly you came tapping, tapping at my chamber-door,
That I scarce was sure I heard you—" Here I opened wide the door.
Darkness there, and nothing more.

Deep into that darkness peering, long I stood there, wondering,
fearing,
Doubting, dreaming dreams no mortal ever dared to dream before;
But the silence was unbroken, and the stillness gave no token,
And the only word there spoken was the whispered word, "Lenore!"
This I whispered, and an echo murmured back the word "LENORE!"
Merely this, and nothing more.

Back into the chamber turning, all my soul within me burning,
Soon again I heard a tapping, something louder than before.
"Surely," said I, "surely that is something at my window-lattice,
Let me see then what thereat is, and this mystery explore—
Let my heart be still a moment, and this mystery explore!
'Tis the wind, and nothing more."

Open here I flung the shutter, when, with many a flirt and flutter,
In there stepped a stately raven of the saintly days of yore.
Not the least obeisance made he, not a minute stopped or stayed he,
But, with mien of lord or lady, perched above my chamber-door—
Perched upon a bust of Pallas just above my chamber-door—
Perched and sat, and nothing more.

Then this ebony bird beguiling my sad fancy into smiling
By the grave and stern decorum of the countenance it wore,
"Though thy crest be shorn and shaven, thou," I said, "art sure
no craven;
Ghastly, grim and ancient raven, wandering from the nightly shore,
Tell me what thy lordly name is on the Night's Plutonian shore."
Quoth the raven, "Nevermore!"

Much I marveled this ungainly fowl to hear discourse so plainly,
Though its answer little meaning, little relevancy, bore;
For we cannot help agreeing that no living human being
Ever yet was blessed with seeing bird above his chamber-door—
Bird or beast upon the sculptured bust upon his chamber-door—
With such a name as "Nevermore!"

But the raven, sitting lonely on the placid bust, spoke only
That one word, as if his soul in that one word he did outpour.

7

Nothing further then he uttered—not a feather then he fluttered—
Till I scarcely more than muttered, "Other friends have flown
    before;
On the morrow he will leave me, as my hopes have flown before."
      Then the bird said, "Nevermore!"

Startled at the stillness broken by reply so aptly spoken,
"Doubtless," said I, "what it utters is its only stock and store,
Caught from some unhappy master, whom unmerciful disaster
Followed fast and followed faster, till his songs one burden bore—
Till the dirges of his hope that melancholy burden bore—
      Of Never—nevermore!"

But the raven still beguiling all my sad soul into smiling,
Straight I wheeled a cushioned seat in front of bird and bust and
    door.
Then upon the velvet sinking, I betook myself to linking
Fancy unto fancy, thinking what this ominous bird of yore—
What this grim, ungainly, ghastly, gaunt and ominous bird of yore—
      Meant in croaking "Nevermore!"

This I sat engaged in guessing, but no syllable expressing
To the fowl, whose fiery eyes now burned into my bosom's core.
This and more I sat divining, with my head at ease reclining
On the cushion's velvet lining that the lamplight gloated o'er,
But whose velvet violet lining, with the lamplight gloating o'er,
      She shall press—ah! nevermore!

Then methought the air grew denser, perfumed from an unseen
    censer,
Swung by seraphim whose footfalls tinkled on the tufted floor.
"Wretch," I cried, "thy God hath lent thee—by these angels he
    hath sent thee—
Respite—respite and nepenthe from thy memories of Lenore!
Quaff, oh, quaff this kind nepenthe, and forget this lost Lenore!"
      Quoth the raven, "Nevermore!"

"Prophet," said I, "thing of evil—prophet still, if bird or devil—
Whether tempter sent or whether tempest tossed thee here ashore,
Desolate, yet all undaunted, on this desert land enchanted—
In this home by Horror haunted—tell me truly, I implore!
Is there—is there balm in Gilead?—tell me—tell me, I implore!"
      Quoth the raven, "Nevermore!"

"Prophet," said I, "thing of evil—prophet still, if bird or devil—
By that heaven that bends above us, by that God we both adore,
Tell this soul, with sorrow laden, if, within the distant Aidenn,
It shall clasp a sainted maiden whom the angels name Lenore;
Clasp a rare and radiant maiden whom the angels name Lenore!"
  Quoth the raven, "Nevermore!"

"Be that word our sign of parting, bird or fiend!" I shrieked
  upstarting—
"Get thee back into the tempest and the Night's Plutonian shore!
Leave no black plume as a token of that lie thy soul has spoken!
Leave my loneliness unbroken! quit the bust above my door!
Take thy beak from out my heart, and take thy form from off my
  door!"
  Quoth the raven, "Nevermore!"

And the raven, never flitting, still is sitting, still is sitting
On the pallid bust of Pallas, just above my chamber-door;
And his eyes have all the seeming of a demon's that is dreaming,
And the lamplight o'er him streaming throws his shadow on the
  floor;
And my soul from out that shadow that lies floating on the floor
  Shall be lifted—NEVERMORE!
        EDGAR A. POE, 1811–1849.

27.—ANCIENT AND MODERN ORATORY.

Is ancient eloquence superior to modern? There is a pre-
liminary point to settle, and that is the *standard* of excellence.
What are we to look at—is it elegance, is it feeling, is it pas-
sion, is it argument, is it logic or rhetoric, or all combined?
Some have a simple test, and that is persuasiveness; the best
oration is the most persuasive, and, *vice versâ*, the most persua-
sive is the best, for it best fulfills the end of eloquence, which
is persuasion.

But there is another element of great importance which
may vary much in orations equally persuasive, and that is
artistic perfection, aptness to satisfy the æsthetic sense, the
critical faculty in man. An oration may be regarded as a
work of art, and subject more or less to the predicates *sym-*

metrical, perfect, beautiful, or the reverse. Indeed, no culti-
vated mind can help taking this view. He who has taste—
that is, the critical faculty which judges of form—must be
shocked with what is out of taste, must admire that which
good taste recommends and sanctions.

Now, it is precisely here that I would take my stand. In
everything else—in vehemence of passion, in depth of feeling,
in cogency of argument, in attractiveness of persuasion—I
admit that the moderns have shown themselves not inferior to
the ancients. But in finish and perfection, in symmetry and
beauty of outward form, I bow to the superiority of the ancient
masters. I regard the orations of Demosthenes as not only
unsurpassed, but as unrivaled specimens of oratoric art.

And now, having pronounced this opinion, if you ask me why,
why this was so, why an old Athenian should have borne away
from all the world the prize of art in oratory, I cannot say, I can-
not satisfy your curiosity. I do not ascribe it to a genial climate
or a productive soil, to successful wars with foreign powers or
noble struggles for national independence, nor to agricultural,
mechanical, professional, political activity, nor to democratic
institutions, to annual magistracies, to vote by ballot or by
bean. I do not deny that these things had their influence, as
furnishing field and opportunity and encouragement to intel-
lectual development. But that matchless *æsthe'sis* of the
Greeks, that unrivaled taste, that wonderful sense of beauty
and harmony and proportion—where that came from is more
than I can tell; I greatly doubt whether it is in any proper
sense the creature of external circumstances.

I hold, then, that the same causes which made a Homer the
first of epic poets, and a Phidias the first of sculptors, and a
Pindar the first of lyric bards, and the builder of the Parthe-
non the first of architects—*the same causes rendered Demos-
thenes the first of orators.* Only let the circumstances offer
fair occasion, and the nation which has the keenest and truest
sense of the beautiful and the perfect will present the highest
master-works of art.

Every oration of Demosthenes is, to my mind, a heroic exhibition of self-denial. So many graces of style and felicities of expression, so many details, sublime, pathetic, brilliant, must have occurred to his rich and copious mind, which ever and anon shows, when such things are necessary, that there was no lack of power to originate them, and yet, in general, he rigorously rejects them, and if he ever employs them, employs them most sparingly. Everywhere he sacrifices the part to the whole, beauty of detail to general effect; and so he holds on in his severe simplicity, rarely allowing any embellishment, just as the architect decorates only the capitals of his columns or the cornice of his roof, trusting to the grand and stately proportions of the completed edifice. How different all this from the general character of modern oratory, and, above all, of American oratory, I need not say.

JAMES HADLEY, 1820–1872.

28.—PUFFING IN LITERATURE.*

A PIOUS Brahmin, it is written, made a vow that on a certain day he would sacrifice a sheep, and on the appointed morning he went forth to buy one. There lived in his neighborhood three rogues who knew of his vow, and laid a scheme for profiting by it. They first met him, and said, " O Brahmin, wilt thou buy a sheep? I have one fit for sacrifice." "It is for that very purpose," said the holy man, "that I came forth this day."

Then the impostor opened a bag, and brought out of it an unclean beast, an ugly dog, lame and blind. Thereon the Brahmin cried out, "Wretch, who touchest things impure, and utterest things untrue, callest thou that cur a sheep?" "Truly," answered the other, "it is a sheep of the finest fleece and of the sweetest flesh. O Brahmin, it will be an offering most acceptable to the gods." "Friend," said the Brahmin, "either thou or I must be blind." Just then one of the

---

* The above extract is from a severe criticism on the poems of Mr. Robert Montgomery, originally published in the Edinburgh Review of 1830.

7 *

accomplices came up. "Praised be the gods," said this second rogue, "that I have been saved the trouble of going to the market for a sheep! This is such a sheep as I wanted. For how much wilt thou sell it?" When the Brahmin heard this, his mind waved to and fro, like one swinging in the air at a holy festival. "Sir," said he to the new-comer, "take heed what thou dost; this is no sheep, but an unclean cur." "O Brahmin," said the new-comer, "thou art drunk or mad."

At this time the third confederate drew near. "Let us ask this man," said the Brahmin, "what the creature is, and I will stand by what he shall say." To this the others agreed, and the Brahmin called out, "O stranger, what dost thou call this beast?" "Surely, O Brahmin," said the knave, "it is a fine sheep." Then the Brahmin said, "Surely the gods have taken away my senses;" and he asked pardon of him who carried the dog, and bought it for a measure of rice and a pot of ghee, and offered it up to the gods, who, being wroth at this unclean sacrifice, smote him with a sore disease in all his joints.

Thus, or nearly thus, if we remember rightly, runs the story of the Sanscrit Æsop. The moral, like the moral of every fable that is worth the telling, lies on the surface. The writer evidently means to caution us against the practices of puffers —a class of people who have more than once talked the public into the most absurd errors.

Macaulay (see p. 59).

--- +◦+ ---

29.—TRIAL OF ROARING RALPH.

Roaring Ralph was one day arraigned before a county court in Kentucky on a charge of horse-stealing. Matters were going hard against him. His many offenses in that line had steeled against him the hearts of all. The proofs of guilt in this particular instance were both strong and manifold. Many an angry and unpitying eye was bent upon the unfortunate fellow when his counsel rose to attempt a defense. This he did in the following terms:

"Gentlemen of the jury," said the man of law, "here is a

man, Captain Ralph Stackpole, indicted before you on the charge of stealing a horse, and the affair is pretty considerably proved on him." Here there was a murmur heard throughout the court, evincing much approbation of the counsel's frankness. "Gentlemen of the jury," continued the orator, elevating his voice, " what I have to say in reply is, first, that that man thar', Captain Ralph Stackpole, did, in the year seventeen seventy-nine, when this good State of Kentucky, and particularly these parts adjacent to Bear's Grass and the mouth thereof, where now stands the town of Louisville, were overrun with yelping Injun savages,—did, I say, gentlemen, meet two Injun savages in the woods on Bear's Grass, and take their scalps, single-handed—a feat, gentlemen of the jury, that an't to be performed every day, even in Kentucky!"

Here there was considerable tumult in the court, and several persons began to swear. "Secondly, gentlemen of the jury," exclaimed the attorney-at-law, with a still louder voice, " what I have to say *secondly*, gentlemen of the jury, is that this same identical prisoner at the bar, Captain Ralph Stackpole, did on another occasion, in the year seventeen eighty-two, meet another Injun savage in the woods—a savage armed with rifle, knife and tomahawk—met him with—you suppose, gentlemen, with gun, axe and scalper, in like manner? No, gentlemen of the jury! with his *fists*, and " (with a voice of thunder) " licked him to death in the natural way! Gentlemen of the jury, pass upon the prisoner—guilty, or not guilty?"

The attorney resumed his seat; his arguments were irresistible. The jurors started up in their box and roared out to a man, "*Not guilty!*" From that moment, it may be supposed, Roaring Ralph could steal horses at his pleasure. Nevertheless, it seems, he immediately lost his appetite for horseflesh; and leaving the land altogether, he betook himself to a more congenial element, launched his broad-horn on the narrow bosom of the Salt, and was soon afterward transformed into a Mississippi alligator, in which amphibious condition, we presume, he roared on till the day of his death.

Robert Bird, 1803–1854.

30.—TO MY HORSE.

COME forth, my brave steed, the sun shines on the vale,
And the morning is bearing its balm on the gale;
Come forth, my brave steed, and brush off as we pass,
With the hoofs of thy speed, the bright dew from the grass!

Let the lover go warble his strains to the fair—
I regard not his rapture, and heed not his care;
But now, as we bound o'er the mountain and lea,
I will weave, my brave steed, a wild measure for thee.

Away and away! I exult in the glow
Which is breathing its pride on my cheek as we go;
And blithely my spirit springs forth as the air
Which is waving the mane of thy dark flowing hair.

Hail, thou gladness of heart and thou freshness of soul
Which have never come o'er me in pleasure's control;
Which the dance and the revel, the bowl and the board,
Though they flushed and they fevered, could never afford.

In the splendor of solitude speed we along
Through the silence but broke by the wild linnet's song;
Not a sight to the eye, not a sound to the ear,
To tell us that sin and that sorrow are near.

Away, and away, and away, then, we pass!
The mole shall not hear thy light hoof on the grass;
Oh the time which is flying whilst I am with thee
Seems as swift as thyself as we bound o'er the lea!

LORD LYTTON (BULWER), 1807–1873.

----◆----

31.—MR. PUFF'S ACCOUNT OF HIMSELF.

SIR, I make no secrets of the trade I follow. Among friends and brother authors I love to be frank on the subject, and to advertise myself *vi'va vo'ce.* I am, sir, a practitioner in panegyric, or, to speak more plainly, a professor of the art of puffing, at your service, or anybody else's. I dare say, now, you conceive half the very civil paragraphs and advertisements you see, to be written by the parties concerned or their friends. No such thing; nine out of ten are manufactured by me, in the way of business.

You must know, sir, that from the first time I tried my hand at an advertisement, my success was such that for some time after I led a most extraordinary life indeed. Sir, I supported myself two years entirely by my misfortunes; by advertisements *To the charitable and humane,* and *To those whom Providence has blessed with affluence!* And, in truth, I deserved what I got, for I suppose man never went through such a series of calamities in the same space of time.

Sir, I was five times made a bankrupt, and reduced from a state of affluence by a train of unavoidable misfortunes; then, sir, though a very industrious tradesman, I was twice burned out, and lost my little all both times. I lived upon those fires a month. I soon after was confined by a most excruciating disorder, and lost the use of my limbs. That told very well, for I had the case strongly attested, and went about to collect the subscriptions myself. I was afterwards twice tapped for a dropsy which declined into a very profitable consumption. I was then reduced to— Oh no! then I became a widow with six helpless children.

F

All this I bore with patience, though I made some occasional attempts at *felo de se;* but as I did not find these rash actions answer, I left off killing myself very soon. Well, sir, at last, what with bankruptcies, fires, gouts, dropsies, imprisonments and other valuable calamities, having got together a pretty handsome sum, I determined to quit a business which had always gone rather against my conscience, and in a more liberal way still to indulge my talents for fiction and embellishments through my favorite channel of diurnal communication ; and so, sir, you have my history.

R. B. Sheridan, 1751–1816.

32.—CALIFORNIA'S PROSPECTS AND DUTIES.

No greater blunder could any man make than expecting to find here, in California, a paradise for idleness and vice. He could stay at home with better prospects far, much more comfort and far less expense. It is true here, if it be true anywhere, that "if a man will not work neither shall he eat." This is the scriptural doctrine, and it is the California doctrine too. It is death to stand still. And so far from complaining, every true man should rejoice, that gold cannot be picked up on the surface and everywhere, but requires, like everything else worth having, hard and patient toil. A man must keep moving, and to some purpose ; for there are none to help a man who will not help himself. It is not idleness or vice which has converted a wilderness with almost miraculous rapidity into thriving cities and towns which already rival those of long-settled communities. It is no mean and solely Mammon-worshiping population which has established courts of justice, the schoolhouse, the church and the press, as among the necessities of a free people. These are the fruits of industry, of intelligence and of religious principle.

But we have still a great work to do here, on this spot, and now. Ignorance is to be enlightened, sin is to be removed and society to be reconstructed on these Pacific shores. This people ought to be, not as *good* as any other, but a great deal *better* than any other. We have the whole past from the beginning of time to build upon. What a universe is here of history, of philosophy, of ethics, of solid experience! To us, under God, it may be given to belt the world with Christian civilization.

If the alphabet of the highest truth was created in the East, and has ever since traveled westward, growing into a complete science, how inspiring the thought that we may carry it round a full circle to its starting-place, restoring fourfold into its bosom, and accomplish the magnificent prophecy, that "righteousness shall cover the earth as the waters cover the seas"! Already what Coleridge saw with the vision of a seer we see growing into reality before our very eyes: "Millions of people, extending from the Atlantic to the Pacific, living under the laws of Alfred, and speaking the language of Milton and Shakspeare." This he called "a grand conception." It is now a grand reality, and becoming grander every hour.

Charles A. Farley.

33.—LORD ULLIN'S DAUGHTER.

A CHIEFTAIN to the Highlands bound cries, "Boatman, do
    not tarry!
And I'll give thee a silver pound to row us o'er the ferry."
"Now, who be ye would cross Lochgyle, this dark and stormy
    water?"
"Oh, I'm the chief of Ulva's isle, and this, Lord Ullin's
    daughter;
And fast before her father's men three days we've fled
    together,
For should he find us in the glen, my blood would stain the
    heather.
His horsemen hard behind us ride; should they our steps
    discover,
Then who will cheer my bonny bride when they have slain
    her lover?"

Out spoke the hardy Highland wight: "I'll go, my chief—
    I'm ready;
It is not for your silver bright, but for your winsome lady,
And, by my word, the bonny bird in danger shall not tarry;
So though the waves are raging white, I'll row you o'er the
    ferry."
By this the storm grew loud apace, the water-wraith was
    shrieking,
And in the scowl of Heaven each face grew dark as they
    were speaking.
And still, as wilder blew the wind, and as the night grew
    drearer,
Adown the glen rode arméd men, their trampling sounded
    nearer.

The boat has left the stormy land, a stormy sea before her,
When, oh! too strong for human hand, the tempest gathered
    o'er her.
And still they rowed amid the roar of waters fast prevailing;
Lord Ullin reached that fatal shore, his wrath was changed
    to wailing.
For sore dismayed, through storm and shade, his child he did
    discover;
One lovely hand she stretched for aid, and one was round
    her lover.
"Come back! come back!" he cried in grief, "across this
    stormy water,
And I'll forgive your Highland chief, my daughter—oh, my
    daughter!"
'Twas vain: the loud waves lashed the shore, return or aid
    preventing;
The waters wild closed o'er his child, and he was left lament-
    ing.

THOMAS CAMPBELL, 1777–1844.

34.—THE PRICE OF LIBERTY.

"ETERNAL vigilance is the price of liberty." "Power is ever stealing from the many to the few." The manna of popular liberty must be gathered each day, or it is rotten. The living sap of to-day outgrows the dead rind of yesterday. The hand intrusted with power becomes, either from human depravity or *esprit de corps*, the necessary enemy of the people. Only by continual oversight can the democrat in office be prevented from hardening into a despot. Only by unintermitted agitation can a people be kept sufficiently awake to principle not to let liberty be smothered in material prosperity. All clouds, it is said, have sunshine behind them, and all evils have some good results.

Never look, therefore, for an age when the people can be quiet and safe. At such times despotism, like a shrouding mist, steals over the mirror of freedom. The Dutch a thousand years ago built against the ocean their bulwark of willow and mud. Do they trust to that? No. Each year the patient, industrious peasant gives so much time from the cultivation of his soil and the care of his children to stop the breaks and replace the willow which insects have eaten, that he may keep the land his fathers rescued from the water, and bid defiance to the waves that roar above his head, as if demanding back the broad fields man has stolen from their realm.

Some men suppose that in order to the people's governing themselves it is only necessary, as Fisher Ames said, that the "Rights of Man be printed, and that every citizen have a copy." As the Epicureans, two thousand years ago, imagined God a being who arranged this marvelous machinery, set it going and then sank to sleep! Republics exist only on the tenure of being constantly agitated. There is no Canaan in politics. As health lies in labor, so there is no republican road to safety but in constant distrust. "In distrust," said Demosthenes, "are the nerves of the mind." Let us see to it that these sentinel nerves are ever on the alert. If the Alps, piled in cold and still sublimity, be the emblem of despotism,

8

the ever-restless ocean is ours, which, girt with the eternal laws
of gravitation, is pure only because never still.

WENDELL PHILLIPS.

35.—A DEMOCRACY HATEFUL TO PHILIP.

THERE are those among you, Athenians, who think to
confound a speaker by asking him, "What, then, is to be
done?" To which I might
reply, "Nothing that you are
doing; everything that you
leave undone!" And it would
be an apt, a true reply. But
I will be more explicit, and
may these men, so ready to
question, be equally ready to
act!

In the first place, Athenians,
admit the incontestable fact
that Philip has violated his
treaties and declared war
against you. On that point

DEMOSTHENES.

let us have no further crimination or recrimination. And
then admit the fact that he is the mortal enemy of Athens,
of its very soil, of all within its walls—ay, of those even who
most flatter themselves that they are high in his good graces.
What Philip most fears and abhors is our liberty, our free
democratic system. For the destruction of that all his snares
are laid, all his projects are shaped.

Is he not consistent in this? Truly, he is well aware that
though he should subjugate all the rest of Greece, his conquest
would be insecure so long as your democracy should stand.
Well does he know that should he experience one of those
reverses to which the lot of humanity is so liable, it would be
into your arms that all of those nations now forcibly held
under his yoke would rush. Is there a tyrant to drive back?
Athens is in the field! Is there a people to be enfranchised?

Lo, Athens, prompt to aid! What wonder, then, that Philip should be impatient so long as Athenian liberty is a spy upon his evil days? Be sure, O my countrymen, that Philip is your irreconcilable foe; that it is against Athens he musters all his armaments; against Athens all his schemes are laid.

What, then, as wise men convinced of these truths, ought you to do? What but to shake off your fatal lethargy, contribute according to your means, summon your allies to contribute and take measures to maintain the troops already under arms, so that if Philip has an army prepared to attack and subjugate all the Greeks, you may have an army ready to succor them and to save? Tell me not of the trouble and expense which this will involve. I grant it all. But consider the dangers that beset you, and how much you will be the gainers by engaging heartily at once in the general cause.

Verily, should some god assure you that however inert and unconcerned you might remain, yet in the end you should not be molested by Philip, still it would be ignominious (bear witness, Heaven!), it would be beneath you, beneath the dignity of your State, beneath the glory of your ancestors, to sacrifice to your own selfish repose the interests of all the rest of Greece. Rather would I perish than recommend such a course. Let some other man urge it upon you, if he will; and listen to him, ye, if you can!

But if my sentiments are yours, if you foresee, as I do, that the more we leave Philip to extend his conquests, the more we are fortifying an enemy whom, sooner or later, we must cope with, why do you hesitate? what wait you? When will you put forth your strength? Wait you the constraint of necessity? What necessity? Can there be a more pressing one for freemen than the prospect of dishonor? Do you wait for that? It is here already; it presses, it weighs on us even now. Now, did I say? Long since was it before us, face to face. Truly, there is still another necessity in reserve—the necessity of slaves—subjugation, blows and stripes. Wait you for them? The gods forbid! The very words are in this place an indignity!

DEMOSTHENES.

36.—THE COMING BARD.

Oh! when at length the expected bard shall come,
Land of our pride, to strike thine echoes dumb
(And many a voice exclaims in prose and rhyme
It's getting late, and he's behind his time),
When all thy mountains clap their hands in joy,
And all thy cataracts thunder, "That's the boy,"—
Say if with him the reign of song shall end,
And Heaven declare its final dividend?

Be calm, dear brother whose impassioned strain
Comes from an alley watered by a drain;
The little Mincio, dribbling to the Po,
Beats all the epics of the Hoang-Ho;
If loved in earnest by the tuneful maid,
Don't mind their nonsense, never be afraid!

The nurse of poets feeds her wingéd brood
By common firesides on familiar food;
In a low hamlet, by a narrow stream,
Where bovine rustics used to doze and dream,
She filled young William's fiery fancy full,
While old John Shakspeare talked of beeves and wool!

No Alpine needle, with its climbing spire,
Brings down for mortals the Promethean fire,
If careless nature have forgot to frame
An altar worthy of the sacred flame.
Unblest by any save the goat-herd's lines,
Mont Blanc rose soaring through his "sea of pines;"
In vain the Arvé and Arveiron dash,
No hymn salutes them but the Ranz des Vaches,
Till lazy Coleridge, by the morning's light,
Gazed for a moment on the fields of white,
And, lo! the glaciers found at length a tongue,
Mont Blanc was vocal, and Chamouni sung!

Children of wealth or want, to each is given
One spot of green, and all the blue of heaven!
Enough if these their outward shows impart;
The rest is thine—the scenery of the heart.
If passion's hectic in thy stanzas glow,
Thy heart's best life-blood ebbing as they flow;
If with thy verse thy strength and bloom distill,
Drained by the pulses of the fevered thrill;
If sound's sweet effluence polarize thy brain,
And thoughts turn crystals in thy fluid strain,—
Nor rolling ocean, nor the prairie's bloom,
Nor streaming cliffs, nor rayless cavern's gloom,
Need'st thou, young poet, to inform thy line;
Thy own broad signet stamps thy song divine!

O. W. HOLMES, 1811.

37.—VIRIATHUS TO THE LUSITANIANS.

Vir-i-a'thus, a Lusitanian shepherd, having escaped the massacre of his people by the Roman proconsul Galba, in the year 150 B. C. (Before Christ), roused and rallied round him his countrymen, and for eight years carried on a war disastrous to Rome. Lusitania comprised the country now known as Portugal.

WHO speaks of Roman pledges? Hear me, Lusitanians! Fresh from a spectacle of Roman perfidy, cowardice, barbarity, I can tell you a tale which will send the blood boiling in torrents of indignation to your hearts. Lured by the pledges of Sulpicius Galba, the Roman pretor, we descended, some thousands of us, from our mountain villages, with our wives and children, and gave up to him our weapons, under a promise of receiving grants of land.

Fatal confidence! No sooner had we parted with our instruments of war than the savage tyrant, the infamous Galba, ordered a general massacre of our people. Brutally was the brutal order carried out. Old men, women, children, the gray-haired, the feeble, the unresisting, were slaughtered in cold blood, with every aggravation of cruelty. My own father, the aged Vir-i-a'thus, was stricken down at my side. I saw the wound on his venerable head—the streaming, precious blood. With dying breath, "Fly," he said, "if not for life, for vengeance!"

That last word compelled me. I wrested a sword from one of the murderers—hewed for myself a lane through the confounded soldiery—sprang on a fleet horse—escaped—and here I am, with my story of wrong and outrage. Well may ye clench your hands! Oh, let them not be empty! Let them close upon the handles of your good blades! Rise, my countrymen! Throw off the yoke of Rome! Arm, and follow me to the field!

Who croaks to us of the power of Rome? The power of Rome lies in her audacity. She dares—and *does!* Let us imitate her in this. Do we not outnumber her legions ten to one? Have we not had enough of Roman extortion—of Roman perfidy! Let the name of Galba be the answer! Rome is an abyss which no treasure wrung from plundered provinces can fill up. Her pretors come, not to govern us justly and humanely, but to amass wealth for their private coffers, without scruple as to the means; and when we will not give up *all* our possessions, even to the poor means of subsistence we share with the beasts, then—then a perfidious massacre is the result.

Rome has driven us to the brink. We must turn upon her or leap the gulf. We *will* turn, my countrymen—shall we not? Why, a rat will turn, even against desperate odds, when he is cornered. And shall we—men, Lusitanians, the sons of brave sires and chaste mothers—shall we stand panic-stricken while Roman ruffians slay and give no quarter—none even to our wives and little ones?

Ask ye for a leader? Ye shall not go far to find one. I claim the office. In my wrongs behold my title. Not one of all my kindred has Rome spared. So now I am all my country's—every sinew, every pulse, every desire of my heart, every faculty of my brain. Here I devote myself, body and soul, to the utter extermination of Roman power from the land. Arm, then, my countrymen, arm, and follow me to victory or death!

SARGENT.

38.—NO ALLIANCES WITH CROWNED HEADS, 1851.

WE should not close our eyes to the fact that a great movement is in progress which threatens the existence of every absolute government in Europe. It will be a struggle between liberal and absolute principles—between republicanism and despotism. Are we to remain cold and indifferent spectators when the time of action shall arrive, and the exciting scene shall be presented to our view? Will it not become our duty to do whatever the interests, honor and glory of our country may require, in pursuance of the law of nations, to give encouragement to that great movement? Should we not recognize the independence of each republic as soon as it shall be established, open diplomatic intercourse, form commercial treaties, and, in short, extend the right hand of fellowship, tendering all the courtesies and privileges which should exist between friendly nations of the same political faith? I think that the bearing of this country should be such as to demonstrate to all mankind that America sympathizes with the popular movement against despotism, whenever and wherever made.

Sir, something has been said about an alliance with England to restrain the march of Russia over the European continent. I am free to say that I desire no alliance with England or with any other crowned head. I am not willing to acknowledge that America needs England as an ally to maintain the principles of our government. Nor am I willing to go to the rescue of England, to save her from the power of the autocrat, until she assimilates her institutions to ours. Hers is a half-way house between despotism and republicanism. She is responsible as much as any power in Europe for the failure of the revolutionary movements which have occurred within the last four years. English diplomacy, English intrigue and English perfidy put down the revolution in Sicily and in Italy, and was the greatest barrier to its success even in Hungary. So long as England shall, by her diplomacy, attempt to defeat liberal movements in Europe, I am utterly averse to an alliance with her to sustain her monarch, her nobles and her privileged classes.

I repeat, I desire no alliance with England. We require no assistance from her, and will yield none to her until she does justice to her own people. The peculiar position of our country requires that we should have an *American policy* in our foreign relations, based upon the principles of our own government and adapted to the spirit of the age. We should sympathize with every liberal movement, recognize the independence of all republics, form commercial treaties and open diplomatic relations with them, protest against all infractions of the laws of nations, and hold ourselves ready to do whatever our duty may require when a case shall arise.

STEPHEN A. DOUGLAS, 1813–1861.

39.—LIFT UP THINE EYES, AFFLICTED SOUL.

LIFT up thine eyes, afflicted soul!
From earth lift up thine eyes,
Though dark the evening shadows roll,
And daylight beauty dies;
One sun is set—a thousand more
Their rounds of glory run,
Where science leads thee to explore
In every star a sun.

Thus, when some long-loved comfort ends,
And nature would despair,
Faith to the heaven of heavens ascends,
And meets ten thousand there;
First faint and small, then clear and bright,
They gladden all the gloom,
And stars that seem but points of light
The rank of suns assume.

JAMES MONTGOMERY, 1771–1855.

40.—WILLIAM TELL AT ALTORF.

CHARACTERS.—*Verner, Tell, Sarnem, Michael.*

Verner. Stay, William Tell.   What means that drum?
      Give heed:
Observe the people.

   Tell. What new show is this?

   Verner. A pole, and on the top of it a cap!

   Tell. Hark! Look at that tall fellow with the sword;
He's going to speak.

   Sarnem. Ye men of Altorf, hear me!
Behold the emblem of your master's power
And dignity.   This is the cap of Gesler,

Your governor, whose pleasure now it is
The cap shall have like honor as himself,
And all shall reverence it with bended knee
And head uncovered.   Those who shall refuse
This act of homage shall be marked and punished.

Verner. A strange device to hit upon, indeed!
Do reverence to a cap?   A pretty freak!

Tell. What!   Grovel to a cap?   Kneel to a cap?
Rare jesting this with men of sober sense!

Verner. No freeborn man will stoop to such disgrace.

Tell. And yet they do it, Verner.   Look!   They do it.
The cravens!   Never call me man again:
I'll herd with brutes.   Am I the same in kind
With yonder servile creature who uncovers
His head and bows—bows to a tyrant's cap?

Verner. Let's slip away before they mark us; come!

Tell. No, no; since I have tasted, I'll feed on.

Verner. See!   There goes one who bows not low enough.
"Bow lower, slave," cries Sarnem, striking him;
And he bows lower.

Tell. Verner, felt you not
That blow?   I did!   My flesh doth tingle with it.

Verner. You tremble, William.   Come, you must not stay.

Tell. Why not?   I'm armed, you see.   I tell you, Verner,
I know no difference 'twixt enduring wrong
And living in the fear of 't.   I do wear
The tyrant's fetters when it only wants
His nod to put them on.   [*Enter* MICHAEL.]

Verner. Hark!   What is this?

Sar. Bow, man!

Michael. For what?

Sar. Obey, and question then!

Mich. I'll question now, perhaps not then obey.

Sar. 'Tis Gesler's will that all
Bow to that cap.

Mich. Were it thy lady's cap,
I'd curtsey to it.

Sar. Do you mock us, friend?

Mich. Not I. I'll bow to Gesler, if you please,
Not to his cap. No, not to any man's.

Sar. I see you love a jest; but jest not now!
Bow to the cap! Do you hear?

Mich. I hear.

Tell. Well done! A man! A man, I say!
The lion thinks as much of cowering
As he does.

Sar. Once for all, bow to that cap!

Tell. Verner, let go my arm!

Sar. Do you hear me, slave?

Mich. Slave?

Tell. Let me go!

Verner. He is not worth it, Tell:
A wild gallant—an idler of the town.

Tell. A man, I say—a man! Don't hold me, Verner!
Let go! You must not hold me.

Sar. Villain, bow
To Gesler's cap!

Mich. No! Not to Gesler's self.

Sar. Guards, seize him!

Tell. Off, you base and hireling pack!
Lay not your brutal touch upon a *man*.
Do not ask *him* to bow. Go, crouch yourselves;
'Tis your vocation, which you should not call
On freeborn men to follow—men who stand
Erect, save in the presence of their Maker.

Sar. What, soldiers! Have ye arms, and do ye shrink
Before this clown? Seize him! Or must I do
Your duty for you?

Tell. Let them try it. Come!
A flock of wolves that did outnumber them
I've scattered just for sport—ay, scattered them
With but a staff not half so thick as this.

(*Wrests Sarnem's weapon from him.* SARNEM *and* SOLDIERS *fly.*)

Verner. Now, Tell, away, before that gilded minion
Returns with help. Come! Be not rash. Away!
  Mich. Whatever happens, Tell, count me your backer.
  Tell. Ye men of Altorf,
What fear ye? See what things ye fear—the shows
And surfaces of men! Why stand you wondering there?
Or is't that cap still holds you thralled to fear?
Be free, then! There! Thus do I trample on
The insolence of Gesler. (*Throws down the pole.*)
             JAMES SHERIDAN KNOWLES, 1794–1862.

41.—IO TRIUMPHE.

Now let us raise a song of praise, like Miriam's song of old—
A song of praise to God the Lord, for blessings manifold!
He lifteth up, he casteth down; he bindeth, maketh free;
He sendeth grace to bear defeat; he giveth victory!
Fling out, fling out the holy flag broad in the swelling air!
Its stars renew their morning song. All hail the symbol fair!
For what the fathers did of yore the sons have learned to do;
And the old legends, half believed, are proven by the new.

Then honor, under God, to those, the noble men who plan,
And unto those of fiery mould who flame in battle's van!
For, oh, the land is safe, is safe; it rallies from the shock;
Ring round, ring round, ye merry bells, till every steeple
    rock!
Loud let the cannon's voice be heard! hang all your banners
    out!
Lift up in your exultant streets the nation's triumph-shout!
Let trumpets bray and wild drums beat; let maidens scatter
    flowers!
The sun bursts thro' the battle-smoke; hurrah! the day is
    ours!
             ELBRIDGE J. CUTTER, Feb. 20, 1862.

42.—THE GOOD GODDESS OF POVERTY.

PATHS sanded with gold, verdant wastes, ravines which the wild-goat loves, great mountains crowned with stars, tumbling torrents, impenetrable forests, let the good goddess pass, the goddess of Poverty! Since the world has existed, since men were in it, she traverses the world, she dwells among men; singing she travels, or working she sings—the goddess, the good goddess of Poverty! Some men assembled to curse her, but they found her too beautiful and too glad, too agile and too strong. "Strip off her wings!" said they; "give her chains, give her stripes, crush her, let her perish—the goddess of Poverty!"

They have chained the good goddess, they have beaten her, and persecuted, but they cannot debase her! She has taken refuge in the souls of poets, of peasants, of artists, of martyrs and of saints—the good goddess, the goddess of Poverty! She has walked more than the Wandering Jew; she has traveled more than the swallow; she is older than the cathedral of Prague; she is younger than the egg of the wren; she has increased more than the strawberry in Bohemian forests—the goddess, the good goddess of Poverty! Many children has she had, and many a divine secret has she taught them; she knows more than all the doctors and all the lawyers—the good goddess of Poverty!

She does all the greatest and most beautiful things that are done in the world; it is she who cultivates the fields and prunes the trees; it is she who drives the herds to pasture, singing the while all sweet songs; it is she who sees the day break and catches the sun's first smile—the good goddess of Poverty! It is she who builds of green boughs the woodman's cabin, and makes the hunter's eye like that of the eagle; it is she who brings up the handsomest children, and who leaves the plow and the spade light in the hands of the old man—the good goddess of Poverty!

It is she who inspires the poet and makes eloquent the violin, the guitar and the flute under the fingers of the wandering

9   G

artist; it is she who crowns his hair with pearls of the dew, and who makes the stars shine for him larger and more clear—the goddess, the good goddess of Poverty! It is she who instructs the dexterous artisan, and teaches him to hew stone, to carve marble, to fashion gold and silver, copper and iron; it is she who makes the flax flexible and fine as hair under the hands of the old wife and the young girl—the good goddess of Poverty!

It is she who sustains the cottage shaken by the storm; it is she who saves rosin for the torch and oil for the lamp; it is she who kneads bread for the family, and who weaves garments for them, summer and winter; it is she who maintains and feeds the world—the good goddess of Poverty! It is she who has built the great castles and the old cathedrals; it is she who builds and navigates all the ships; it is she who carries the sabre and the musket; it is she who makes war and conquests; it is she who buries the dead, cares for the wounded and shelters the vanquished—the good goddess of Poverty!

Thou art all gentleness, all patience, all strength and all compassion, O good goddess! it is thou who dost reunite all thy children in a holy love, givest them charity, faith, hope, O goddess of Poverty! Thy children will one day cease to bear the world on their shoulders; they will be recompensed for all their pains and labors. The time shall come when there shall be neither rich nor poor on the earth, but when all men shall partake of its fruits and enjoy equally the bounties of Providence; but thou shalt not be forgotten in their hymns, O good goddess of Poverty!

They will remember that thou wert their fruitful mother and their robust nurse. They will pour balm into thy wounds, and of the fragrant and rejuvenated earth they will make for thee a couch, where thou canst at length repose, O good goddess of Poverty! Until that day of the Lord, torrents and woods, mountains and valleys, wastes swarming with little flowers and little birds, paths sanded with gold without a master, let pass the goddess, the good goddess of Poverty!

George Sand.

43.—SANITARY LAWS.

SIR, when the religious man reflects that our bodies are God's workmanship, he sees that the laws impressed upon them can be no less than God's laws. If these laws, then, are God's laws, we are bound to recognize and obey them. We are bound to obey a law which God has impressed upon the body, on the same principle that we are bound to obey a law which he has impressed upon the soul. And, here, how pertinent and forcible is the great idea that when we know a law to be God's law, it matters not by what means we may have arrived at the knowledge—the law becomes imperatively and equally binding upon us! Between the law of the body and the law of the soul there may, indeed, sometimes arise what we call a conflict of duty, when the subordinate obligation of the former must yield to the supremacy of the latter; but this refers to relative importance, and not to inherent obligation.

My general conclusion, then, is that it is the duty of all the governing minds in society, whether in office or out of it, to diffuse a knowledge of these beautiful and beneficent laws of health and life throughout the length and breadth of the state—to popularize them; to make them, in the first place, the common acquisition of all, and through education and custom the common inheritance of all, so that the healthful habits naturally growing out of their observance shall be inbred in the people; exemplified in the personal regimen of each individual; incorporated into the economy of every household; observable in all private dwellings and in all public edifices, especially in those buildings which are erected by capitalists for the residence of their work-people, or for renting to the poorer classes; obeyed, by supplying cities with pure water; by providing public baths, public walks and public squares; by rural cemeteries; by the drainage and sewerage of populous towns;—in fine, by a religious observance of all those sanitary regulations with which modern science has blessed the world.

HORACE MANN, 1796–1859.

44.—TELL'S BIRTHPLACE.

MARK this holy chapel well!
The birthplace this of William Tell.
Here first an infant to her breast
Him his loving mother prest,
And kissed the babe, and blessed the day,
And prayed as mothers used to pray:
"Vouchsafe him health, O God, and give
The child thy servant still to live!"

But God had destined to do more
Through him than through an armèd power:
God gave him reverence of laws,
Yet stirring blood in Freedom's cause—
A spirit to his rocks akin,
The eye of the hawk and the fire therein!
To Nature and to Holy Writ
Alone did God the boy commit;
Where flashed and roared the torrent, oft
His soul found wings, and soared aloft!

The straining oar, the chamois chase,
Had formed his limbs to strength and grace;
On wave and wind the boy would toss,
Was great, nor knew how great he was!
He knew not that his chosen hand
(Made strong by God) his native land
Would rescue from the shameful yoke
Of slavery,—the which he broke!

STOLBERG (*imitated by* COLERIDGE).

45.—THE INFLUENCE OF INVENTORS.

SIR, in calling a meeting to do honor to the dead inventor whose invention can never die—the inventor of the electric telegraph—our city has shown itself to be on a level with the science and the humanity of the age. Our civilization, sir, depends for its progress upon the ever fresh supply of those intellects who wrest from reluctant Nature the secrets she so jealously hoards and hides. Certain inventions do not merely extend the dominion of human intelligence, but they at the same time are the beneficent creators of new wealth to satisfy human needs.

Great Britain spent a thousand millions of pounds sterling —five thousand millions of dollars—in her twenty years' war with revolutionary and imperial France. Now, who supplied the sinews of that long and terrible war? Is not the answer plain? They were supplied by James Watt and Richard Arkwright, two men who gave to their country labor-saving machines which were equivalent to the manual labor of five hundred millions of men. English statesmen and English generals, with all their blunders, could not waste wealth as fast as Watt and Arkwright created it. And the first Napoleon was at last overwhelmed, not by Pitt, Percival, Liverpool or Wellington, but by two illustrious inventors, one of whom began life as a mathematical-instrument-maker and the other as a common barber; these were the men who overthrew

Napoleon.' And I doubt whether we, with all our familiarity with the worth of industrial invention, can still realize the enormous, the unutterable debt of gratitude we owe to such of our countrymen as Whitney, Fulton, Howe, McCormick and Morse.

As to Morse and his invention, you all of you of course remember the well-known lines of Byron as he witnessed a thunder-storm among the Alps. He wishes he might wreak his thoughts upon expression—compress them into one word— "and that one word were lightning;" but Morse made the lightning not only converse, he made it to write also; he has forced it not only to flash terror, but to flash intelligence; he has made it to be the obedient, humble servant of the meanest as well as of the greatest of men and women. Under his control it condescends even to be careless or insipid, a retailer of gossip or thrall of scandal-mongers.

You all recollect the remark of the old lady when she saw a telegraph pole with its wires set up before her country cottage. "Now," she spitefully said, "I suppose no one can whip a child without its being known all over creation!" Certainly not, my good woman; the press of Calcutta and St. Petersburg will hear every slap you give, and hold you to strict account for all unnecessary infantile castigation.

Even the restive Yankee who, asking the operator in the early days of telegraphy how long it would take to send a message to Washington, and on being told five minutes replied that he could not wait—even he can now be satisfied. By the blessed difference in time he can be consoled by the assurance that this telegram from Liverpool will arrive several hours before the operator sent it. In short, Franklin drew the lightning from the skies; Morse sent it over the earth and commanded it to do the behests of his fellow-men.

But this taming of the seemingly untamable lightning has wrought noble as well as brilliant results. It enables great nations to communicate with each other in a minute of time. It enables the merchant who is rusticating at Newport or Saratoga to direct the course of his ships, separated from him though they be by ten or twenty thousand miles; and it equalizes prices by the transmission of intelligence that prevents monopoly. It enables the press to annihilate space and bring every morning, Europe, Asia and Africa to your very doors; and last, though not least, it makes every throb of the human heart, every tear and tender anxiety for absent friends, kinsmen, parents, lovers, known everywhere, and brings San Francisco, St. Louis, Chicago, Philadelphia, New York, Boston, London, Vienna, Paris, Berlin, Rome, Naples, and even Hong Kong, into one great metropolitan city.   E. P. WHIPPLE.

46.—ON ENGLISH INTERFERENCE, Oct., 1862.

Do not think I am going to predict what is going to happen in America, or to set myself up as a judge of the Americans. What I wish to say is a few words to throw light on our relations as a nation with the American people. We all regret this dreadful war, but to attempt to scold the Americans for fighting, or to think of reaching them with arguments when they are standing in mortal combat, a million of men armed and fighting to the death, would be the greatest waste of intellect we could commit.

There are motives at work among the large majority of the people of America which seem to me to drive them to this dreadful contest rather than see their country broken into two nations. Leaving the dreams aside, what appears to be in the present day the tendency among the races of man? Certainly not a desire to separate, but to agglomerate, to bring together in greater concentration different races speaking the same language and professing the same religion. What is going on in Italy? What is it that stirs the heart of Germany? What is it that moves Hungary? It is the nations wishing to come together. It is very odd that statesmen here who have a profound sympathy with the movement in Italy in favor of unity cannot appreciate the force of that motive in the present contest in America. Three-fourths of the whole population in America are now contending against disunion; they are fol-

lowing the instinct which is impelling the Italian, the German
and the other populations of Europe.

Let the foreigner once interfere in that quarrel, and you will
have in America a united people—united to repel the intru-
sion.   And let me remind you that your interference would
not obtain for you cotton.   If the great Western States—the
great, growing region of the Mississippi—determine to carry
on the war, and say, "We will never make peace while the
mouths of the Mississippi, which drain 27,000 miles of navi-
gable water into the ocean, remain in the hands of a foreign
power," we could never expect to put a period to it.   You
must remember that you have to go 1000 miles up the Mis-
sissippi before you get to that vast region, peopled by eight or
ten millions of souls, that will be the future depository of the
wealth and numbers of that great continent; and whatever
the will of that people is, New York is but the broker of their
opinion, and New York, Pennsylvania and New England must
go with them.

It is as idle, then, as the talk of children, for France and
England to pretend that they can go there and reach that
population.   For my part, I think the language which is used
sometimes in certain quarters with regard to the power of this
country to go and impose its will upon the population of
America almost savors of the ludicrous.   When America had
but 2,500,000 of population, we could not enforce our will
upon it.   And when you consider the tendency of modern
armaments, and when you have to deal with civilized people
having the same mechanical appliances as yourselves, and
when that people number ten, twenty, thirty millions, it is next
to impossible for any force to be transported across the Atlan-
tic which will effect a conquest.

Englishmen are very apt to think that they can do anything
by force.   Let them banish that idea; their interference in
this case would only do harm, and in the end you would not
get your cotton.   Even if you could, what price would you
pay for it?   I know something of the way in which money is
voted in the House of Commons for warlike armaments even

in a time of peace, and I venture to say that it would be cheaper to keep all the population engaged in the cotton man-ufacture—ay, to keep them on turtle, champagne and veni-son—than to send to America to obtain that cotton by force of arms. It would involve you in a war, and six months of a war would cost more money than would be required to main-tain this population comfortably for ten years.

RICHARD COBDEN.

47.—A CRY TO ARMS.

Ho, woodmen of the mountain side! ho, dwellers in the vales!
Ho, ye who by the chafing tide have roughened in the gales!
Leave barn and byre, leave kin and cot, lay by the bloodless spade,
Let desk and case and counter rot, and burn your books of trade.

The despot ravages your lands, and till he flies or fears,
Your fields must grow but armëd bands, your sheaves be sheaves
  of spears.
Give up to mildew and to rust the useless tools of gain,
And feed your country's sacred dust with floods of crimson rain.

Come with the weapons at your call, with musket, pike or knife;
He wields the deadliest blade of all who lightest holds his life.
The arm that drives its unbought blows with all a patriot's scorn
Might brain a tyrant with a rose, or stab him with a thorn.

Does any falter? Let him turn to some brave maiden's eyes,
And catch the holy fires that burn in those sublunar skies.
Oh, could you like your women feel, and in their spirit march,
A day might see your lines of steel beneath the victor's arch.

What hope, O heaven, would not grow warm when thoughts like
  these give cheer?
The lily calmly braves the storm, and shall the palm tree fear?
No! rather let its branches court the rack that sweeps the plain,
And from the lily's regal port learn how to breast the strain.

Ho, woodmen of the mountain side! ho, dwellers in the vales!
Ho, ye who by the roaring tide have roughened in the gales!
Come! flocking gayly to the fight, from forest, hill and lake!
We battle for our country's right, and for the lily's sake!

HENRY TIMROD, 1829–1867.

48.—CATILINE EXPELLED.

At length, Romans, we are rid of Catiline. We have driven him forth, drunk with fury, breathing mischief, threatening to  revisit us with fire and sword. He is gone—he is fled—he has broken away—he has escaped! No longer within the very walls of the city shall he plot her ruin. We have forced him from secret plots into open rebellion. The bad citizen is now the avowed traitor. His flight is the confession of his treason. Would that his attendants had not been so few! Be speedy, ye companions of his dissolute pleasures, be speedy, and you may overtake him before night on the Aurelian road. Let him not languish, deprived of your society. Haste to join the congenial crew that compose his army; *his* army, I say, for who doubts that the army under Manlius expect Catiline for their leader? And such an army!—outcasts from honor and fugitives from debt; gamblers and felons; miscreants whose dreams are of rapine, murder and conflagration!

CICERO.

Against these gallant troops of your adversary, prepare, O Romans, your garrisons and armies! and first to that maimed and battered gladiator oppose your consuls and generals; next, against that miserable, outcast horde lead forth the strength and flower of all Italy. On the one side contends purity, on the other side pollution; here integrity, there treachery; here piety, there profanity; here constancy, there rage; here integrity, there corruption; here continence, there licentiousness; in short, equity, temperance, fortitude, prudence, struggle with iniquity, luxury, cowardice, rashness—every virtue with every vice; and finally the contest lies between well-grounded hope and absolute despair. In such a conflict, were every human aid to fail, would not the gods themselves empower such conspicuous virtue to triumph over such complicated vice?

CICERO.*

49.—A DIVIDED REPUBLIC, 1861.

FELLOW-CITIZENS, there are some persons who maintain that this republic could be separated, and that two rival republics could live on prosperously and peaceably side by side. No more false or fatal thought ever crept into an American bosom. You might as well tell me that the boat which has been turned adrift above the cataract of Niagara will have a prosperous and a peaceful voyage. Stand amid the ruins of crumbling empires in the Old World, and the lesson of their experience will be that your dream of a divided republic is a delusion. Go into the cemetery of nations, and hold your ear to the sepulchres of those young and generous and high-spirited nations that have perished through the convulsions of civil strife, and in heart-breaking accents the answer will come, " It is a delusion."

And if you will not listen to the voices of the past, go into Mexico and South America and ask the inhabitants of those bright lands, blest with a climate the most delightful on the earth, occupying a soil of exhaustless fertility, and living amid lakes, rivers and mountains of grandeur and inspiration; they will lift up their bowed heads amid demoralization, poverty and dishonor, and they will tell you it is a delusion.

Fellow-citizens, I rejoice to believe—may I not say to know? —that the spirit of loyalty at this time dwells richly and abundantly in the popular heart of America. But I do beseech you—you who have a deep stake in the present and in the future of our country—you, men of culture and of moral power—I do implore you, by all means possible, add yet to the power and to the fervor of that loyalty. If it grows cool

---

* Marcus Tullius Cicero, the greatest of Roman orators, was born at Arpinum, 106 B. C., 216 years after the death of Demosthenes. He was proscribed by Antony after the assassination of Cæsar, and murdered, in the sixty-fourth year of his age, by a party of soldiers, headed by a man whose life he had once saved by his eloquence.

amid the calculations of avarice, or craven under the discouragements of defeat, our country will be overcome. What we now need is a patriotism that will abide the ordeal of fire—a patriotism that is purged of all selfishness and all fear, which is heroic and exhaustless, which vows with every throb of life, with every pulse, that it will rally—if stricken down it will rise again—and that under the pressure of no circumstances of defeat, of sorrow or of suffering shall the national flag be abandoned or the honor of the country compromised.

What we need is a patriotism which rises fully to the comprehension of the actual and the awful perils in which our institutions are placed, and which is willing to devote every power of body and mind and fortune to their deliverance—a patriotism which, obliterating all party lines and entombing all party issues, says to the President of the United States, Here are our lives and our estates ; use them freely, use them boldly, but use them successfully. For, looking upon the graves of our fathers, and upon the cradles of our children, we have sworn that though all things else should perish, this country and this Union shall live.   JOSEPH HOLT.

50.—HEAR BOTH SIDES.

A MAN in his carriage was riding along,
    A gayly-dressed wife by his side ;
In satin and laces she looked like a queen,
    And he like a king in his pride.

A wood-sawyer stood on the street as they passed :
    The carriage and couple he eyed,
And said, as he worked with his saw on a log,
    "I wish I was rich, and could ride."

The man in the carriage remarked to his wife,
    "One thing I would have if I could :
I would give all my wealth for the strength and the health
    Of that man who is sawing the wood."

IT were better, O Athenians! to die ten thousand deaths than to be guilty of a servile acquiescence in the usurpation of Philip. Not only is he no Greek, and no way allied to Greece, but he sprang from a part of the barbarian world unworthy to be named—from Macedonia, where formerly we could not find a slave fit to purchase. And why is it that the insolence of this man is so tamely tolerated? Surely there must be some cause why the Greeks, who were once so jealous of their liberty, now show themselves so basely submissive. It is this, Athenians! They were formerly impelled by a sentiment which was more than a match for Persian gold—a sentiment which maintained the freedom of Greece, and wrought her triumphs by sea and land, over all hostile powers. It was no subtle or mysterious element of success. It was simply this— an abhorrence of traitors, of all who accepted bribes from those princes who were prompted by the ambition of subduing, or the base intent of corrupting, Greece.

To receive bribes was accounted a crime of the blackest dye—a crime which called for all the severity of public justice. No petitioning for mercy, no pardon, was allowed. Those favorable conjunctures with which fortune oftentimes assists the supine against the vigilant, and renders men, even when most regardless of their interests, superior to those who exert their utmost efforts, could never be sold by orator or general, as in these degenerate days. Our mutual confidence, our settled hatred and distrust of all tyrants and barbarians, could not be impaired or turned aside by the force of money.

But now, opportunity, principles, private honor and the public good are exposed to sale as in a market, and in exchange we have that pernicious laxity which is destroying the safety, the very vitals, of Greece. Let a man receive a bribe, he is envied; let him confess it, he provokes laughter; let him be convicted, he is pardoned! His very accusation only awakens resentment, so thoroughly is public sentiment corrupted. Richer, more powerful, better prepared, than ever

10

before, we lose all our advantages through these traffickers in their country's welfare.

How was it formerly? Listen to the decree which your ancestors inscribed upon a brazen column erected in the citadel: "Let Arthmius of Zelia, the son of Pythonax, be accounted infamous, and an enemy to the Athenians and their allies, both he and all his race!" Then comes the reason for his sentence: "Because he brought gold from Media into Peloponne'sus." This is the decree. Think upon it! Think what wisdom, what dignity, appeared in this action of our ancestors! This receiver of bribes they declare an enemy to them and their confederates, and that he and his posterity shall be infamous. And the sentence imported more; for in the laws relating to capital cases it is enacted that "when the legal punishment of a man's crime cannot be inflicted, he may be put to death." And it was accounted meritorious to *kill* him!

"Let not the infamous man," says the law, "be permitted to live," implying that the citizen is free from guilt who executes this sentence. Such was the detestation in which bribery was held by our fathers. And hence was it that the Greeks were a terror to the barbarians—not the barbarians to the Greeks. Hence was it that wars were fair and open, that battles were fought, not with *gold*, but *steel*, and won, if won at all, not by *treachery*, but by *force of arms!*   DEMOSTHENES.

52.—TO-MORROW.

To-morrow, didst thou say?
Methought I heard Horatio say, To-morrow.
Go to—I will not hear of it.   To-morrow!
'Tis a sharper who stakes his penury
Against thy plenty; who takes thy ready cash,
And pays thee naught but wishes, hopes and promises,
The currency of idiots: injurious bankrupt,
That gulls the easy creditor!   To-morrow!
It is a period nowhere to be found

In all the hoary registers of Time,
Unless, perchance, in the fool's calendar!
Wisdom disclaims the word, nor holds society
With those who own it. No, my Horatio,
'Tis Fancy's child, and Folly is its father;
Wrought of such stuff as dreams are, and as baseless
As the fantastic visions of the evening.

But soft, my friend; arrest the present moments,
For, be assured, they are all arrant tell-tales;
And though their flight be silent, and their path
Trackless as the winged couriers of the air,
They post to heaven, and there record thy folly.
Because, though stationed on the important watch,
Thou, like a sleeping, faithless sentinel,
Didst let them pass, unnoticed, unimproved.
And know for that thou slumberest on the guard,
Thou shalt be made to answer at the bar
For every fugitive; and when thou thus
Shalt stand impleaded at the high tribunal
Of hoodwinked Justice, who shall tell thy audit?

Then stay the present instant, dear Horatio!
Imprint the marks of wisdom on its wings;
'Tis of more worth than kingdoms—far more precious
Than all the crimson treasures of life's fountains!
Oh, let it not elude thy grasp, but like
The good old patriarch upon record,
Hold the fleet angel fast until he bless thee!

NATHANIEL COTTON, 1707–1788.

53.—AN APPEAL TO ARMS.

Mr. President, it is natural to man to indulge in the illusions of hope. We are apt to shut our eyes against a painful truth, and listen to the song of that siren till she transforms us into beasts. Is this the part of wise men engaged in a great and arduous struggle for liberty? Are we disposed to be of the number of those who, having eyes, see not, and having ears, hear not the things which so nearly concern their temporal salvation? For my part, whatever anguish of spirit it may cost, I am willing to know the whole truth, to know the worst and to provide for it.

PATRICK HENRY.

I have but one lamp by which my feet are guided, and that is the lamp of experience. I know of no way of judging of the future but by the past. And judging by the past, I wish to know what there has been in the conduct of the British ministry for the last ten years to justify those hopes with which gentlemen have been pleased to solace themselves and the House? Is it that insidious smile with which our petition has been lately received? Trust it not, sir; it will prove a snare to your feet. Suffer not yourselves to be betrayed with a kiss.

Ask yourself how this gracious reception of our petition comports with those warlike preparations which cover our waters and darken our land. Are fleets and armies necessary to a work of love and reconciliation? Have we shown ourselves so unwilling to be reconciled that force must be called in to win back our love? Let us not deceive ourselves, sir.

These are the implements of war and subjugation, the last arguments to which kings resort. I ask gentlemen, sir, what means this martial array, if its purpose be not to force us to submission? Can gentlemen assign any other possible motive for it? Has Great Britain any enemy in this quarter of the world, to call for all this accumulation of navies and armies? No, sir; she has none. They are meant for us—they can be meant for no other.

They are sent over to bind and rivet upon us those chains which the British ministry have been so long forging. And what have we to oppose to them? Shall we try argument? Sir, we have been trying that for the last ten years. Have we anything new to offer upon the subject? Nothing. We have held the subject up in every light of which it is capable, but it has been all in vain. Shall we resort to entreaty and humble supplication? What terms shall we find which have not been already exhausted? Let us not, I beseech you, sir, deceive ourselves longer. Sir, we have done everything that could be done to avert the storm which is now coming on. We have petitioned; we have remonstrated; we have supplicated; we have prostrated ourselves before the throne, and have implored its interposition to arrest the tyrannical hands of the ministry and the Parliament. Our petitions have been slighted, our remonstrances have produced additional violence and insult, our supplications have been disregarded, and we have been spurned with contempt from the foot of the throne!

In vain, after these things, may we indulge the fond hope of peace and reconciliation. There is no longer any room for hope. If we wish to be free—if we mean to preserve inviolate those inestimable privileges for which we have been so long contending—if we mean not basely to abandon the noble struggle in which we have been so long engaged, and which we have pledged ourselves never to abandon until the glorious object of our contest shall be obtained—we must *fight!* I repeat it, sir, we must FIGHT! An appeal to ARMS and to the God of hosts is all that is left us!

PATRICK HENRY, 1736–1799.

54.—ABRAM AND ZIMRI.

ABRAM and Zimri owned a field together—
A level field hid in a happy vale;
They plowed it with one plow, and in the spring
Sowed, walking side by side, the fruitful seed.
In harvest, when the glad earth smiled with grain,
Each carried to his home one-half the sheaves,
And stored them with much labor in his barns.
Now, Abram had a wife and seven sons,
But Zimri dwelt alone within his house.

One night, before the sheaves were gathered in,
As Zimri lay upon his lonely bed
And counted in his mind his little gains,
He thought upon his brother Abram's lot,
And said, "I dwell alone within my house,
But Abram hath a wife and seven sons,
And yet we share the harvest sheaves alike.
He surely needeth more for life than I;
I will arise, and gird myself, and go
Down to the field, and add to his from mine."

So he arose, and girded up his loins,
And went out softly to the level field;
The moon shone out from dusky bars of clouds,
The trees stood black against the cold blue sky,
The branches waved and whispered in the wind.
So Zimri, guided by the shifting light,
Went down the mountain path, and found the field,
Took from his store of sheaves a generous third,
And bore them gladly to his brother's heap,
And then went back to sleep and happy dreams.

Now, that same night, as Abram lay in bed,
Thinking upon his blissful state in life,
He thought upon his brother Zimri's lot,
And said, " He dwells within his house alone,

He goeth forth to toil with few to help,
He goeth home at night to a cold house,
And hath few other friends but me and mine "
(For these two tilled the happy vale alone);
" While I, whom Heaven hath very greatly blessed,
Dwell happy with my wife and seven sons,
Who aid me in my toil and make it light,
And yet we share the harvest sheaves alike.
This surely is not pleasing unto God;
I will arise and gird myself, and go
Out to the field, and borrow from my store,
And add unto my brother Zimri's pile."

So he arose and girded up his loins,
And went down softly to the level field;
The moon shone out from silver bars of clouds,
The trees stood black against the starry sky,
The dark leaves waved and whispered in the breeze.
So Abram, guided by the doubtful light,
Passed down the mountain path and found the field,
Took from his store of sheaves a generous third,
And added them unto his brother's heap;
Then he went back to sleep and happy dreams.

So the next morning with the early sun
The brothers rose, and went out to their toil;
And when they came to see the heavy sheaves,
Each wondered in his heart to find his heap,
Though he had given a third, was still the same.

Now, the next night went Zimri to the field,
Took from his store of sheaves a generous share,
And placed them on his brother Abram's heap,
And then lay down behind his pile to watch.
The moon looked out from bars of silvery cloud,
The cedars stood up black against the sky,
The olive branches whispered in the wind.

Then Abram came down softly from his home,
And looking to the right and left, went on;
Took from his ample store a generous third,
And laid it on his brother Zimri's pile.
Then Zimri rose, and caught him in his arms,
And wept upon his neck, and kissed his cheek,
And Abram saw the whole, and could not speak,
Neither could Zimri. So they walked along
Back to their homes, and thanked their God in prayer
That he had bound them in such loving bands.

Clarence Cook.

55.—IN DEFENSE OF THE FRENCH REVOLUTION.*

In looking at the French revolution, one thing should never be forgotten—the people were driven to it in the first instance. The principles which they laid down were the simplest and the broadest, such as human nature left to itself everywhere recognizes.

"A man's a man for a' that,"

we often say and sing, and no class objects at present to our doing so, and yet that was the principle of the French revolution. "All ye are brethren" is a Christian doctrine, and yet that was the principle of the French revolution. Clothe them in hateful colors as you may, you cannot strip from the eye of posterity the fact that the principles of the French revolution— the principles of liberty, equality and human rights—are sacred and eternal principles belonging to all morality and religion. They were so judged at the time by men who had eyes to see and hearts to feel—by men like that pure, noble-minded, genuine Christian philanthropist, Roscoe, of Liverpool, who hailed the annunciation of such principles with the whole fervor of his soul, and when the National Convention put

* From a speech delivered in London on the twenty-ninth anniversary of the battle of Waterloo, 1844.

forth its celebrated Declaration of Rights invoked all the powers of nature to give it sanction.

Crimes, no doubt, there were—sanguinary and enormous crimes—perpetrated during the course of the French revolution. But be it remembered that these acts were done in self-defense. The revolution itself was completed peacefully, and no proof whatever is capable of being adduced that a peaceably accomplished event would not have remained had it been let alone. But the fact is there was a ceaseless struggle for a counter-revolution—a struggle carried on continually within and stimulated from without. The revolution was never secure for a day; there were always persons in different ranks of society plotting. Foreign gold was circulating there to bribe domestic treason, and all Europe in arms was thundering on the frontiers. Is it wonderful that crimes were committed in self-defense in the circumstances in which they were placed? Blockade a man in his own house—bribe his servants—put gunpowder under his bed—set fire to his dwelling, already surrounded by banditti—and then you must not be surprised if his conduct is *rather* extravagant and he becomes somewhat violent.

Let there be no exaggeration here. In describing this event we speak as though the streets of Paris had for years and years flowed with blood. Much there was, indeed, shed of noble blood. Many fell under the guillotine who deserved statues raised to their honor and a niche in history—many who, if they had lived in England at no great distance of time, would have had their chance of being hanged under the reign of terror of William Pitt; for if the French literary, philosophic and patriotic men suffered, we must not forget the fate of our honest Hardy in England. We must not forget that not only men of the shoemaking class, but that our Holcrofts and Thelwalls and Horne Tookes—our men of philosophy, literature, art and genius—held their lives for a while in peril; and it was by no virtue of the then ruling power that we did not commit some crimes as foul as any of those that stained the progress of the French revolution.

"And what was the use of this grand victory at Waterloo?" will be the child's question to its teacher. Well, the battle of Waterloo replaced the Bourbons; and where are they now? Behold Louis Philippe, the son of Monsieur Egalité, upon the throne of France, sitting there nominally as "the citizen king," by the voice of the people, and not "by the grace of God!" •And after him, what?

The Bourbons had reigned fifteen years, and the price of those fifteen years of Bourbon rule was twenty-three years of hard fighting. For every hour during which they reigned over France a hundred lives had been sacrificed upon the battle-field, to say nothing of the tears and the miseries and the horrors that attend a state of war, and the wretchedness which it propagates to the remotest distances. The reign of an archangel would have been dearly purchased at such a cost as that.   W. J. Fox, 1790-1856.

56.—ON PARTING WITH MY BOOKS.

As one who, destined from his friends to part,
Regrets his loss, but hopes again erewhile
To share their converse and enjoy their smile,
And tempers, as he may, affliction's dart,
Thus, loved associates! chiefs of elder art!
Teachers of wisdom! who could once beguile
My tedious hours, and lighten every toil,
I now resign you, nor with fainting heart;
For pass a few short years, or days, or hours,
And happier seasons may their dawn unfold,
And all your sacred fellowship restore;
When, freed from earth, unlimited its powers,
Mind shall with mind direct communion hold,
And kindred spirits meet to part no more.
                    WM. ROSCOE, 1753-1831.

THE FALL OF WOLSEY.

57.—VANITY OF HUMAN WISHES.

In full-blown dignity see Wolsey stand,
Law in his voice and fortune in his hand;
To him the Church, the realm, their powers consign,
Through him the rays of regal bounty shine;
Turned by his nod the stream of honor flows,
His smile alone security bestows;
Still to new heights his restless wishes tower;
Claim leads to claim, and power advances power;
Till conquests unresisted cease to please,
And rights subverted left him none to seize.

At length his sovereign frowns : the train of state
Mark the keen glance, and watch the sign to hate;
Where'er he turns he meets a stranger's eye,
His suppliants scorn him and his followers fly;
Now drops at once the pride of awful state,
The golden canopy, the glittering plate,
The regal palace, the luxurious board,
The liveried army, and the menial lord.
With age, with cares, with maladies, oppressed,
He seeks the refuge of monastic rest.
Grief aids disease, remembered folly stings,
And his last sighs reproach the faith of kings.

Speak, thou whose thoughts at humble peace repine,
Shall Wolsey's wealth with Wolsey's end be thine?
Or liv'st thou now, with safer pride content,
The wisest justice on the banks of Trent?
For why did Wolsey, near the steeps of fate,
On weak foundations raise th' enormous weight—
Why, but to sink beneath misfortune's blow,
With louder ruin, to the gulfs below?

When first the college rolls receive his name,
The young enthusiast quits his ease for fame ;
Resistless burns the fever of renown,
Caught from the strong contagion of the gown ;
O'er Bodley's dome his future labors spread,
And Bacon's mansion* trembles o'er his head.
Are these thy views? proceed, illustrious youth,
And virtue guard thee to the throne of truth !
Yet should thy soul indulge the generous heat,
Till captive science yields her last retreat ;
Should reason guide thee with her brightest ray,
And pour on misty doubt resistless day;
Should no false kindness lure to loose delight,
Nor praise relax, nor difficulty fright;

*There was a tradition that the study of Friar Bacon, built on an arch
over the bridge, would fall when a man greater than Bacon should pass
under it.

Should tempting novelty thy cell refrain,
And sloth effuse her opiate fumes in vain;
Should beauty blunt on fops her fatal dart,
Nor claim the triumph of a lettered heart;
Should no disease your torpid veins invade,
Nor melancholy's phantom haunt thy shade,
Yet hope not life from grief or danger free,
Nor think the doom of man reversed for thee:
Deign on the passing world to turn thine eyes,
And pause a while from learning to be wise;
There mark what ills the scholar's life assail—
Toil, envy, want, the patron and the jail;
See nations slowly wise and meanly just
To buried merit raise the tardy bust: .
If dreams yet flatter, once again attend,
Hear Lydiat's life and Galileo's end.

On what foundation stands the *warrior's* pride,
How just *his* hopes, let Swedish Charles decide;
A frame of adamant, a soul of fire,
No dangers fright him and no labors tire;
O'er love, o'er fear, extends his wide domain,
Unconquered lord of pleasure and of pain;
No joys to him pacific sceptres yield,
War sounds the trump, he rushes to the field;
Behold surrounding kings their power combine,
And one capitulate, and one resign;
Peace courts his hand, but spreads her charms in vain;
"Think nothing gained," he cries, "till naught remain,
On Moscow's walls till Gothic standards fly,
And all be mine beneath the polar sky."
The march begins in military state,
And nations on his eye suspended wait;
Stern famine guards the solitary coast,
And winter barricades the realms of frost;
He comes, nor want nor cold his course delay;
Hide, blushing glory, hide Pultowa's day!

11

The vanquished hero leaves his broken bands,
And shows his miseries in distant lands;
Condemned a needy supplicant to wait,
While ladies interpose and slaves debate.
But did not chance at length her error mend?
Did no subverted empire mark his end?
Did rival monarchs give the fatal wound,
Or hostile millions press him to the ground?
His fall was destined to a barren strand,
A petty fortress and a dubious hand;
He left the name at which the world grew pale
To point a moral, or adorn a tale.

                    SAMUEL JOHNSON, 1709–1784.

58.—A PLEA FOR BREVITY.

HAVE mercy, O ye orators, ministers and talkers generally,
have mercy on your hearers. Let your words be measured
by the sands of the hour-glass, and not by an eight-day clock.
Bethink you of the innumerable throng of speakers and writers
our country has nourished, and lay to heart the significant
fact that the first bronze statue raised on her soil was to Frank-
lin, whose brevity was proverbial, his most wordy speech being
hardly a span's length. Many of our public speakers and
sermonizers are so long coming to the point that they remind
one of the Dutch gymnast who took a start of a mile to make
a leap, but being well out of breath when he arrived at the
point, sat himself down and rested, and afterward made the
leap at leisure.

The oration of a late Senator in Congress, celebrated as
having outlasted the French Revolution of 1830 by twenty-
four hours, could now scarcely be brought to light by a Bow
street detective. Jeremiah Mason, one of the most successful
lawyers ever known at any bar, was always short—seldom
more than a half an hour; and Webster was brief, sententious

and pithy. Camping down before a jury is a late Yankee invention.

Do you say it costs labor to be brief? Of course it does. Mere words are cheap and plenty enough, but ideas that rouse and set multitudes thinking come as gold comes—from the quarry. Your fifteen-minute man must be a worker, not easily satisfied and much given to blotting.

How well do I remember the many hours I sat, in my juvenile days, watching the sounding-board suspended over the pulpit in the old church where I was wont to worship, wondering when it would come down, as tradition had it that it would in case the preacher uttered anything wrong! But it never fell (political preachers were then unknown), proof positive of the worth of the venerable pastor. What a blessing nowadays would such sounding-boards be, hung over every forum, wound up to the half-hour pitch, and sure to clap down on the speaker at the right moment! They would extinguish many a politician, moralist and divine, but relieve much suffering.

59.—HOW SLEEP THE BRAVE.

How sleep the brave, who sink to rest
By all their country's wishes blest!
When Spring, with dewy fingers cold,
Returns to deck their hallowed mould,
She there shall dress a sweeter sod
Than Fancy's feet have ever trod.

By fairy hands their knell is rung;
By forms unseen their dirge is sung;
There Honor comes, a pilgrim gray,
To bless the turf that wraps their clay;
And Freedom shall a while repair
To dwell, a weeping hermit, there.

WILLIAM COLLINS, 1720–1756.

60.—THE UNITED STATES AND THE STATES, 1788.

MR. CHAIRMAN, it has been advanced as a principle that
no government but a despotism can exist in a very extensive
country. This is a melancholy consideration, indeed. If it

were founded on truth, we
ought to dismiss the idea of a
republican government even
for the State of New York.
But the position has been mis-
apprehended. Its application
relates only to democracies,
where the body of the people
meet to transact business, and
where representation is un-
known. The application is
wrong in respect to all rep-
resentative governments, but

ALEXANDER HAMILTON.   especially in relation to a con-

federacy of States, in which the supreme legislature has only
general powers, and the civil and domestic concerns of the
people are regulated by the laws of the several States.

After all our doubts, suspicions and speculations on the sub-
ject, we must return at last to this important truth, that when
we have formed a constitution upon free principles, and given
a proper balance to the different branches of the administra-
tion, we may with safety supply all the powers necessary to
answer in the most ample manner the purposes of government.

I insist that it never can be the interest or desire of the
national legislature to destroy the State governments. The
blow aimed at the members must give a fatal wound to the
head, and the destruction of the States must be at once a
political suicide. But imagine for a moment that a political
frenzy should seize the government; suppose they should make
the attempt. Certainly, sir, it would be for ever impracticable.
This has been sufficiently demonstrated by reason and expe-
rience. It has been proved that the members of republics

have been, and ever will be, stronger than the head.   Let us attend to one general historical example.

In the ancient feudal governments of Europe, there were, in the first place, a monarch; subordinate to him, a body of nobles; and subject to these, the vassals, or the whole body of the people.   The authority of the kings was limited, and that of the barons considerably independent.   The histories of the feudal wars exhibit little more than a series of successful encroachments on the prerogatives of monarchy.

Here, sir, is one great proof of the superiority which the members in limited governments possess over their head.   As long as the barons enjoyed the confidence and attachment of the people they had the strength of the country on their side, and were irresistible.   I may be told in some instances the barons were overcome; but how did this happen?   Sir, they took advantage of the depression of the royal authority, and the establishment of their own power, to oppress and tyrannize over their vassals.   As commerce enlarged, and wealth and civilization increased, the people began to feel their own weight and consequence; they grew tired of their oppressions, united their strength with that of their prince, and threw off the yoke of the aristocracy.

These very instances prove what I contend for.   They prove that in whatever direction the popular weight leans the current of power will flow—wherever the popular attachments be, there will rest the political superiority.   Sir, can it be supposed that the State governments will become the oppressors of the people?   Will they forfeit their affections?   Will they combine to destroy the liberties and happiness of their fellow-citizens for the sole purpose of involving themselves in ruin?   God forbid!   The idea, sir, is shocking!   It outrages every feeling of humanity and every dictate of common sense.

ALEXANDER HAMILTON.*

*Born in Nevis, one of the West India Islands, in 1737, Hamilton entered the American army before he was nineteen.   With Madison and Jay, he wrote the "Federalist."   He was the first Secretary of the Treasury of the United States.   He was shot by Aaron Burr in a duel in 1804.

11

61.—PRIDE SHALL HAVE A FALL.

CHARACTERS.—*Mr. Lofty, Mr. Bluff, Mr. Girard.*

Bluff. Friend Lofty, I am delighted to see you. I did not expect to meet you in Philadelphia.

Lofty. Sir, you have the advantage of me. I cannot call you by name.

Bluff. What! don't you recollect Bluff, the shipbuilder? Were we not once on a jury together?

Lofty. Very likely, Mr. Bluff; but that is hardly a reason for pledging eternal friendship.

Bluff. I don't know that, friend Lofty.

Lofty [*aside*]. Friend Lofty! what impudence!

Bluff. Make a friend when you can, and be a friend when you can, is my maxim. Now, I left New York in such a hurry that I forgot to take a letter of introduction to the man we are both calling on—old Stephen Girard. Are you acquainted with him?

Lofty. I never saw him in my life, Mr. Buff.

Bluff. Bluff, if you please, sir—Benjamin Bluff, at your service. As I was about to say, if you do not know Mr. Girard personally, you have brought letters, perhaps?

Lofty. Certainly, sir; I should not presume to call on a gentleman without an introduction of some sort.

Bluff. Well, now, friend Lofty, you can do me a favor. Lying at my pier on the North River is the Flying Cloud, as fine a ship as ever walked the waters.

Lofty. That is no concern of mine, Mr. Bluff. I do not see what I can have to do with your Flying Cloud.

Bluff. I want a cargo for her, and Stephen Girard is the man who can give her one, and you are the man who can say a good word to him for me as a fellow New Yorker.

Lofty. Impossible, Mr. Bluff! You and I move in very different circles, Mr. Bluff. In short, Mr. Bluff, you will please not to claim my acquaintance before Mr. Girard.

Bluff. Not claim acquaintance? Surely you know the firm of Babbitt & Bluff.

Lofty. In the way of business, yes. Oh, a very respectable firm, no doubt!

Bluff. Is our note good at the banks?

Lofty. Unexceptionable, Mr. Bluff.

Bluff. Why, then— But no matter, sir—no matter! Here comes Mr. Girard's gardener.

[*Enter* Mr. Girard, *with a hoe and watering-pot.*]

Lofty. Come here, my good man. I am Mr. Lofty; when can I see Mr. Girard?

Girard. What do you want to see him for?

Lofty. I am waiting to see him on business.

Gir. So I supposed. But what is the business?

Lofty. That's *my* business, my good man. You must not ask impertinent questions.

Gir. Oh, I humbly beg your pardon, sir. I hope you will excuse my bad manners. We farmers, you know, are a rough, awkward set. [*Makes an awkward bow.*]

Bluff. Don't say a word against farmers, old fellow. My father was a farmer. An honest, industrious farmer is better than a king.

Gir. Who are you, and who asked your opinion?

Bluff. Who am I?—Benjamin Bluff. Who asked my opinion?—Nobody. But this is a free country, and I can give my opinions unasked if I choose. So put that in your pipe and smoke it, Old Squaretoes.

Gir. And what do you want of old Girard?

Bluff. I want him to give me a cargo for the Flying Cloud, bound for Marseilles, and as staunch and well-conditioned a craft as floats.

Gir. The times are hard, and Girard is a stingy, close-fisted, grasping, disobliging, malicious, avaricious, miserly old—

Bluff. Avast, there, avast! Stop that, stop that, my friend! Are you not ashamed of yourself, to abuse after this fashion the employer whose bread you are eating?

Gir. Why, everybody knows what old Girard is, and there is no harm in speaking it out. Because he pays me wages must I hold my tongue?

Bluff. You must hold it so far as to speak only what you know. Did he ever wrong you to the amount of a cent? Did he ever do you an injustice?

Gir. I can't say he ever did.

Bluff. Did you ever know to a certainty of his wronging any man?

Gir. I can't say I ever did; but I have heard all sorts of reports.

Bluff. Reports! All that you *know* of him is in his favor, and yet, on the strength of mere *reports*, you try to prejudice a stranger against him.

Gir. I don't know what right you have to talk to me in this way, Benjamin Bluff. I'm not to be brow-beaten by you, Benjamin Bluff!

Bluff. Come, sir, put down the hoe and the watering-pot, the honest implements of the gardener, and take up the bludgeon of the highwayman; it is not so dastardly a weapon as the tongue of the slanderer.

Gir. Well, well, since you talk to me in this style, I will settle your business for you with old Girard. I have more influence with him than any one of his clerks.

Lofty. Influence? Did you say you had influence with old Girard?

Gir. I can wind him round my finger. He will do anything I advise him to.

Lofty. Then I will tell you what I want.

Gir. Tell me? Why, just now I was an impertinent fellow for asking what you wanted.

Lofty. Here is a dollar for you, my good man.

Gir. Keep it for the next beggar. There are some bruises that money will not heal.

Lofty. The truth is, old Girard has a couple of promissory notes of mine for ten thousand dollars, due next week, and I want him to renew them for six months. Do you think he will do it?

Gir. I know he will not. He can make a better use of his money. Besides, he is whimsical, and will not like you.

Lofty. Then I am ruined. But I'll not believe you. After all, you are only Mr. Girard's gardener.

Gir. That's true—I am only his gardener. But, then, he does his own gardening.

Bluff. It is Mr. Girard himself!

Lofty. My dear Mr. Girard, a thousand pardons for my stupidity in not recognizing you at once.

Gir. No apologies, I beg you. I hate apologies. Old Ben Franklin used to say that a man who is good at apologies is generally good for nothing else.

Lofty. I have brought letters from our mutual friends in New York—letters of introduction, sir, letters which will tell you who I am and what my standing is. I belong, sir, to one of the oldest families in the State.

Gir. Put up your letters, sir. You have introduced yourself more truly than any letters can do.

Lofty. What a provoking blunder!

Bluff. Well, I have spoiled my chances, and may as well go. Good-bye to you, Mr. Girard.

Gir. Stop, Benjamin Bluff. Stop and dine with me, Benjamin Bluff. You want a cargo for your ship, Benjamin Bluff? You shall have it, Benjamin Bluff. Is there anything else I can do for you, Benjamin Bluff?

Bluff. Really, Mr. Girard, really, you take me by surprise; I am very, very much obliged.

Gir. Didn't I say Girard was a whimsical old fellow?

Bluff. Coming a stranger to you, and without letters, I had no right to expect this kindness.

Gir. What do I care for letters? I can measure a man by the glance of his eye, by the tone of his voice, by his gait, by the toss of his head, the grasp of his hand. I like you, Benjamin Bluff, and you shall have as many cargoes as you want, Benjamin Bluff.

Lofty. My dear Mr. Girard, if you would have the goodness to read this letter—

Gir. I desire to have nothing to do with you or your letters. The notes must be paid or go to protest—unless—unless—

Lofty. Unless what, my dear sir?

Gir. Unless Benjamin Bluff says I must grant your request. Are you his friend?

Bluff [*aside to Lofty*]. Do not be uneasy, sir. You told me not to claim your acquaintance before him, and I'll not do it. As you said, we move in different circles.

Lofty. Oh, the fool that I have been!

Bluff. Do you really think so?

Lofty. I do, indeed.

Bluff. So do I. But PRIDE SHALL HAVE A FALL, and yours is in the dust. The old proverb is true.

Lofty. Gentlemen, I will bid you good-morning.

Bluff. Stop a moment, sir. Mr. Girard, I think we must try and do something for my old friend Lofty.

Lofty. Ah, Mr. Bluff, how contemptible seems my pride by the side of your great generosity!

Bluff. I think we must give him the extension, Mr. Girard.

Gir. Oh, if he's a friend of yours, that alters the case. It shall be just as you say, Benjamin Bluff.

Bluff. We must help him out of his difficulties.

Gir. It shall be done, Benjamin Bluff.

Lofty. Gentlemen, my wife and children thank you. *My* thanks are not worth your taking.

Gir. Well, Mr. Lofty, join us at the dinner-table. We all have our weak points. Let us try to forgive and to forget.

Lofty. And, if possible, to *reform.*

Gir. What say you, Benjamin Bluff?

Bluff. That I'm too much of a sinner myself, sir, to refuse forgiveness to the fellow-man who sees his error.

Lofty. Gentlemen, it is hard to change one's character in a minute; but I think I now see as I never saw before the littleness of pride.

Gir. Enough said, Mr. Lofty! A fault heartily confessed is half repaired. Perhaps we may all be better for this meeting. Who knows?   SARGENT.

STRATFORD-ON-AVON, WHERE SHAKSPEARE WAS BORN.

62.—SCENES FROM MACBETH.

CHARACTERS—*Macduff, Prince Malcolm, Rosse.*

Macduff. See, who comes here?

Malcolm. My countryman; but yet I know him not.

Macd. My ever-gentle cousin, welcome hither.

Mal. I know him now. Kind powers, betimes remove
The means that makes us strangers!

Rosse. Sir, amen.

Macd. Stands Scotland where it did?

Rosse. Alas, poor country,
Almost afraid to know itself! it cannot
Be called our mother, but our grave; where nothing,
But who knows nothing, is once seen to smile;
Where sighs and groans, and shrieks that rend the air,
Are made, not marked; where violent sorrow seems

A modern ecstasy; the dead man's knell
Is there scarce asked for whom; and good men's lives
Expire before the flowers in their caps—
Dying or ere they sicken.

    Macd. Oh, relation
Too nice, and yet too true!

    Mal. What is the newest grief?

    Rosse. That of an hour's age doth hiss the speaker;
Each minute teems a new one.

    Macd. How does my wife?

    Rosse. Why, well.

    Macd. And all my children?

    Rosse. Well, too.

    Macd. The tyrant has not battered at their peace?

    Rosse. No; they were well at peace when I did leave
    them.

    Macd. Be not a niggard of your speech: how goes it?

    Rosse. When I came hither to transport the tidings
Which I have heavily borne, there ran a rumor
Of many worthy fellows that were out,
Which was to my belief witnessed the rather
For that I saw the tyrant's power afoot.
Now is the time of help; your eye in Scotland
Would create soldiers, and make women fight,
To doff their dire distresses.

    Mal. Be't their comfort
We're coming thither; gracious England hath
Lent us good Siward and ten thousand men;
An older, and a better soldier, none
That Christendom gives out.

    Rosse. Would I could answer
This comfort with the like! But I have words
That would be howled out in the desert air,
Where hearing should not catch them.

    Macd. What concern they?
The general cause? Or is it a fee-grief
Due to some single breast?

Rosse. No mind that's honest,
But in it shares some woe, though the main part
Pertains to you alone.

Macd. If it be mine,
Keep it not from me, quickly let me have it!

Rosse. Let not your ears despise my tongue for ever,
Which shall possess them with the heaviest sound
That ever yet they heard.

Macd. Ah! I guess at it!

Rosse. Your castle is surprised; your wife and babes
Savagely slaughtered! To relate the manner
Were, on the quarry of these murdered deer,
To add the death of you.

Mal. Merciful powers!
What, man! ne'er pull your hat upon your brows;
Give sorrow words; the grief that does not speak
Whispers the o'er-fraught heart, and bids it break.

Macd. My children too?

Rosse. Wife, children, servants, all that could be found.

Macd. And I must be from thence! My wife killed too?

Rosse. I have said.

Mal. Be comforted.
Let's make us medicines of our great revenge,
To cure this deadly grief.

Macd. He has no children— All my pretty ones?
Did you say all? what, all? Oh, hell-kite! all?
What, all my pretty chickens and their dam,
At one fell swoop?

Mal. Dispute it like a man.

Macd. I shall do so!
But I must also feel it as a man.
I cannot but remember such things were
That were most precious to me; did Heav'n look on,
And would not take their part? Sinful Macduff,
They were all struck for thee! Naught that I am,
Not for their own demerits, but for mine,
Fell slaughter on their souls!

12

Mal. Be this the whetstone of your sword! let grief
Convert to wrath: blunt not the heart, enrage it.

Macd. Oh, I could play the woman with mine eyes,
And braggart with my tongue. But, gentle powers!
Cut short all intermission: front to front
Bring thou this fiend of Scotland and myself;
Within my sword's length set him: if he 'scape,
Then Heav'n forgive him too!

Mal. This tune goes manly;
Come, go we to the king: our power is ready;
Our lack is nothing but our leave. Macbeth
Is ripe for shaking, and the powers above
Put on their instruments. Receive what cheer you may;
The night is long that never finds a day.

SHAKSPEARE, 1564–1616.

63.—WHO'S READY?

HEAVEN help us! Who's ready? There's danger before!
Who's armed and who's mounted? The foe's at the door!
The smoke of his cannon hangs black o'er the plain,
His shout rings exultant while counting our slain;
And onward and onward he presses his line.
Who's ready? Oh, forward, for yours and for mine!

II.

No halting, no discord! the moments are fates;
To shame or to glory they open the gates:
There's all we hold dearest to lose or to win;
The web of the future to-day we must spin,
And bid the hours follow with knell or with chime!
Who's ready? Oh, forward, while yet there is time!

III.

Earth's noblest are praying at home and o'er sea,
"God keep the great nation united and free!"

Her tyrants watch, eager to leap at our life
If once we should falter or faint in the strife;
Our trust is unshaken, though legions assail.
Who's ready? Oh, forward, and Right shall prevail.

IV.

Who's ready? "All ready!" undaunted we cry;
"For Country, for Freedom, we'll fight till we die;
No traitor at midnight shall pierce us in rest,
No alien at noonday shall stab us abreast;
The God of our fathers is guiding us still.
All forward! we're ready, and conquer we will!"

EDNA DEAN PROCTOR.

64.—MAGNANIMITY IN POLITICS.

A REVENUE from America transmitted hither? Do not delude yourselves. You never can receive it—no, not a shilling! Let the colonies always keep the idea of their civil rights associated with your government, and they will cling and grapple to you. These are ties which, though light as air, are strong as links of iron. But let it once be understood that your government may be one thing and their privileges another, the cement is gone, the cohesion is loosened! Do not entertain so weak an imagination as that your

EDMUND BURKE.

registers and your bonds, your affidavits and your sufferances, your cockets and your clearances, are what form the great securities of your commerce. These things do not make your government. Dead instruments, passive tools, as they are, it is the spirit of the English communion that gives all their life and efficacy to them. It is the spirit of the English constitution which, infused through the mighty mass, pervades, feeds, unites, invigorates, vivifies, every part of the empire, even down to the minutest member.

Do you imagine that it is the land tax which raises your revenue, that it is the annual vote in the committee of supply which gives you your army, or that it is the mutiny bill which inspires it with bravery and discipline? No! Surely, no! It is the love of the people, it is their attachment to their government from the sense of the deep stake they have in such a glorious institution, which gives you your army and navy, and infuses into both that liberal obedience without which your army would be a base rabble and your navy nothing but rotten timber.

All this, I know well enough, will sound wild and chimerical to the profane herd of those vulgar and mechanical politicians who have no place among us—a sort of people who think that nothing exists but what is gross and material, and who, therefore, far from being qualified to be directors of the great movement of empire, are not fit to turn a wheel in the machine. But to men truly initiated and rightly taught, these ruling and master principles, which, in the opinion of such men as I have mentioned, have no substantial existence, are, in truth, everything and all in all. Magnanimity in politics is not seldom the truest wisdom, and a great empire and little minds go ill together. Let us get an American revenue, as we have got an American empire. English privileges have made it all that it is ; English privileges alone will make it all it can be!

The American colonists draw from you as with their lifeblood their love of liberty. We cannot falsify the pedigree of this fierce people and persuade them that they are not sprung from a nation in whose veins the blood of freedom circulates. The language in which they would hear you tell them this tale would detect the imposition. Your speech would betray you.

EDMUND BURKE, 1730–1797.

65.—THE FATAL BRAWL.*

CHARACTERS—*Macgregor, Lamont, Argyle, Ross, Linzie.*

SCENE—A room in Macgregor's house.

[*Enter* LAMONT.]

Lamont. What, ho! Who hears? A stranger claims a
    refuge—
Refuge and help! Is no one in the house?
[*Soliloquizes.*] 'Twas a hot chase, but I have distanced them.
My brain still whirls—the wine is not yet out.
What have I done? Oh fatal, fatal frenzy!
Now it comes back—the dire reality!
Oh irretrievable and utter wreck
Of all my hopes, made in one drunken moment!
This morning rich in all that graces life,
And now a miserable homicide,
A hunted fugitive!

[*Enter* MACGREGOR.]

Macgregor. A stranger here?
I knew not any one was in the room.
Did no one wait upon you?
  Lam. No. I entered
By stealth one of the windows in the basement,
And made my way unchallenged to this room.
I am pursued—my life is in your hands;
I throw myself for shelter on your mercy!
  Mac. Pursued? For what? No crime, I hope?
  Lam. No crime
Premeditate in act or in intent—
Nothing to stain my honor; yet a deed
To blacken all my future—ay, to make it
One long sigh of repentance!
At a tavern,
A few miles off, a party of us stopped

* Founded on an actual occurrence which took place in Scotland about
the year 1625. In the incidents here represented there is hardly any de-
parture from the facts as they are on record.

12 *

And dined. The wine flashed freely. We partook
More than our brains could carry. Up there came
Another party of young men, elated,
Like us, with wine. Quick wakener of contention,
Politics grew the theme—high words ensued—
The lie was given ; a blow—a fatal blow !—
Was struck, and I the giver ! The receiver
Fell backward—hit the curbstone with his neck—
Rose—staggered—dropped—and died !

    Mac. Unhappy chance !

    Lam. When the appalling fear that I had killed him
Grew to conviction, I stood motionless
And mute with horror. Then a cry of *vengeance!*
Broke from his friends. Mine, overpowered, urged me
To fly. I ran, scarce knowing how or why,
But with such speed I soon left my pursuers
Far out of sight. At length I reached this house,
And here I stand a suppliant.

    Mac. Your reliance
Shall not be disappointed. On my hearth
You stand a sacred guest. Let that suffice.
Why do you start?

    Lam. Because your tartan tells me
My foes are of your clan.

    Mac. And what of that ?
Did a Macgregor ever yet betray
Or friend or foe ? Did a disloyal host
Ever yet bear our name ? Fear not. Your trust
Shall be respected. If I heard aright,
The deed was one of passion, not of malice.

    Lam. Oh, not of malice—not of brooding malice !
But momentary anger—anger that,
Quick as the lightning, was as quickly ended,
Leaving a desolation and regret !
Oh, in that fatal wine-cup there was melted
A pearl of price—the relish of a life !
Never again the morning sunlight reddening

My window-pane shall wake a thrill of joy!
Never again the smile of innocence
Shall be reflected from these alien lips!
That sad, appealing look my victim gave me
In his last dying throe will paint itself
On the void air, and make my memory
A funeral chamber for the dreadful image
For ever.

    Mac. I'll not try to blunt the edge
Of your great sorrow. 'Tis a wholesome pain.
That man is less than man who can destroy
The sacred human life and feel no awe,
No swelling of compunction. I'd not trust him!
To time and to God's mercy I commit you.   ·   ·

       [*An impatient knocking is heard outside of the house.*]

    Lam. [*listens*]. Hark! They have tracked me here! They
        knock for entrance.
I hear their voices. Now the door is opened!
They're on the stairs. In their revenge and fury,
Attempt to stay them, they will dash you down.

    Mac. Enter that room. Whatever you may hear,
Be mute and do not stir. Fear not for me.

       [*Exit* LAMONT.   *Enter* ARGYLE *and* ROSS.]

    Argyle. He is not here!

    Ross. I know not that. Macgregor,
A fugitive is sheltered in this house.
Deny it not. Show us his hiding-place.

    Mac. Unmannerly clown! And if a fugitive
Were here, am I the man to give him up
On such a summons? Master Archie Ross,
Go home, and bid your teachers keep you there
Till you can show a touch of gentle breeding
When you accost a gentleman.

    Argyle. Macgregor,
You'll blame us not for our disdain of forms
When you hear all. You'll readily give up

The miscreant when you learn he is the slayer
Of your own son—of Albert!

Mac. No! No! No!
Albert Macgregor slain?   A trick—a trick
To get possession of the fugitive,
To make me play the recreant—the traitor.

Ross. So!   He admits it!   He admits the culprit
Is in this house!

Mac. I admit nothing.   Boy,
If what you say is true—that he—my son—
Is slain (and now the anguish of my heart
Confirms the direful blow)—is't not enough
For one day's woe that I'm bereft of *him?*
Would ye bereave me of my honor too?

Argyle. Macgregor, your own words betray the fact
That here our man is harbored.
We must pass through this door.   [*Going toward* LAMONT'S
        place of exit.]

Mac. Must pass, Argyle!   Back, trifler!   *Must*, indeed!
'Tis a Macgregor you are dealing with.
Must is a word that he's not wont to hear
In his own house, or elsewhere.

Argyle [*bowing*]. Then, Macgregor,
I pray you *suffer* us to pass.

[ROSS *and* ARGYLE *approach as if to lay hands on him.   He
        seizes a club from the wall, and they fall back.*]

Mac. Stand back !
This is my house, and I am master of it!
Keep a respectful distance.

Argyle. Give us up
The wretch at once, or we'll call in assistance.

Mac. Then you shall know what desperation is,
And we'll have havoc.   Would you madden me?

Ross. The man you shelter is a murderer—
The murderer of your son!   [*A pause.*]

Argyle. You hear, Macgregor?

Mac. Were he the murderer of all my clan,

If he had made my hearth a sanctuary,
If I had given my word to shelter him,
So help me Heaven, I'd perish, hacked in pieces,
Ere I would violate the sacred pledge !
[Enter LINZIE.]

   Linzie. Where is the homicide?
   Ross. Concealed within,
As we believe. Macgregor bars our entrance.
A loving father, truly,
To try to screen the murderer of his son !
   Mac. What wouldst *thou* be?   The murderer of my honor !
Reviler, mocker of a father's anguish,
Think you I could have loved my son so well
Carried I here the stuff traitors are made of?
Think you the bitterness of my bereavement,
Sharp as it is beyond your poor conception,
Could parallel the pang of treachery
In a true heart—in a Macgregor's heart?
   Linzie. You've done your best, Macgregor !   On your head
No blame can fall.   Away, and let us enter.
We must have life for life.   Lamont must die.
   Mac. Lamont!   You said *Lamont ?*
   Linzie. The son and heir
Of your most deadly foe.
   Argyle. Did we omit
To mention that?   Now you'll not hesitate
To give him up!
   Mac. A double sanctity
Invests him now.   If I had wavered, that
One mention had confirmed me.
   Linzie. We waste time.
Enter we *must*, by soft means or by hard.
   Mac. Well, Master Linzie, enter if you dare !
Why do you wait?   Why waste the time you grudge?
[LAMONT appears through the door.]

   Lam. From further parley I relieve you all!
Macgregor, I absolve you from your pledge.

Thanks for your noble dealing—for the honor,
Stronger than vengeance, tenderer than love,
That would protect one who has thrown a blight
On all your joys.
Now, seekers of my life, come on and take it!
Be quick! Ye'll only ease me of a burden
My act has rendered hateful.

 Linzie. Ho, secure him!

 Mac. [*shielding Lamont*]. I'd like to see the rash one who
  will venture
To lay a finger, save in gentleness,
Upon this youth. Back, tamperers with my honor!
Out of my house! That man who tarries longer
Is in great danger. Out of my house, I say!

 [*He threatens them with his weapon, and drives them out. A pause.*
*MACGREGOR stands aside and covers his face with his hands. LAMONT
draws near to him and kneels.*]

 Lam. Macgregor, I am kneeling at your feet!
Not for my *life*—oh, not to thank you, sir, `
For that poor boon which one ungoverned impulse
Has emptied of all value—but in token
Of veneration for true nobleness,
Of the prostration of my wretchedness,
Of sympathy, of sorrow, of remorse!

 Mac. Oh, I am childless.

 Lam. [*rising*]. That thought is like a knife
In my own heart. Let there be expiation!
[*Calls.*] Linzie! Argyle! Come, seize me!

 Mac. Reckless boy!
Would you thus frustrate all my pains to save you?
Judge you so poorly of me as to think
I nurse a brute revenge that blood of yours
Alone can satisfy?—that my affliction
Such balm could mitigate?

 Lam. Oh, let me die!

 Mac. No! Be a man, and live! Look up, Lamont!
Hark! I hear angry voices. Your pursuers

In thicker numbers crowd.   They will be here
In half a minute.   Come!   This way lies safety.
They little know the secrets of my hold.
We'll foil them.   Do not doubt it.   You shall hide
Here in my house till I can guide you safely
To Inverary to your friends.   Delay not.
Will you bring added woe upon my head?
Moments are precious.   Come!
   Lam. One word from you,
And only one, shall from this spot uproot me
And that word is *forgiveness*.
   Mac. I forgive you—
As I would be forgiven, I forgive you.
   Lam. [*gives him his hand*].   Lead on, then, my preserver!
Oh, let my future tell how much you lift
From this despairing heart in that one word,
You do *forgive* me!
Now guide me and bestow me as you will.
Henceforth above all prayers shall rise *this* prayer,*
That I may live to comfort and requite you!

SARGENT.

GOD RULES.

CEASE, then, nor order imperfection name;
Our proper bliss depends on what we blame.
All nature is but art, unknown to thee;
All chance, direction, which thou canst not see;
All discord, harmony not understood;
All partial evil, universal good;
And spite of pride, in erring reason's spite,
One truth is clear, Whatever is, is right.   POPE.

---

* The prayer was signally fulfilled. It happened that in the year 1633 there was an unjust act passed by the government, under which Macgregor lost his property and was hunted for his life. And now Lamont had the opportunity for which he had longed. Macgregor took shelter in his house. Lamont received him with tears of welcome, provided liberally for him and his family, and thanked Heaven for the gracious opportunity.

ROBERT BRUCE AND WILLIAM WALLACE.

66.—BANNOCKBURN.

Scots who have with Wallace bled,
Scots whom Bruce has often led,
Welcome to your gory bed,
    Or to victory!

Now's the day and now's the hour:
See the front of battle lower,
See approach proud Edward's power—
    Chains and slavery!

Who will be a traitor knave,
Who can fill a coward's grave,
Who so base as be a slave,
    Let him turn and flee!

Who for Scotland's king and law
Freedom's sword will strongly draw,
Freeman stand, or freeman fa',
    Let him follow me!

By oppression's woes and pains,
By your sons in servile chains,
We will drain our dearest veins
    But they shall be free.

Lay the proud usurper low;
Tyrants fall in every foe,
Liberty's in every blow—
    Let us do or die!
ROBERT BURNS, 1750–1798.

67.—NOTHING IN IT.

Leech. But you don't laugh, Coldstream! Come, man, be amused, for once in your life—you don't laugh.

Sir Charles. Oh yes, I do. You mistake; I laughed twice, distinctly—only, the fact is, I am bored to death!

Leech. Bored? What! after such a feast as that you have given us? Look at me—I'm inspired! I'm a king at this moment, and all the world is at my feet!

Sir C. My dear Leech, you began life late. You are a young fellow—forty-five—and have the world yet before you. I started at thirteen, lived quick, and exhausted the whole round of pleasure before I was thirty. I have tried everything, heard everything, done everything, know everything; and here I am, a man of thirty-three, literally used up—completely *blasé.*

Leech. Nonsense, man! Used up, indeed, with your wealth, with your twenty estates in the sunniest spots in England, not to mention that Utopia within four walls in the *Rue de Provence,* in Paris.

Sir C. I'm dead with *ennui!*

Leech. Ennui! poor Crœsus!

Sir C. Crœsus! no, I'm no Crœsus! My father—you've seen his portrait, good old fellow!—he certainly did leave me a little matter of twelve thousand pounds a year, but, after all—

Leech. Oh, come!

Sir C. Oh, I don't complain of it.

Leech. I should think not.

13   K

Sir C. Oh no ; there are some people who can manage to do on less—on credit.

Leech. I know several. My dear Coldstream, you should try change of scene.

Sir C. I have tried it ; what's the use?

Leech. But I'd gallop all over Europe.

Sir C. I have—there's nothing in it.

Leech. Nothing in all Europe ?

Sir C. Nothing ! Oh dear, yes ! I remember at one time I did somehow go about a good deal.

Leech. You should go to Switzerland.

Sir C. I have been. Nothing there—people say so much about everything ! There certainly were a few glaciers, some monks, and large dogs, and thick ankles, and bad wine, and Mont Blanc ; yes, and there was ice on top, too ; but I prefer the ice at Gunter's—less trouble, and more in it.

Leech. Then, if Switzerland wouldn't do, I'd try Italy.

Sir C. My dear Leech, I've tried it over and over again, —and what then ?

Leech. Did not Rome inspire you ?

Sir C. Oh, believe me, Tom, a most horrible hole ! People talk so much about these things. There's the Colosseum, now, round, very round—a goodish ruin enough ; but I was disappointed with it. Capitol, tolerable high ; and St. Peter's, marble and mosaics and fountains—dome certainly not badly scooped, but there was nothing in it.

Leech. Come, Coldstream, you must admit we have nothing like St. Peter's in London.

Sir C. No, because we don't want it ; but if we wanted such a thing, of course we should have it. A dozen gentlemen meet, pass resolutions, institute, and in twelve months it would be run up ; nay, if that were all, we'd buy St. Peter's itself and have it sent over.

Leech. Ha, ha ! well said ; you're quite right. What say you to beautiful Naples ?

Sir C. Not bad ; excellent watermelons and goodish opera ; they took me up Vesuvius—a horrid bore ! It smoked a good deal, certainly, but altogether a wretched mountain. Saw the crater—looked down, but there was nothing in it.

Leech. But the bay.

Sir C. Inferior to Dublin! The Campagna? a swamp! Greece? a morass! Athens? a bad Edinburgh! Egypt? a desert! The Pyramids? humbugs! Nothing in any of them.

Leech. Nothing in the Pyramids?

Sir C. Nothing. You bore me. Is it possible you cannot invent something that would make my blood boil in my veins, my hair stand on end, my heart beat, my pulse rise?—that would produce an excitement, an emotion, a sensation, a palpitation? But no!

Leech. I've an idea.

Sir C. You? An idea? What is it?

Leech. What if you should—marry?

Sir C. Hum! well, not bad. There's novelty about the notion; it never did strike me to— Oh, but no! I should be bored with the exertion of choosing. If a wife, now, could be had like a dinner—for the ordering.

Leech. She can—by you. Take the first woman that comes; on my life, she'll not refuse twelve thousand pounds a year.

Sir C. Come, I don't dislike the project; I almost feel something like a sensation coming. I haven't felt so excited for some time. It's a novel enjoyment—a surprise. I'll try it.

CHARLES MATHEWS.

68.—A LESSON FOR CRITICS.

ONCE on a time a Nightingale, whose singing
Had with her praises set the forest ringing,
Consented at a concert to appear.
Of course her partial friends all flocked to hear,
And with them many a critic, wide awake
To note a flaw or carp at a mistake.
   She sang as only nightingales can sing,

And when she had ended,
There was a general cry of " Bravo !   Splendid !"
    While she, poor thing !
Abashed and fluttering, to her nest retreated,
Alarmed at having been so wildly greeted.
    The turkeys gobbled their delight ; the geese,
Who rarely failed to hiss a new performer,
In their approval now grew warm and warmer :
    It seemed as if the applause would never cease.

But 'mong the swelling critics on the ground
An Ass was present, pompous and profound,
Who said, "My friends, I'll not dispute the honor
That you would do our little prima donna ;
Although her upper notes are very shrill,
And she defies all method in her trill,
    She has some talent, and, upon the whole,
With study may some cleverness attain :
    Then, her friends tell me she's a virtuous soul ;
        But, but—"
" But !" growled the Lion, wrathful.   " By my mane,
I never knew an ass who did not strain
To qualify a good thing with a *but!* "
" Nay," said the Goose, approaching with a strut,
" Don't interrupt him, sire ; pray let it pass ;
The Ass is honest, if he *is* an Ass."

" I was about," said Long Ear, " to remark
    That there is something lacking in her whistle—
        Something magnetic,
        To waken chords, emotions, sympathetic,
And kindle in a donkey's breast a spark
    Like—like, for instance, a good juicy thistle."

The assembly tittered, but the Fox, with gravity,
    Said, at the Lion winking,
" Our learnëd friend, with his accustomed suavity,
    Has given his opinion without shrinking.

But out of justice to the Nightingale,
 He should inform us, as no doubt he will,
What sort of music 'tis that does not fail
 His sensibilities to rouse and thrill."

" Why," said the critic, with a look potential,
 And pricking up his ears, delighted much
At Reynard's tone and manner deferential—
 " Why, sir, there's nothing can so deeply touch
My feelings, and so carry me away,
 As a fine, mellow, animating bray."

" I thought so," said the Fox, without a pause;
 " As far as you're concerned, your judgment's true :
You do not like the Nightingale because
 The Nightingale is not an Ass—like you!"

SARGENT.

69.—IRISH ALIENS AND BRITISH VICTORIES.

The following eloquent remarks were made in the British House of Commons in 1837, in reply to Lord Lyndhurst, who had spoken of the Irish as "aliens." Sheil was born in Dublin, Ireland, in 1791. He died in 1851.

I SHOULD be surprised, indeed, if, while you are doing us wrong, you did not profess your solicitude to do us justice. From the day on which Strongbow set his foot upon the shore of Ireland, Englishmen were never wanting in protestations of their deep anxiety to do us justice. Even Strafford, the deserter of the people's cause—the renegade Wentworth, who gave evidence in Ireland of the spirit of instinctive tyranny which predominated in his character—even Strafford, while he trampled upon our rights and trod upon the heart of the country, protested his solicitude to do justice to Ireland! What marvel is it, then, that gentlemen opposite should deal in such vehement protestations?

There is, however, one man of great abilities—not a mem-

13 *

ber of this House, but whose talents and whose boldness have placed him in the topmost place in his party—who, disdaining all imposture, and thinking it best to appeal directly to the religious and national antipathies of the people of this country—abandoning all reserve and flinging off the slender veil by which his political associates affect to cover, although they cannot hide, their motives—distinctly and audaciously tells the Irish people that they are not entitled to the same privileges as Englishmen, and pronounces them, in any particular which could enter his minute enumeration of the circumstances by which fellow-citizenship is created, in race, identity and religion, to be aliens—to be aliens in race, to be aliens in country, to be aliens in religion! Aliens! Good heavens! was Arthur, duke of Wellington, in the House of Lords, and did he not start up and exclaim, "HOLD, I HAVE SEEN THE ALIENS DO THEIR DUTY"?

The duke of Wellington is not a man of an excitable temperament—his mind is of a cast too martial to be easily moved; but notwithstanding his habitual inflexibility, I cannot help thinking that when he heard his countrymen (for we are his countrymen) designated by a phrase as offensive as the abundant vocabulary of his eloquent confederate could supply—I cannot help thinking that he ought to have recollected the many fields of fight in which we have been contributors to his renown. "The battles, sieges, fortunes that he has passed" ought to have come back upon him. He ought to have remembered that, from the earliest achievement in which he displayed that military genius which has placed him foremost in the annals of modern warfare, down to that last and surpassing combat which has made his name imperishable—from Assaye to Waterloo—the Irish soldiers, with whom your armies are filled, were the inseparable auxiliaries to the glory with which his unparalleled successes have been crowned.

Whose were the arms that drove your bayonets at Vimieira through the phalanxes that never reeled in the shock of war before? What desperate valor climbed the steeps at Badajos? All his victories should have rushed and crowded back upon his memory—Vimieira, Badajos, Salamanca, Albuera, Toulouse, and, last, of all, the greatest——* Tell me—for you were there—I appeal to the gallant soldier before me, from whose opinion I differ, but who bears, I know, a generous heart in an intrepid breast—tell me—for you must needs remember—on that day when the destinies of mankind were trembling in the balance, while death fell in showers, when the artillery of France was leveled with a precision of the most deadly science, when her legions, incited by the voice and inspired by the example of their mighty leader, rushed again and again to the onset,—tell me if for an instant, when to hesitate for an instant was to be lost, the "aliens" blenched?

And when, at length, the moment for the last and decided movement had arrived, and the valor which had so long been wisely checked was at last let loose—when, with words familiar but immortal, the great captain commanded the great assault—tell me if Catholic Ireland with less heroic valor than the natives of this your own glorious country precipitated herself upon the foe? The blood of England, Scotland and of Ireland flowed in the same stream and drenched the same field. When the chill morning dawned, their dead lay cold and stark together; in the same deep pit their bodies were deposited; the green corn of spring is now breaking from their commingled dust; the dew falls from Heaven upon their union in the grave. Partakers in every peril, in the glory shall we not be permitted to participate? and shall we be told, as a requital, that we are estranged from the noble country for , whose salvation our life-blood was poured out?

RICHARD LALOR SHEIL, 1791–1851.

* The tone of suspension should be given at *greatest*, the dash indicating a sudden break in the speaker's remarks. The battle he there refers to is Waterloo, fought against Napoleon, June 18, 1815. The opposing forces were commanded by Wellington, whose "words" to which the orator alludes were, "Up, Guards, and at them!" Sir Henry Hardinge was the "gallant soldier" to whom Sheil appealed.

Pronounce *Assaye* (in Hin-dos-tan') *As-si'ye; Vimieira* (in Portugal) *Vim-e-a-e'ra; Badajos* (in Spain) *Bad-a-hōs; Albuera* (in Spain) *Al-boo-ā'ra; Toulouse* (in France) *Too-looz'.*

70.—NORA'S VOW.

HEAR what Highland Nora said:
"The earlie's son I will not wed,
  Should all the race of nature die,
  And none be left but he and I.
  For all the gold, for all the gear,
  And all the lands both far and near,
  That ever valor lost and won,
  I would not wed the earlie's son!"

"A maiden's vows," old Callum spoke,
"Are lightly made and lightly broke;
  The heather on the mountain's height
  Begins to bloom in purple light:
  The frost-wind soon shall sweep away
  That luster deep from glen and brae;
  Yet Nora, ere its bloom be gone,
  May blithely wed the earlie's son."

"The swan," she said, "the lake's clear breast
May barter for the eagle's nest;
  The Awe's fierce stream may backward turn,
  Ben-Cruaichan fall and crush Kilchurn;
  Our kilted clans, when blood is high,
  Before their foes may turn and fly;
  But *I*, were all these marvels done,
  Would never wed the earlie's son."

Still in the water-lily's shade
Her wonted nest the wild swan made;
Ben-Cruaichan stands as fast as ever,
Still downward foams the Awe's fierce river;
To shun the clash of foeman's steel,
No Highland brogue has turned the heel;
But Nora's heart is lost and won—
She's wedded to the earlie's son!

SIR WALTER SCOTT, 1771–1832.

71.—IMPEACHMENT OF WARREN HASTINGS.

My lords, there is one thing, and one thing only, which defies all mutation: that which existed before the world and will survive the fabric of the world itself—I mean justice; that justice which, emanating from the Divinity, has a place in the breast of every one of us, given us for our guide with regard to ourselves and with regard to others, and which will stand after this globe is burned to ashes, our advocate or our accuser, before the great Judge when he comes to call upon us for the tenor of a well-spent life.

My lords, I do not mean now to go farther than just to remind your lordships of this—that Mr. Hastings's government was one whole system of oppression, of robbery of individuals, of spoliation of the public and of supersession of the whole system of the English government, in order to vest in the worst of the natives all the power that could possibly exist in any government, in order to defeat the ends which all governments ought, in common, to have in view.   In the name of the Commons of England, I charge all this villainy upon Warren Hastings, in this last moment of my application to you.

My lords, what is it that we want here to a great act of national justice? Do we want a cause? You have the cause of oppressed princes, of undone women of the first rank, of desolated provinces and of wasted kingdoms.

Do you want a criminal? When was there so much iniquity ever laid to the charge of any one? No, my lords, you must not look to punish any other such delinquent from India. Warren Hastings has not left substance enough in India to nourish such another delinquent.

Is it a prosecutor you want? You have before you the Commons of Great Britain as prosecutors—and I believe, my lords, that the sun, in his beneficent progress round the world,' does not behold a more glorious sight than that of men separated from a remote people by the material bounds and barriers of nature, united by the bond of a social and moral community—all the Commons of England resenting as their own the indignities and cruelties that are offered to all the people of India.

Do we want a tribunal? My lords, no example of antiquity, nothing in the modern world, nothing in the range of human imagination, can supply us with a tribunal like this. We commit safely the interests of India and humanity into your hands. Therefore it is with confidence that, ordered by the Commons, I impeach Warren Hastings, Esquire, of high crimes and misdemeanors.

I impeach him in the name of the Commons of Great Britain in Parliament assembled, whose parliamentary trust he has betrayed.

I impeach him in the name of all the Commons of Great Britain, whose national character he has dishonored.

I impeach him in the name of the people of India, whose laws, rights and liberties he has subverted; whose properties he has destroyed; whose country he has laid waste and desolate.

I impeach him in the name and by the virtue of those eternal laws of justice which he has violated.

I impeach him in the name of human nature itself, which he has cruelly outraged, injured and oppressed, in both sexes, in every age, rank, situation and condition of life.

EDMUND BURKE.

72.—THE CURSE OF TYRANNY.

THE race or tribe
That willingly accepts a tyrant's chain,
Content to take his word for law, content
To merge the general reason and the sense
Of common life and free-born patriotism,
Of common wealth and common law, and all
That banded freemen cherish and defend,
In craven admiration of his power,
Or skill, or knowledge, genius, yea, or wish
To serve his country,—this same race is lost.
The warrant for its death hath been made out
In the high court of God, and it shall die
And rot into the dust. Be the pretense
More shining than Sidonian blazonry—
Call it obedience, order, due respect
For that which is above you, what you will ;
Be the bribe carried in the tyrant's hand
Desirable beyond all utterance—
Security for property and life,
Peace in the city, plenty in the store,
And empire over half a world, no less—
He who shall cast a stain on liberty,
Or palliate the rule of one sole will
O'er any nation imaging the God
Whose children are the common brood of men,
Is traitor to his kind, and poisoner
Of the living wells where drinks the soul of man.

PETER BAYNE.

73.—TRUE AND FALSE SCIENCE.

As all is not gold that glitters, so all is not science that bears the name. Dean Swift, in his day, humorously complained that Grub street had migrated to the Royal Society. Well, we cannot say that things are as bad as that, but certainly there are some ragged and suspicious-looking fellows lurking about the premises; and as the duty of the press, like *Dogberry's*, is to comprehend all vagroms, so we bid these stand. For example, a German doctor was around the other day, who informed us that with matter and force he could very easily reconstruct everything there is in the universe. He did not tell us what matter and force are apart from the mind which conceives them as phenomenal relations, but he was sure of his point, and that was enough.

Then, there is another of these outside teachers of science who has contrived a vast process of cosmic evolutions, who tells us that a great while ago—ten thousand years—no, a hundred million of millions of millions of years ago—a nebulous gas was diffused through the immensity of space, which first twisted itself into a solar system ; then into a world ; then into first layers of mineral strata ; then into vegetable sporules, into animal motions, into human vortices, called societies, into Iliads, Parthenons and Shakespeares, and at last into a grand philosophy of evolution—the crown and consummation of the whole; which may all be true, though the birth strikes me as hardly worthy of so long and so tremendous a parturition.

Again, a third convinces himself and his admirers that the universe is considerably defective, and that, like Alphonso of Castile, if he had been consulted in the making of it, he could have given many useful hints toward its improvement. And so, too, when the deepest human instincts in all ages have repeated what the Hebrew peasant said gazing into the clear depths of the Eastern skies, "The heavens declare the glory of God, and the firmament showeth his handiwork," our modern philosopher cries, "Pish! the heavens declare the glory of Copernicus, Kepler and Newton."

Then there is another French litterateur, who with all his
undeniable merits, masquerades a little too much in the habil-
iments of science, who is very sure that mind and motion are
but the obverse sides of the same essential phenomenon, the
one coming in by the front door of the consciousness, and the
other by the back door of the sense. When you talk, he says,
of the martyr's faith, the hero's devotion, the mother's love,
the poet's fancy, the artist's genius, the lover's rapture, you
are only giving so many different names to so many dif-
ferent movements of little molecules in the brain—up,
down, hither, thither, this way, that way, etc.; but my
opinion is that the ingenious gentleman will find, when he
comes to the truth of the case, that what he terms mole-
cules are only maggots, of which a very fine specimen has
found its cradle and home in his own capacious cranium.
Now, if this be science, we must exclaim with the poet,

> "O star-eyed Science! hast thou wandered there
> To waft us back the tidings of despair?"

Is this all the tidings ye bring from the empyrean? What! is
there nothing at the central wheel of life but a blind, dumb,
insensible, unknowable force—a force without love, without
intelligence, without desire or purpose—an eyeless Samson who
goes grinding on for ever at his mill, and crushing onward for
ever in a fruitless battle against death, and nothing new?
"Great God!" as Wordsworth says:

> "I'd rather be
> A pagan, suckled in a creed outworn,
> So might I, standing on this pleasant lea,
> Have glimpses that would make it less forlorn,
> Have sight of Proteus rising from the sea,
> Or hear old Triton blow his wreathèd horn!"

No! These are conjectures that impose upon us their own
fantastic offsprings for the legitimate offsprings of science.
Science is exact, and certain, and authoritative, because deal-
ing with fact and the systematic co-ordination of facts only.
She does not wander away into the void inane. She has noth-
ing to do with questions of primal origin or of ultimate des-

14

tinies, not because they are unimportant questions or insoluble, but because they transcend her instruments and her methods. She leaves them to philosophy, which proceeds not by demonstration and proof, but by insight, by intuition and by moral reasoning, or she leaves them to revelation, in whose supernal light alone they can be properly illuminated and fully seen.

PARKE GODWIN.

74.—TO A WINTER WIND.

LOUD wind, strong wind, sweeping o'er the mountains,
   Fresh wind, free wind, blowing from the sea,
Pour forth thy vials like streams from airy fountains,
      Draughts of life to me!

Clear wind, cold wind, like a northern giant,
   Stars brightly threading thy cloud-driven hair,
Thrilling the blank night with a voice defiant,
      Lo! I meet thee there!

Wild wind, bold wind, like a strong-armed angel,
   Clasp me round—kiss me with thy kisses divine!
Breathe in my dull heart thy secret sweet evangel—
      Mine, and only mine!

Fierce wind, mad wind, howling through the nations,
   Knew'st thou how leapeth that heart as thou goest by,
Ah! thou wouldst pause a while in a sudden patience,
      Like a human sigh.

Sharp wind, keen wind, cutting as word arrows,
   Empty thy quiverful! pass on! what is't to thee
Though in some mortal eyes life's whole bright circle narrows
      To one misery?

Loud wind, strong wind, stay thou in the mountains!
   Fresh wind, free wind, trouble not the sea!
Or lay thy deathly hand upon my heart's warm fountains,
      That I hear not thee!   MRS. MULOCK CRAIK.

HOLLAND HOUSE, RESIDENCE OF ADDISON.

75.—FUTURE GROWTH OF THE SOUL.

AMONG other excellent arguments for the immortality of the soul there is one drawn from its perpetual progress to its perfection, without a possibility of ever arriving at it, which is a hint that I do not remember to have seen opened and improved on by others, though it seems to me to carry great weight. How can it enter into the thoughts of man that the soul, which is capable of such immense perfections and of receiving new improvements to all eternity, shall fall away into nothing almost as soon as it is created?

Would an infinitely wise Being make such glorious beings for so mean and brief a purpose? Would he give us talents not to be exerted, capacities never to be gratified? How can we find that wisdom that shines in all his works, in the formation of man, without looking on this world as only a nursery for the next, and believing that the several generations which rise up and disappear in quick succession are only to receive their first rudiments of existence here, and afterwards to be transplanted into a more friendly climate, where they may spread and flourish to all eternity?

There is not a more pleasing consideration in religion than this of the perpetual progress which the soul makes toward the perfection of its nature without ever arriving at a period in it. To look upon the soul as going on from strength to strength, to consider that she is to shine for ever with new accessions of glory, that she will still be adding virtue to virtue, and knowledge to knowledge, carries in it something wonderfully agreeable to that ambition which is natural to the mind of man.

Methinks this single consideration, of the progress of a finite spirit to perfection, will be sufficient to extinguish all envy in inferior natures, and all contempt in superior. That cherubim that now appears as a God to a human soul knows very well that the period will come about in eternity when the human soul shall be as perfect as he himself now is—nay, when she shall look down on that degree of perfection as much as she now falls short of it. It is true the higher nature still advances and preserves his superiority, but he knows that how high soever the station may be of which he stands possessed, the inferior nature will mount up to it, and shine in the same degree of glory. With what astonishment and veneration may we look into our own souls, where there are such hidden sources of perfection!

JOSEPH ADDISON, 1672–1719.

76.—AGAINST INORDINATE SPECULATION.

INDUSTRY is the natural, sure way to wealth. This is so true that it is impossible an industrious, free people should want the necessaries and comforts of life or an idle enjoy them under any form of government. Money is so far useful to the public as it promoteth industry, and credit, having the same effect, is of the same value with money; but money or credit circulating through a nation from hand to hand, without producing labor and industry in the inhabitants, is direct gaming.

It is not impossible for cunning men to make such plausible

schemes as may draw those who are less skillful into their own
and the public ruin. But surely there is no man of sense and
honesty but must see and own, whether he understands the
game or not, that it is an evident folly for any people, instead
of prosecuting the old honest methods of industry and frugal-
ity, to sit down to a public gaming-table and play off their
money one to another.

The more methods there are in a state for acquiring riches
without industry or merit, *the less there will be of either in that
state;* this is as evident as the ruin that attends it. Besides,
when money is shifted from hand to hand in such a blind, for-
tuitous manner that some men shall from nothing acquire in
an instant vast estates without the least desert, while others
are as suddenly stripped of plentiful fortunes and left on the
parish by their own avarice and credulity, what can be hoped
for on the one hand but abandoned luxury and wantonness, or
on the other but extreme madness and despair?

In short, all projects for growing rich by sudden and extra-
ordinary methods, as they operate violently on the passions of
men, and encourage them to despise the slow, moderate gains
that are to be made by an honest industry, must be ruinous to
the public, and even the winners themselves will at length be
involved in the public ruin. God grant the time be not near
when men shall say (as if it were a state that had passed
away), "This island was *once* inhabited by a religious, brave,
sincere people, of plain, uncorrupt manners, respecting inbred
worth rather than titles and appearances, assertors of liberty,
lovers of their country, jealous of their own rights, and unwill-
ing to infringe the rights of others; improvers of learning
and the useful arts, enemies to luxury, tender of other men's
lives and prodigal of their own; inferior in nothing to the old
Greeks or Romans, and superior to each of those people in the
perfections of the other."

GEORGE BERKELEY,* 1684–1753.

* Berkeley, bishop of Cloyne, was a native of Ireland, and the author of
several philosophical and scientific works. In the year 1728 he sailed for
America, and resided nearly two years in Newport, Rhode Island. He
was the friend of Pope and Swift.

77.—WOODHULL.

General Nathaniel Woodhull was born at Mastic, Long Island, in 1722, and was engaged in several gallant actions during the war of the American Revolution. At the time of the invasion of Long Island by the royal forces, in 1776, he was overtaken at Jamaica, with two or three companions, by a detachment of the seventeenth regiment of British dragoons and the seventy-first regiment of infantry. He gave up his sword in token of surrender; but the subordinate officer who first approached ordered him to say, "God save the king!" This Woodhull refused to do, for which the officer struck him severely over the head with his sword; and of the effects of the wound Woodhull died.

'Twas when Long Island's heights beheld
　　The king's invading horde,
That, by outnumbering foes compelled,
　　Our chief gave up his sword.

Then spoke the victor: "Now from me
　　No mercy shall you wring,
Unless, base rebel, on your knee,
　　You cry, 'God save the king!'"

With reverent but undaunted tone
　　Then Woodhull made reply:
"No king I own, save one alone,
　　The Lord of earth and sky!

"But far from me the wish that ill
　　Your monarch should befall;
So freely, and with right good will,
　　I'll say, God save us all!"

Shouted the foeman, "Paltering slave!
　　Repeat, without delay,
'God save the king,' nor longer brave
　　The fury that can slay!"

But Woodhull said, "Unarmed, I hear;
　　Yet threats cannot appall!
Ne'er passed these lips the breath of fear,
　　And so—God save us all!"

"Then, rebel, rue thy stubborn will,"
    The ruffian victor cried,
"This weapon shall my threat fulfill;
    So perish in thy pride!"

Rapid as thought the murderous blow
    Fell on the prisoner's head;
With warrior rage he scanned his foe,
    Then, staggering, sank and bled.

But anger vanished with his fall;
    His heart the wrong forgave:
Dying, he sighed, "God save you all,
    And me, a sinner, save!"

                              SARGENT.

78.—THE WEATHERCOCK.

Old Fickle. What reputation, what honor, what profit can accrue to you from such conduct as yours? One moment you tell me you are going to become the greatest musician in the world, and straight you fill my house with fiddlers.

Tristram Fickle. I am clear out of that scrape now, sir.

Old F. Then from a fiddler you are metamorphosed into a philosopher; and for the noise of drums, trumpets and hautboys, you substitute a vile jargon more unintelligible than was ever heard at the tower of Babel.

Tri. You are right, sir. I have found out that philosophy is folly; so I have cut the philosophers of all sects, from Plato and Aristotle down to the puzzlers of modern date.

Old F. How much had I to pay the cooper the other day for barreling you up in a large tub, when you resolved to live like Diogenes?

Tri. You should not have paid him anything, sir, for the tub would not hold. You see the contents are run out.

Old F. No jesting, sir; this is no laughing matter. Your follies have tired me out. I verily believe you have taken the whole round of arts and sciences in a month, and have been of fifty different minds in half an hour.

Tri. And by that shown the versatility of my genius.

Old F. Don't tell me of versatility, sir! Let me see a little steadiness. You have never yet been constant to anything but extravagance.

Tri. Yes, sir; one thing more.

Old F. What is that, sir?

Tri. Affection for you. However my head may have wandered, my heart has always been constantly attached to the kindest of parents; and from this moment I am resolved to lay my follies aside and pursue that line of conduct which will be most pleasing to the best of fathers and of friends.

Old F. Well said, my boy—well said! You make me happy indeed! Now, then, my dear Tristram, let me know what you really mean to do.

Tri. To study the law.

Old F. The law!

Tri. I am most resolutely bent on following that profession.

Old F. No!

Tri. Absolutely and irrevocably fixed.

Old F. Better and better! I am overjoyed. Why, 'tis the very thing I wished. Now I am happy! [*Tristram makes gestures as if speaking.*] See how his mind is engaged!

Tri. Gentlemen of the jury—

Old F. Why, Tristram!

Tri. This is a cause—

Old F. Oh, my dear boy! I forgive you all your tricks. I see something about you now that I can depend on. [*Tristram continues making gestures.*]

Tri. I am for the plaintiff in this cause—

Old F. Bravo, bravo! Excellent boy! I'll go and order your books directly.

Tri. 'Tis done, sir.

Old F. What, already?

Tri. I ordered twelve square feet of books when I first thought of embracing the arduous profession of the law.

Old F. What! do you mean to read by the foot?

Tri. By the foot, sir; that is the only way to become a solid lawyer.

Old F. Twelve square feet of learning! Well!

Tri. I have likewise sent for a barber.

Old F. A barber! What, is he to teach you to shave close?

Tri. He is to shave one half my head, sir.

Old F. You will excuse me if I cannot perfectly understand what that has to do with the study of the law.

Tri. Did you never hear of Demosthenes, sir, the Athenian orator? He had half his head shaved, and locked himself up in a coal-cellar.

Old F. Ah, he was perfectly right to lock himself up, after having undergone such an operation as that. He certainly would have made rather an odd figure abroad.

Tri. I think I see him now, awaking the dormant patriotism of his countrymen—lightning in his eye and thunder in his voice; he pours forth a torrent of eloquence resistless in its force; the throne of Philip trembles while he speaks; he denounces, and indignation fills the bosom of his hearers; he exposes the impending danger, and every one sees impending ruin; he threatens the tyrant, they grasp their swords; he calls for vengeance, their thirsty weapons glitter in the air, and thousands reverberate the cry! One soul animates a nation, and that soul is the soul of the orator!

Old F. Oh what a figure he will make on the King's Bench! But come, I will tell you what my plan is, and then you will see how happily this determination of yours will further it. You have [*Tristram makes extravagant gestures, as if speaking*] often heard me speak of my friend Briefwit, the barrister.

Tri. Who is against me in this cause.

Old F. He is a most learned lawyer.

Tri. But as I have justice on my side—

Old F. Zounds! he doesn't hear a word I say! Why, Tristram!

Tri. I beg your pardon, sir; I was prosecuting my studies.

Old F. Now attend.

Tri. As my learned friend observes— Go on, sir; I am all attention.

Old F. Well, my friend the counselor—

Tri. Say learned friend, if you please, sir. We gentlemen of the law always—

Old F. Well, well, my learned friend—

Tri. A black patch!

Old F. Will you listen and be silent?

Tri. I am mute as a judge.

Old F. My friend, I say, has a ward who is very handsome, and who has a very handsome fortune. She would make you a charming wife.

Tri. This is an action—

Old F. Now, I have hitherto been afraid to introduce you to my friend, the barrister, because I thought your lightness and his gravity—

Tri. Might be plaintiff and defendant.

Old F. But now you are grown serious and steady, and have resolved to pursue his profession, I will shortly bring you together; you will obtain his good opinion, and all the rest follows, of course.

Tri. A verdict in my favor.

Old F. You marry and sit down, happy for life.

Tri. In the King's Bench.

Old F. Bravo! Ha, ha, ha! But now run to your study— run to your study, my dear Tristram, and I'll go and call upon the counselor.

Tri. I remove by *habeas corpus.*

Old F. Pray have the goodness to make haste, then. [*Hurrying him off.*]

Tri. Gentlemen of the jury, this is a cause— [*Exit.*]

Old F. The inimitable boy! I am now the happiest father living. What genius he has! He'll be lord chancellor one day or other, I dare be sworn. I am sure he has talents. Oh how I long to see him at the bar!

JOHN TILL ALLINGHAM.

79.—LYRICS BY TENNYSON.

I.

THE GOLDEN YEAR.

WE sleep, and wake, and sleep, but all things move;
The Sun flies forward to his brother Sun;
The dark Earth follows wheeled in her ellipse;
And human things returning on themselves
Move onward, leading up the golden year.

Ah, though the times when some new thought can bud
Are but as poets' seasons when they flower,
Yet seas that daily gain upon the shore
Have ebb and flow conditioning their march,
And slow and sure comes up the golden year.

Then wealth no more shall rest in mounded heaps,
But smit with freer light shall slowly melt
In many streams to fatten lower lands,
And light shall spread, and man be liker man,
Through all the seasons of the golden year.

Shall eagles not be eagles? wrens be wrens?
If all the world were falcons, what of that?
The wonder of the eagle were the less,
But he not less the eagle. Happy days
Roll onward, leading up the golden year!

Fly, happy, happy sails, and bear the Press—
Fly, happy with the mission of the Cross;
Knit land to land, and, blowing havenward,
With silks, and fruits, and spices clear of toll,
Enrich the markets of the golden year.

But we grow old. Ah, when shall all men's good
Be each man's rule, and universal peace
Lie like a shaft of light across the land,
And like a lane of beams athwart the sea,
Through all the circles of the golden year?

II.
MEMORIES.

Tears, idle tears, I know not what they mean;
Tears from the depth of some divine despair
Rise in the heart, and gather to the eyes,
In looking on the happy autumn fields,
And thinking of the days that are no more.

Fresh as the first beam glittering on a sail
That brings our friends up from the underworld,
Sad as the last which reddens over one
That sinks with all we love below the verge;
So sad, so fresh, the days that are no more.

Ah, sad and strange as in dark summer dawns
The earliest pipe of half-awakened birds
To dying ears, when unto dying eyes
The casement slowly grows a glimmering square;
So sad, so strange, the days that are no more.

Dear as remembered kisses after death,
And sweet as those by hopeless fancy feigned
On lips that are for others; deep as love,
Deep as first love, and wild with all regret,
Oh death in life, the days that are no more!

III.

BUGLE SONG.

The splendor falls on castle walls,
  And snowy summits old in story;
The long light shakes across the lakes,
  And the wild cataract leaps in glory.
Blow, bugle, blow! set the wild echoes flying;
Blow, bugle; answer, echoes, dying, dying, dying!

Oh hark, oh hear! how thin and clear,
  And thinner, clearer, farther going!
Oh sweet and far, from cliff and scar,
  The horns of Elfland faintly blowing!
Blow! let us hear the purple glens replying;
Blow, bugle; answer, echoes, dying, dying, dying!

Oh love, they die in yon rich sky;
  They faint on hill, or field, or river:
Our echoes roll from soul to soul,
  And grow for ever and for ever.
Blow, bugle, blow! set the wild echoes flying,
And answer, echoes, answer, dying, dying, dying!

IV.

WELCOME TO ALEXANDRA.

Welcome her, thunders of fort and of fleet!
Welcome her, thundering cheer of the street!
Welcome her, all things youthful and sweet,
Scatter the blossoms under her feet!
Break, happy land, into earlier flowers!
Make music, O bird, in the new budded bowers.
Welcome her, welcome her, all that is ours!

15

Warble, O bugle, and, trumpet, blare!
Flags, flutter out upon turrets and towers!
Flames, on the windy headland flare!
Utter your jubilee, steeple and spire!
Clash, ye bells, in the merry March air!
Flash, ye cities, in rivers of fire!
Welcome her, welcome the land's desire.

V.

INDEPENDENCE ON FORTUNE.

Turn, Fortune, turn thy wheel and lower the proud;
Turn thy wild wheel through sunshine, storm and cloud;
　　Thy wheel and thee we neither love nor hate.

Turn, Fortune, turn thy wheel with smile or frown;
With that wild wheel we go not up or down;
　　Our hoard is little, but our hearts are great.

Smile, and we smile, the lords of many lands;
Frown, and we smile, the lords of our own hands;
　　For man is man, and master of his fate.

Turn, turn thy wheel above the staring crowd;
Thy wheel and thou are shadows in the cloud;
　　Thy wheel and thee we neither love nor hate.

VI.

THE FOOLISH VIRGINS.

Late, late, so late! and dark the night and chill!
Late, late, so late! but we can enter still.
　　Too late, too late! ye cannot enter now.

No light had we—for that we do repent;
And learning this, the Bridegroom will relent.
　　Too late, too late! ye cannot enter now.

No light, so late! and dark and chill the night!
Oh, let us in, that we may find the light!
　　Too late, too late! ye cannot enter now.

Have we not heard the Bridegroom is so sweet?
Oh, let us in, though late, to kiss his feet.
 No, no, too late! ye cannot enter now.

80.—CONDEMNATION OF SOCRATES.

SOCRATES was the reverse of a skeptic. No man ever looked upon life with a more positive and practical eye. No man ever pursued his mark with a clearer perception of the road which he was to travel. No man ever combined, in like manner, the absorbing enthusiasm of a missionary with the acuteness, the originality, the inventive resources and the generalizing comprehension of a philosopher.

SOCRATES.

And yet this man was condemned to death—condemned by a hostile tribunal of more than five hundred citizens of Athens, drawn at hazard from all classes of society. In the most momentous trial that up to that time the world had witnessed, a majority of six turned the scale. And the vague charges on which Socrates was condemned were that he was a vain babbler, a corrupter of youth and a setter-forth of strange gods.

It would be tempting to enlarge on the closing scene of his life—a scene which Plato has invested with such immortal glory—on the affecting farewell to the judges; on the long thirty days which passed in prison before the execution of the verdict; on his playful equanimity amid the uncontrollable emotions of his companions; on the gathering in of that solemn evening when the fading of the sunset hues on the top of the Athenian hills was the signal that the last hour was at hand; on the introduction of the fatal hemlock.

And then there should be represented the immovable countenance of Socrates, the firm hand, the burst of frantic lamentation from all his friends, as, with his habitual ease and cheerfulness, he drained the cup to its dregs; then the solemn silence enjoined by himself; the pacing to and fro; the strong religious persuasions attested by his last words; the cold palsy· of the poison creeping from the extremities to the heart; the gradual torpor ending in death. But I must forbear.

Oh for a modern spirit like his! Oh for one hour of Socrates! Oh for one hour of that voice whose questioning would make men see what they knew and what they did not know, what they meant and what they only thought they meant, what they believed in truth and· what they only believed in name, wherein they agreed and wherein they differed!

That voice is indeed silent, but there is a voice in each man's heart and conscience which, if we will, Socrates has taught us to use rightly. That voice still enjoins us to give to ourselves a reason for the hope that is in us—both hearing and asking questions. It tells us that the fancied repose which self-inquiry disturbs is more than compensated by the real repose which it gives, that a wise. questioning is the half of knowledge, and that a life without self-examination is no life at all.

81.—INVECTIVE AGAINST MR. CORRY.

The following speech was delivered in the Irish Parliament, February 14, 1800, in reply to Mr. Corry, who had said that Grattan, instead of. having a voice in the councils of his country, should have been standing as a culprit at the bar. A duel, in which Corry was wounded in the arm, was provoked by this severe retort from Grattan. We do not commend the spirit of either the retort or of the duel, but the former has been rarely paralleled in power since the days of Demosthenes.

HAS the gentleman done? Has he completely done? He was unparliamentary from the beginning to the end of his speech. There was scarce a word that he uttered that was not a violation of the privileges of the House. But I did not call him to order. Why? Because the limited talents of some men render it impossible for them to be severe without being unparliamentary. But before I sit down I shall show him how to be severe and parliamentary at the same time. On any other occasion, I should think myself justifiable in treating with silent contempt anything which might fall from that honorable member; but there are times when the insignificance of the accuser is lost in the magnitude of the accusation.

I know the difficulty the honorable gentleman labored under when he attacked me, conscious that, on a comparative view of our characters, public and private, there is nothing he could say which would injure me. The public would not believe the charge. I despise the falsehood. If such a charge were made by an honest man, I would answer it in the manner I shall do before I sit down. But I shall first reply to it as if it were *not* made by an honest man.

The honorable gentleman has called me "an unimpeached traitor." I ask, Why not "traitor," unqualified by an epithet? I will tell him: it was because he dare not. It was the act of a coward who raises his arm to strike, but has not courage to give the blow. I will not call him villain, because it would be unparliamentary, and he is a privy councilor. I will not call him fool, because he happens to be chancellor of the exchequer.

But I say he is one who has abused the privilege of Parliament and freedom of debate, to the uttering language which, if spoken out of the House, I should answer only with a blow. I care not how high his station, how low his character, how contemptible his speech; whether a privy councilor or a parasite, my answer would be a blow.

He has charged me with being connected with the rebels. The charge is utterly, totally and meanly false! Does the honorable gentleman rely on the report of the House of Lords for the foundation of his assertion? If he does, I can prove to the committee there was a physical impossibility of that report being true. But I scorn to answer any man for my conduct, whether he be a political coxcomb, or whether he brought himself into power by a false glare of courage or not.

The right honorable gentleman says I fled from the country after exciting rebellion, and that I have returned to raise another. The charge is false. The civil war had not commenced when I left the kingdom, and I could not have re-

15 *

turned without taking part. On the one side there was the camp of the rebel, on the other the camp of the minister, a greater traitor than the rebel. The stronghold of the constitution was nowhere to be found.

I agree that the rebel who rose against the government should have suffered, but I missed on the scaffold the right honorable gentleman. Two desperate parties were in arms against the constitution. The right honorable gentleman belonged to one of those parties, and deserved death. I could not join the rebel, I could not join the government. I was therefore absent from a scene where I could not be active without self-reproach, nor indifferent with safety.

Many honorable gentlemen thought differently from me; I respect their opinions, but I keep my own, and I think now, as I thought then, that the treason of the minister against the liberties of the people was infinitely worse than the rebellion of the people against the minister.

I have returned, not, as the right honorable member has said, to raise another storm; I have returned to discharge an honorable debt of gratitude to my country, that conferred a great reward for past services, which, I am proud to say, was not greater than my desert. I have returned to protect that constitution, of which I was the parent and the founder, from the assassination of such men as the honorable gentleman and his unworthy associates. They are corrupt, they are seditious, and they, at this very moment, are in a conspiracy against their country.

I have returned to refute a libel as false as it is malicious, given to the public under the appellation of a report of the committee of the Lords. Here I stand for impeachment or trial. I dare accusation. I defy the honorable gentleman, I defy the government, I defy their whole phalanx : let them come forth! I tell the ministers I shall neither give them quarter nor take it. I am here to lay the shattered remains of my constitution on the floor of this House in defense of the liberties of my country.

HENRY GRATTAN, 1746–1820.

82.—ROME.

O ROME! my country! city of the soul!
  The orphans of the heart must turn to thee,
Lone mother of dead empires! and control
  In their shut breasts their petty misery.
What are our woes and sufferance? Come and see
  The cypress, hear the owl, and plod your way
O'er steps of broken thrones and temples, ye
  Whose agonies are evils of a day—
  A world is at our feet as fragile as our clay.

The Niobe of nations! there she stands,
  Childless and crownless in her voiceless woe,
An empty urn within her withered hands,
  Whose holy dust was scattered long ago;
The Scipios' tomb contains no ashes now;
  The very sepulchres lie tenantless
Of their heroic dwellers: dost thou flow,
  Old Tiber! through a marble wilderness?
  Rise, with thy yellow waves, and mantle her distress!

The Goth, the Christian, Time, War, Flood and Fire
  Have dealt upon the seven-hilled city's pride;
She saw her glories star by star expire,
  And up the steep barbarian monarchs ride

Where the car climbed the capitol; far and wide
　Temple and tower went down, nor left a site:
Chaos of ruins! who shall trace the void,
　O'er the dim fragments cast a lunar light,
　And say, " here was, or is," where all is doubly night?

The double night of ages, and of her,
　Night's daughter, Ignorance, hath wrapped and wrap
All round us; we but feel our way to err:
　The ocean hath his chart, the stars their map,
　And Knowledge spreads them on her ample lap;
　But Rome is as the desert, where we steer
Stumbling o'er recollections; now we clap
　Our hands, and cry "Eureka!" "It is clear,"
　When but some false mirage of ruin rises near.

Alas! the lofty city! and alas!
　The trebly hundred triumphs! and the day
When Brutus made the dagger's edge surpass
　The conqueror's sword in bearing fame away!
Alas for Tully's voice, and Virgil's lay,
　And Livy's pictured page!—but these shall be
Her resurrection; all beside—decay.
　Alas for earth, for never shall we see
　That brightness in her eye she bore when Rome was free!

LORD BYRON, 1788–1824.

83.—ON THE IRISH DISTURBANCE BILL.

I DO not rise to fawn or cringe to this House; I do not rise
to supplicate you to be merciful toward the nation to which I
belong—toward a nation which, though subject to England,
yet is distinct from it. It is a distinct nation; it has been
treated as such by this country, as may be proved by history
and by seven hundred years of tyranny. I call upon this
House, as you value the liberty of England, not to allow the
present nefarious bill to pass.

In it are involved the liberties of England, the liberty of the press and of every other institution dear to Englishmen. Against the bill I protest, in the name of the Irish people, and in the face of Heaven. I treat with scorn the puny and pitiful assertions that grievances are not to be complained of, that our redress is not to be agitated; for in such cases remonstrances cannot be too strong, agitation cannot be too violent, to show to the world with what injustice our fair claims are met, and under what tyranny the people suffer.

The clause which does away with trial by jury—what in the name of Heaven is it, if it is not the establishment of a revolutionary tribunal? It drives the judge from his bench, it does away with that which is more sacred than the throne itself—that for which your king reigns, your lords deliberate, your commons assemble. If ever I doubted before of the success of our agitation for repeal, this bill, this infamous bill— the way in which it has been received by the House; the manner in which its opponents have been treated; the personalities to which they have been subjected; the yells with which one of them has this night been greeted,—all these things dissipate my doubts, and tell me of its complete and early triumph.

Do you think those yells will be forgotten? Do you suppose their echo will not reach the plains of my injured and insulted country—that they will not be whispered in her green valleys and heard from her lofty hills? Oh they will be heard there! Yes, and they will not be forgotten. The youth of Ireland will bound with indignation; they will say, " We are eight millions, and you treat us thus, as though we were no more to your country than the isle of Guernsey or of Jersey!"

I have done my duty. I stand acquitted to my conscience and my country. I have opposed this measure throughout, and I now protest against it, as harsh, oppressive, uncalled for, unjust—as establishing an infamous precedent by retaliating crime against crime, as tyrannous—cruelly and vindictively tyrannous!

DANIEL O'CONNELL, 1775–1847.

M

84.—ON RECONCILIATION WITH AMERICA.

January 20, 1775.

Dr. Franklin, who was present at the debate, said of this speech that "he had seen, in the course of his life, sometimes eloquence without wisdom, and often wisdom without eloquence; in the present instance he saw both united, and both, as he thought, in the highest degree possible."

AMERICA, my lords, cannot be reconciled to this country—she ought not to be reconciled—till the troops of Britain are withdrawn. How can America trust you, with the bayonet at her breast? How can she suppose that you mean less than bondage or death? I therefore move that an address be presented to his Majesty, advising that immediate orders be despatched to General Gage for removing his Majesty's forces from the town of Boston. The way must be immediately opened for reconciliation. It will soon be too late. An hour now lost in allaying ferments in America may produce years of calamity.

Never will I desert, for a moment, the conduct of this weighty business. Unless nailed to my bed by the extremity of sickness, I will pursue it to the end. I will knock at the door of this sleeping and confounded ministry, and will, if it be possible, rouse them to a sense of their danger.

I contend not for indulgence but for justice to America. What is our right to persist in such cruel and vindictive acts against a loyal, respectable people? They say you have no right to tax them without their consent. They say truly. Representation and taxation must go together; they are inseparable. I therefore urge and conjure your lordships immediately to adopt this conciliating measure. If illegal violences have been, as it is said, committed in America, prepare the way—open the door of possibility—for acknowledgment and satisfaction; but proceed not to such coercion—such proscription; cease your indiscriminate inflictions; amerce not thirty thousand, oppress not three millions, irritate them not to unappeasable rancor, for the fault of forty or fifty.

Such severity of injustice must for ever render incurable the wounds you have inflicted. What though you march from town to town, from province to province? What though you enforce a temporary and local submission? How shall you secure the obedience of the country you leave behind you in your progress? How grasp the dominion of eighteen hundred miles of continent, populous in numbers, strong in valor, liberty and the means of resistance?

The spirit which now resists your taxation in America is the same which formerly opposed loans, benevolences and ship-money in England—the same spirit which called all England on its legs, and by the Bill of Rights vindicated the English constitution—the same spirit which established the great fundamental essential maxim of your liberties, *that no subject of England shall be taxed but by his own consent.* This glorious Whig spirit animates three millions in America who prefer poverty with liberty to gilded chains and sordid affluence, and who will die in defense of their rights as men, as freemen.

What shall oppose this spirit, aided by the congenial flame glowing in the breast of every Whig in England? "'Tis liberty to liberty engaged" that they will defend themselves, their families and their country. In this great cause they are immovably allied: it is the alliance of God and nature, immutable, eternal, fixed as the firmament of heaven.

LORD CHATHAM.

85.—CITY MEN IN THE COUNTRY.

Come back to your mother, ye children, for shame,
Who have wandered like truants for riches or fame!
With a smile on her face and a sprig in her cap,
She calls you to feast from her bountiful lap.

Come out from your alleys, your courts and your lanes,
And breathe, like young eagles, the air of our plains;
Take a whiff from our fields, and your excellent wives
Will declare it's all nonsense insuring your lives.

Come, you of the law, who can talk, if you please,
Till the man in the moon will allow it's a cheese,
And leave " the old lady that never tells lies "
To sleep with her handkerchief over her eyes.

Ye healers of men, for a moment decline
Your feats in the rhubarb and ipecac line;
While you shut up your turnpike, your neighbors can go
The old roundabout road to the regions below.

You clerk, on whose ears are a couple of pens,
And whose head is an ant-hill of units and tens,
Though Plato denies you, we welcome you still
As a featherless biped, in spite of your quill.

Poor drudge of the city, how happy he feels,
With the burrs on his legs and the grass at his heels,
No *dodger* behind his bandannas to share,
No constable growling, " You mustn't walk there ! "

In yonder green meadow, to memory dear,
He slaps a musquito and brushes a tear;
The dew-drops hang round him on blossoms and shoots;
He breathes but one sigh for his youth and his boots.

There stands the old schoolhouse, hard by the old church;
That tree at its side had the flavor of birch:
Oh, sweet were the days of his juvenile tricks,
Though the prairie of youth had so many " big licks ! "

By the side of yon river he weeps and he slumps,
The boots fill with water, as if they were pumps;
Till, sated with rapture, he steals to his bed,
With a glow in his heart and a cold in his head.

'Tis past—he is dreaming—I see him again;
The ledger returns as by legerdemain;
His neckcloth is damp with an easterly flaw,
And he holds in his fingers an omnibus straw.

He dreams the chill gust is a blossomy gale,
That the straw is a rose from his dear native vale ;
And murmurs, unconscious of space and of time,
" A. 1—Extra super.—Ah, isn't it prime ! "

Oh what are the prizes we perish to win
To the first little " shiner " we caught with a pin !
No soil upon earth is as dear to our eyes
As the soil we first stirred in terrestrial pies !

Then come from all parties and parts to our feast ;
Though not at the " Astor," we'll give you, at least,
A bite of an apple, a seat on the grass,
And the best of old—water—at nothing a glass.

OLIVER WENDELL HOLMES.

86.—REPEAL CLAIMED AS A RIGHT.
January 20, 1775.

IT is not repealing this or that act of Parliament—it is not repealing a piece of parchment—that can restore America to our bosom. You must repeal her fears and her resentments, and you may then hope for her love and gratitude. But now, insulted with an armed force posted at Boston, irritated with a hostile array before her eyes, her concessions, if you *could* force them, would be suspicious and insecure, the dictates of fear and the extortions of force! But it is more than evident that you *cannot* force them, principled and united as they are, to your unworthy terms of submission. Repeal, therefore, my lords, I say !

But bare repeal will not satisfy this enlightened and spirited people. You must go through the work. You must declare you have no right to tax. Then they may trust you. There is no time to be lost. Every moment is big with dangers. While I am speaking, the decisive blow may be struck, and millions involved in the consequence. The very first drop of blood shed in civil and unnatural war will make a wound

16

which years, perhaps ages, may not heal. It will be *immed-icab'ile vulnus.*

When your lordships look at the papers transmitted to us from America—when you consider their decency, firmness and wisdom—you cannot but respect their cause, and wish to make it your own. I must declare and avow that in the master States of the world I know not the people nor the senate who, under such a complication of difficult circum-stances, can stand in preference to the delegates of America assembled in General Congress at Philadelphia. For genuine sagacity, for singular moderation, for solid wisdom, manly spirit, sublime sentiments and simplicity of language—for everything respectable and honorable—they stand unrivaled.

I trust it is obvious to your lordships that all attempts to impose servitude upon such men, to establish despotism over such a mighty continental nation, must be vain, must be fatal. This wise people speak out. They do not hold the language of slaves. They tell you what they mean. They do not ask you to repeal your laws as a favor. They claim it as a right —they demand it. They tell you they will not submit to them. And I tell you the acts must be repealed. We shall be forced ultimately to retract. Let us retract while we can, not when we must. I say we must necessarily undo these violent, oppressive acts. They *must* be repealed. You *will* repeal them. I pledge myself for it that you will, in the end, repeal them. I stake my reputation on it. I will con-sent to be taken for an idiot if they are not finally repealed.*

Avoid, then, this humiliating, this disgraceful necessity. Every motive of justice and of policy, of dignity and of pru-dence, urges you to allay the ferment in America by a re-moval of your troops from Boston, by a repeal of your acts of Parliament. On the other hand, every danger and every hazard impend to deter you from perseverance in your present ruinous measures—foreign war hanging over your heads by

---

* This prediction was verified. After a fruitless war of three years, the repeal of the offensive acts was sent out as a peace-offering to the col-onists, but it was too late.

a slight and brittle thread—France and Spain watching your conduct, and waiting the maturity of your errors!

To conclude, my lords: if the ministers thus persevere in misadvising and misleading the king, I will not say that they can alienate the affections of his subjects from the crown, but I will affirm that they will make his crown not worth his wearing; I will not say that the king is betrayed, but I will pronounce that the kingdom is undone.

LORD CHATHAM.

VIEW OF LUCKNOW.

87.—THE RELIEF OF LUCKNOW.

IN the summer of 1857 the British garrison in Lucknow were reduced to perilous straits. They were besieged by the native rebels in a largely outnumbering force. Cruel, vindictive and remorseless, these mutineers, could they enter the city, would put all the men, women and children to a fearful death. They had advanced their batteries and mines so far that in less than an hour the city must fall, unless relief should be at hand. And relief was at hand, though no one was aware of it. Havelock with 2500 men was approaching, but amid the din and smoke of the cannonade nothing could be heard or seen.

"On every side," says a lady who was present, "death stared us in the face. No human skill could avert it any longer. The engineers told us that soon all would be over. We women strove to encourage one another, and to perform such light duties as we could. I had gone out to try and make myself useful, in company with Jessie Brown, the wife of a corporal in my husband's regiment. Poor Jessie had been in a state of restless excitement, and at last, overcome with fatigue, she lay down, wrapped up in her plaid, on the ground.

"She fell, at length, into a profound slumber, motionless and apparently breathless, her head resting in my lap. I myself could no longer resist the inclination to sleep, in spite of the continual roar of the cannon. Suddenly I was roused by a wild scream close to my ear; and my companion started upright beside me, her arms raised and her head bent forward, in the attitude of listening. A look of intense delight broke over her countenance; she grasped my hand, drew me toward her, and exclaimed, 'Do you not hear it? I'm not dreaming. I hear the slogan of the Highlanders. We're saved—saved!'

"Then, kneeling down, she prayed with passionate fervor. I was bewildered; my English ears heard only the roar of artillery, and I thought my poor Jessie was raving; but she darted to the batteries, and cried to the men, 'Courage! courage! Hark to the slogan—the slogan of the Macgregors, the grandest of them all! Here's help at last!' The soldiers ceased firing, and all listened in intense anxiety. Gradually, however, there rose a murmur of disappointment, and the wailing of the women who had flocked to the spot burst out anew as the colonel shook his head. Our dull lowland ears heard nothing but the rattle of musketry.

"A few moments more of suspense, and Jessie, who had sunk on the ground, sprang to her feet, and cried, in a voice so clear and piercing that it was heard along the whole line, 'Will ye believe it *now?* The slogan of the Macgregors has ceased, indeed, but it is now the slogan of the Campbells—

The Campbells are coming, ho, ho! ho, ho! Do ye hear?
Do ye hear?'

"At that moment we seemed indeed to hear the voice of
deliverance in the distance; the pibroch of the Highlanders
brought us tidings of relief, for now there was no longer any
doubt of the fact that the Campbells were coming. That
sharp, penetrating, ceaseless sound which rose above all other
sounds could come neither from the advance of the enemy
nor from the work of the sappers. No, it was indeed the blast
of the Scottish bagpipes, now shrill and harsh, as threatening
vengeance on the foe, then in softer tones seeming to promise
succor to friends.

"Never, surely, was such a scene as that which followed.
All, by one simultaneous impulse, fell upon their knees, and
nothing was heard but bursting sobs and the murmured voice
of prayer. Then all arose, and from a thousand lips rang out
a great shout of joy. We were saved." On came Havelock
and his men; they hewed a passage through the rebel masses
up to the very walls of Lucknow, and snatched their country-
men from the horrors of their impending fate.

88.—LITTLE BILLEE.

THERE were three sailors of Bristol city
    Who took a boat and went to sea;
But first with beef and captain's biscuits
    And pickled pork they loaded she.

There was gorging Jack and guzzling Jimmy,
    And the youngest he was little Billee.
Now, when they got as far as the equator,
    They'd nothing left but one split pea.

Says gorging Jack to guzzling Jimmy,
    "I am extremely hungaree."
To gorging Jack says guzzling Jimmy,
    "We've nothing left, we must eat we."

16 *

Says gorging Jack to guzzling Jimmy,
   " With one another we shouldn't agree!
There's little Bill, he's young and tender,
   We're old and tough, so let's eat he."

" Oh, Billy, we're going to kill and eat you,
   So undo the button of your chemie."
When Billy received this information,
   He used his pocket handkerchie.

" First let me say my catechism,
   Which my poor mammy taught to me."
" Make haste, make haste," says guzzling Jimmy,
   While Jack pulled out his snickersee.

So Billy went up to the main-top gallant mast,
   And down he fell on his bended knee.
He scarce had come to the twelfth commandment
   When up he jumps: " There's land I see :

" Jerusalem and Madagascar,
   And North and South Amerikee :
There's the British flag a-riding at anchor,
   With Admiral Napier, K. C. B."

But when they got aboard of the admiral's,
   He hanged fat Jack and flogged Jimmee ;
But as for little Bill, he made him
   The captain of a seventy-three.
                  W. M. THACKERAY.

89.—CAIUS GRACCHUS TO THE ROMANS.

Caius Gracchus, born B. C. 163, was the son of that Cornelia who once said, pointing to her two boys, "These are my jewels!" Tiberius, his elder brother, an advocate of popular rights, was slain by the aristocratic party.

IT is now ten years, O Romans! since my brother, Tiberius Gracchus, was elected your tribune. In what a condition did he find you! The great body of the people pining in abject poverty; thousands suffering for the want of daily bread, eager to labor, but without a clod of earth they could call their own! A few men, rapacious, insatiate, reckless, claiming to be the aristocracy—the aristocracy!—having amassed enormous wealth by extortion and fraud, lorded it over you with remorseless rigor.

The class of small landed proprietors had disappeared. Mercenary idlers, their fingers itching for bribes, political tricksters, hungry usurers, desperate gamblers, all the vilest abettors of lawless power, had usurped the places of men once the strength and glory of the republic. Incalculable distress among the millions, unbounded wealth and prodigality among the hundreds—such was the state of things.

The rich might crush and plunder the poor with impunity, for your rulers were corrupt, your judges cowardly and venal, and money could buy them all to aid in any act of spoliation. And bribery at elections—open, unblushing, flagrant—kept in power the men who were thus sapping the life-blood of the country. Do I exaggerate? Do I not rather too faintly picture the deep woe and degradation of the people—the rapacity, arrogance and depravity of their oppressors?

It was at such a time that Tiberius Gracchus presented himself to you for the tribuneship, and was elected. His affectionate heart had been wrung by the spectacle of your distresses. He had seen with indignation the atrocious system under which you were plundered and downtrodden. He resolved upon your rescue. He flung defiance at your domestic tyrants. He swiftly put an end to that system of fraud by which they robbed you of the public lands.

No shelter of wealth, no privilege of rank or of high place, could save the guilty from his honest wrath, his fiery denunciation. In vain did they retort with the cheap words "demagogue!" "factionist!" "anarchist!" There was that truthfulness in his very tones, that simplicity and nobleness in his very bearing, that dignity and gentleness in his very rage against wrong, that carried conviction of his sincerity to every heart.

Oh how they grew pale with anger, those aristocrats, as they called themselves, when they felt their power melting away, when they saw the people recovering their rights, under the resistless eloquence of that young, devoted spirit! He must be silenced, this audacious tribune, this questioner of the incorruptibility of the privileged classes, this friend and leader of the people—he must be silenced. A bloody revenge must be taken for the fears, which he has made these plunderers endure, of being deprived of their illegally-got possessions.

Alas! the foul deed was done. In a tumult instigated for the purpose your illustrious tribune, this champion of the poor, this friend of the friendless, was slain. His very body, which his friends sought from his murderers, was refused them, and your sacred river was made more sacred by receiving in its bosom all of Tiberius Gracchus that could perish.

And now, men of Rome, if you ask, as those who fear me have asked, why have I left my questorship in Sardinia without leave from the Senate, here is my answer: I must either have come to you without leave or not at all. And if you ask why I have come at all, here is my reply: I have come to present myself for the office my brother held, and for serving you in which he was brutally murdered.

I have come to vindicate his memory, to reinaugurate his policy. I have come—I avow it frankly—to strip the privileged classes of their privileges, to restore popular rights, to uplift the crushed, to bring down the oppressor.

I come with clean hands, O Romans! with no coffers filled with gold from desolated provinces and a ruined people. I can offer no bribe for votes. I come back as poor as I went—poor in all but hatred of tyrants and zeal to serve my country. Shall I be your tribune?*

SARGENT.

* Caius Gracchus was elected tribune B. C. 124. He entered boldly upon his patriotic policy, and carried out many important reforms; but the aristocracy, growing desperate, induced a creature of their own to outbid him in extreme measures, and brought about a state of things which resulted in the defeat and subsequent death of Caius Gracchus.

90.—NOW.

THE venerable Past is past;
  No longer in its shade we'll stay:
'Twas good, no doubt—'tis gone at last—
  There dawns another day!
Why should we sit where ivies creep,
And shroud ourselves in charnels deep,
Or the world's Yesterdays deplore?
Why should we see with dead men's eyes,
  Looking at *Was* from morn to night,
When the beauteous *Now*, the divine *To Be*,
  Woo with their charms our living sight?
Why should we hear but echoes dull,
When the world of sound, so beautiful,
  Will give us music of our own?
Why in the darkness will we grope,
When the sun in heaven's resplendent cope
  Shines as bright as ever it shone?

Abraham saw no brighter stars
  Than those which burn for me and thee;
When Homer heard the lark's sweet song,
  Or night-bird's lovelier melody,
They were such sounds as Shakspeare heard,
Or Chaucer, when he blessed the bird—
Such lovely sounds as we can hear!

Great Plato saw the vernal year
Send forth its tender flowers and shoots,
And luscious autumn pour its fruits;
And *we* can see the lilies blow,
The corn-fields wave, the rivers flow.
For us all bounties of the earth,
For us its wisdom, love and mirth,
If we daily walk in the sight of God,
And prize the gifts he has bestowed!

The Present needs us.   Every age
Bequeaths the next, for heritage,
No lazy luxury or delight,
But strenuous labor for the right;
For *Now*, the child and sire of Time,
  Demands the deeds of earnest men,
To make it better than the Past,
  And stretch the circle of its ken.

For *Now* is ever good and fair;
'Tis ever new and ever bright,
Would we but fashion it aright,
Of past infinitude the heir,
And we of it.   So let us live
That from the Past we may receive
Light from the Now, from Now a joy
Fate shall not mar, nor Time destroy!

CHARLES MACKAY.

IT having been announced to me, my young friends, that you were about forming a fire company, I have called you together to give you such directions as long experience in a first-quality engine company qualifies me to communicate. The moment you hear an alarm of fire, scream like a pair of panthers. Run any way except the right way, for the farthest way round is the nearest way to the fire. If you happen to run on the top of a wood-pile, so much the better; you can then get a good view of the neighborhood.

If a light breaks on your view, " break " for it immediately, but be sure you don't jump into a bow-window. Keep yelling all the time; and if you can't make night hideous enough yourself, kick all the dogs you come across, and set them yelling too; 'twill help amazingly. A brace of cats dragged up stairs by the tail would be a " powerful auxiliary."

When you reach the scene of the fire, do all you can to convert it into a scene of destruction. Tear down all the fences in the vicinity. If it be a chimney on fire, throw salt down it; or if you can't do that, perhaps the best plan would be to jerk off the pump-handle and pound it down. Don't forget to yell all the while, as it will have a prodigious effect in frightening off the fire. The louder the better, of course, and the more ladies in the vicinity, the greater necessity for " doing it up brown."

Should the roof begin to smoke, get to work in good earnest, and make any man " smoke " that interrupts you. If it is summer, and there are fruit trees in the lot, cut them down, to prevent the fire from roasting the apples. *Don't forget to yell !* Should the stable be threatened, carry out the cow-chains. Never mind the horse; he'll be alive and kicking; and if his legs don't do their duty, let them pay for the roast. Ditto as to the hogs—let them save their own bacon or smoke for it.

When the roof begins to burn, get a crow-bar and pry away the stone steps; or if the steps be of wood, procure an axe and chop them up. Next, cut away the wash-boards in the basement story; and if that don't stop the flames, let the chairboards on the first floor share the same fate. Should the "devouring· element" still pursue the "even tenor of its way," you had better ascend to the second story. Pitch out the pitchers and tumble out the tumblers. *Yell all the time!*

If you find a baby abed, fling it into the second-story window of the house across the way, but let the kitten carefully down in a work-basket. Then draw out the bureau drawers and empty their contents out of the back window, telling somebody below to upset the slop-barrel and rain-water hogshead at the same time. Of course you will attend to the mirror. The farther it can be thrown, the more pieces will be made. If anybody objects, smash it over his head.

Do not, under any circumstances, drop the tongs down from the second story; the fall might break its legs, and render the poor thing a cripple for life. Set it straddle of your shoulders, and carry it down carefully. Pile the bed-clothes carefully on the floor, and throw the crockery out of the window. By the time you have attended to all these things, the fire will be arrested, or the building be burnt down. In either case your services will be no longer needed, and of course you require no further directions.

92.—THE SOUTH DURING THE REVOLUTION.

If there be one State in the Union, Mr. President—and I say it not in a boastful spirit—that may challenge comparison with any other for a uniform, zealous, ardent and uncalculating devotion to the Union, that State is South Carolina. Sir, from the very commencement of the Revolution up to this hour, there is no sacrifice, however great, she has not cheerfully made—no service she has ever hesitated to perform. She has adhered to you in your prosperity, but in your adversity she has clung to you with more than filial affection. No matter what was the condition of her domestic affairs—

though deprived of her resources, divided by parties or surrounded with difficulties—the call of the country has been to her as the voice of God. Domestic discord ceased at the sound ; every man became at once reconciled to his brethren, and the sons of Carolina were all seen crowding together to the temple, bringing their gifts to the altar of their common country.

What, sir, was the conduct of the South during the Revolution ? Sir, I honor New England for her conduct in that glorious struggle. But great as is the praise which belongs to her, I think at least equal honor is due to the South. They espoused the quarrel of their brethren with a generous zeal which did not suffer them to stop to calculate their interest in the dispute. Favorites of the mother-country, possessed of neither ships nor seamen to create a commercial rivalship, they might have found in their situation a guarantee that their trade would be for ever fostered and protected by Great Britain. But trampling on all considerations either of interest or of safety, they rushed into the conflict, and fighting for principle, periled all in the sacred cause of freedom.

Never was there exhibited in the history of the world higher examples of noble daring, dreadful suffering and heroic endurance than by the Whigs of Carolina during the Revolution. The whole State, from the mountains to the sea, was overrun by an overwhelming force of the enemy. The fruits of industry perished on the spot where they were produced, or were consumed by the foe. The "plains of Carolina" drank up the most precious blood of her citizens. Black and smoking ruins marked the places which had been the habitations of her children. Driven from their homes into the gloomy and almost impenetrable swamps, even there the spirit of liberty survived, and South Carolina, sustained by the example of her Sumpters and her Marions, proved by her conduct that though her soil might be overrun, the spirit of her people was invincible.

ROBERT Y. HAYNE, 1791-1839.

17   N

93.—THE ARSENAL AT SPRINGFIELD.

THIS is the arsenal.   From floor to ceiling,
  Like a huge organ, rise the burnished arms ;
But from their silent pipes no anthem pealing
  Startles the villages with strange alarms.

Ah ! what a sound will rise, how wild and dreary,
  When the death angel touches those swift keys !
What loud lament and dismal Miserere
  Will mingle with their awful symphonies !

I hear even now the infinite fierce chorus,
  The cries of agony, the endless groan,
Which, through the ages that have gone before us,
  In long reverberations reach our own.

The tumult of each sacked and burning village,
  The shout that every prayer for mercy drowns,
The soldiers' revels in the midst of pillage,
  The wail of famine in beleaguered towns ;

The bursting shell, the gateway wrenched asunder,
  The rattling musketry, the clashing blade,
And ever and anon, in tones of thunder,
  The diapason of the cannonade!

Is it, O man, with such discordant noises,
  With such accursëd instruments as these,
Thou drownest nature's sweet and kindly voices,
  And jarrest the celestial harmonies?

Were half the power that fills the world with terror,
  Were half the wealth bestowed on camps and courts,
Given to redeem the human mind from error,
  There were no need of arsenals or forts.

Down the dark future, through long generations,
  The echoing sounds grow fainter, and then cease;
And like a bell, with solemn, sweet vibrations,
  I hear once more the voice of Christ say, "Peace!"

Peace! and no longer from its brazen portals
  The blast of War's great organ shakes the skies;
But beautiful as songs of the immortals,
  The holy melodies of love arise.

HENRY W. LONGFELLOW.

94.—FALSE NOTIONS OF VIGOR.

I CANNOT describe the horror and disgust which I felt at hearing Mr. Perceval call upon the then ministry for measures of vigor in Ireland. If I lived at Hampstead upon stewed meats and claret, if I walked to church every Sunday before eleven young gentlemen of my own begetting, with their faces washed and their hair pleasantly combed, if the Almighty had blessed me with every earthly comfort, how awfully would I pause before I sent forth the flame and the sword over the cabins of the poor, brave, generous, open-hearted peasants of Ireland!

How easy it is to shed human blood; how easy it is to per-
suade ourselves that it is our duty to do so, and that the de-
cision has cost us a severe struggle; how much, in all ages,
have wounds and shrieks and tears been the cheap and vulgar
resources of the rulers of mankind; how difficult and how
noble it is to govern in kindness, and to found an empire upon
the everlasting basis of justice and affection!

But what do men call vigor? To let loose hussars, and to
bring up artillery, to govern with lighted matches, and to cut,
and push, and prime. I call this not vigor, but the sloth of
cruelty and ignorance. The vigor I love consists in finding
out wherein subjects are aggrieved, in relieving them, in study-
ing the temper and genius of a people, in consulting their pre-
judices, in selecting proper persons to lead and manage them
in the laborious, watchful and difficult task of increasing pub-
lic happiness by allaying each particular discontent. In this
way only will Ireland ever be subdued.

But this, in the eyes of Mr. Perceval, is imbecility and
meanness; houses are not broken open, women are not insult-
ed, the people seem all to be happy—they are not ridden over
by horses and cut by whips. Do you call this vigor? Is this
government?

Rev. Sydney Smith, 1771–1845.

95.—PLAIN LANGUAGE FROM TRUTHFUL JAMES.

Which I wish to remark—and my language is plain—
That for ways that are dark, and for tricks that are vain,
The heathen Chinee is peculiar, which the same I would rise
　　to explain.

Ah Sin was his name, and I shall not deny
In regard to the same what that name might imply;
But his smile it was pensive and childlike, as I frequent re-
　　marked to Bill Nye.

It was August the third, and quite soft were the skies;
Which it might be inferred that Ah Sin was likewise,
Yet he played it that day upon William and me in a way I
    despise.

Which we had a small game, and Ah Sin took a hand;
It was euchre—the same he did not understand;
But he smiled as he sat at the table with the smile that was
    childlike and bland.

Yet the cards they were stocked in a way that I grieve,
And my feelings were shocked at the state of Nye's sleeve,
Which was stuffed full of aces and bowers, and the same with
    intent to deceive.

But the hands that were played by that heathen Chinee
And the points that he made were quite frightful to see,
Till at last he put down a right bower, which the same Nye
    had dealt unto me.

Then I looked up at Nye, and he gazed upon me;
And he rose with a sigh, and said, "Can this be?
We are ruined by Chinese cheap labor;" and he went for
    that heathen Chinee.

In the scene that ensued I did not take a hand,
But the floor it was strewed like the leaves on the strand
With the cards that Ah Sin had been hiding in the game "he
    did not understand."

In his sleeves, which were long, he had twenty-four packs,
Which was coming it strong, yet I state but the facts;
And we found on his nails, which were taper, what is frequent
    in tapers—that's wax.

Which is why I remark--and my language is plain—
That for ways that are dark, and for tricks that are vain,
The heathen Chinee is peculiar, which the same I am free to
    maintain.

BRET HARTE.

17 *

BENJAMIN FRANKLIN.

96.—ON THE FEDERAL CONSTITUTION.

SIR, I agree to this constitution, with all its faults—if they are such—because I think a general government necessary for us, and there is no form of government but what may be a blessing to the people if well administered, and I believe further that this is likely to be well administered for a course of years, and can only end in despotism, as other forms have done before it, when the people shall become so corrupted as to need despotic government, being incapable of any other.

I doubt, too, whether any other convention we can obtain may be able to make a better constitution. For when you assemble a number of men to have the advantage of their joint wisdom, you inevitably assemble with those men all their prejudices, their passions, their errors of opinion, their local interests and their selfish views. From such an assembly can a perfect production be expected? It therefore astonishes me, sir, to find this system approaching so near to perfection as it does, and I think it will astonish our enemies, who are waiting with confidence to hear that our counsels are confounded, like those of the builders of Babel, and that our States are on the point of separation, only to meet hereafter for the purpose of cutting one another's throats.

Thus I consent, sir, to this constitution, because I expect no better, and because I am not sure that this is not the best. The opinions I have had of its errors I sacrifice to the public good. I have never whispered a syllable of them abroad. Within these walls they were born, and here they shall die. If every one of us, in returning to his constituents, were to report the objections he has had to it, and endeavor to gain partisans in support of them, we might prevent its being generally received, and thereby lose all the salutary effects and great advantages resulting naturally in our favor among foreign nations, as well as among ourselves, from our real or apparent unanimity.

Much of the strength and efficacy of any government in procuring and securing happiness to the people depends on opinion—on the general opinion of the goodness of that government, as well as of the wisdom and integrity of its governors. I hope, therefore, that for our own sakes, as a part of the people, and for the sake of our posterity, we shall act heartily and unanimously in recommending this constitution wherever our influence may extend, and turn our future thoughts and endeavors to the means of having it well administered.

BENJAMIN FRANKLIN. 1706–1790.

—◦◇◦—

97.—NOTHING TO WEAR.

Miss FLORA McFLIMSEY, of Madison Square,
   Has made three separate journeys to Paris,
And her father assures me, each time she was there,
   That she and her friend Mrs. Harris
Spent six consecutive weeks, without stopping,
In one continuous round of shopping—
Shopping alone and shopping together,

At all hours of the day, and in all sorts of weather,
For all manner of things that a woman can put
On the crown of her head, or the sole of her foot,
Or wrap round her shoulders, or fit round her waist,
Or that can be sewed on, or pinned on, or laced,
Or tied on with a string, or stitched on with a bow,
In front or behind, above or below:
Dresses for home, and the street, and the hall,
Dresses for winter, spring, summer and fall!

And yet, tho' 'tis hardly three months since the day
All this merchandise went in twelve carts up Broadway,
This same Miss McFlimsey, of Madison Square,
When asked to a ball, was in utter despair,
Because she had nothing whatever to wear!
But the fair Flora's case is by no means surprising;
   I find there exists the greatest distress
In our female community, solely arising
   From this unsupplied destitution of dress,
Whose unfortunate victims are filling the air
With the pitiful wail of "Nothing to wear!"

Oh, ladies, dear ladies, the next sunny day,
Please trundle your hoops just out of Broadway,
   To the alleys and lanes where misfortune and guilt
   Their children have gathered, their hovels have built;
Where hunger and vice, like twin beasts of prey,
   Have hunted their victims to gloom and despair;
Raise the rich, dainty dress and the fine broidered skirt,
Pick your delicate way through the dampness and dirt,
   Grope through the dark dens, climb the rickety stair
To the garret, where wretches, the young and the old,
Half starved and half naked, lie crouched from the cold;
See those skeleton limbs, those frost-bitten feet
All bleeding and bruised by the stones of the street;
Then home to your wardrobes, and say if you dare,
Spoiled children of fashion, you've nothing to wear!

And oh, if perchance there *should* be a sphere
Where all is made right which so puzzles us here;
Where the glare and the glitter and tinsel of time
Fade and die in the light of that region sublime;
Where the soul, disenchanted of flesh and of sense,
Unscreened by its trappings, and shows, and pretense,
Must be clothed for the life and the service above
With purity, truth, faith, meekness and love,—
O daughters of earth! foolish virgins, beware!
Lest in that upper realm you have nothing to wear!

Wm. A. Butler.

98.—THE BELLS.

Hear the sledges with the bells—silver bells! What a world of merriment their melody foretells! How they tinkle, tinkle, tinkle, in the icy air of night! While the stars that over-sprinkle all the heavens seem to twinkle with a crystalline delight. Keeping time, time, time, in a sort of Runic rhyme, to the tintinnabulation that so musically wells from the bells, bells, bells, bells, bells, bells, from the jingling and the tinkling of the bells.

Hear the mellow wedding-bells—golden bells! What a world of happiness their harmony foretells! Through the balmy air of night, how they ring out their delight! From the molten-golden notes, all in tune, what a liquid ditty floats to the turtle-dove that listens, while she gloats on the moon! Oh, from out the sounding cells, what a gush of euphony voluminously wells! How it swells! How it dwells on the Future! How it tells of the rapture that impels to the swinging and the ringing of the bells, bells, bells, of the bells, bells, bells, bells, bells, bells, bells, to the rhyming and the chiming of the bells!

Hear the loud alarum bells—brazen bells! What a tale of terror, now, their turbulency tells! In the startled ear of night, how they scream out their affright! Too much horrified to speak, they can only shriek, shriek, shriek, out of tune, in a clamorous appealing to the mercy of the fire—in a mad expostulation with the deaf and frantic fire leaping higher, higher, higher, with a desperate desire, and a resolute endeavor, now, now to sit, or never, by the side of the pale-faced moon. Oh, the bells, bells, bells! What a tale their terror tells of despair! How they clang, and clash, and roar! What a horror they outpour on the bosom of the palpitating air! Yet the ear, it fully knows, by the twanging and the clanging, how the danger ebbs and flows; yet the ear distinctly tells, in the jangling and the wrangling, how the danger sinks and swells, by the sinking or the swelling in the anger of the bells—of the bells, bells, bells, bells, bells, bells, bells, in the clamor and the clangor of the bells.

Hear the tolling of the bells—iron bells! What a world of solemn thought their monody compels! In the silence of the night, how we shiver with affright at the melancholy menace of their tone! For every sound that floats from the rust within their throats is a groan. And the people, ah! the people, they that dwell up in the steeple all alone, and who tolling, tolling, tolling, in that muffled monotone, feel a glory in so rolling on the human heart a stone: they are neither man nor woman, they are neither brute nor human—they are ghouls; and their king it is who tolls; and he rolls, rolls, rolls, rolls, a pæan from the bells! And his merry bosom swells with the pæan of the bells! And he dances and he yells; keeping time, time, time, in a sort of Runic rhyme, to the pæan of the bells—of the bells; keeping time, time, time, in a sort of Runic rhyme, to the throbbing of the bells—of the bells, bells, bells, to the sobbing of the bells; keeping time, time, time, as he knells, knells, knells, in a happy Runic rhyme, to the rolling of the bells—of the bells, bells, bells—to the tolling of the bells, of the bells, bells, bells, bells, bells, bells, bells, to the moaning and the groaning of the bells.

EDGAR A. POE.

99.—THE GRANDMOTHER'S APOLOGY.

AND Willy, my eldest born, is gone, you say, little Anne?
Ruddy and white, and strong on his legs, he looked like a man.
And Willy's wife has written: she never was overwise,
Never the wife for Willy; he wouldn't take my advice.

For, Anne, you see, her father was not the man to save,
Hadn't a head to manage, and drank himself into his grave.
Pretty enough—very pretty; but I was against it for one.
Eh! but he wouldn't hear me: and Willy, you say, is gone.

Willy, my beauty, my eldest boy, the flower of the flock,
Never a man could fling him, for Willy stood like a rock.
Here's a leg for a babe of a week!" says the doctor; and he would be
    bound
There was not his like that year in twenty parishes round.

Strong of his hands, and strong on his legs, but still of his tongue!
I ought to have gone before him: I wonder he went so young.
I cannot cry for him, Anne: I·have not long to stay;
Perhaps I shall see him the sooner, for he lived far away.

Why do you look at me, Anne? You think I am hard and cold;
But all my children have gone before me, I am so old:
I cannot weep for Willy, nor can I weep for the rest;
Only at your age, Anne, I could have wept with the best.

For mine is a time of peace, it is not often I grieve;
I am oftener sitting at home in my father's farm at eve:
And the neighbors come and laugh and gossip, and so do I;
I find myself often laughing at things that have long gone by.

To be sure the preacher says our sins should make us sad,
But mine is a time of peace, and there is grace to be had ;
And God, not man, is the Judge of us all when life shall cease;
And in this Book, little Anne, the message is one of peace.

And age is a time of peace, so it be free from pain,
And happy has been my life, but I would not live it again.
I seem to be tired a little, that's all, and long for rest;
Only at your age, Anne, I could have wept with the best.

So Willy has gone, my beauty, my eldest-born, my flower;
But how can I weep for Willy? he has gone but for an hour—
Gone for a minute, my son, from this room into the next;
I, too, shall go in a minute.   What time have I to be vext?

And Willy's wife has written: she never was overwise.
Get me my glasses, Anne; thank God that I keep my eyes.
There is but a trifle left you when I shall have passed away.
But stay with the old woman now: you cannot have long to stay.

ALFRED TENNYSON.

100.—AGAINST MR. PITT,* 1741.

SIR, I was unwilling to interrupt the course of this debate
while it was carried on with calmness and decency by men
who do not suffer the ardor of opposition to cloud their reason
or transport them to such expressions as the dignity of this
assembly does not admit.   I have hitherto deferred to answer
the gentleman who declaimed against the bill with such fluency
of rhetoric and such vehemence of gesture—who charged the
advocates for the expedients now proposed with having no re-

* William Pitt, afterward Lord Chatham, and father of another William
Pitt, whose fame equals, though it does not eclipse, that of his father.
Both Walpole's remarks and Pitt's reply bear signs of touches from Dr.
Jonnson's pen, in whose Register of Debates they first appeared.

gard to any interest but their own, and with making laws only to consume paper, and threatened them with the defection of their adherents and the loss of their influence upon this new discovery of their folly and their ignorance. Nor, sir, do I now answer him for any other purpose than to remind him how little the clamors of rage and the petulancy of invective contribute to the end for which this assembly is called together; how little the discovery of truth is promoted, and the security of the nation established, by pompous diction and theatrical emotions.

Formidable sounds and furious declamation, confident assertions and lofty periods, may affect the young and inexperienced, and perhaps the gentleman may have contracted his habits of oratory by conversing more with those of his own age than with such as have had more opportunities of acquiring knowledge, and more successful methods of communicating their sentiments.

If the heat of his temper, sir, would suffer him to attend to those whose age and long acquaintance with business give them an indisputable right to deference and superiority, he would learn in time to reason rather than declaim, and to prefer justness of argument and an accurate knowledge of facts to sounding epithets and splendid superlatives, which may disturb the imagination for a moment, but which leave no lasting impression on the mind. He will learn, sir, that to accuse and prove are very different, and that reproaches unsupported by evidence affect only the character of him who utters them. Excursions of fancy and flights of oratory are indeed pardonable in young men, but in no other; and it would surely contribute more, even to the purpose for which some gentlemen appear to speak—that of depreciating the conduct of the administration—to prove the inconveniences and injustice of this bill than barely to assert them, with whatever magnificence of language or appearance of zeal, honesty or compassion.

Sir Robert Walpole, 1676–1745.

18

101.—REPLY TO SIR ROBERT WALPOLE, 1741.

SIR, the atrocious crime of being a young man, which the honorable gentleman has, with such spirit and decency, charged upon me, I shall neither attempt to palliate nor deny, but content myself with wishing that I may be one of those whose follies may cease with their youth, and not of that number who are ignorant in spite of their experience.

Whether youth can be imputed to any man as a reproach, I will not, sir, assume the province of determining; but surely age may become justly contemptible if the opportunities which it brings have passed away without improvement, and vice appears to prevail when the passions have subsided. The wretch who, after having seen the consequences of a thousand errors, continues still to blunder, and whose age has only added obstinacy to stupidity, is surely the object of either abhorrence or contempt, and deserves not that his gray hairs should secure him from insult. Much more, sir, is *he* to be abhorred who, as he has advanced in age, has receded from virtue, and become more wicked, with less temptation, who prostitutes himself for money which he cannot enjoy, and spends the remains of his life in the ruin of his country.

But youth, sir, is not my only crime; I have been accused of acting a theatrical part. A theatrical part may either imply some peculiarities of gesture, or a dissimulation of my real sentiments and an adoption of the opinions and language of another man.

In the first sense, sir, the charge is too trifling to be confuted, and deserves to be mentioned only to be despised. I am at liberty, like every other man, to use my own language; and though perhaps I may have some ambition to please this gentleman, I shall not lay myself under any restraint, nor very solicitously copy his diction or his mien, however matured by age or modeled by experience.

But if any man shall, by charging me with theatrical behavior, imply that I utter any sentiments but my own, I shall treat him as a calumniator and a villain; nor shall any protection shelter him from the treatment he deserves. I shall, on such an occasion, without scruple, trample upon all those forms within which wealth and dignity entrench themselves, nor shall anything but age restrain my resentment—age, which always brings with it *one* privilege, that of being insolent and supercilious without punishment.

But with regard, sir, to those whom I have offended, I am of opinion that if I had acted a borrowed part I should have avoided their censure; the heat that offended them is the ardor of conviction and that zeal for the service of my country which neither hope nor fear shall influence me to suppress. I will not sit unconcerned while my liberty is invaded, nor look in silence upon public robbery. I will exert my endeavors at whatever hazard to repel the aggressor and drag the thief to justice, whoever may protect him in his villainy, and whoever may partake of his plunder.

MR. PITT (*afterward* LORD CHATHAM).

102.—BILL AND JOE.

COME, dear old comrade, you and I
Will steal an hour from days gone by—
The shining days when life was new,
And all was bright as morning dew,
The lusty days of long ago,
When you were Bill and I was Joe.

Your name may flaunt a titled trail,
Proud as a cockerel's rainbow tail;
And mine as brief appendix wear
As Tam O'Shanter's luckless mare;
To-day, old friend, remember still
That I am Joe and you are Bill.

You've won the great world's envied prize,
And grand you look in people's eyes,

With H O N. and L L. D.,
In big brave letters, fair to see.
Your fist, old fellow! off they go!
How are you, Bill?   How are you, Joe?

You've worn the judge's ermine robe;
You've taught your name to half the globe;
You've sung mankind a deathless strain;
You've made the dead past live again:
The world may call you what it will,
But you and I are Joe and Bill.

The chaffing young folks stare and say,
"See those old buffers, bent and gray;
They talk like fellows in their teens!
Mad, poor old boys!   That's what it means,"
And shake their heads; they little know
The throbbing hearts of Bill and Joe;—

How Bill forgets his hour of pride,
While Joe sits smiling at his side;
How Joe, in spite of time's disguise,
Finds the old schoolmate in his eyes—
Those calm, stern eyes that melt and fill
As Joe looks fondly up at Bill.

Ah, pensive scholar, what is fame?
A fitful tongue of leaping flame;
A giddy whirlwind's fickle gust,
That lifts a pinch of mortal dust:
A few swift years, and who can show
Which dust was Bill, and which was Joe?

The weary idol takes his stand,
Holds out his bruised and aching hand,
While gaping thousands come and go—
How vain it seems, this empty show!—

Till all at once his pulses thrill :
'Tis poor old Joe's " God bless you, Bill ! "

And shall we breathe in happier spheres
The names that pleased our mortal ears,
In some sweet lull of harp and song,
For earth-born spirits none too long,
Just whispering of the world below,
Where this was Bill, and that was Joe?

No matter ; while our home is here
No sounding name is half so dear :
When fades at length our lingering day,
Who cares what pompous tombstones say ?
Read on the hearts that love us still,
Hic jacet Joe.   *Hic jacet* Bill.

OLIVER WENDELL HOLMES.

103.—FALSE COLORING LENT TO WAR.

On every side of me I see causes at work which go to spread a most delusive coloring over war, and to remove its shocking barbarities to the background of our contemplations altogether. I see it in the history which tells me of the superb appearance of the troops and the brilliancy of their successive charges. I see it in the poetry which lends the

THOMAS CHALMERS.

magic of its numbers to the narrative of blood, and transports its many admirers, as by its images and its figures and its nodding plumes of chivalry it throws its treacherous embellishments over a scene of legalized slaughter.

I see it in the music which represents the progress of the

18 *   O

battle, and where, after being inspired by the trumpet-notes of preparation, the whole beauty and tenderness of a drawing-room are seen to bend over the sentimental entertainment; nor do I hear the utterance of a single sigh to interrupt the death tones of the thickening contest, and the moans of the wounded men, as they fade away upon the ear and sink into lifeless silence.

All, all goes to prove what strange and half-sighted creatures we are. Were it not so, war could never have been seen in any other aspect than that of unmingled hatefulness, and I can look to nothing but to the progress of Christian sentiment upon earth to arrest the strong current of the popular and prevailing partiality for war. Then only will an imperious sense of duty lay the check of severe principle on all the subordinate tastes and faculties of our nature.

Then will glory be reduced to its right estimate, and the wakeful benevolence of the gospel, chasing away every spell, will be turned by the treachery of no delusion whatever from its simple but sublime enterprises for the good of the species. Then the reign of truth and quietness will be ushered into the world, and war—cruel, atrocious, unrelenting war—will be stripped of its many and its bewildering fascinations.

THOMAS CHALMERS, 1780–1847.

104.—TO-DAY AND TO-MORROW.

HIGH hopes that burned like stars sublime go down i' the heavens
    of freedom,
And true hearts perish in the time we bitterliest need 'em,
But never sit we down and say there's nothing left but sorrow;
We walk the wilderness to-day—the promised land to-morrow.

Our birds of song are silent now, there are no flowers blooming;
Yet life holds in the frozen bough, and freedom's spring is coming,
And freedom's tide comes up alway, tho' we may stand in sorrow,
And our good bark, aground to-day, shall float again to-morrow.

Through all the long, long night of years the people's cry ascendeth,
And earth is wet with blood and tears, but our meek sufferance
  endeth.
The few shall not for ever sway—the many toil in sorrow ;
The powers of hell are strong to-day, but Christ shall rise to-
  morrow.

Tho' hearts brood o'er the past, our eyes with smiling futures
  glisten,
For, lo! our day bursts up the skies : lean out your souls and listen !
The world rolls freedom's radiant way, and ripens with her sorrow ;
Keep heart ! who bears the Cross to-day shall wear the Crown to-
  morrow !

O youth, flame-earnest, still aspire with energies immortal !
To many a heaven of desire our yearnings ope the portal ;
And tho' age wearies by the way and hearts break in the furrow,
We'll sow the golden grain to-day—the harvest reap to-morrow !

Build up heroic lives and all be like a sheathen sabre,
Ready to flash out at God's call, O chivalry of labor !
Triumph and toil are twins, and aye joy suns the clouds of sorrow,
And 'tis the martyrdom to-day brings victory to-morrow.

GERALD MASSEY.

—◦—

105.—DANGERS OF OUR PROSPERITY.

THE danger, my countrymen, is that we shall become
intoxicated by our amazing physical triumphs. Because,
within the memory of most of us, the lightning has been har-
nessed to the newsman's car, and the steam-engine has not only
brought the ends of the earth into proximity, but has also
provided a working power which, requiring no nutriment and
susceptible of no fatigue, almost releases living creatures from
the necessity of toil,—because of these most marvelous discov-
eries, we are in danger of believing that like wonders may be
achieved in the social and moral world.

But be it remembered that in all our discoveries no substitute has been found for conscience, and no machine to take the place of reason. The telegraph cannot legislate, nor the locomotive educate. The mind is still the mind, and must obey its own higher laws. Our most pressing needs are such as no mechanism can supply. What we most lack is true, earnest, sincere, faithful, loyal, self-sacrificing men. Without these it is in vain that we extend our territory from ocean to ocean, and quarry gold as we do rocks. These physical accessions, coming so suddenly upon us, do but increase our peril. Adversity we might bear, and be the better for it, but how shall we bear this gush of seeming prosperity? Seeming, I say, because time alone can determine whether it is real.

If, my countrymen, with all these excitements, we do not become a nation of reckless adventurers—gamblers perhaps would be the proper word—if we do not cut ourselves entirely loose from our ancient moorings, but still hold fast to our integrity, our very continence will prove that there is still some sterling virtue left. For never was there so much reason for the prayer, "Deliver us from temptation." After all our conquests, the most difficult yet remains—the victory over ourselves. We have now to answer, under untried difficulties, that gravest of questions, "What constitutes a state?" And the answer must be like that which was given long, long ago:

"Not high-raised battlement or labored mound,
      Thick wall or moated gate,
   Not cities proud, with spires and turrets crowned,
      Not bays and broad-armed ports,
   Where, laughing at the storm, rich navies ride;
      Not starred and spangled courts,
   Where low-browed Baseness wafts perfume to Pride;
      No, men, high-minded men—
   With powers as far above dull brutes endued
      In forest, brake, or den,
   As beasts excel cold rocks and brambles rude;
   Men who their duties know,
      But know their rights, and, knowing, dare maintain."

                              TIMOTHY WALKER.

106.—DESTRUCTION OF THE PHILISTINES.

Mr. Thyer remarks of this piece: "One may without extravagance say that the poet seems to exert no less force of genius in describing than Samson does in executing."

MILTON.

OCCASIONS drew me early to the
    city,
And as the gates I entered with
    sunrise,
The morning trumpets festival
    proclaimed
Through each high street; little I
    had despatched,
When all abroad was rumored
    that this day
Samson should be brought forth,
    to show the people
Proof of his mighty strength in
    feats and games;
  I sorrowed at his captive state, but minded
  Not to be absent at that spectacle.

  The building was a spacious theatre,
  Half round, on two main pillars vaulted high,
  With seats where all the lords, and each degree
  Of sort, might sit, in order to behold;
  The other side was open, where the throng
  On banks and scaffolds under sky might stand;
  I among these aloof obscurely stood.

  The feast and noon grew high, and sacrifice
  Had filled their hearts with mirth, high cheer, and wine,
  When to their sports they turned. Immediately
  Was Samson as a public servant brought,
  In their state livery clad; before him pipes
  And timbrels; on each side went armèd guards,
  Both horse and foot; before him and behind,
  Archers and slingers, cataphracts and spears.

At sight of him the people with a shout
Rifted the air, clamoring their god with praise,
Who had made their dreadful enemy their thrall.
He, patient, but undaunted, where they led him,
Came to the place; and what was set before him,
Which without help of eye might be essayed,
To heave, pull, draw or break, he still performed,
All with incredible, stupendous force,
None daring to appear antagonist.

At length, for intermission sake, they led him
Between the pillars; he his guide requested
(For so from such as nearer stood we heard),
As over-tired, to let him lean a while
With both his arms on those two massy pillars
That to the archëd roof gave main support.
He, unsuspicious, led him; which when Samson
Felt in his arms, with head a while inclined,
And eyes fast fixed, he stood, as one who prayed,
Or some great matter in his mind revolved:
At last, with head erect, thus cried aloud:

"Hitherto, lords, what your commands imposed
I have performed, as reason was, obeying,
Not without wonder or delight beheld;
Now of my own accord such other trial
I mean to show you of my strength, yet greater,
As with amaze shall strike all who behold."

This uttered, straining all his nerves, he bowed.
As with the force of winds and waters pent,
When mountains tremble, those two massy pillars
With horrible convulsion to and fro
He tugged, he shook, till down they came, and drew
The whole roof after them with burst of thunder
Upon the heads of all who sat beneath—
Lords, ladies, captains, counselors or priests,

Their choice nobility and flower, not only
Of this, but each Philistian city round,
Met from all parts to solemnize this feast!

Samson, with these immixed, inevitably
Pulled down the same destruction on himself;
The vulgar only 'scaped who stood without.

JOHN MILTON, 1608–1674.

107.—THE NOBLEST PUBLIC VIRTUE.

THERE is a sort of courage to which—I frankly confess it
—I do not lay a claim; a boldness to which I dare not aspire;
a valor which I cannot covet. I cannot lay myself down in
the way of the welfare and happiness of my country. That I
cannot, I have not the courage to do. I cannot interpose the
power with which I may be invested—a power conferred not
for my personal benefit or aggrandizement, but for my coun-
try's good—to check her onward march to greatness and glory.
I have not courage enough—I am too cowardly for that!

I would not, I dare not, lie down and place my body across
the path that leads my country to prosperity and happiness.
This is a sort of courage widely different from that which a
man may display in his private conduct and personal rela-
tions. Personal or private courage is totally distinct from
that higher and nobler courage which prompts the patriot to
offer himself a voluntary sacrifice to his country's good.

Apprehensions of the imputation of the want of firmness
sometimes impel us to perform rash and inconsiderate acts.
It is the greatest courage to be able to bear the imputation of
the *want* of courage. But pride, vanity, egotism, so unamiable
and offensive in private life, are vices which partake of the
character of crimes in the conduct of public affairs. The un-
fortunate victim of these passions cannot see beyond the little
petty, contemptible circle of his own personal interest. All

his thoughts are withdrawn from his country and concentrated on his consistency, his firmness, himself.

The high, the exalted, the sublime emotions of a patriotism which, soaring toward heaven, rises far above all mean, low or selfish things, and is absorbed by one soul-transporting thought of the good and glory of one's country, are never felt in his impenetrable bosom. That patriotism which, catching its inspiration from on high, and leaving at an immeasurable distance below all lesser, groveling, personal interests and feelings, animates and prompts to deeds of self-sacrifice, of valor, of devotion and of death itself,—that is public virtue, that is the noblest, the sublimest of all public virtues!

HENRY CLAY, 1777–1852.

108.—THE MODERN PUFFING SYSTEM.

FROM AN EPISTLE TO SAMUEL ROGERS, ESQ.

UNLIKE those feeble gales of praise
Which critics blew in former days,
Our modern puffs are of a kind
That truly, really, "raise the wind;"
And since they've fairly set in blowing,
We find them the best "trade-winds" going.

What steam is on the deep—and more—
Is the vast power of Puff on shore;
Which jumps to glory's future tenses
Before the present even commences,
And makes "immortal" and "divine" of us.
Before the world has read one line of us.

In old times, when the god of song
Drove his own two-horse team along,
Carrying inside a bard or two
Booked for posterity "all through,"

Their luggage a few close-packed rhymes
(Like yours, my friend, for after-times),
So slow the pull to Fame's abode
That folks oft slumbered on the road;
And Homer's self sometimes, they say,
Took to his night-cap on the way.

But now how different is the story
With our new galloping sons of glory,
Who, scorning all such slack and slow time,
Dash to posterity in no time!
Raise but one general blast of puff
To start your author—that's enough!

In vain the critics set to watch him
Try at the starting-post to catch him:
He's off—the puffers carry it hollow—
The critics, if they please, may follow;
Ere they've laid down their first positions,
He's fairly blown through six editions!

In vain doth Edinburgh* dispense
Her blue-and-yellow pestilence
(That plague so awful in my time
To young and touchy sons of rhyme);
The Quarterly, at three months' date,
To catch the Unread One, comes too late;
And nonsense, littered in a hurry,
Becomes "immortal," spite of Murray.†

Thomas Moore, 1780–1852.

---

* An allusion to the "Edinburgh Review," the Edinburgh edition of which has blue covers, backed with yellow. In his younger days Moore was so much offended by a criticism which appeared in the "Review" on his poems, that he sent a challenge to Francis Jeffrey, the editor. A hostile meeting took place August 11, 1806, but the police interfered and nobody was hurt. Moore and Jeffrey lived to be good friends.

† Murray, the publisher of the "London Quarterly Review."

THE BIRTHPLACE OF WASHINGTON.

109.—WASHINGTON'S BIRTHDAY.

I RISE, gentlemen, to propose to you the name of that great man in commemoration of whose birth, and in honor of whose character and services, we have here assembled. I am sure that I express a sentiment common to every one present when I say that there is something more than ordinarily solemn and affecting in this occasion.

We are met to testify our regard for him whose name is intimately blended with whatever belongs most essentially to the prosperity, the liberty, the free institutions and the renown of our country. That name was of power to rally a nation in the hour of thick-thronging public disasters and calamities; that name shone amid the storm of war, a beacon-light to cheer and guide the country's friends; its flame, too, like a meteor, to repel her foes. That name in the days of peace was a loadstone, attracting to itself a whole people's confidence, a whole people's love and the whole world's respect; that name, descending with all time, spread over the whole earth and uttered in all the languages belonging to the tribes and races of men, will for ever be pronounced with affectionate gratitude by every one in whose breast there shall arise an aspiration for human rights and human liberty.

Gentlemen, we are at the point of a century from the birth of Washington; and what a century it has been! During its course the human mind has seemed to proceed with a sort of geometric velocity, accomplishing more than had been done in fives or tens of centuries preceding. Washington stands at the commencement of a new era as well as at the head of the New World. A century from the birth of Washington has changed the world. The country of Washington has been the theatre on which a great part of that change has been wrought, and Washington himself a principal agent by which it has been accomplished. His age and his country are equally full of wonders, and of both he is the chief.

It is the spirit of human freedom, the new elevation of individual man, in his moral, social and political character, leading the whole long train of other improvements, which has most remarkably distinguished the era. Society has assumed a new character; it has raised itself from *beneath* governments to a participation *in* governments; it has mixed moral and political objects with the daily pursuits of individual men, and with a freedom and strength before altogether unknown it has applied to these objects the whole power of the human understanding. It has been the era, in short, when the social principle has triumphed over the feudal principle; when society has maintained its rights against military power, and established on foundations never hereafter to be shaken its competency to govern itself.

If the prediction of the poet, uttered a few years before Washington's birth, be true—if indeed it be designed by Providence that the proudest exhibition of human character and human affairs shall be made on this theatre of the Western world—if it be true that

> " The first four acts already past,
> A fifth shall close the drama with the day;
> Time's noblest offspring is the last,"

—how could this imposing, swelling final scene be appropri-
ately opened, how could its intense interest be adequately sus-
tained, but by the introduction of just such a character as
our Washington?

DANIEL WEBSTER, 1782–1852.

———◆———

110.—THE ROLLING STONE.

CHARACTERS.—*Mr. Carp, Charles Veer.*

Enter MR. CARP *and* CHARLES VEER, *in opposite directions.*
CHARLES *has a rake and pitchfork, which he soon lays down.*

Carp. Why, nephew, what is the meaning of this? The last
time I saw you, you were feeling a sick man's pulse, and trying
to look wise.

Veer. True, uncle, I prescribed for that man.

Carp. Poor fellow! Did he recover?

Veer. Did he recover? He certainly did *not.* I had the
honor of giving him the last dose he ever took.

Carp. Then you gave up medicine and your patient to-
gether, eh? Well, you did right. Not one man in a hundred
succeeds as a doctor. The profession is trying to the health,
lacerating to the feelings, petrifying to the conscience. Besides,
what with hydropaths, homœopaths, gymnasts, quacks and
healing mediums, the regular practitioner is crowded to the
wall.

Veer. So I thought, and accordingly entered my name in
the law-office of Messrs. Wheedle & Grab.

Carp. Law? Worse still! It gets a man into the habit of
trying to make the *worse* appear the *better* reason. Profession
crowded. Business demoralizing. Keep away from the law.

Veer. I did most faithfully, till at last I took to trade.

Carp. If there is anything uncertain, it is trade. Seventy-
five merchants in a hundred break down before they have
been in business ten years. Never be a merchant. You
failed, I suppose?

Veer. Oh no! I couldn't get a chance to fail. Nobody would give me any credit. So, after a dash at authorship and a week's trial at school-teaching, I fixed—yes, *fixed*—upon an occupation to which I mean to be faithful.

Carp. As for authorship, it is too precarious for any but vagabonds ; and as for school-teaching, put me into a tread-mill rather. But what is this new occupation you have taken up ?

Veer. Ecce Signum! Don't you see? It is the one occupation for a rational man. I am a tiller of the soil. Yes, I have found a harbor at last. *In-ve'ni port'um.* Behold my rake and my pitchfork. Blessed tools ! Hay-making! Fragrance, health and all rural charms are in the very sound. Hay-making !

Carp. Hay-making! Bah! I could have told you something about farming. It has been proved from statistical tables that farmers—

Veer. Upset the statistical tables—smash them—burn them —if they insinuate anything against farmers !

Carp. Be quiet. They prove, I say, that farmers suffer more from diseases of the brain than any other class.

Veer. Statistics prove that, do they ?

Carp. To be sure they do.

Veer. Do you know what else statistics prove? I will tell you. They prove that old gentlemen of leisure and of choleric temper, like yourself, generally go off in an apoplexy before they reach the age of sixty.

Carp. Statistics are a humbug. You can prove anything by statistics. Here is a newspaper from California proving by statistics that the country has lost money by the discovery of gold.

Veer [*taking the newspaper*]. Allow me. Ah! What have we here? [*Reads.*] "Enormous deposits of silver!" "In a single day, two men took out fifty thousand dollars' worth of silver !" [*Paces the stage.*]

Carp. What's the matter, Charles? Are you bitten by anything?

Veer. Fifty thousand dollars in one day! Think of that!

19 *

[*Kicks the rake.*] Uncle, fit me out for Utah, and you shall have fifty per cent. of my mining profits.

Carp. Mining profits, indeed! Chills and fevers! Rattle-snakes and grizzly bears!

Veer. Uncle of mine, do you approve of a man's living at all? What is a poor fellow to do? Tell me that. Shall I stand still?

Carp. By no means.

Veer. Shall I go on—keep moving?

Carp. No. Your pushing men always get a stumble.

Veer. What in the name of common sense, then, shall I do? I will tell you what I will do: I will stick to the farm. Who is more independent than a tiller of the soil? See him go forth in the morning, "pride in his port, defiance in his eye," his pitchfork on his shoulder. His way is through green fields, by babbling brooks, in the shadow of primeval forests. Oh *how* happy, did he but *know* his happiness!

Carp. Bravo, nephew! What a fortune you would make on the stage!

Veer. Eh? The stage? Did you say the stage? Not a bad idea, that! Do you really think I should succeed on the stage? Come, now, there you are not so far in the wrong. Figure—well, though *I* say it, figure not bad! Height—just the thing to a hair! Garrick, Kean, and Booth were all under five feet four. Face—well, if I were to pronounce it a re-markably fine face, I should merely be stating a notorious fact in a very mild way.

Carp. Refreshing modesty!

Veer. Voice—let me give you a touch from Hamlet.

Carp. Spare me. I never wronged you. [*Looks at his watch.*]

Veer. Put up that watch and listen! "What a piece of work is a man! How noble in reason! How infinite in facul-ties! In form and moving, how express and admirable! In action—" [*In gesticulating he nearly hits* CARP.]

Carp. Be careful.

Veer. "In action, how like an angel! In apprehension,

how like a god! The beauty of the world! the paragon of animals!"

Carp. I take back my compliment. That will do.

Veer. Perhaps the dagger scene in Macbeth, or the mad scene in Lear, or the defiance in Coriolanus, would better suit my style. " Is this a dagger that—"

Carp. That will do, sir. My nose isn't a dagger.

Veer. " I tax not you, ye elements, with unkindness."

Carp. That will do, my boy.

Veer. Boy?

> "Measureless liar, thou hast made my heart
> Too great for what contains it. ' Boy !' O slave !
> Cut me to pieces, Volsces ; men and lads,
> Stain all your edges on me. ' Boy !' False hound !
> If you have writ your annals true, 'tis there
> That, like an eagle in a dove-cote, I
> Fluttered your Volscians in Co-ri'o-li !
> Alone I did it. ' Boy !' "

Carp. That will do, I say. That will do.

Veer. To be sure it will do! Who could do it better? The pit would rise at me.

Carp. Yes, rise to hoot you from the boards.

Veer. The ladies would wave their handkerchiefs.

Carp. Yes, wave you off out of their sight. Ah! you'll never make an actor, nephew; and if you *could*, is not the actor's vocation the most hazardous, the most humiliating, the most—

Veer. I have it! I'll be a lecturer.

Carp. That would be a blow indeed to your family. Spare them the disgrace. A lecturer is another name for a bore. Punch and Judy are worth the whole mob of gentlemen who lecture.

Veer. Thou darkener of counsel! Did you never hear the old proverb, " A rolling stone gathers no moss"? I will stay where I am. My grasp is on the handle of the plow, and I'll not look back.

Carp. Hear him! How long will this farming frolic last?

Veer. Last? As long as I can swing a scythe or handle a spade! "Let not ambition mock my useful toil!" Come and see my improvements.

Carp. When a farmer asks me to see his improvements, I always have an attack of rheumatism. I know he means to take me to his pig-stye. No, I thank you. Improvements, indeed! The very word is enough. I hate improvements. Go your own way. Good-bye, Mr. *Farmer.*   [*Exit.*

Veer. There's a nice man for a rich uncle! No matter. [*Takes his rake and pitchfork.*] Here are my weapons. *Steady* is the word now. I'll wring from this coy, reluctant soil a living of some kind, and with it a treasure that silver cannot purchase—content.   [*Exit.*   SARGENT.

111.—THE DYING TRUMPETER.

UPON the field of battle the dying trumpeter lay,
And from his side the life-blood was streaming fast away.
His deadly wound is burning, and yet he cannot die
Till his company returning bring news of victory.

Hark! as he rises reeling upon the bloody ground—
Hark! o'er the field is pealing a well-known trumpet's sound.
It gives him life and vigor; he grasps his horse's mane,
He mounts and lifts his trumpet to his dying lips again.

And all his strength he gathers to hold it in his hand,
Then pours in tones of thunder, "Victoria!" o'er the land.
"Victoria!" sounds the trumpet! "Victoria!" all around;
"Victoria!" like loud thunder it runs along the ground.

And in that blast so thrilling the trumpeter's spirit fled;
He breathed his last breath in it, and from his horse fell dead.
The company returning stood silent round their friend;
"That," said the old field-marshal—"that was a happy end!"

JULIUS MOSEN.

112.—A PRISONER'S MEDITATIONS.

To live at liberty is doubtless much better than living in a prison, but even here the reflection that God is present with us, that worldly joys are brief and fleeting and that true happiness is to be sought in the conscience, not in external objects, can give a real zest to life. In less than one month after my captivity I had made up my mind as to the part I should adopt.

SILVIO PELLICO.

Having been incapable of the mean action of purchasing impunity by procuring the destruction of others, I saw that the only prospect that lay before me was the scaffold, or long-protracted imprisonment. It was necessary that I should prepare myself. "I will live," thought I, "so long as I shall be permitted; and when they take my life, I will do as the unfortunate have done before me: when the last moment arrives, I can die!"

At the beginning of my captivity I was fortunate enough to meet a friend. It was neither the governor nor any of his under-jailers, but a poor deaf-and-dumb boy five or six years old, the offspring of thieves who had paid the penalty of the law. The little fellow used to come under my window, smile and bow to me. I threw him a piece of bread; he took it and gave a leap of joy; then ran to his companions, divided it, and returned to eat his own share under my window. This boy seemed delighted whenever I deigned to notice him; and one day, on being permitted to enter my prison, he uttered a cry of joy and ran to embrace my knees. I took him up in my arms, and he threw his little hands about my neck and lavished on me the tenderest caresses.

How much affection in his smile and manner! how eagerly I longed to have him to educate, to raise him from his abject condition, and snatch him, perhaps, from ruin! I never even learned his name; he himself did not know that he had one. He seemed always happy—as light-hearted as if he had been the child of a grandee. Strange happiness, thought I, in a receptacle of so much pain and sorrow!

From this little teacher I learned, at least, that the mind need not depend on situation, but may be rendered independent of external things. Govern the imagination, and all will be well with us, wherever we may be placed. A day is soon over; and if at night we can retire to rest without actual pain and hunger, it matters little whether it be within the walls of a prison or of a palace. The mind is its own place.

But how govern the imagination? I began to try, and sometimes thought I had succeeded to a miracle, but at other times the enchantress triumphed, and I was repeatedly astonished to find tears starting into my eyes. "Still, slavery, still thou art a bitter draught!"   SILVIO PELLICO.*

———◆◇◆———

113.—THE SECOND WAR WITH ENGLAND, 1812.

IF we are not fully prepared for war, let the sublime fact be soon exhibited that a free and valiant nation, with our numbers and a just cause, is always a powerful nation, is always ready to defend its essential rights. In the Congress of 1774, among other arguments used to prevent a war and discourage separation from Great Britain, the danger of having our towns battered down and burnt was zealously urged. The venerable Christopher Gadsden, of South Carolina, rose and replied to it in these memorable words: "Our seaport towns, Mr. President, are composed of brick and wood. If they are destroyed, we have clay and timber enough to rebuild them. But if the liberties of our country are destroyed, where shall we find the materials to replace *them?*"

* Author of "My Prisons," born near Turin, in Piedmont, 1780, died 1854. He was imprisoned by the Austrian authorities on account of supposed hostility to the government.

During the siege of Boston, General Washington consulted Congress upon the propriety of bombarding the town. Mr. Hancock was then President of Congress. After General Washington's letter was read, a solemn silence ensued. This was broken by a member making a motion that the House should resolve itself into a committee of the whole, in order that Mr. Hancock might give his opinion upon the important subject, as he was so deeply interested, from having all his estate in Boston. After he left the chair, he addressed the chairman of the committee of the whole in the following words : " It is true, sir, nearly all the property I have in the world is in houses and other real estate in the town of Boston ; but if the expulsion of the British army—if the liberties of our country—require their being burnt to ashes, *issue the order for that purpose immediately.*"

What inspiring lessons of duty do examples like these inculcate ! War, fellow-citizens, is a great evil, but not the greatest of evils. Submission to injustice is worse. Loss of honor is worse. A peace purchased by mean and inglorious sacrifices is worse. That sordid or that self-indulgent spirit which would lead a man to prize the satisfaction of avarice or of worldly ease above country, above manliness, above freedom, is worse, far worse.

I am no apologist of war. I hate and deplore it. It should be the last resort of nations. It should be shunned on every principle, Christian and humane. It brings tremendous evils in its train. It foments some of the vilest passions of our nature. But an ignoble peace may be even more demoralizing than a sanguinary war. It may corrupt all the springs of a people's energy and magnanimity. It may make them servile, sensual, selfish. It may be such an incubus on a nation's character that every true patriot must feel crushed and degraded under its weight, till he could almost exclaim with disgraced Cassio, "Oh, I have lost my reputation ! I have lost the immortal part of myself, and what remains is bestial. My reputation, Iago, my reputation !"

T. C. BROWN.

114.—THE BATTLE OF FONTENOY, May 11, 1745.

By our camp-fires rose a murmur at the dawning of the day,
And the tread of many footsteps spoke the advent of the fray ;
And as we took our places, few and pithy were our words,
While some were tightening horse-girths and some were girding
    swords.

The trumpet blast has sounded our footmen to array ;
The willing steed has bounded, impatient for the fray ;
The green flag is unfolded, while rings the cry of joy,
"Heaven speed dear Ireland's banner to-day at Fontenoy !"

We looked upon that banner, and the memory arose
Of our homes and perished kindred where the Lee or Shannon
    flows ;
We looked upon that banner, and we swore to God on high
To smite to-day the Saxon's might, to conquer or to die !

Loud swells the charging trumpet—'tis a voice from our own land ;
God of battles, God of vengeance, guide to-day the patriot's brand !
There are stains to wash away, there are memories to destroy
In the best blood of the Briton to-day at Fontenoy !

Plunge deep the fiery rowels in a thousand reeking flanks ;
Down, chivalry of Ireland, down on the British ranks !
Now shall their serried columns beneath our sabres reel ;
Thro' their ranks, then, with the war-horse ! thro' their bosoms with
    the steel !

With one shout for good King Louis and the fair land of the vine,
Like the wrathful Alpine tempest we swept upon their line :
Then rang along the battle-field triumphant our hurrah,
And we smote them down, still cheering "*Erin slanthagal go
    bragh !*"

As prized as is the blessing from an aged father's lip,
As welcome as the haven to the tempest-driven ship,
As dear as to the lover the smile of gentle maid,
Is this day of long-sought vengeance to the swords of the brigade.

See their shattered forces flying, a broken, routed line—
See, England, what brave laurels for your brow to-day we twine.
Oh, thrice blessed the hour that witnessed the Briton turn to flee
From the chivalry of Erin and France's *fleur de lis !*

As we lay beside our camp-fires when the sun had passed away,
And thought upon our brethren who had perished in the fray,
We prayed to God to grant us (and then we'd die with joy)
One day upon our own dear land like this of Fontenoy !

BARTHOLOMEW DOWLING.

115.—ETHAN ALLEN'S ACCOUNT OF THE CAPTURE OF TICONDEROGA.

ETHAN ALLEN.

WHILE I was waiting an opportunity to signalize myself, directions were privately sent to me from Connecticut to raise the Green Mountain boys, and if possible with them to surprise and take the fortress of Ticonderoga. This enterprise I cheerfully undertook. I made a forced march from Bennington, and arrived at the lake opposite to Ticonderoga on the evening of the ninth day of May, 1775, with two hundred and thirty valiant Green Mountain boys. It was with the utmost difficulty I procured boats to cross the lake. However, I landed eighty-three men near the garrison, and sent the boats back for the rear-guard, commanded by Colonel Seth Warner, but the day began to dawn, and I found myself under the necessity of attacking the fort before the rear could cross the lake; and as this was viewed as a hazardous business, I harangued the officers and soldiers in the manner following :

"Friends and fellow-soldiers : You have for a number of years past been a scourge and terror to arbitrary power. Your valor has been famed abroad, and it has been acknowledged at home, as appears by the advice and orders to me from the General Assembly of Connecticut to surprise and take this garrison. I now propose to advance before you, and in person to conduct you through the wicket-gate ; for we must this morning either quit our pretensions to valor or possess ourselves of this fortress in a few minutes. And

20

inasmuch as it is a desperate attempt, which none but the bravest of men dare undertake, I do not urge it on any contrary to his will. You that will undertake it voluntarily, poise your firelocks."

The men being at this time drawn up in three ranks, each poised his firelock. I ordered them to face to the right, and at the head of the centre file marched them immediately to the wicket-gate aforesaid, where I found a sentry posted who instantly snapped his fusee at me. I ran immediately toward him, and he retreated through the covered way into the parade within the garrison, gave a halloo and ran under a bomb-proof. My party, who followed me into the fort, I formed on the parade in such a manner as to face the two barracks, which faced each other.

The garrison being asleep, except the sentries, we gave three huzzas, which greatly surprised them. One of the sentries made a pass at one of my officers with a charged bayonet, and slightly wounded him. My first thought was to kill the sentry with my sword, but in an instant I altered the design and fury of the blow to a slight cut on the side of the head, upon which he dropped his gun and asked quarter, which I readily granted him, and demanded of him the place where the commanding officer slept. He showed me a pair of stairs in the front of a barrack, on the west part of the garrison, which led up to a second story in said barrack, to which I immediately repaired and ordered the commander, Captain de la Place, to come forth instantly or I would sacrifice the whole garrison, at which the captain came immediately to the door with his breeches in his hand, when I ordered him to deliver me the fort instantly. He asked me by what authority I demanded it. I answered him, " *In the name of the Great Jehovah and the Continental Congress.*"

The authority of the Congress being very little known at that time, he began to speak again. But I interrupted him, and with my drawn sword over his head once more demanded an immediate surrender of the garrison, with which he then complied.

ETHAN ALLEN, 1737–1789.

116.—HENRY V. TO HIS TROOPS.

ONCE more unto the breach, dear friends, once more,
Or close the wall up with our English dead !
In peace there's nothing so becomes a man
As modest stillness and humility ;
But when the blast of war blows in our ears,
Then imitate the action of the tiger !
Stiffen the sinews, summon up the blood,
Disguise fair nature with hard-favored rage ;
Then lend the eye a terrible aspect ;
Let it pry through the portage of the head
Like the brass cannon ;
Now set the teeth, and stretch the nostril wide ;
Hold hard the breath, and bend up every spirit
To his full height ! On, on, you noblest English,
Whose blood is fetched from fathers of war proof !—
Fathers that, like so many Alexanders,
Have in these parts from morn till even fought,
And sheathed their swords for lack of argument.
I see you stand like greyhounds in the slips,
Straining upon the start. The game's afoot ;
Follow your spirit ; and, upon this charge,
Cry, God for Harry, England, and St. George !

SHAKSPEARE.

117.—MOSES AT THE FAIR.

Jenkinson, having thrown aside his disguise as a quack doctor, enters
with a box under his arm, encounters Moses and sets down his box.

Jenkinson. A wonderful man ! A wonderful man !

Moses. Ah, a patient of that impudent quack doctor.

Jen. Quack doctor, sir ? Would there were more such !
One draught of his aqua soliginus has cured me of a sweating
sickness that was on me now these six years, and carried a
large imposthume off my throat that scarce let me eat, drink
or sleep except in an upright posture, and now it has gone as

clean, saving your presence, as [*picks his pocket*] that, sir. Oh, a wonderful man! I came here at full length in a cart, but I shall ride back as upright as a gate-post if I can but come by a horse.

Moses [*aside*]. A customer for the colt; he seems a simple fellow. I have a horse to sell, sir.

Jen. Oh! I warrant me you are one of those cozening horse-jockeys that take in poor honest folk. I know no more of horses than you do of Greek.

Moses. Nay. [*Aside.*] But I must appear simple. I assure you, sir, that you need not fear being cozened by me. I have a good stout colt for sale that has been worked in the plow these two years; you can but step aside and look at him.

Jen. Well, as for that, I don't care if I do; but, bless me! I was forgetting my wares.   [*Takes up his box.*

Moses. What have you there?

Jen. [*mysteriously*]. Ah! that's a secret. They're my wares. There's a good twelve pounds' worth under the lid of that box. But you'll not talk about it, or I might be robbed; the fair's full of rogues. Perhaps you're one of 'em; you look mighty sharp!

Moses. Nay, my good man, I am as honest as thyself. [*Aside.*] Though perhaps not such a simpleton!

Jen. Well, I don't care if I do look at thy horse. [*Aside.*] And you may say good-bye to him. But you're sure he's quiet to ride and drive?

Moses. I've driven him myself, and I am not one that driveth furiously, and you may believe he's quiet to ride when I tell you he's carried my mother, an old lady, and never thrown her. [*Aside.*] It's true she tumbled off once, but that was her fault, and not the colt's.

Jen. Then I don't care if I say a bargain. How much is it to be? I don't like paying more than ten guineas.

Moses [*aside*]. He's not worth half the money! You shall name your own price. [*Aside.*] And then nobody can say I cheated him.

Jen. What say you to nine guineas, and the odd half guinea for saddle and bridle?

Moses. Nay, I would not drive a hard bargain; I'm content.

Jen. Stop a bit, and I'll show the money. [*Pretends to search his pockets.*] Eh? Oh, nay, 'tis t'other pocket; no! Oh, I'm a ruined man! I be robbed—thieves! I be robbed!

Moses. Robbed? This comes of carrying money. "Cantabit vacuus coram latro'ne viator," as Juvenal says. But I will lend thee enough to take thee home again. [*Going to put his hand in his pocket.*

Jen. [*prevents him*]. Nay, good young man, I have friends enow in this place who will do that for me. It is the loss of the horse that vexes me. Hold! perhaps, though I can no longer buy, you may be willing to make a barter?

Moses. Why, the practice of barter was much used among the ancients; and, indeed, the Lacedemonians had no coined money until after the time of Lycurgus, as you are aware.

Jen. No, I can't say I know the family. But will you exchange your horse against my wares? There's a good twelve pounds' worth of 'em.

Moses. What are they? Depro'me—that is, bring them forth.

Jen. [*opens his box*]. A gross of green spectacles, fine pebbles and silver rims.   [*Taking a pair out of case.*

Moses. A gross of green spectacles.   [*Taking a pair.*

Jen. A dozen dozen.

Moses. Let's see. [*Aside, calculates.*] Twelve times twelve is—and twenty one's into—go—yes, a capital bargain! I accept; you take the colt and I'll take the spectacles. [*Offering to take the box.*

Jen. Nay, nay! I'll give you the box when you've given me the colt; so come!

Moses. A gross of green spectacles! Huzza! [*Aside.*] I'll retail them for twice the money. "Nocte pluit tota redeunt spectacula ma'ne"—"There come back spectacles many."

20 *

Ha, ha! the silly fellow! Well, it's not my fault; he will cheat himself—ha, ha! Oh, Moses is a simpleton, is he? Moses can't make a bargain, can't he?   [*Exit.*

Jen. Of all the green spectacles I ever sold, I must say you're the greenest.   J. S. COYNE.

118.—MARY QUEEN OF SCOTS.

IT was a laboring bark that slowly held its way,
And o'er its lee the coast of France in the light of evening lay;
And on the deck a lady sat who looked with tearful gaze
Upon the fast-receding hills within the distant haze.
The past was fair, like those dear hills so far behind her bark;
The future, like the gathering night, was ominous and dark.
One gaze again, one long, last gaze: "Adieu, dear France, to thee!"
The breeze comes forth—she's there alone upon the wide, wide sea

The scene was changed. It was an eve of raw and surly mood,
And in a turret-chamber high of ancient Holyrood
Sat Mary, listening to the rain and sighing with the winds,
That seemed to suit the stormy state of men's uncertain minds.
The touch of care had blanched her cheeks, her smile was sadder now,
The weight of royalty had lain too heavy on her brow;

And traitors to her councils came, and rebels to the field;
The Stuart *sceptre* well she swayed, but the *sword* she could not wield.
She thought of all her blighted hopes, the dreams of youth's brief day,
And summoned Rizzio with his lute, and bade the minstrel play
The songs she loved in early years, the songs of gay Navarre,
The songs perchance that erst were sung by gallant Chatelar:
They half beguiled her of her cares, they soothed her into smiles,
They won her thoughts from bigot zeal and fierce domestic broils.

But hark, the tramp of armëd men! the Douglas' battle-cry!
They come, they come! and, lo! the scowl of Ruthven's hollow eye!
Around an unarmed man they crowd—Ruthven in mail complete,
George Douglas, Ker of Fawdonside, and Rizzio at their feet!
With rapiers drawn and pistols bent they seized their wretched prey,
Wrenched Mary's garments from his grasp, and stabbed him where
    he lay.
I saw George Douglas raise his arm, I saw his dagger gleam;
Then sounded Rizzio's dying cry and Mary's piteous scream.
I saw her writhe in Darnley's arms as in a serpent's fold:
The coward! he was pale as death, but would not loose his hold.
And then the torches waved and shook, and louder grew the din,
And up the stairs and thro' the doors the rest came trooping in.
But Mary Stuart brushed aside the burning tears that fell:
"Now for my father's arm!" she gasped; "my woman's heart, fare-
    well!"

The scene was changed. It was a lake with one small lonely isle,
And there, within the prison walls of its baronial pile,
Stern men stood menacing their queen till she should stoop to sign
The traitorous scroll that snatched the crown from her ancestral line.
"My lords, my lords," the captive said, "were I but once more free,
With ten good knights on yonder shore to aid my cause and me,
That parchment would I rend and give to any wind that blows,
And reign a queen, a Stuart yet, in spite of all my foes!"
A red spot burned upon her cheek—streamed her rich tresses down,
She wrote the words; she stood erect—a queen without a crown!

The scene was changed. A royal host a royal banner bore,
And the faithful of the land stood round their smiling queen once
    more;
She checked her steed upon a hill, she saw them marching by,
She heard their shouts, she read success in every flashing eye.

The tumult of the strife begins; it roars, it dies away,
And Mary's troops and banners now—oh, where and what are they?
Scattered, struck down or flying far, defenseless and undone—
Ah, me! to see what she has lost, to think what guilt has won!
Away, away! her gallant steed must act no laggard's part;
Yet vain his speed to bear her from the anguish at her heart.

Last scene of all.   Beside the block a sullen headsman stood,
Gleamed in his hand the murderous axe that soon must drip with
        blood.
With slow and stately step there came a lady thro' the hall,
And breathless silence chained the lips and touched the hearts of all:
Rich were the sable robes she wore; her white veil round her fell,
And from her neck there hung a cross—the cross she loved so well!
I knew that queenly form again, though blighted was its bloom—
Though grief and care had decked it out, an offering for the tomb.
I knew the eye, tho' faint its light, that once so brightly shone;
I knew the voice, still musical, that thrilled with every tone;
I knew the ringlets, almost gray, once threads of living gold;
I knew that bounding step of grace, that symmetry of mold.
And memory sought her far away in that calm convent aisle,
Could hear her chant her vesper-hymn, could mark her holy smile;
Could see her as in youth she looked upon her bridal morn,
A new star in the firmament to light and glory born!
Alas, the change! her daring foot had touched a triple throne—
Now see her on the scaffold stand, beside the block, *alone!*
A little dog that licks her hand the last of all the crowd
Who sunned themselves beneath her glance or round her footsteps
        bowed!
Her neck is bare—the axe descends—the soul has passed away!
The bright, the beautiful, is now a bleeding piece of clay.

LOCHLEVEN CASTLE, WHERE MARY WAS IMPRISONED.

119.—IMPRISONMENT OF BONNIVARD.

FAILING in his enterprise for the liberation of Geneva, Bonnivard was transported to the castle of Chillon, where a dreadful captivity awaited him. Bound by the middle of his body to a chain the other end of which was attached to an iron ring in a pillar, he remained in this condition six years, free to move the length only of his chain, and able to recline only where it allowed him to extend himself.

CHILLON.

The pavement was hollowed by his measured tread; but the thought that his captivity would perhaps avail nothing for the enfranchisement of his country, and that Geneva and he were doomed to perpetual fetters, must have been more wearing to his mind than his steps to the stone.

> "Chillon! thy prison is a holy place,
>   And thy sad floor an altar; for 'twas trod
> Until his very steps have left a trace,
>   Worn, as if thy cold pavement were a sod,
> By Bonnivard! May none those marks efface!
>   For they appeal from tyranny to God."

How happened it in this long night, which no day broke in upon and where the silence was disturbed by no sound save that of the waves of the lake dashing against the walls of his dungeon—how happened it that the mind did not overpower the body, or the body the mind? Why was it that the jailer, on going his rounds some morning, did not find his prisoner either dead or mad? One besetting, one eternal idea—was it not enough to break the heart or paralyze the brain?

And during this time—during these six years, during this eternity—not a cry, not a murmur, as his jailers testified, escaped from the prisoner; although, without doubt, when the tempest was unloosed—when the gale tore up the waves, when the rain and the blast lashed the walls—he too had his utterance, for then his voice might be lost in the great voice of nature, for then God only could distinguish his cries and sobs; and the next day his jailers, who had not feasted on his despair, would find him calm and resigned, the tempest in his heart subdued and hushed, like that in the sky.

Ah! without that—without that—would he not have dashed his brains out against the pillar to which he was chained? Could he have awaited that day when his countrymen simultaneously burst into his prison to rescue and to honor him? A hundred voices then exclaimed, "Bonnivard, thou art free!" "And Geneva?" "Is also free!"

ALEXANDRE DUMAS.

120.—DEMOCRACY ADVERSE TO SOCIALISM.

DEMOCRACY, socialism? Why profess to associate what, in the nature of things, can never be united? Can it be, gentlemen, that this whole grand movement of the French Revolution is destined to terminate in that form of society which the socialists have with so much fervor depicted?—a society marked out with compass and rule, in which the state is to charge itself with everything, and the individual is to be nothing; in which society is to absorb all force, all life, and in which the only end assigned to man is his personal comfort? What! was it for such a society of beavers and of bees—a society rather of skillful animals than of men free and civilized—was it for such that the French Revolution was accomplished? Not so! It was for a greater, a more sacred end—one more worthy of humanity.

But socialism professes to be the legitimate development of

democracy. I shall not search, as many have done, into the true etymology of this word *democracy*. I shall not, as gentlemen did yesterday, traverse the garden of Greek roots to find the derivation of this word. I shall point you to democracy where I have seen it, living, active, triumphant; in the only country in the world where it truly exists, where it has been able to establish and maintain even to the present time something grand and durable to claim our admiration—in the New World, in America.

There shall you see a people among whom all conditions of men are more on an equality even than among us; where the social state, the manners, the laws, everything, is democratic; where all emanates from the people, and returns to the people; and where, at the same time, every individual enjoys a greater amount of liberty, a more entire independence, than in any other part of the world, at any period of time—a country, I repeat it, essentially democratic, the only democracy in the wide world at this day, and the only republic *truly* democratic which we know of in history. And in this republic you will look in vain for socialism. Not only have the theories of the socialists gained no possession there of the public mind, but they have played so trifling a part in the discussions and affairs of that great nation that they have not even reached the dignity of being feared.

America is at this day that country of the whole world where the sovereignty of democracy is most practical and complete, and it is at the same time that where the doctrines of the socialists, which you pretend to find so much in accordance with democracy, are the least in vogue—the country of the whole universe where the men sustaining those doctrines would have the least chance of making an impression. For myself, personally, I do not see, I confess, any objection to the emigration of these proselyting gentlemen to America, but I warn them that they will not find there any field for their labors.

No, gentlemen, democracy and socialism are the antip'o-des of each other. While democracy extends the sphere of individual independence, socialism contracts it. Democracy develops a man's whole manhood, socialism makes him an agent, an instrument, a cipher. Democracy and socialism assimilate on one point only—the equality which they introduce; but mark the difference: democracy seeks equality in liberty, while socialism seeks it in servitude and constraint.

ALEXIS DE TOCQUEVILLE.

121.—THE PLATFORM OF THE CONSTITUTION, 1838.

A PRINCIPAL object in his late political movements, the gentleman himself tells us, was to unite the entire South. And against whom or against what does he wish to unite the

entire South? Is not this the very essence of local feeling and local regard? Is it not the acknowledgment of a wish and object to create political strength by uniting political opinions geographically? While the gentleman wishes to unite the entire South, I pray to know, sir, if he expects me to turn toward the polar star, and acting on the same principle, to utter a cry of Rally! to the whole North?

DANIEL WEBSTER.

Heaven forbid! To the day of my death neither he nor others shall hear such a cry from me.

Finally, the honorable member declares that he shall now march off under the banner of State rights. March off from whom? March off from what? We have been contending for great principles. We have been struggling to maintain the liberty and to restore the prosperity of the country; we have made these struggles here in the national councils with the old flag—the true American flag, the eagle and the stars and stripes—waving over the chamber in which we sit. He now tells us, however, that he marches off under the State rights banner!

Let him go. I remain. I am where I ever have been and ever mean to be. Here, standing on the platform of the general constitution—a platform broad enough and firm enough to uphold every interest of the whole country—I shall still be found. Intrusted with some part in the administration of that constitution, I intend to act in its spirit and in the spirit of those who framed it. Yes, sir. I would act as if our fathers who formed it for us and who bequeathed it to us were looking on me—as if I could see their venerable forms bending down to behold us from the abodes above! I would act, too, as if the eye of posterity was gazing on me.

Standing thus as in the full gaze of our ancestors and our posterity, having received this inheritance from the former to be transmitted to the latter, and feeling that if I am born for any good in my day and generation it is for the good of the country, no local policy, no local feeling, no temporary impulse, shall induce me to yield my foothold on the constitution and the Union. I move off under no banner not known to the whole American people and to their constitution and laws. No, sir! these walls, these columns, "fly from their firm base as soon as I."

I came into public life, sir, in the service of the United States. On that broad altar my earliest and all my public vows have been made. I propose to serve no other master. So far as depends on any agency of mine, they shall continue *united* States—united in interest and affection, united in everything in regard to which the constitution has decreed their union, united in war for the common defense, the common renown and the common glory, and united, compacted, knit firmly together in peace for the common prosperity and happiness of ourselves and our children!

DANIEL WEBSTER, 1782–1852.

———◦◦◦———

122.—KENELM CHILLINGLY.

Kenelm. What is there in my conduct, sir, that occasions you displeasure?

Sir Peter. Not displeasure, Kenelm, but anxiety. You see, my dear son, that it is my wish you should distinguish yourself in the world. Oratory is the talent most appreciated in a free country, and why should you not be an orator? Demosthenes says that delivery, delivery, delivery, is the art of oratory; and your delivery is excellent, graceful, self-possessed, classical.

Kenelm. Pardon me, my dear father, Demosthenes does not say delivery, nor action, as the word is commonly rendered; he says "acting or stage-playing"—*hupokrisis,* the art by which a man delivers a speech in a feigned character, whence we get the word *hypocrisy.* Hypocrisy, hypocrisy, hypocrisy, is, according to Demosthenes, the triple art of the orator. Do you wish me to become triply a hypocrite?

Sir Peter. Kenelm, I am ashamed of you. You know as well as I do that it is only by metaphor that you can twist the word ascribed to the great Athenian into the sense of *hypocrisy.* But assuming it, as you say, to mean not *delivery,* but *acting,* I understand why your *debut* as orator was not successful. Your delivery was excellent, your acting defective. An orator should please, conciliate, persuade, prepossess. You did the reverse of all this; and though you produced a great effect, the effect was so decidedly to your disadvantage that it would have lost you an election on any hustings in England.

Kenelm. Am I to understand, my dear father, that you would commend to your son the adoption of deliberate falsehood for the gain of a selfish advantage?

Sir Peter. Deliberate falsehood? You impertinent puppy!

Kenelm. Puppy! puppy! Father of mine, does not a well-bred puppy always take after its parents?

Sir Peter. Well, well, you dog, never lose your temper. Look you, Kenelm, these quips and humors of yours are amusing enough to an eccentric man like myself, but they will not do for the world. And how, at your age, and with the advantages you have had, you could have made so silly a speech as you did yesterday, I do not understand.

Kenelm. My dear father, the ideas I expressed are the new ideas most in vogue.

Sir Peter. Boy, boy, such ideas would turn the world topsy-turvy.

Kenelm. New ideas always do tend to turn old ideas topsy-turvy. And the world, after all, is only an idea which is turned topsy-turvy with every successive century.

Sir Peter. You make me sick of the word *ideas.* Leave off your metaphysics, and study real life.

Kenelm. It is real life which I have been studying. It is sham life which you wish me to study. To oblige you, I am willing to commence it. I dare say it is very pleasant. *Real* life is not; on the contrary, it is dull.

Sir Peter. Have you no young friends among your fellow-collegians?

Kenelm. Friends! certainly not, sir; but I believe I have some enemies, who answer the same purpose as friends, only they don't embarrass one so much—are not so mischievous.

Sir Peter. Do you mean to say that you lived alone at Cambridge?

Kenelm. No; I lived a good deal with Aristoph'anes, and a little with Conic Sections and Hydrostatics.

Sir Peter. Books? *Dry* company!

Kenelm. More innocent, at least, than *moist* company. Did you ever get drunk, sir?

Sir Peter. Drunk?

Kenelm. I tried to do so once with the young companions whom you would commend to me as friends. I don't think I succeeded, but I woke with a headache. Real life at college abounds with headache.

Sir Peter. Kenelm, my boy, one thing is clear—you must travel.

Kenelm. As you please, sir. Marcus Antoni'nus says that it is all one to a stone whether it is thrown upward or downward. When shall I start?

Sir Peter. Very soon. Among your other studies, may I inquire if you have included that which no man has ever yet thoroughly mastered—the study of woman?

Kenelm. Every one who receives a classical education is introduced into female society. We have to encounter Pyrrha, Lydia, Corinna, and many more, all of the same sort.

Sir Peter. Then it is only females who lived two thousand or three thousand years ago, or more probably never lived at all, whose intimacy you have cultivated? Have you never admired any *real* women?

Kenelm. Real women! I never met one. Never met a woman who was not a sham—a sham from the moment she is told to be pretty-behaved, conceal her sentiments and look fibs when she does not speak them. But if I am to learn sham life, I suppose I must put up with sham women.

Sir Peter. Have you been crossed in love, that you speak so bitterly of the sex?

Kenelm. I don't speak bitterly of the sex. Examine any woman on her oath, and she'll own she's a sham, always has been, and always will be, and is proud of it.

Sir Peter. I am glad your mother is not by to hear you. You will think differently one of these days. Meanwhile, to turn to the other sex, is there no young man of your own rank with whom you would like to travel?

Kenelm. Certainly not. I hate quarreling.

Sir Peter. As you please. But you cannot go quite alone; I will find you a good traveling servant. Your allowance will be whatever you like to fix it at; you have never been extravagant, and, boy, I love you. Amuse yourself, enjoy yourself, and come back cured of your oddities, but preserving your honor.

Kenelm. If ever I am tempted to do a base thing, may I remember whose son I am! I shall then be safe.

Dramatized from LORD LYTTON (BULWER).

123.—BATTLE HYMN, AND FAREWELL TO LIFE.

Theodore Körner, the martial poet of Germany, born in the year 1791
fell in battle August 25, 1813, when scarcely twenty-two years old.

FATHER of earth and heaven, I call thy name!
 Round me the smoke and shout of battle roll;
My eyes are dazzled with the rustling flame—
 Father, sustain an untried soldier's soul.
 Or life, or death, whatever be the goal
That crowns or closes round the struggling hour,—
 Thou knowest if ever from my spirit stole
One deeper prayer, 'twas that no cloud might lower
On my young fame! Oh hear, God of eternal power!

21 *

Now for the fight! Now for the cannon-peal!
  Forward, through blood and toil and cloud and fire!
Glorious the shout, the shock, the clash of steel,
  The volley's roll, the rocket's blasting spire!
  They shake! like broken waves their squares retire!
On them, hussars! Now give them rein and heel;
  Think of the orphaned child, the murdered sire:
Earth cries for blood! In thunder on them wheel!
This hour to Europe's fate shall set the triumph-seal!

My deep wound burns; my pale lips quake in death;
  I feel my fainting heart resign its strife;
  And reaching now the limit of my life,
Lord, to thy will I yield my parting breath!
Yet many a dream hath charmed my youthful eye,
  And must life's fairy visions all depart?
  Oh, surely, no! for all that fired my heart
To rapture here shall live with me on high.
And that fair form that won my earliest vow,
  That my young spirit prized all else above,
  And now adored as freedom, now as love,
Stands in seraphic guise before me now!
  And as my failing senses fade away,
  It beckons me on high, to realms of endless day!

THEODORE KÖRNER.

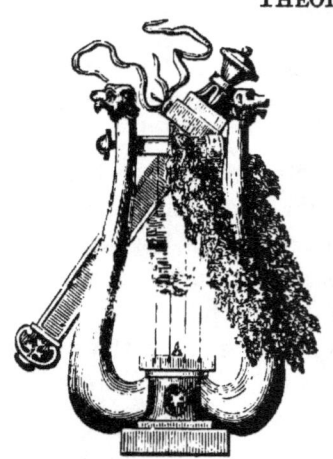

124.—IN FAVOR OF AMERICAN INDEPENDENCE.

Delivered in Philadelphia, August 1, 1776, twenty-seven days after the Declaration of Independence.

My countrymen, from the day on which an accommodation takes place between England and America on any other terms than as independent States I shall date the ruin of this country. We are now, to the astonishment of the world, three millions of souls united in one common cause. This day we are called on to give a glorious example of what the wisest and best of men were rejoiced to view only in speculation. This day presents the world with the most august spectacle that its annals ever unfolded—millions of freemen voluntarily and deliberately forming themselves into a society for their common defense and common happiness. Immortal spirits of Hampden, Locke and Sydney! will it not add to your benevolent joys to behold your posterity rising to the dignity of *men*, evincing to the world the reality and expediency of your systems, and in the actual enjoyment of that equal liberty which you were happy when on earth in delineating and recommending to mankind?

Other nations have received their laws from conquerors; some are indebted for a constitution to the sufferings of their ancestors through revolving centuries. The people of this country alone have formally and deliberately chosen a government for themselves, and with open, uninfluenced consent bound themselves into a social compact. And, fellow-countrymen, if it ever was granted to mortals to trace the designs of Providence and interpret its manifestations in favor of their cause, we may, with humility of soul, cry out, NOT UNTO US, NOT UNTO US, BUT TO THY NAME BE THE PRAISE. The confusion of the devices of our enemies and the rage of the elements against them have done almost as much toward our success as either our counsels or our arms.

The time at which this attempt on our liberties was made, when we were ripened into maturity, had acquired a knowledge of war, and were free from the incursions of intestine enemies; the *gradual* advances of our oppressors, enabling us to prepare for our defense; the unusual fertility of our lands; the clemency of the seasons; the success which at first attended our feeble arms, producing unanimity among our friends and compelling our internal foes to acquiescence,—these are all strong and palpable marks and assurances that Providence IS YET GRACIOUS UNTO ZION, THAT IT WILL TURN AWAY THE CAPTIVITY OF JACOB!

Driven from every other corner of the earth, freedom of thought and the right of private judgment in matters of conscience direct their course to this happy country as their last asylum. Let us cherish the noble guests! Let us shelter them under the wings of universal toleration! Be this the seat of UNBOUNDED RELIGIOUS FREEDOM! She will bring with her in her train Industry, Wisdom and Commerce. Our union is now complete. You have in the field armies sufficient to repel the whole force of your enemies. The hearts of your soldiers beat high with the spirit of freedom. Go on, then, in your generous enterprise, with gratitude to Heaven for past success and confidence of it in the future! For my own part, I ask no greater blessing than to share with you the common danger and the common glory. If I have a wish dearer to my soul than that my ashes may be mingled with those of a Warren and a Montgomery, it is THAT THESE AMERICAN STATES MAY NEVER CEASE TO BE FREE AND INDEPENDENT!

SAMUEL ADAMS, 1722–1803.

125.—REFORM IRRESISTIBLE.

SIR, I have from the beginning of these discussions supported reform on two grounds: first, because I believe it to be in itself a good thing; and secondly, because I think the dangers of withholding it to be so great that even if it were an evil it would be the less of two evils. We have heard it said a hundred times during these discussions that the people are more free than ever they were, that the government is more democratic than ever it was; and this is urged as an argument against reform. I admit the fact, but I deny the inference. The history of England is the history of a government constantly giving way—sometimes peaceably, sometimes after a violent struggle, but constantly giving way—before a nation which has been constantly advancing. It is not sufficient to look merely at the form of government. We must look to the state of the public mind.

The worst tyrant that ever had his neck wrung in modern Europe might have passed for a paragon in Persia or Morocco. Our Indian subjects submit patiently to a monopoly of salt. We tried a stamp-duty—a duty so light as to be hardly perceptible—on the fierce breed of the old Puritans, and we lost an empire. The government of Louis XVI. was certainly a much better and milder government than that of Louis XIV., yet Louis XIV. was admired, and even loved, by his people; Louis XVI. died on the scaffold. Why? Because, though the government had made many steps in the career of improvement, it had not advanced so rapidly as the nation.

These things are written for our instruction. There is a change in society. There must be a corresponding change in the government. You may make the change tedious; you may make it violent; you may—God in his mercy forbid!—you may make it bloody; but avert it you cannot. Of this I am assured, that, by means lawful or unlawful, to a termination happy or unhappy, this contest must speedily come. Agitations of the public mind so deep and so long continued as those which we have witnessed do not end in nothing. In peace or in convulsion, by the law or in spite of the law, through the Parliament or over the Parliament, reform must be carried. Therefore be content to guide that movement which you cannot stop; fling wide the gates to that force which else will enter through the breach.

MACAULAY (see p. 59).

126.—ON MECHANICS' INSTITUTES.

Delivered at Manchester, England, 1843.

I DON'T know whether, at this time of day, we need tc trouble ourselves very much to rake up the ashes of the dead-and-gone objections that were wont to be urged by all men of all parties against institutions such as this whose interests we are met to promote, but their philosophy was always to be summed up in the unmeaning application of one short sentence. How often have we heard from a large class of men, wise in their generation, who would really seem to be born and bred for no other purpose than to pass into currency counterfeit and mischievous scraps of wisdom, as it is the sole pursuit of some other crim-

CHARLES DICKENS.

inals to utter base coin,—how often have we heard from them, as an all-convincing argument, that "*A little learning is a dangerous thing*"!

Why, a little hanging was considered a very dangerous thing, according to the same authorities, with this difference —that because a little hanging was dangerous we had a great deal of it, and because a little learning was dangerous we were to have none at all. Why, when I hear such cruel absurdities gravely reiterated, I do sometimes begin to doubt whether the parrots of society are not more pernicious to its interests than its birds of prey. I should be glad to hear such people's estimate of the comparative danger of a "little learning" and a vast amount of ignorance; I should be glad to know which they consider the most prolific parent of misery and crime.

Descending a little lower in the social scale, I should be glad to assist them in their calculations by carrying them into certain jails and nightly refuges I know of, where my own heart dies within me when I see thousands of immortal creatures condemned, without alternative or choice, to tread, not what our great poet calls "the primrose path" to the everlasting bonfire, but one of jagged flints and stones, laid down by brutal ignorance, and held together like the solid rocks by years of this most wicked axiom.

The old doggerel rhyme so often written in the beginning of books says that

> "When house and lands are gone and spent,
> Then learning is most excellent,"

but I should be strongly disposed to reform the adage, and say that

> "Though house and land be never got,
> Learning can give what they can *not.*"

And this I know—that the first purchasable blessing earned by every man who makes an effort to improve himself in such a place as the Athenæum is self-respect—an inward dignity of character which, once acquired and righteously maintained, nothing, no, not the hardest drudgery nor the direst poverty, can vanquish.

Though he should find it hard for a season even to keep the wolf hunger from his door, let him but once have chased the dragon ignorance from his hearth, and self-respect and hope are left him. You could no more deprive him of these sustaining qualities by loss or destruction of his worldly goods than you could by plucking out his eyes take from him an internal consciousness of the bright glory of the sun.

The man who lives from day to day by the daily exercise in his sphere of hands or head, and seeks to improve himself in such a place as the Athenæum, acquires for himself that property of soul which has in all times upheld struggling men of every degree, but self-made men especially and always. He secures to himself that faithful companion which, while it has

ever lent the light of its countenance to men of rank and emi-
nence who have deserved it, has ever shed its brightest consola-
tions on men of low estate and almost hopeless means. It
took its patient seat beside Sir Walter Raleigh in his dungeon
study in the Tower, it laid its head upon the block with More,
but it did not disdain to watch the stars with Ferguson the
shepherd's boy; it walked the streets in mean attire with
Crabbe; it was a poor barber here in Lancashire with Ark-
wright; it was a tallow-chandler's son in Boston with Frank-
lin; it worked at shoemaking with Bloomfield in his garret;
it followed the plow with Burns; and high above the noise of
the loom and hammer it whispers courage even at this day in
ears I could name in Sheffield and in Manchester.

CHARLES DICKENS, 1812–1870.

127.—THE POWER OF SHORT WORDS.

THINK not that strength lies in the big round word,
   Or that the brief and plain must needs be weak.
To whom can this be true who once has heard
   The cry for help, the tongue that all men speak
When want, or woe, or fear is in the throat,
   So that each word gasped out is like a shriek
Pressed from the sore heart, or a strange wild note
   Sung by some fay or fiend? There is a strength
Which dies if stretched too far or spun too fine,
   Which has more height than breadth, more depth than
      length.
Let but this force of thought and speech be mine,
   And he that will may take the sleek fat phrase
Which glows and burns not, though it gleam and shine—
   Light but not heat—a flash but not a blaze!

Nor mere strength is it that the short word boasts:
   It serves of more than fight or storm to tell—
The roar of waves that clash on rock-bound coasts,
   The crash of tall trees when the wild winds swell,

The roar of guns, the groans of men that die
  On blood-stained fields.   It has a voice as well
For them that far off on their sick-beds lie;
  For them that weep, for them that mourn the dead;
For them that laugh, and dance, and clap the hand;
  To Joy's quick step, as well as Grief's slow tread,
The sweet, plain words we learnt at first keep time;
  And though the theme be sad, or gay, or grand,
With each, with all, these may be made to chime,
In thought, or speech, or song, in prose or rhyme.

JOSEPH ADDISON ALEXANDER, 1809–1860.

128.—HOTSPUR READING THE LETTER.

"BUT for my own part, my lord, I could be well contented
to be there, in respect of the love I bear your house." He
could be contented! Why is he not, then? In respect of the
love he bears our house! He shows in this he loves his own
barn better than he loves our house. Let me see some more.
(*Reads.*) "The purpose you undertake is dangerous." Why,
that's certain; 'tis dangerous to take a cold, to sleep, to drink:
but I tell you, my lord fool, out of this nettle danger we
pluck the flower safety. (*Reads.*) "The purpose you under-
take is dangerous, the friends you have named uncertain, the
time itself unsorted, and your whole plot too light for the
counterpoise of so great an opposition." Say you so? say you
so? I say unto you again, You are a shallow, cowardly hind,
and you lie! What a lack-brain is this! By the Lord, our
plot is a good plot as ever was laid, our friends true and con-
stant; a good plot, good friends, and full of expectation—an
excellent plot, very good friends. What a frosty-spirited rogue
is this! Why, my lord of York commends the plot and the
general course of the action. 'Zounds! an I were now by this
rascal, I could brain him with his lady's fan. Is there not my
father, my uncle and myself? lord Edmund Mortimer, my
lord of York and Owen Glendower? Is there not, besides, the
Douglas? Have I not all their letters, to meet me in arms

22

by the ninth of the next month, and are they not, some of them, set forward already? What a pagan rascal is this—an infidel! Ha! you shall see now in very sincerity of fear and cold heart will he to the king and lay open all our proceedings. Oh, I could divide myself and go to buffets for moving such a dish of skimmed milk with so honorable an action! Hang him! let him tell the king—we are prepared; I will set forward to-night.*   SHAKSPEARE.

129.—LOCHINVAR.

SCOTT.

OH, young Lochinvar is
    come out of the west;
Through all the wide bor-
    der his steed was the best;
And save his good broad-
    sword, he weapon had
    none;
He rode all unarmed, and
    he rode all alone.
So faithful in love and so
    dauntless in war,
There never was knight like
    the young Lochinvar.

He stayed not for brake and
    he stopped not for stone;
He swam the Eske River where ford there was none;
But ere he alighted at Netherby gate,
The bride had consented, the gallant came late;
For a laggard in love and a dastard in war
Was to wed the fair Ellen of brave Lochinvar.

So boldly he entered the Netherby hall,
Among bridesmen and kinsmen, and brothers and all.

* Hotspur is a choleric, easily roused character, blunt, impulsive, courageous. The passages in quotation-marks are supposed to be parts of the letter he is reading.

Then spoke the bride's father, his hand on his sword—
For the poor craven bridegroom said never a word—
" Oh, come ye in peace here, or come ye in war,
    Or to dance at our bridal, young Lord Lochinvar?"

"'I long wooed your daughter—my suit you denied:
Love swells like the Solway, but ebbs like its tide—
And now am I come with this lost love of mine
To lead but one measure, drink one cup of wine.
There are maidens in Scotland more lovely by far,
That would gladly be bride to the young Lochinvar!"

The bride kissed the goblet, the knight took it up;
He quaffed off the wine and he threw down the cup.
She looked down to blush, and she looked up to sigh,
With a smile on her lips, and a tear in her eye.
He took her soft hand ere her mother could bar;
" Now tread we a measure!" said young Lochinvar.

So stately his form, and so lovely her face,
That never a hall such a galliard did grace;
While her mother did fret and her father did fume,
And the bridegroom stood dangling his bonnet and plume,
And the bride-maidens whispered, " 'Twere better, by far,
To have matched our fair cousin with young Lochinvar!"

One touch to her hand and one word in her ear,
When they reached the hall door, and the charger stood near;
So light to the croup the fair lady he swung,
So light to the saddle before her he sprung.
" She is won! we are gone! over bank, bush and scaur;
They'll have fleet steeds that follow!" quoth young Lochinvar

There was mounting 'mong Græmes of the Netherby clan;
Forsters, Fenwicks and Musgraves, they rode and they ran;
There was racing and chasing on Cannobie Lee,
But the lost bride of Netherby ne'er did they see!
So daring in love and so dauntless in war,
Have ye e'er heard of gallant like young Lochinvar!

                    SIR WALTER SCOTT, 1771–1832.

130.—LOVEJOY'S LAST SPEECH.

MEN of Alton, you come together for the purpose of driving out a confessedly innocent man for no cause but that he dares to think and speak as his conscience and his God dictate. Will conduct like this stand the scrutiny of your country, of posterity—above all, of the judgment-day? For remember the Judge of that day is no respecter of persons. Pause, I beseech you, and reflect. The present excitement will soon be over, the voice of conscience will at last be heard, and in some season of honest thought, even in this world, as you review the scenes of this hour you will be compelled to say, "He was right, he was right."

But you have been exhorted to be lenient and compassionate, and in driving me away to affix no unnecessary disgrace upon me. Sir, I reject all such compassion! Disgrace me? You cannot disgrace me. Scandal and calumny and falsehood have already done their worst. My shoulders have borne the burden till it sits easy upon them. You may hang me up as the mob hung up the martyrs of Vicksburg, you may burn me at the stake as they did McIntosh at St. Louis, or you may tar and feather me or throw me into the Mississippi, as you have often threatened to do; but you cannot disgrace me. I, and I only, can disgrace myself, and the deepest of all disgraces would be at a time like this to deny my Master by forsaking his cause.

Again, you have been told that I have a family who are dependent on me, and this has been given as a reason why I should be driven off as gently as possible. It is true, Mr. Chairman, I am a husband and a father, and this it is that adds the bitterest ingredient to the cup of sorrow I am called to drink. Yet I am not unhappy. I have counted the cost, and stand prepared freely to offer up my all in the service of God. I am commanded to forsake father and mother and wife and children for Jesus' sake; and as his professed disciple, I stand prepared to do it. The time for fulfilling this pledge in my case it seems to me has come.

Sir, I dare not flee away from Alton. Should I attempt it, I should feel that the angel of the Lord with his flaming sword was pursuing me wherever I went. It is because I fear God that I am not afraid of all who oppose me in this city. No, sir; the contest has commenced here, and here it must be finished. Before God and you all I here pledge myself to continue in it, if need be, till death. If I fall, my grave shall be made in Alton.

ELIJAH P. LOVEJOY.

131.—ST. PAUL AT ATHENS.

BEHOLD St. Paul at Athens; think of the matchless splendor which blazed upon his view as he rolled his eyes round the enchanting panorama that encircled the hill of Mars. On the one hand, as he stood upon the summit of the rock, beneath the canopy of heaven was spread a glorious prospect of mountains, islands, seas and skies; on the other, quite within his view, was the plain of Marathon, where the wrecks of former generations and the tombs of departed heroes mingled together in silent desolation. Behind him towered the lofty Acropolis, crowned with the pride of Grecian architecture.

There, in the zenith of their splendor and the perfection of

22 *

their beauty, stood those peerless temples the very fragments of which are viewed by modern travelers with an idolatry almost equal to that which reared them. Stretched along the plain below him, and reclining her head on the slope of the neighboring hills, was Athens, mother of the arts and sciences, with her noble offspring sporting by her side. The Porch, the Lyceum and the Grove, with the stations of departed sages and the forms of their living disciples, were all presented to the apostle's eye. What mind possessing the slightest pretension to classic taste can think of his situation, and such sublime and captivating scenery, without a momentary rapture? Yet there, even there, did this accomplished scholar stand as insensible to all this grandeur as if nothing was before him but the treeless, turfless desert. Absorbed in the holy abstractions of his own mind, he saw no charms, felt no fascination, but on the contrary was pierced with the most poignant distress; and what was the cause?

"He saw the city wholly given to idolatry." To him it presented nothing but a magnificent mausoleum, decorated, it is true, with the richest productions of the sculptor and the architect, but, still, where the souls of men lay dead in trespasses and sins; while the dim light of philosophy that still glimmered in the schools appeared but as the lamp of the sepulchre, shedding its pale and sickly ray around these gorgeous chambers of death.

JOHN A. JAMES.

132.—THE OLD GRENADIER'S STORY.

'TWAS the day beside the Pyramids—it seems but an hour ago—
That Kleber's Foot stood firm in squares, returning blow for blow.
The Mamelukes were tossing their standards to the sky,
When I heard a child's voice say, "My men, *teach me the way to die!*"

'Twas a little drummer with his side torn terribly with shot,
But still he feebly beat his drum, as though the wound were not.
And when the Mameluke's wild horse burst with a scream and cry,
He said, "O men of the Forty-third, *teach me the way to die!*

"My mother has got other sons with stouter hearts than mine,
But none more ready blood for France to pour out free as wine.
Yet still life's sweet," the brave lad moaned, "fair are this earth and
    sky;
Then, comrades of the Forty-third, *teach me the way to die!*"

I saw Salenche of the granite heart wiping his burning eyes—
It was by far more pitiful than mere loud sobs and cries;
One bit his cartridge till his lip grew black as winter sky,
But still the boy moaned, "Forty-third, *teach me the way to die!*"

Oh, never saw I sight like that! the sergeant flung down flag,
Even the fifer bound his brow with a wet and bloody rag,
Then looked at locks and fixed their steel, but never made reply,
Until he sobbed out once again, "*Teach me the way to die!*"

Then, with a shout that flew to God, they strode into the fray:
I saw their red plumes join and wave, but slowly melt away.
The last who went—a wounded man—bade the poor boy good-bye,
And said, "We men of the Forty-third *teach you the way to die!*"

I never saw so sad a look as the poor youngster cast,
When the hot smoke of cannon in cloud and whirlwind passed.
Earth shook, and heaven answered; I watched his eagle eye
As he faintly moaned, "The Forty-third *teach me the way to die!*"

Then, with a musket for a crutch, he leaped into the fight;
I, with a bullet in my hip, had neither strength nor might,
But proudly beating on his drum, a fever in his eye,
I heard him moan, "The Forty-third *taught me the way to die!*"

They found him on the morrow stretched on a heap of dead;
His hand was in the grenadier's who at his bidding bled;
They hung a medal round his neck and closed his dauntless eye;
On the stone they cut, "The Forty-third *taught him the way to die!*"

'Tis forty years from then till now—the grave gapes at my feet,
Yet when I think of such a boy, I feel my old heart beat;
And from my sleep I sometimes wake, hearing a feeble cry,
And a voice that says, "Now, Forty-third, *teach me the way to die!*"
                         GEORGE WALTER THORNBURY.

133.—LAST SPEECH OF MADAME ROLAND.

NOT to its own times merely does the generous mind feel that it belongs. It comprehends in its regard the whole human race, and extends its care even to posterity. It was my lot to be the friend of men proscribed and sacrificed by those who hated them for their superiority. And I must perish in my turn! I have a double claim to death at your hands.

MADAME ROLAND.

When innocence walks to the scaffold at the command of error and of guilt, every step she takes is an advance to glory. Might I be the last victim of that furious spirit of party by which you are impelled, with what joy would I quit this unfortunate earth, which swallows up the friends of virtue and drinks the blood of the just!

Truth! Friendship! Country!—sacred objects, sentiments dear to my heart—accept my last sacrifice! My life was devoted to you, and you will render my death easy and glorious. Righteous Heaven, enlighten this wretched people for whom I invoke liberty. Liberty? Ah! that is for noble minds, not for weak beings who enter into a covenant with guilt, and try to varnish cowardice and selfishness with the name of prudence; not for corrupt wretches who rise from the bed of vice or from the mire of indigence to feast their eyes on the noble blood that streams from the scaffold.

Oh no! Liberty is the portion of a people who delight in humanity, who revere justice, despise flattery and venerate truth. While you are *not* such a people, O my fellow-citizens, in vain will you talk of liberty. Instead of liberty you will have licentiousness, and to that you all in your turns will fall victims. You will ask for bread, and will get—corpses! And at length you will bow down your necks to the yoke and find your vile refuge in the rule of a despot.

I make no concealment of my sympathies, my opinions. I know that a Roman mother was once sent to the scaffold for lamenting the death of her son. I know that in times of delusion and party rage he who dares avow himself the friend of the proscribed exposes himself to their fate. But I do not fear death. I never feared anything but guilt, and I will not purchase life at the price of a lie. Woe to the times, woe to the people, among whom to do homage to disregarded truth is to incur their hate! Happy he who, under such circumstances, is bold enough to defy that hate—as I do!

Madame Roland.*

134.—THE CLOUD AND THE SUNBEAM.

Characters—*Robert Touchwood, J. Jaundice Thorn, Vivian Bright.*

Touchwood. Heigh-ho! This is one of my doleful days. Somehow, the drugs I swallow don't seem to do me any good. I've felt worse ever since I took that last bottle of Humm's Unfailing Remedy. [*Feels of his pulse.*] There's something wrong about this pulse. Too much febrile action. I am afraid my lungs are affected. [*Drums on his chest.*] Shouldn't wonder if I was dropsical; or is it an apoplectic tendency? I am feeling rather queer about the head—or is it about the heart?

Enter Thorn.

Thorn. Good-morning, Touchwood!

Touch. Well met, Thorn!

* Born in Paris, in 1754, she became the wife of a French statesman in 1779. During the Reign of Terror she was arrested on the fall of the party to which she belonged, and condemned to death. All her eloquence and courage could not save her from the guillotine. She died in 1793 with the utmost heroism, one of her last exclamations being, "O Liberty! how many crimes are committed in thy name!"

Thorn. Aren't you imprudent?

Touch. Imprudent in what?

Thorn. In venturing out in such a raw east wind. I didn't like the sound of that cough of yours the other night at the concert. If I'm right, you lost an aunt not long ago by pulmonary consumption?

Touch. True; 'twas my stepmother's sister. Anything in that to excite alarm?

Thorn. Not if you're careful, perhaps. How gray you're getting behind the ears!

Touch. Am I? It's the effect of disease, I suppose.

Thorn. Yes. You can't be more than twenty-five; at this rate, you'll look like an old man at thirty—if you live so long. Have you seen Miss Laura Blythe lately?

Touch. Not since the concert. Why do you ask?

Thorn. She's on the point of being engaged to Vapid.

Touch. I noticed he was very attentive.

Thorn. You had some hopes in that quarter yourself, hadn't you?

Touch. I should have knelt at her feet long ago could I have presumed that such a melancholy wreck as I am might win the favor of a sprightly, beautiful young woman like Laura.

Thorn. Ah! In your state of health you shouldn't think of marriage. By the way, I found in the New York Slasher a notice of your book, and cut it out. Here it is. [*Produces piece cut from a newspaper.*]

Touch. Is it friendly?

Thorn. Not exactly. It pronounces the book an abortion, and says the best thing in it is the last line on page 480, and that's the word *finis*. Perhaps you'd like to read the notice?

Touch. No, I'd rather not. I've concluded that the book is a failure. I've given up all hope of having a kind word said of it. Was a fool to write it, and a greater fool to publish it.

Thorn. Yes; I've heard two or three of your friends make the same remark. Are you engaged at one o'clock?

Touch. No. Why do you ask?

Thorn. I'd like to take you to see a picture.

Touch. I'll go. What is it?

Thorn. Death on the Pale Horse. Wait here till I come back.   [*Exit.*

Touch. Poor Thorn! He sees I'm low-spirited, and does his best to entertain me; but what can you do where the nervous system is shattered as mine is? How vain the attempt to amuse and cheer! As well try to inflate a punctured balloon or give buoyancy to a waterlogged ship! Heigh-ho!'

Enter VIVIAN.

Vivian. Ah, Robert! You're just the man I wanted to see. The cream of the morning to you! Glad to see you out this lovely day. Why, how well you're looking!

Touch. Do you think so?

Vivian. Think so? I know so. You've improved wonderfully within a week.

Touch. I think it must be the effect of Gargle's Alterative that I've been trying. I'll order another case.

Vivian. Stuff and nonsense! You're getting well in spite of your vile mixtures, not in consequence of them. Throw physic to the dogs! Come and pass a month with me at Surfside. There inhale such oxygen as Nature offers free of cost, and my life on it, you'll be a well man before you've been with us a week. What say you? Wife and children will be delighted. Cars start at a quarter past one. Will you go?

Touch. I'll think of it seriously.

Vivian. Seriously? No! Think of it gayly. I fix only one condition: it is that you leave all your de—de—detestable drugs behind. We don't tolerate such trash at Surfside.

Touch. You'll let me take my Gargle's Alterative and my Pike's Elixir?

Vivian. Not a drop! Come, Touchwood, consent! We'll talk over old times, old schoolmates, old frolics. Do you remember the trick we played on Master Grimshaw that day he kept us after school to thrash us? Ah, Touchwood, you were a sad rogue!

Touch. Ha, ha, ha! Those were jolly times! But, I say, Vivian, you used to put me up to all the mischief I was ever guilty of.

Vivian. No, no! Do you remember the time we drove off with Squire Chapman's team? Who plied the whip till the old horse scampered down the hill like mad, and frightened the whole population?

Touch. Ha, ha, ha! We were wild ones.

Vivian. What do you say to my invitation? My cousin Laura Blythe is with us. What's the matter? You don't seem to like that.

Touch. If she's with you, of course Charles Vapid will be your guest.

Vivian. No, he'll not. The little coxcomb has received his walking ticket. He'll not trouble Laura again. By the way, if it weren't for betraying confidence, I'd tell you something my wife told me about Laura's preferences. But it will make you blush, so I'll keep it to myself.

Touch. No, let me hear it, Vivian—let me hear it.

Vivian. You shall hear it on the beach at Surfside, under a clear starlight, with the ocean before us and my pine forest for a background. But I'm getting poetical; and speaking of poetry, what a capital notice of your book there is in the last London Critic!

Touch. I didn't know there had been one.

Vivian. Is it possible? Why, my dear fellow, the Critic fills two or three of its pages with quotations—says 'tis *the* book of the season, and winds up with a hope that such a pen as Mr. Touchwood's will not be suffered to lie idle.

Touch. Does the Critic say all that?

Vivian. All that, and more. Now that we've got our cue from England, how you will be puffed, my dear fellow! How you will be *interviewed!* What baskets of letters you'll have, begging your autograph! What importunities to sit for your portrait! We shall have you in the illustrated weeklies; we shall see you looking out on us with a benignant smile from the shop windows; we shall find paragraphs like this in the daily papers—ahem!—"We learn that Mr. Robert Touchwood is passing a week or two with a distinguished party at a friend's house at Surfside." So you see some of the glory will be reflected on us. You can't deprive us of that. Ha, ha, ha!

Touch. Ha, ha, ha! Why, Vivian, you are getting extravagant.

Vivian. No, sir. 'Twill happen within a twelvemonth. I feel it in my bones.

Touch. Good! Vivian, I'll go with you to Surfside.

Vivian. Under the conditions?

Touch. Under the conditions.

Vivian. You agree that all pills, elixirs, patent medicines and drugs shall be forfeited as contraband?

Touch. I agree.

Vivian. Why, man, the very thought of the thing has sent back the color to your cheeks and added five pounds to your weight. At this rate you'll eat me out of house and home before the month is ended.

Touch. We'll be jolly, eh, Vivian?

Vivian. Jolly! We'll be jubilant. We'll outscream the sea-gulls and outroar the breakers. We'll astonish old Neptune with our fun.

Re-enter THORN.

Thorn. I'm punctual, you see, Touchwood. Are you ready to go and see that picture?

Vivian. What picture, may I be allowed to ask?

Thorn. Death on the Pale Horse.

Vivian. Avaunt and quit my sight! Death on the Pale Horse, indeed! No, sir! He goes to see Life on the Black Mare. You shall ride my little Bessie, Robert. Gentle as a kitten, and fleet as a locomotive. Will go a mile in 2.40, easy.

Touch. You must excuse me, Thorn. I am going to Surfside.

Thorn. I hope not, with that pulmonary difficulty of yours.

23

I was going to propose driving you this afternoon over to the new cemetery. I've picked out a very nice lot for you. Beautifully shaded with cypresses, weeping willows and copper beeches.

Vivian. Avaunt, I say! Vanish, Vapor! Dissipate, Cloud! Dry up, Wet Blanket! You miserable killjoy! You born hearse-driver! You walking *memento mori!* Out of my sight!

Thorn. Positively, Mr. Bright, I can't comprehend such turbulent hilarity, such heartless frivolity, on the part of a rational being in a dying world. I can't comprehend it.

Vivian. Of course you can't, any more than an owl can comprehend a rainbow. Look deeper, you impious saint, and you'd see life under death, joy under sorrow. But you prefer lingering in the charnel-house to penetrating to the beatitudes beyond the veil. Suit your own taste, but don't think to throw your black crape over our heads. Let me catch you within a mile of Surfside, and I'll set my dogs on you. Go!

Thorn. Good-morning, Mr. Touchwood. Should you want a lawyer or a clergyman at any time, I shall be happy to show my friendship. [*Exit.*

Vivian. Ha, ha, ha! His friendship! The friendship of frost for roses!

Touch. Ha, ha, ha! I'm glad he's gone.

Vivian. And now for Surfside and Laura!

Touch. Done! I feel ten years younger already, my boy! We'll have high times.

Vivian. High times? We'll have picnics and regattas and chowder-parties every day. We'll have a band playing on the lawn and entertain the whole village.

Touch. We'll go up in a balloon.

Vivian. Bravo! We'll have a perpetual breach of the peace. Come on. We mustn't miss the cars. [*Exeunt.*

SARGENT.

135.—POLITICS AND METAPHYSICS.

CALHOUN.

THE great question at issue has not been directly and fairly met. Is this a federal union? a union of States, as distinct from that of individuals? Is the sovereignty in the several States or in the American people in the aggregate?

The very language which we are compelled to use when speaking of our political institutions affords proof conclusive as to its real character. The terms *union, federal, united,* all imply a combination of sovereignties, a confederation of States. They are never applied to an association of individuals. Who ever heard of the United States of New York, of Massachusetts or of Virginia? Who ever heard the term *federal* or *union* applied to the aggregation of individuals into one community?

Nor is the other point less clear—that the sovereignty is in the several States, and that our system is a union of twenty-four sovereign powers under a constitutional compact, and not of a divided sovereignty between the States severally and the United States. In spite of all that has been said, I maintain that sovereignty is in its nature indivisible. It is the supreme power in a State, and we might just as well speak of half a square or half a triangle as of half a sovereignty. It is a gross error to confound the *exercise* of sovereign powers with sovereignty itself, or the *delegation* of such powers with the *surrender* of them. A sovereign may delegate his powers to be exercised by as many agents as he may think proper, under such conditions and with such limitations as he may impose; but to surrender any portion of his sovereignty to another is to annihilate the whole.

The Senator from Delaware calls this "metaphysical reasoning," which he says he cannot comprehend. If by metaphysics he means that scholastic refinement which makes distinctions without difference, no one can hold it in more utter contempt than I do; but if, on the contrary, he means the power of analysis and combination—that power which reduces the most complex idea into its elements, which traces causes to their first principle, and by the power of generalization and combination unites the whole in one harmonious system—then, so far from deserving contempt, it is the highest attribute of the human mind. It is the power that raises man above the brute—that distinguishes his faculties from mere sagacity, which he holds in common with inferior animals.

It is this power which has raised the astronomer from being a mere gazer at the stars to the high intellectual eminence of a Newton or a Laplace, and astronomy itself from a mere observation of insulated facts into that noble science which displays to our admiration the system of the universe.

And shall this high power of the mind, which has effected such wonders when directed to the laws that control the material world, be for ever prohibited, under a senseless cry of *metaphysics*, from being applied to the high purpose of political science and legislation? I hold them to be subject to laws as fixed as matter itself, and to be as fit a subject for the application of the highest intellectual power. Denunciation may indeed fall upon the philosophical inquirer into these first principles, as it did upon Galileo and Bacon when they first unfolded the great discoveries which have immortalized their names. But the time will come when truth will prevail in spite of prejudice and denunciation, and when politics and legislation will be considered as much a science as astronomy and chemistry.

JOHN C. CALHOUN, 1782–1850.

WE are two travelers, Roger and I.
  Roger's my dog—come here, you scamp!
Jump for the gentleman—mind your eye!
  Over the table—look out for the lamp!
The rogue is growing a little old;
  Five years we've tramped through wind and weather,
And slept out-doors when nights were cold,
  And ate and drank and starved together.

We've learned what comfort is, I tell you—
  A bed on the floor, a bit of rosin,
A fire to thaw our thumbs (poor fellow!
  The paw he holds up there's been frozen),
Plenty of catgut for my fiddle
  (This out-door business is bad for strings),
Then a few nice buckwheats hot from the griddle,
  And Roger and I set up for kings.

No, thank ye, sir—I never drink;
  Roger and I are exceedingly moral.
Aren't we, Roger?—see him wink!
  Well, something hot, then—we won't quarrel.
He's thirsty, too—see him nod his head?
  What a pity, sir, that dogs can't talk!
He understands every word that's said,
  And he knows good milk from water-and-chalk.

The truth is, sir, now I reflect,
  I've been so sadly given to grog
I wonder I've not lost the respect
  (Here's to you, sir!) even of my dog.
But he sticks by through thick and thin;
  And this old coat, with its empty pockets
And rags that smell of tobacco and gin,
  He'll follow while he has eyes in his sockets.

23. *

There isn't another creature living
   Would do it, and prove, through every disaster,
So fond, so faithful and so forgiving
   To such a miserable, thankless master!
No, sir—see him wag his tail and grin!
   By George! it makes my old eyes water!
That is, there's something in this gin
   That chokes a fellow. But no matter.

We'll have some music if you're willing,
   And Roger (hem! what a plague a cough is, sir!)
Shall march a little. Start, you villain!
   Stand straight! 'Bout face! Salute your officer!
Put up that paw! Dress! Take your rifle!
   (Some dogs have arms, you see!) Now hold your
Cap while the gentleman gives a trifle
   To aid a poor old patriot soldier.

March! Halt! Now show how the rebel shakes
   When he stands up to hear his sentence.
Now tell us how many drams it takes
   To honor a jolly new acquaintance.
Five yelps—that's five; he's mighty knowing.
   The night's before us, fill the glasses!
Quick, sir! I'm ill—my brain is going!
   Some brandy—thank you—there! it passes!

Why not reform? That's easily said;
   But I've gone through such wretched treatment,
Sometimes forgetting the taste of bread,
   And scarce remembering what meat meant,
That my poor stomach's past reform;
   And there are times when, mad with thinking,
I'd sell out heaven for something warm
   To prop a horrible inward sinking.

Is there a way to forget to think?
   At your age, sir, home, fortune, friends,

A dear girl's love— But I took to drink—
   The same old story; you know how it ends.
If you could have seen these classic features—
   You needn't laugh, sir; they were not then
Such a burning libel on God's creatures:
   I was one of your handsome men!

If you had seen her, so fair and young,
   Whose head was happy on this breast,
If you could have heard the songs I sung
   When the wine went round, you wouldn't have guessed
That ever I, sir, should be straying
   From door to door with fiddle and dog,
Ragged and penniless, and playing
   To you to-night for a glass of grog.

She's married since—a parson's wife;
   'Twas better for her that we should part—
Better the soberest, prosiest life
   Than a blasted home and a broken heart.
I have seen her? Once. I was weak and spent;
   On the dusty road a carriage stopped,
But little she dreamed, as on she went,
   Who kissed the coin that her fingers dropped!

You've set me to talking, sir; I'm sorry;
   It makes me wild to think of the change!
What do you care for a beggar's story?
   Is it amusing? you find it strange?
I had a mother so proud of me!
   'Twas well she died before— Do you know
If the happy spirits in heaven can see
   The ruin and wretchedness here below?

Another glass, and strong, to deaden
   This pain, then Roger and I will start.
I wonder has he such a lumpish, leaden,
   Aching thing in place of a heart?

He is sad sometimes, and would weep if he could,
  No doubt remembering things that were—
A virtuous kennel, with plenty of food,
  And himself a sober, respectable cur.

I'm better now; that glass was warming—
  You rascal, limber your lazy feet!
We must be fiddling and performing
  For supper and bed, or starve in the street.
Not a very gay life to lead, you think?
  But soon we shall go where lodgings are free
And the sleepers need neither victuals nor drink—
  The sooner the better for Roger and me!

J. T. Trowbridge.

137.—RESULTS OF THE AMERICAN WAR, 1780.

FOX.

WE are charged with expressing joy at the triumphs of America. True it is that in former sessions I proclaimed it as my sincere opinion that if the ministry had succeeded in their first scheme against the liberties of America, the liberties of this country would have been at an end. Thinking this, as I did, in the sincerity of an honest heart, I rejoiced at the resistance which the ministry had met. That great and glorious statesman the late Lord Chatham, feeling for the liberties of his native country, thanked Heaven that America had resisted.

But it seems "all the calamities of the country are to be ascribed to the wishes and the joy and the speeches of opposition." Oh, miserable and unfortunate ministry! oh, blind and incapable men! whose measures are framed with so little foresight and executed with so little firmness that they not only crumble to pieces, but bring ruin on the country, merely because one rash, weak or wicked man in the House of Commons makes a speech against them!

But who is he who arraigns gentlemen on this side of the House with causing by their inflammatory speeches the misfortunes of their country? The accusation comes from one whose inflammatory harangues have led the nation, step by step, from violence to violence, in that inhuman, unfeeling system of blood and massacre which every honest man must detest, and which every good man must abhor and every wise man condemn! And this man imputes the guilt of such measures to those who had all along foretold the consequences, who had prayed, entreated and supplicated not only for America, but for the credit of the nation and its eventual welfare, to arrest the hand of power, meditating slaughter and directed by injustice!

What was the consequence of the sanguinary measures recommended in those bloody, inflammatory speeches? Though Boston was to be starved, though Hancock and Adams were proscribed, yet at the feet of these very men the Parliament of Great Britain was obliged to kneel, flatter and cringe; and as it had the cruelty at one time to denounce vengeance against these men, so it had the meanness afterward to implore their forgiveness. Shall he who called the Americans "Hancock and his crew"—shall he presume to reprehend any set of men for inflammatory speeches?

It is this accursed American war that has led us, step by step, into all our present misfortunes and national disgraces. What was the cause of our wasting forty millions of money and sixty thousand lives? The American war! What was it that produced the French rescript and a French war? The American war! What was it that produced the Spanish manifesto and Spanish war? The American war! What was it that armed forty-two thousand men in Ireland with the arguments carried on the points of forty thousand bayonets? The American war! For what are we about to incur an additional debt of twelve or fourteen millions? This accursed, cruel, diabolical American war!

CHARLES JAMES FOX, 1749–1806.

138.—HOW THEY BROUGHT THE GOOD NEWS FROM GHENT TO AIX.

I SPRANG to the stirrup, and Joris, and he;
I galloped, Dirck galloped, we galloped all three;
" Good speed!" cried the watch, as the gate-bolts undrew;
" Speed!" echoed the wall to us galloping through;
Behind shut the postern, the lights sank to rest,
And into the midnight we galloped abreast.

Not a word to each other; we kept the great pace
Neck by neck, stride by stride, never changing our place;
I turned in my saddle and made its girths tight,
Then shortened each stirrup, and set the pique right,
Rebuckled the cheek-strap, chained slacker the bit,
Nor galloped less steadily Roland a whit.

'Twas moonset at starting; but while we drew near
Lokēren, the cocks crew and twilight dawned clear;
At Boom a great yellow star came out to see;
At Düffeld 'twas morning as plain as could be;
And from Mecheln church-steeple we heard the half chime,
So Joris broke silence with, " Yet there is time!"

At Aerschot up leaped of a sudden the sun,
And against him the cattle stood black every one,
To stare through the mist at us galloping past,
And I saw my stout galloper, Roland, at last,
With resolute shoulders, each butting away
The haze, as some bluff river headland its spray—

And his low head and crest, just one sharp ear bent back
For my voice, and the other pricked out on his track;
And one eye's black intelligence—ever that glance
O'er its white edge at me, his own master, askance!

And the thick heavy spume-flakes which aye and anon
His fierce lips shook upward in galloping on.

By Hasselt, Dirck groaned; and cried Joris, "Stay spur!
Your Ross galloped bravely, the fault's not in her,
We'll remember at Aix"—for one heard the quick wheeze
Of her chest, saw the stretched neck and staggering knees,
And sunk tail, and horrible heave of the flank,
As down on her haunches she shuddered and sank.

So we were left galloping, Joris and I,
Past Looz and past Tongrés, no cloud in the sky;
The broad sun above laughed a pitiless laugh,
'Neath our feet broke the brittle bright stubble like chaff;
Till over by Dalhem a dome-spire sprang white,
And "Gallop!" gasped Joris, "for Aix is in sight!"

"How they'll greet us!" and all in a moment his roan
Rolled neck and croup over, lay dead as a stone;
And there was my Roland to bear the whole weight
Of the news which alone could save Aix from her fate,
With his nostrils like pits full of blood to the brim,
And with circles of red for his eye-sockets' rim.

Then I cast loose my buff-coat, each holster let fall,
Shook off both my jack-boots, let go belt and all,
Stood up in the stirrup, leaned, patted his ear,
Called my Roland his pet-name, my horse without peer;
Clapped my hands, laughed and sang, any noise, bad or
    good,
Till at length into Aix Roland galloped and stood.

And all I remember is, friends flocking round,
As I sat with his head 'twixt my knees on the ground,
And no voice but was praising this Roland of mine,
As I poured down his throat our last measure of wine,
Which—the burgesses voted by common consent—
Was no more than his due who brought good news from
    Ghent.   Robert Browning.

139.—MARIE ANTOINETTE, 1790.*

It is now sixteen or seventeen years since I saw the queen of France, then the dauphiness, at Versailles; and surely never lighted on this orb, which she hardly seemed to touch, a more delightful vision. I saw her just above the horizon, decorating and cheering the elevated sphere she just began to move in, glittering like the morning star, full of life, and splendor, and joy. Oh what a revolution! and what a heart must I have to contemplate without emotion that elevation and that fall!

MARIE ANTOINETTE.

Little did I dream, when she added titles of veneration to those of enthusiastic, distant, respectful love, that she should ever be obliged to carry the sharp antidote against disgrace concealed in that bosom; little did I dream that I should have lived to see such disasters fallen upon her in a nation of gallant men, in a nation of men of honor and of cavaliers! I thought ten thousand swords must have leaped from their scabbards to avenge even a look that threatened her with insult.

But the age of chivalry is gone; that of sophisters, economists and calculators has succeeded, and the glory of Europe is extinguished for ever. Never, never more shall we behold that generous loyalty to rank and sex, that proud submission, that dignified obedience, that subordination of the heart, which kept alive even in servitude itself the spirit of an exalted freedom!

* Born, 1755; beheaded, 1792.

The unbought grace of life, the cheap defense of nations, the nurse of manly sentiment and heroic enterprise, is gone! It is gone—that sensibility of principle, that chastity of honor, which felt a stain like a wound, which inspired courage whilst it mitigated ferocity, which ennobled whatever it touched, and under which vice itself lost half its evil by losing all its grossness.

EDMUND BURKE (see p. 135).

140.—WILLIAM PENN UNDER ARREST.
A DIALOGUE AS IT ACTUALLY OCCURRED.

In England, in the year 1670, William Penn, afterward the founder of Pennsylvania, was persecuted for his religious opinions, which were those of the Quakers. He was tyrannically arrested for speaking at a Quaker meeting in Wheeler street, in London, and brought before a magistrate named Sir John Robinson. We abridge from Dixon's life of Penn the conversation which took place in court on this occasion.

Sir John Robinson. What is this person's name?

Constable. Mr. Penn, sir.

Rob. Is your name Penn?

Penn. Dost thou not know me?

Rob. I don't know you; I don't desire to know such as you.

Penn. If not, why didst thou send for me hither?

Rob. Is that your name, sir?

Penn. Yes, yes, my name is Penn; I am not ashamed of my name.

Rob. Constable, where did you find him?

Constable. At Wheeler street, at a meeting, speaking to the people.

Rob. You mean he was speaking to an unlawful assembly!

Constable. I don't know, indeed, sir. He was there, and he was speaking.

Penn. I freely acknowledge that I was in Wheeler street, and I spoke to an assembly of people there.

Rob. He confesses it.

Penn. I do so; I am not ashamed of my testimony.

24

Rob. Mr. Penn, I am sorry for you. You are an ingenious gentleman—all the world must allow that—and you have a plentiful estate. Why should you render yourself unhappy by associating with such simple people?

Penn. I confess I have made it my choice to relinquish the company of those that are ingeniously wicked, to converse with those who are honestly simple.

Rob. I wish thee wiser.

Penn. I wish thee better.

Rob. You have been as bad as other folks.

Penn. When and where? I charge thee tell the company to my face.

Rob. Abroad, and at home too.

Penn. I make this bold challenge to all men—justly to accuse me with ever having been heard to swear, utter a curse or speak one obscene word. I trample thy slander under my feet!

Rob. Well, Mr. Penn, I have no ill-will toward you. Your father was my friend, and I have a great deal of kindness for you.

Penn. Thou hast an ill way of expressing it.

Rob. Well, I must send you to Newgate for six months; and when they are expired, you will come out.

Penn. Is that all? Thou well knowest that a longer imprisonment has not daunted me. This is not the way to compass your ends.

Rob. You bring yourself into trouble. You *will* be heading of parties, and drawing people after you.

Penn. Thou mistakest. I would have thee and all men know that I scorn that religion which is not worth suffering for, and able to sustain those that are afflicted for its sake. Thy religion persecutes, mine forgives. I leave you all in perfect charity.

Rob. Send a corporal with a file of musketeers with him.

Penn. No, no; send thy lackey. I know the way to Newgate.

———◦◦◦———

141.—THE BATTLE.*

Heavy and solemn,
  a cloudy column,
Through the green plain
  they marching came.
Measureless spread, like
  a table dread,
For the wild grim dice
  of the iron game.
Looks are bent on the
  shaking ground,
Hearts beat loud with a
  knelling sound;
Swift by the breasts that
  must bear the brunt

SCHILLER.

Gallops the major along the front;
     "Halt!"
And fettered they stand at the stark command,
And the warriors, silent, halt!

Proud in the blush of morning glowing,
What on the hill-top shines in flowing?
"See you the foeman's banners waving?"
"We see the foeman's banners waving!"
"God be with ye, children and wife!"
Hark to the music—the trump and the fife—
How they ring through the ranks which they rouse to the
  strife!
Thrilling they sound, with their glorious tone,
Thrilling they go through the marrow and bone!
Brothers, God grant, when this life is o'er,
In the life to come that we meet once more!

See the smoke how the lightning is cleaving asunder!
Hark! the guns, peal on peal, how they boom in their
  thunder!

*Translation of Sir E. Bulwer Lytton.

From host to host, with kindling sound,
The shouting signal circles round;
Ay, shout it forth to life or death,
Freer already breathes the breath!
The war is waging, slaughter raging,
And heavy through the reeking pall
      The iron death-dice fall!
Nearer they close, foes upon foes.
"Ready!" from square to square it goes.

They kneel as one man, from flank to flank,
And the fire comes sharp from the foremost rank.
Many a soldier to earth is sent,
Many a gap by the balls is rent;
O'er the corse before springs the hinder man,
That the line may not fail to the fearless van.
To the right, to the left, and around and around,
Death whirls in its dance on the bloody ground.
God's sunlight is quenched in the fiery fight,
Over the host falls a brooding night!
Brothers, God grant, when this life is o'er,
In the life to come that we meet once more!

The dead men lie bathed in the weltering blood,
And the living are blent in the slippery flood,
And the feet, as they reeling and sliding go,
Stumble still on the corses that sleep below.
"What! Francis!" "Give Charlotte my last farewell."
As the dying man murmurs, the thunders swell.
"I'll give—O God! are their guns so near?
Ho, comrades!—yon volley!—look sharp to the rear!—
I'll give thy Charlotte thy last farewell;
Sleep soft! where death thickest descendeth in rain,
The friend thou forsakest thy side may regain!"
Hitherward, thitherward, reels the fight,
Dark and more darkly day glooms into night;
Brothers, God grant, when this life is o'er,
In the life to come that we meet once more!

Hark to the hoofs that galloping go !
  The ádjutants flying !
The horsemen press hard on the panting foe,
  Their thunder booms, in dying—
          Victory !
Terror has seized on the dastards all,
  And their colors fall !
          Victory !

Closed is the brunt of the glorious fight ;
And the day, like a conqueror, bursts on the night.
Trumpet and fife swelling choral along,
The triumph already sweeps marching in song.
Farewell, fallen brothers; though this life be o'er,
There's another in which we shall meet you once more !
                    SCHILLER, 1759–1805.

142.—DECLARATION OF IRISH RIGHTS.

THE English opposition are right—mere trade will not satisfy Ireland. They judge of us by other great nations—by the nation whose political life has been a struggle for liberty, America ! They judge of us with a true knowledge and just deference for our character, that a country enlightened as Ireland, chartered as Ireland, armed as Ireland and injured as Ireland will be satisfied with nothing less than liberty.

What ! has England lost thirteen provinces, has she reconciled herself to this loss, and will she not be reconciled to the liberty of Ireland ? Take notice that the very constitution which I move you to declare for Ireland, Great Britain herself offered to America ! What ! has England offered this to the *resistance* of America, and will she refuse it to the *loyalty* of Ireland ?

I shall hear of ingratitude. I name the argument to despise it and the men who make use of it. I know the men who use it are not grateful; they are insatiate, they are public extortioners who would stop the tide of public prosperity and turn it to the channel of their own emolument. I know

24 *

of no species of gratitude which should prevent my country from being free, no gratitude which should oblige Ireland to be the slave of England. In cases of robbery and usurpation, nothing is an object of gratitude except the thing stolen, the charter spoliated.

A nation's liberty cannot, like her treasure, be melted and parceled out in gratitude. No man can be grateful or liberal of his conscience, nor woman of her honor, nor nation of her liberty. There are certain unimpartable, inherent, invaluable properties not to be alienated from the person, whether body politic or body natural. With the same contempt do I treat that charge which says that Ireland is insatiable. Ireland asks nothing but that which Great Britain has robbed her of—her rights and privileges. To say that Ireland will not be satisfied with liberty because she is not satisfied with slavery is folly. I laugh at that man who supposes that Ireland will not be content with a free trade and a free constitution; and would any man advise her to be content with less?

I might, as a constituent, come to your bar and demand my liberty. I do call upon you by the laws of the land and their violation, by the instruction of eighteen centuries, by the arms, inspiration and providence of the present moment, tell us the rule by which we shall go, assert the law of Ireland, declare the liberty of the land. I will not be answered by a public lie in the shape of an amendment; neither, speaking for the subject's freedom, am I to hear of faction. I wish for nothing but to breathe in this our island, in common with my fellow-subjects, the air of liberty.

I have no ambition, unless it be the ambition to break your chain and contemplate your glory. I never will be satisfied so long as the meanest cottager in Ireland has a link of the British chain clanking to his rags. He may be naked—he shall not be in irons. And I do see the time is at hand, the spirit is gone forth, the declaration is planted; and though great men should apostatize, yet the cause will live, and though the public speaker should die, yet the immortal fire shall outlast the organ which conveyed it, and the breath of liberty, like the word of the holy man, will not die with the prophet, but survive him.

Henry Grattan (see p. 314.)

143.—THE LOVE OF LIFE.

Our attachment to every object around us increases, in general, from the length of our acquaintance with it. "I would not choose," says a French philosopher, "to see an old post pulled up with which I had been long acquainted."

GOLDSMITH.

Chinvang the Chaste, ascending the throne of China, commanded that all who were unjustly detained in prison during the preceding reign should be set free. Among the number who came to thank their deliverer on this occasion there appeared a majestic old man, who, falling at the emperor's feet, addressed him thus:

"Great father of China, behold a wretch, now eighty-five years old, who was shut up in a dungeon at the age of twenty-two. I was imprisoned, though a stranger to crime, and without being even confronted by my accusers. I have now lived in solitude and darkness for more than sixty years, and am grown familiar with distress. As yet, dazzled with the splendor of that sun to which you have restored me, I have been wandering here and there to find out some friend that would assist or relieve or remember me, but my friends, my family and relations are all dead, and I am forgotten. Permit me then, O Chinvang, to wear out the wretched remains of life in my former prison; the walls of my dungeon are to me more pleasing than the most splendid palace; I have not long to live, and shall be unhappy except I spend the rest of my days where my youth was passed—in that prison from whence you were pleased to release me."

The old man's passion for confinement is similar to that we

all have for life. We are habituated to the prison, we look round with discontent, are displeased with the abode, and yet the length of our captivity only increases our fondness for the cell. The trees we have planted, the houses we have built, or the posterity we have begotten, all serve to bind us closer to earth and embitter our parting. Life sues the young like a new acquaintance; the companion, as yet unexhausted, is at once instructive and amusing, its company pleases, yet for all this it is but little regarded. To us who are declined in years life appears like an old friend; its jests have been anticipated in former conversations, it has no new story to make us smile, no new improvement with which to surprise, yet still we love it; destitute of every enjoyment, still we love it—husband the wasting treasure with increasing frugality, and feel all the poignancy of anguish in the fatal separation.

OLIVER GOLDSMITH, 1728–1774.

144.—COUNT CANDESPINA'S STANDARD.

Now one by one the wearied knights had fallen or basely flown,
And on the mound where his post was fixed O-le'a stood alone.
" Yield up the banner, gallant knight, thy lord lies on the plain ;
Thy duty has been nobly done ; I would not see thee slain."
" Spare pity, king of Aragon ; I would not hear thee lie ;
My lord is looking down from heaven to see his standard fly."

"Yield, madman, yield ! thy horse is down, thou hast nor lance nor shield ;
Fly ! I will grant thee time." "This flag can neither fly nor yield."
They girt the standard round about, a wall of flashing steel ;
But still they heard the battle-cry, "Olea for Castile !"
And there, against all Aragon, full armed with lance and brand,
Olea fought until the sword snapped in his sturdy hand.

Among the foe, with that high scorn that laughs at earthly fears,
He hurled the broken hilt, and drew his dagger on the spears.
They hewed the hauberk from his breast, the helmet from his head ;
They hewed the hands from off his limbs, from every vein he bled.
Clasping the standard to his heart, he raised one dying peal
That rang as if a trumpet blew—"Olea for Castile !"

GEORGE H. BOKER.

145.—SPEECH OF SERGEANT BUZFUZ.

You heard from my learnëd friend, gentlemen of the jury, that this is an action for a breach of promise of marriage, in which the damages are laid at fifteen hundred pounds. The plaintiff, gentlemen, is a widow—yes, gentlemen, a widow. The late Mr. Bardell some time before his death became the father, gentlemen, of a little boy. With this little boy, the only pledge of her departed exciseman, Mrs. Bardell shrank from the world and courted the retirement and tranquillity of Goswell street, and here she placed in her front-parlor window a written placard bearing this inscription : "Apartments furnished for a single gentleman. Inquire within."

Mrs. Bardell's opinions of the opposite sex, gentlemen, were derived from a long contemplation of the inestimable qualities of her lost husband. She had no fear—she had no distrust; all was confidence and reliance. " Mr. Bardell," said the widow, " was a man of honor—Mr. Bardell was a man of his word—Mr. Bardell was no deceiver—Mr. Bardell was once a single gentleman himself; to single gentlemen I look for protection, for assistance, for comfort and consolation; in single gentlemen I shall perpetually see something to remind me of what Mr. Bardell was when he first won my young and untried affections; to a single gentleman, then, shall my lodgings be let."

Actuated by this beautiful and touching impulse (among the best impulses of our imperfect nature, gentlemen), the lonely and desolate widow dried her tears, furnished her first floor, caught her innocent boy to her maternal bosom and put the bill up in her parlor window. Did it remain there long? No. The serpent was on the watch, the train was laid, the mine was preparing, the sapper and miner was at work! Before the bill had been in the parlor window three days—three days, gentlemen—a being, erect upon two legs and bearing all the outward semblance of a man and not of a monster, knocked at the door of Mrs. Bardell's house. He inquired within; he took the lodgings, and on the very next

day he entered into possession of them.   This man was Pick-
wick—Pickwick, the defendant!

Of this man I will say little.   The subject presents but few
attractions; and I, gentlemen, am not the man, nor are you,
gentlemen, the men, to delight in the contemplation of revolt-
ing heartlessness and of systematic villainy.   I say systematic
villainy, gentlemen ; and when I say systematic villainy, let
me tell the defendant, Pickwick, if he be in court, as I am in-
formed he is, that it would have been more decent in him,
more becoming, if he had stopped away.   Let me tell him,
further, that a counsel in the discharge of his duty is neither
to be intimidated, nor bullied, nor put down, and that any.
attempt to do either the one or the other will recoil on the
head of the attempter, be he plaintiff or be he defendant,
be his name Pickwick, or Noakes, or Stoakes, or Stiles, or
Brown, or Thompson.

I shall show you, gentlemen, that for two years Pickwick
continued to reside constantly and without interruption or in-
termission at Mrs. Bardell's house.   I shall show you that
Mrs. Bardell during the whole of that time waited on him,
attended to his comforts, cooked his meals, looked out his linen
for the washerwoman when it went abroad, darned, aired and
prepared it for wear when it came home, and, in short, enjoyed
his fullest trust and confidence.   I shall show you that on
many occasions he gave halfpence, and on some occasions even
sixpence, to her little boy.   I shall prove to you that on one
occasion, when he returned from the country, he distinctly and
in terms offered her marriage, previously, however, taking
special care that there should be no witnesses to their solemn
contract; and I am in a situation to prove to you, on the tes-
timony of three of his own friends—most unwilling witnesses,
gentlemen, most unwilling witnesses—that on that morning
he was discovered by them holding the plaintiff in his arms
and soothing her agitation by his caresses and endearments.

And now, gentlemen, but one word more.   Two letters
have passed between these parties—letters that must be viewed
with a cautious and suspicious eye—letters that were evidently

intended at the time, by Pickwick, to mislead and delude any third parties into whose hands they might fall. Let me read the first: "Garraway's, twelve o'clock—Dear Mrs. B.: Chops and tomato sauce. Yours, Pickwick." Gentlemen, what does this mean? Chops and tomato sauce! Yours, Pickwick! Chops! Gracious Heavens! And tomato sauce! Gentlemen, is the happiness of a sensitive and confiding female to be trifled away by such shallow artifices as these?

The next has no date whatever, which is in itself suspicious: "Dear Mrs. B.: I shall not be at home to-morrow. Slow coach." And then follows this very remarkable expression: "Don't trouble yourself about the warming-pan." The warming-pan! Why, gentlemen, who *does* trouble himself about a warming-pan? Why is Mrs. Bardell so earnestly entreated not to agitate herself about this warming-pan, unless (as is no doubt the case) it is a mere cover for hidden fire—a mere substitute for some endearing word or promise, agreeably to a preconcerted system of correspondence, artfully contrived by Pickwick with a view to his contemplated desertion? And what does this allusion to the slow coach mean? For aught I know, it may be a reference to Pickwick himself, who has most unquestionably been a criminally slow coach during the whole of this transaction, but whose speed will now be very unexpectedly accelerated, and whose wheels, gentlemen, as he will find to his cost, will very soon be greased by you.

But enough of this, gentlemen. It is difficult to smile with an aching heart. My client's hopes and prospects are ruined, and it is no figure of speech to say that her occupation is gone indeed. The bill is down, but there is no tenant! Eligible single gentlemen pass and repass, but there is no invitation for them to inquire within or without! All is gloom and silence in the house; even the voice of the child is hushed: his infant sports are disregarded when his mother weeps.

But Pickwick, gentlemen, Pickwick, the ruthless destroyer of this domestic oasis in the desert of Goswell street—Pickwick, who has choked up the well and thrown ashes on the sward—

Pickwick, who comes before you to-day with his heartless tomato sauce and warming-pans,—Pickwick still rears his head with unblushing effrontery, and gazes without a sigh on the ruin he has made! Damages, gentlemen, heavy damages, is the only punishment with which you can visit him—the only recompense you can award to my client! And for those damages she now appeals to an enlightened, a high-minded, a right-feeling, a conscientious, a dispassionate, a sympathizing, a contemplative jury of her civilized countrymen!

Charles Dickens.

146.—LINES FROM GRAY'S ELEGY

IN A COUNTRY CHURCHYARD.

THOMAS GRAY.

Can storied urn or ani-
mated bust
　Back to its mansion call
　the fleeting breath?
Can Honor's voice pro-
voke the silent dust,
　Or Flattery soothe the
　dull, cold ear of death?
Perhaps in this neglected
spot is laid
　Some heart once preg-
　nant with celestial fire,
Hands that the rod of em-
pire might have swayed,
　Or waked to ecstasy the
　living lyre.

But Knowledge to their eyes her ample page,
　Rich with the spoils of time, did ne'er unroll;
Chill Penury repressed their noble rage,
　And froze the genial current of the soul.

Full many a gem of purest ray serene
　　The dark, unfathomed caves of ocean bear;
Full many a flower is born to blush unseen,
　　And waste its sweetness on the desert air.
Some village Hampden, that with dauntless breast
　　The little tyrant of his fields withstood—
Some mute, inglorious Milton—here may rest;
　　Some Cromwell guiltless of his country's blood.

The applause of listening senates to command,
　　The threats of pain and ruin to despise,
To scatter plenty o'er a smiling land,
　　And read their history in a nation's eyes,
Their lot forbade; nor circumscribed alone
　　Their growing virtues, but their crimes confined;
Forbade to wade through slaughter to a throne,
　　And shut the gates of mercy on mankind;
The struggling pangs of conscious truth to hide,
　　To quench the blushes of ingenuous shame,
Or heap the shrine of luxury and pride
　　With incense kindled at the Muse's flame!

Far from the madding crowd's ignoble strife
　　Their sober wishes never learned to stray;
Along the cool, sequestered vale of life
　　They kept the noiseless tenor of their way.
Yet even these bones from insult to protect
　　Some frail memorial, still erected nigh,
With uncouth rhymes and shapeless sculpture decked,
　　Implores the passing tribute of a sigh.
Their name, their years, spelt by the unlettered Muse,
　　The place of fame and elegy supply;
And many a holy text around she strews,
　　To teach the rustic moralist to die.

For who, to dumb forgetfulness a prey,
　　This pleasing, anxious being e'er resigned,

25　　　　　　　　　　T

Left the warm precincts of the cheerful day,
    Nor cast one longing, lingering look behind?
On some fond breast the parting soul relies,
    Some pious drops the closing eye requires;
Even from the tomb the voice of nature cries,
    Even in our ashes live their wonted fires.

THOMAS GRAY, 1716–1771.

147.—ROBESPIERRE'S LAST SPEECH.*

THE enemies of the republic call me tyrant! Were I such, they would grovel at my feet. I should gorge them with gold, I should grant them impunity for their crimes, and they would be grateful! Were I such, the kings we have vanquished, far from denouncing Robespierre, would lend him their guilty support. There would be a covenant between them and me. Tyranny must have tools.

But the enemies of tyranny, whither does *their* path tend? To the tomb and to immortality! What tyrant is my protector? To what faction do I belong? Yourselves! What faction, since the beginning of the revolution, has crushed and annihilated so many detected traitors? You, the people, our principles, are that faction—a faction to which I am devoted, and against which all the scoundrelism of the day is banded!

The confirmation of the republic has been my object, and I know that the republic can be established only on the eternal basis of morality. Against me and against those who hold kindred principles the league is formed. My life? Oh, my life I abandon without a regret! I have seen the Past, AND I FORESEE THE FUTURE!

What friend of his country would wish to survive the moment he could no longer serve it—when he could no longer defend innocence against oppression? Wherefore should I continue in an order of things where intrigue eternally tri-

---

* This translation was originally made for Sargent's Standard Speaker.

umphs over truth, where justice is mocked, where passions the most abject or fears the most absurd override the sacred interests of humanity? How support the misery of seeing traitors to the cause of human rights conceal their hideous souls under the veil of virtue, of patriotism, of philanthropy?

In witnessing the multitude of vices which the torrent of the revolution has rolled in turbid communion with its civic virtues, I confess that I have sometimes feared that I should be sullied in the eyes of posterity by the impure neighborhood of unprincipled men who had thrust themselves into association with the sincere friends of humanity, and I rejoice that these conspirators against my country have now, by their reckless rage, traced deep the line of demarkation between themselves and all true men.

Question history, and learn how all the defenders of liberty, in all times, have been overwhelmed by calumny. But their traducers died also. The good and the bad disappear alike from the earth, but in very different conditions.

O Frenchmen! O my countrymen! Let not your enemies, with their desolating doctrines, degrade your souls and enervate your virtues! No, Chaumette,* no! Death is *not* "an eternal sleep"! Citizens, efface from the tomb that motto graven by sacrilegious hands, which spreads over all nature a funeral crape, takes from oppressed innocence its support, and affronts the beneficent dispensation of death! Inscribe rather thereon these words: "Death is the commencement of immortality!" I leave to the oppressors of the people a terrible testament, which I proclaim with the independence befitting one whose career is so nearly ended; it is the awful truth,—" Thou shalt die!" †

MAXIMILIAN ROBESPIERRE, 1759–1794.

* Chaumette was a member of the Convention who was opposed to the public recognition, advocated by Robespierre, of God and a future state.

† The day after this speech—delivered July 28, 1794, and addressed to an assembly bent on his destruction—Robespierre was executed at the early age of thirty-five, under circumstances of accumulated horror. His fate is a warning to rulers who would cement even the best of governments with blood. Robespierre's character is still an enigma, some regarding him as an honest fanatic and others as a crafty demagogue.

148.—AGAINST SUBMISSION TO BRITISH RULE.

You may be told that your forts have been taken, your country ravaged, and that your armies have retreated; and that, therefore, God is not with you. It is true that some forts

have been taken, that our country is ravaged, and that our Maker is displeased with us; but it is also true that the King of heaven is not, like the king of Britain, implacable. If we turn from our sins, He will turn from his anger.

Let a general reformation of manners take place; let universal charity, public spirit and private virtue be inculcated, encouraged and prac-

JOHN JAY.

ticed; unite in preparing for a vigorous defense of your country, as if all depended on your own exertions; and when you have done all these things, then rely upon the good Providence of God for success, in the full confidence that without his blessing all our efforts will inevitably fail.

Cease, then, to desire the flesh-pots of Egypt, and remember her taskmasters and her oppression. No longer hesitate about rejecting all dependence on a king who would rule you with a rod of iron. Freedom is now in your power; value the heavenly gift. Remember that if you dare to neglect or despise it you offer an insult to the divine Bestower. Do not despair of keeping it.

After the armies of Rome had been repeatedly defeated by Hannibal, that imperial city was besieged by this brave and experienced general at the head of a numerous and victorious army. But so far were her glorious citizens from being dismayed by the loss of so many battles, and of all their country —so confident were they in their own virtue and the protection of Heaven—that the very land on which the Carthaginians were encamped was sold at public auction *for more than the usual price!* These heroic citizens disdained to receive the protection of the enemy, or to regard his proclamations. They invoked the protection of the supreme Being—they defended their city with undaunted courage—they repelled the enemy and recovered their country.

Blush, then, ye degenerate spirits who give over all for lost because your enemies have marched through three or four counties in this and a neighboring State—ye who basely fly to have the yoke of slavery fixed on your necks! Rouse, brave citizens! Do your duty like men. Consider that from the earliest ages of the world, religion, liberty and reason have been bending their course toward the setting sun. The holy gospels are yet to be preached in these western regions. Do not believe that the Almighty will suffer slavery and the gospel to go hand in hand. It cannot, it will not, be!

JOHN JAY, 1745–1829.

149.—VICTORY OR RUIN.

IT is the judgment of the American people that there shall be no compromise—that ruin to themselves or ruin to the nation's foes is the only alternative. It is only by resolutions of this kind that nations can rise above great dangers and overcome them in crises like this. It was only by turning France into a camp—resolved that Europe might exterminate but should not subjugate her—that France became the leading empire of Europe.

It is by such a resolve that the American people, coercing a reluctant government to draw the sword and stake the national existence on the integrity of the republic, are now anything but the fragments of a nation before the world, the scorn and hiss of every petty tyrant. It is because the people of the United States, rising to the height of the occasion, dedicated this generation to the sword—pouring out the blood of their children as of no account, and avowing before high Heaven that there should be no end to this conflict but absolute ruin or absolute triumph—that we now are what we are, that the banner of the republic, still pointing onward, floats proudly in the face of the enemy. It is only by this earnest and abiding resolution that the American people will survive in history. And this will save us. We shall succeed, and not fail.

For I have an abiding confidence in the firmness, the patience, the endurance, of the American people; and having vowed to stand in history on the great resolve to accept of nothing but victory or ruin, victory is ours. And if with such heroic resolve we fall, we fall with honor, and transmit the name of liberty, committed to our keeping, untarnished, to go down to future generations.

The historian of our decline and fall, contemplating the ruins of the last great republic and drawing from its fate lessons of wisdom on the waywardness of men, shall drop a tear as he records with sorrow the vain heroism of that people who dedicated and sacrificed themselves to the cause of freedom, and by their example will keep alive her worship in the hearts of men till happier generations shall learn to walk in her paths.

Yes, sir, if we must fall, let our last hours be stained by no weakness; if we must fall, let us stand amid the crash of the falling republic and be buried in its ruins, so that history may take note that men lived in the middle of the nineteenth century worthy of a better fate, but chastised by God for the sins of their forefathers. Let the ruins of the republic remain to testify to the latest generations our greatness and our heroism. And let Liberty, crownless and childless, sit upon these ruins, crying aloud in a sad wail to the nations of the world, " I nursed and brought up children, and they have rebelled against me."

HENRY WINTER DAVIS, 1817–1865.

SHAKSPEARE READING BEFORE QUEEN ELIZABETH.

150.—REGRETS OF DRUNKENNESS.

Iago. What! be you hurt, lieutenant?

Cassio. Past all surgery!

Iago. Marry, Heaven forbid!

Cassio. Reputation! reputation! reputation! Oh, I have lost my reputation! I have lost the immortal part of myself, and what remains is bestial. My reputation, Iago, my reputation!

Iago. As I am an honest man, I thought you had received some bodily wound; there is more offense in that than in reputation. Reputation is an idle and most false imposition, oft got without merit and lost without deserving. What, man! There are ways to recover the general again. Sue to him, and he is yours.

Cassio. I will rather sue to be despised than to deceive so good a commander with so light, so drunken and so indiscreet an officer. Drunk? and speak parrot? and squabble? swagger? swear? and discourse fustian with one's own shadow? O thou invisible spirit of wine! if thou hast no name to be known by, let us call thee Devil.

Iago. What was he that you followed with your sword? what had he done to you?

Cassio. I know not.

Iago. Is it possible?

Cassio. I remember a mass of things, but nothing distinctly— a quarrel, but nothing wherefore. Oh, that men should put an enemy in their mouths to steal away their brains! that we should with joy, pleasure, revel, and applause, transform ourselves into beasts!

Iago. Why, but you are now well enough; how came you thus recovered?

Cassio. It has pleased the devil Drunkenness to give place to the devil Wrath; one imperfection shows me another t make me frankly despise myself.

Iago. Come, you are too severe a moraler. As the time, the place and the condition of this country stands, I could heartily wish this had not befallen; but since it is as it is, mend it for your own good.

Cassio. I will ask him for my place again; he shall tell me I am a drunkard! Had I as many mouths as Hydra, such an answer would stop them all. To be now a sensible man, by and by a fool, and presently a beast! Oh, strange! Every inordinate cup is unblessed, and the ingredient is a devil.

Iago. Come, come! good wine is a good familiar creature, if it be well used; exclaim no more against it; and, good lieutenant, I think you think I love you.

Cassio. I have well approved it, sir. I drunk!

Iago. You or any man living may be drunk some time, man! I'll tell you what you shall do. Our general's *wife* is now the general; confess yourself freely to her; importune her; she'll help to put you in your place again. She is of so free, so kind, so apt, so blessed a disposition, she holds it a vice in her goodness not to do more than she is requested. This broken joint between you and her husband entreat her to splinter; and my fortunes against any lay worth naming, this crack of your love shall grow stronger than it was before.

Cassio. You advise me well.

Iago. I protest in the sincerity of love and honest kindness.

Cassio. I think it freely; and betimes in the morning I will beseech the virtuous Desdemona to undertake for me.

Iago. You are right. Good-night, lieutenant. I must to watch.

Cassio. Good-night, honest Iago.

WILLIAM SHAKSPEARE, 1564–1616.

151.—ON ENGLISH SLAVERY.

I TRUST that at length the time is come when Parliament will no longer bear to be told that slave-owners are the best law-givers on slavery—no longer suffer our voice to roll across the Atlantic in empty warnings and fruitless orders. Tell me not of rights; talk not of the property of the planter in his slaves. I deny his right; I acknowledge not the property. The principles, the feelings, of our common nature, rise in rebellion against it. Be the appeal made to the understanding or to the heart, the sentence that rejects it is the same!

In vain you tell me of laws that sanction such a claim. There is a law above all the enactments of human codes; the same throughout the world, the same in all times. Such as it was, before the daring genius of Columbus pierced the night of ages, and opened, to one world, the sources of power, wealth and knowledge, to another, all unutterable woes, such is it at this day: it is the law written by the finger of God on the heart of man; and by that law, unchangeable and eternal, while men despise fraud, and loathe rapine, and hate blood, they shall reject with indignation the wild and guilty fantasy, that man can hold property in man!

In vain you appeal to treaties—to covenants between nations. The covenants of the Almighty, whether the old covenant or the new, denounce such unholy pretensions. To these laws did they of old refer who maintained the African trade. Such treaties did they cite, and not untruly; for by one shameful compact you bartered the glories of Blenheim for the traffic in blood. Yet, in despite of law and of treaty, that infernal traffic is now destroyed, and its votaries put to death like other pirates.

How came this change to pass? Not assuredly by Parliament leading the way, but the country at length awoke; the indignation of the people was kindled; it descended in thunder, and smote the traffic, and scattered its guilty profits to the winds. Now, then, let the planters beware; let their assemblies beware; let the government at home beware; let the Parliament beware!

The same country is once more awake—awake to the condition of negro slavery; the same indignation kindles in the bosom of the same people; the same cloud is gathering that annihilated the slave-trade; and if it shall descend again, they on whom its crash may fall will not be destroyed before I have warned them; but I pray that *their* destruction may turn away from us the more terrible judgment of God!

LORD BROUGHAM, 1779–1868.

152.—THE ACT OF HABEAS CORPUS.

CURRAN.

IN the act of *habeas corpus* we have a solemn legislative declaration "that it is incompatible with liberty to send any subject out of the realm under pretense of any crime supposed or alleged to be committed in a foreign jurisdiction, except that crime be capital." Such were the bulwarks which our ancestors placed about the sacred temple of liberty, such the ramparts by which they sought to bar out the ever-toiling ocean of an arbitrary power, and thought (generous credulity!) that they *had* barred it out from their posterity for ever. Little did they foresee the future race of vermin that would work their way through those mounds and let back the inundation.

The Habeas Corpus Act declares the transmission of all persons to be illegal, except only persons charged with capital crimes. But to support the construction that takes in all possible offenses of all possible degrees, you have been told, and upon the grave authority of notable cases, that the enacting part of a statute may go beyond its preamble. Can you, my lords, bring your minds easily to believe that such a tissue of despotism and folly could have been the sober and deliberate intention of the legislature?

I am not ignorant that this extraordinary construction has received the sanction of another court, nor of the surprise and dismay with which it smote upon the general heart of the bar. I am aware that I may have the mortification of being told in another country of that unhappy decision, and I foresee in what confusion I shall hang down my head when I am told it.

But I cherish, too, the consolatory hope that I shall be able to tell them that I had an old and learnëd friend whom I would put above all the sweepings of their hall, who was of a different opinion; who had derived his ideas of civil liberty from the purest fountains of Athens and of Rome; who had fed the youthful vigor of his studious mind with the theoretic knowledge of their wisest philosophers and statesmen; and who had refined that theory into the quick and exquisite sensibility of moral instinct by contemplating the practice of their most illustrious examples; by dwelling on the sweet-souled piety of Cimon, on the anticipated Christianity of Socrates, on the gallant and pathetic patriotism of Epaminondas, on that pure austerity of Fabricius, whom to move from his integrity would have been more difficult than to have pushed the sun from his course.

I would add that if he had seemed to hesitate, it was but for a moment—that his hesitation was like the passing cloud that floats across the morning sun and hides it from view, and does so for a moment hide it by involving the spectator without even approaching the face of the luminary. And this soothing hope I draw from the dearest and tenderest recollections of my life; from the remembrance of those Attic nights and those refections of the gods which we have partaken with those admired and respected and beloved companions who have gone before us—over whose ashes the most precious tears of Ireland have been shed.*

Yes, my good lord, I see you do not forget them; I see their sacred forms passing in sad review before your memory; I see your pained and softened fancy recalling those happy meetings, where the innocent enjoyment of social mirth became expanded into the nobler warmth of social virtue, and the horizon of the board became enlarged into the horizon of man; where the swelling heart conceived and communicated the pure and generous purpose; where my slenderer and younger taper imbibed its borrowed light from the more matured and redundant fountain of yours. Yes, my lord, we can remember those nights without any other regret than that they can nevermore return; for

> "We spent them not in toys, or lust, or wine;
> But search of deep philosophy,
> Wit, eloquence and poesy—
> Arts which I loved, for they, my friend, were thine."

John Philpot Curran, 1750–1817.

* Here, according to the original report, Lord Avonmore (who sat upon the bench, and who was "the old and learned friend" to whom Curran was alluding) could not refrain from tears. In the midst of Curran's legal argument, "this most beautiful episode," says Charles Phillips "bloomed like a green spot amid the desert. Mr. Curran told me himself that when the court rose, the tipstaff informed him he was wanted immediately in chamber by one of the judges of the Exchequer. He, of course, obeyed the judicial mandate; and the moment he entered, poor Lord Avonmore, whose cheeks were still wet with the tears extorted by this heart-touching appeal, clasped him to his bosom." A coolness caused by political differences which had for some time existed between them gave place to a renewal of friendship, which was not again interrupted. Curran was wont to say that he inherited from his father a homely face and small figure, while from his mother he inherited his intellect. Curran excelled in pathos, as the extract we have quoted shows.

153.—THE VILLAGE PREACHER.

NEAR yonder copse, where once the garden smiled,
And still where many a garden flower grows wild,
There, where a few torn shrubs the place disclose,
The village preacher's modest mansion rose.
A man he was to all the country dear,
And passing rich with forty pounds a year.

26

Remote from towns he ran his godly race,
Nor e'er had changed, nor wished to change, his place;
Unskillful he to fawn or seek for power
By doctrines fashioned to the varying hour!
Far other aims his heart had learned to prize,
More bent to raise the wretched than to rise.
His house was known to all the vagrant train;
He chid their wanderings, but relieved their pain.
The long remembered beggar was his guest,
Whose beard descending swept his agéd breast;
The ruined spendthrift, now no longer proud,
Claimed kindred there, and had his claims allowed;
The broken soldier, kindly bade to stay,
Sat by his fire, and talked the night away;
Wept o'er his wounds, or, tales of sorrow done,
Shouldered his crutch, and showed how fields were won.
Pleased with his guests, the good man learned to glow,
And quite forgot their vices in their woe;
Careless their merits or their faults to scan,
His pity gave ere charity began.

Thus to relieve the wretched was his pride,
And even his failings leaned to virtue's side;
But in his duty prompt in every call,
He watched and wept, he prayed and felt for all.
And as a bird each fond endearment tries,
To tempt her new-fledged offspring to the skies,
He tried each art, reproved each dull delay,
Allured to brighter worlds, and led the way.

Beside the bed where parting life was laid,
And sorrow, guilt and pain by turns dismayed,
The reverend champion stood. At his control
Despair and anguish fled the struggling soul!
Comfort came down the trembling wretch to raise,
And his last faltering accents whispered praise.

At church, with meek and unaffected grace,
His looks adorned the venerable place;
Truth from his lips prevailed with double sway,
And fools, who came to scoff, remained to pray.
The service past, around the pious man,
With steady zeal, each honest rustic ran;
Even children followed with endearing wile,
And plucked his gown, to share the good man's smile.
His ready smile a parent's warmth expressed,
Their welfare pleased him, and their cares distressed;
To them his heart, his love, his griefs, were given,
But all his serious thoughts had rest in heaven.
As some tall cliff that lifts its awful form,
Swells from the vale, and midway leaves the storm,
Though round its breast the rolling clouds are spread,
Eternal sunshine settles on its head.

OLIVER GOLDSMITH (see p. 283).

———◦◇◦———

154.—TAXES THE PRICE OF GLORY.

JOHN BULL can inform Jonathan what are the inevitable consequences of being too fond of glory—taxes. Taxes upon every article which enters into the mouth, or covers the back, or is placed under the foot; taxes upon everything which it is pleasant to see, hear, feel, smell or taste; taxes upon warmth, light and locomotion; taxes on everything on earth and the waters under the earth; on everything that comes from abroad or is grown at home; taxes on the raw material; taxes on every fresh value that is added to it by the industry of man; taxes on the sauce which pampers man's appetite, and the drug that restores him to health; on the ermine which decorates the judge and the rope that hangs the criminal; on the poor man's salt and the rich man's spice; on the brass nails of the coffin and the ribbons of the bride;—at bed or board, couchant or levant, we must pay.

The schoolboy whips his taxed top; the beardless youth

manages his taxed horse with a taxed bridle on a taxed road; and the dying Englishman, pouring his medicine, which has paid seven per cent., into a spoon that has paid fifteen per cent., flings himself back upon his chintz bed, which has paid twenty-two per cent., makes his will on an eight-pound stamp, and expires in the arms of an apothecary, who has paid a license of a hundred pounds for the privilege of putting him to death. His whole property is then immediately taxed from two to ten per cent. Besides the probate, large fees are demanded for burying him in the chancel; his virtues are handed down to posterity on taxed marble; and he is then gathered to his fathers—to be taxed no more.

In addition to all this, the habit of dealing with large sums will make the government avaricious and profuse; and the system itself will infallibly generate the base vermin of spies and informers, and a still more pestilential race of political tools and retainers of the meanest and most odious description; while the prodigious patronage which the collecting of this splendid revenue will throw into the hands of government will invest it with so vast an influence, and hold out such means and temptations to corruption, as all the virtue and public spirit, even of republicans, will be unable to resist. Every wise Jonathan should remember this.

SYDNEY SMITH, 1768–1845.

155.—INVOCATION.

ANSWER me, burning stars of night! where is the spirit gone
That past the reach of human sight as a swift breeze hath flown?
And the stars answered me, "We roll in light and power on high;
But of the never-dying soul, ask that which cannot die."

O many-toned and chainless wind! thou art a wanderer free!
Tell me if *thou* its place canst find, far over mount and sea?
And the wind murmured in reply, "The blue deep I have crossed,
And met its barks and billows high, but not what thou hast lost."

Ye clouds that gorgeously repose around the setting sun,
Answer! have ye a home for those whose earthly race is run?

The bright clouds answered, "We depart, we vanish from the sky;
Ask what is deathless in thy heart, for that which cannot die."

Speak, then, thou voice of God within, thou of the deep, low tone!
Answer me through life's restless din, where is the spirit flown?
And the voice answered, " Be thou still ! Enough to know is given;
Clouds, winds and stars, *their* part fulfill, *thine* is to trust in Heaven."

FELICIA HEMANS.

THE HOUSE OF COMMONS IN 1781.

156.—THE AMERICAN WAR DENOUNCED, 1781.

GENTLEMEN have passed the highest eulogiums on the
American war. Its justice has been defended in the most
fervent manner. A noble lord in the heat of his zeal has
called it a holy war. For my part, although the honorable
gentleman who made this motion, and some other gentlemen,
have been more than once in the course of the debate severely
reprehended for calling it a wicked and accursèd war, I am
persuaded and would affirm that it was a most accursèd,

26 *

wicked, barbarous, cruel, unnatural, unjust and diabolical war!

It was conceived in injustice; it was nurtured and brought forth in folly; its footsteps were marked with blood, slaughter, persecution and devastation—in truth, everything which went to constitute moral depravity and human turpitude was to be found in it. It was pregnant with misery of every kind.

The mischief, however, recoiled on the unhappy people of this country, who were made the instruments by which the wicked purposes of the authors of the war were effected. The nation was drained of its best blood, and of its vital resources of men and money. The expense of the war was enormous—much beyond any former experience.

And yet what has the British nation received in return? Nothing but a series of ineffective victories or severe defeats—victories celebrated only by a temporary triumph over our brethren, whom we would trample down and destroy; victories which filled the land with mourning for the loss of dear and valued relatives slain in the impious cause of enforcing unconditional submission, or victories attended with narratives of the glorious exertions of men struggling in the holy cause of liberty, though struggling in the absence of all the facilities and advantages which are in general deemed the necessary concomitants of victory and success.

Where was the Englishman who, on reading the narrative of those bloody and well-fought contests, could refrain from lamenting the loss of so much British blood spilt in such a cause, or from weeping, on whatever side victory might be declared?

WILLIAM PITT, 1759–1806.*

---

* Second son of Lord Chatham, he became a member of the House of Commons in 1781, when in his twenty-second year. Burke said of him, " He is not merely a chip of the old block, but he is the old block itself." At the age of twenty-four Pitt became prime minister of England and virtual leader of the House of Commons. The subjoined remarks were made in reference to a resolution declaring that immediate measures ought to be taken for concluding peace with the American Colonies.

157.—ON ADMINISTRATIVE REFORM, 1855.

I COME now to a third objection to Administrative Reform— an objection common among young gentlemen who are not particularly fit for anything but spending money which they have not got. It is usually comprised in the observation, " How very extraordinary it is that these Administrative Reform fellows can't mind their own business !"

I think it will occur to all that a very sufficient mode of disposing of this objection is to say that *it is our own business we mind* when we come forward in this way, and it is to prevent it from being mismanaged by *them.*

There is an old story and a true one, which has a pointed moral at the end of it. Ages ago a barbarous mode of keeping accounts on notched sticks was introduced into the Court of Exchequer, and the accounts were kept much as Robinson Crusoe kept his calendar on the desert island. In the course of considerable revolutions of time, the celebrated Cocker* was born and died; Walkingame, of "The Tutor's Assistant," and well versed in figures, was also born and died; a multitude of accountants, bookkeepers and actuaries were born and died. Still official routine inclined to these notched sticks, as if they were pillars of the constitution, and still the Exchequer accounts continued to be kept on certain splints of elm wood called "tallies."

In the reign of George III. an inquiry was made by some revolutionary spirit, whether, pens, ink and paper, slates and pencils, being in existence, this obstinate adherence to an obsolete custom ought to be continued, and whether a change ought not to be effected.

All the red tape in the country grew redder at the bare mention of this bold and original conception, and it took till 1826 to get these sticks abolished. In 1834 it was found that there was a considerable accumulation of them, and the question then was, What was to be done with such worn-out, worm-eaten, rotten old bits of wood ? I dare say there was a

---

* Author of Cocker's Arithmetic.

vast amount of memoranduming and despatch-boxing on this mighty subject. The sticks were housed at Westminster, and it would naturally occur to any intelligent person that nothing could be easier than to allow them to be carried away for firewood by the miserable people who live in the neighborhood.

However, the sticks never *had* been useful, and official routine required that they never *should* be; and so the order went forth that they were to be privately and confidentially burned. It came to pass that they *were* burned in a stove in the House of Lords. The stove, over-gorged with these preposterous sticks, set fire to the paneling; the paneling set fire to the House of Lords; the House of Lords set fire to the House of Commons; the two houses were reduced to ashes. Architects were called in to build others; we are now in the second million of the cost thereof. The national pig is not nearly over the stile yet; and the little old woman, Britannia, hasn't yet got home.

Said the noble lord at the head of the government when Mr. Layard asked him for a day for his motion, "Let the honorable gentleman find a day for himself."

> "Now, in the name of all the gods at once,
> Upon what meat doth this our Cæsar feed,
> That he is grown so great?"

If our Cæsar will excuse me, I would take the liberty of reversing that cool and lofty sentiment, and I would say, "First lord, your duty is to see that no man is left to find a day for himself. See you, who take the responsibility of government, who aspire to it, live for it, intrigue for it, scramble for it, who hold to it tooth and nail when you can get it, see that no man is left to find a day for himself. Woe the day when the dangerous man shall have a day for himself, because the head of the government failed in his duty in not anticipating it by a brighter and a better one!"

Name you the day, first lord; make a day; work for a day beyond your little time, Lord Palmerston, and history in return may then—not otherwise—find a day for you.

CHARLES DICKENS (see p. 250.)

158.—ON BURGOYNE'S SURRENDER, 1777.

To what, my lords, shall we attribute these disasters to our arms? To what but want of wisdom in our council, want of ability in our ministers? You have ransacked every corner of Lower Saxony for mercenaries; but forty thousand Hessian boors can never conquer ten times the number of American freemen. You have searched the darkest wilds of America for the scalping-knife; but all your attempts to draw strength from the inhuman alliance have proved as

LORD CHATHAM.

abortive as they are wicked. You may ravage—you cannot conquer—it is impossible—you cannot conquer—the Americans. You talk of your numerous friends among them, who will annihilate the Congress, and of your powerful forces who will disperse their army; I might as well talk of driving them before me with this crutch.

That America is lost to us, even the accounts published by administration seem to admit. General Washington has proved himself three times an abler general than Sir William Howe; for with a force much inferior in number, and infinitely inferior in every other respect, as asserted from an authority not to be questioned, he has been able to baffle every attempt of ours, and left us in such a situation that, if not assisted by our fleet, our troops in the neighborhood of Philadelphia must probably share the same unhappy fate with those under General Burgoyne.

Do we ever consider what we owe to America? Since our last war, what has occasioned the rise in the value of English estates? America—that colony which, I now fear, we have for ever lost. She has been the great support of this country; has multiplied our resources; has supplied us with soldiers and sailors; has given our manufacturers employment, and opened new markets to our merchants.

And for what have we sacrificed all these advantages? The pursuit of a peppercorn!* And how have we treated America? Let her petitions rejected, her complaints unanswered, her dutiful representations treated with contempt, be the reply. Let our endeavors to establish despotism on the ruins of constitutional liberty, our measures to enforce taxation at the point of the sword, show what we have done! Ministers have betrayed us into disastrous war, and what are the fruits? Let the catastrophe that has overwhelmed Burgoyne proclaim!

The men you called cowards, poltroons, runaways and knaves are become victorious over your veteran troops! And in the midst of victory, and in the flush of conquest, these men have set ministers an example of moderation and magnanimity. Yes, my lords, to the very troops sent out to execute the diabolical orders for the employment of savages, the Americans have granted terms of capitulation due only to the makers of fair and honorable war. Such is American progress in civilization. And let me tell you the day is not far distant when America will vie with these kingdoms, not only in arms, but in arts.

Oh, but if America is not to be conquered, she is to be treated with! Conciliation is at length thought of! Terms are to be offered! And who are the persons that are to treat on the part of England? Why, the very men who have been the authors of our misfortunes! The very men who have en-

---

* Mr. Nugent had said that a peppercorn in acknowledgment of the right to tax America was of more value than millions without it.

deavored, by the most pernicious policy, to enslave the American people! *They* would be the mediators to conciliate those who have survived the Indian tomahawk and the Hessian bayonet! Can your lordships entertain the most distant prospect of success from the efforts of negotiators like these? No! The Americans have virtue, and must detest the principles of such men.

LORD CHATHAM (see p. 49).

159.—THE SOUL OF ELOQUENCE.

How shall we learn to sway the minds of men
By eloquence? to rule them, to persuade?
Do you seek genuine and worthy fame?
Reason and honest feeling want no arts
Of utterance, ask no toil of elocution!

And when you speak in earnest, do you need
A search for words? Oh, these fine holiday phrases,
In which you robe your worn-out commonplaces,
These scraps of paper which you crimp and curl
And twist into a thousand idle shapes,
These filigree ornaments, are good for nothing!
Cost time and pains, please few, impose on no one;
Are unrefreshing as the wind that whistles
In autumn 'mong the dry and wrinkled leaves.

If feeling does not prompt, in vain you strive.
If from the soul the language does not come,
By its own impulse, to impel the hearts
Of hearers with communicated power,
In vain you strive, in vain you study earnestly,
Toil on for ever, piece together fragments,
Cook up your broken scraps of sentences,
And blow, with puffing breath, a struggling light,
Glimmering confusedly now, now cold in ashes—
Startle the schoolboys with your metaphors—

And, if such food may suit your appetite,
Win the vain wonder of applauding children !

But never hope to stir the hearts of *men*,
And mould the souls of many into one,
By words which come not native from the heart.
                        GOETHE (*translated by John Anster*).

160.—A REPUBLIC OR A MONARCHY ?

On the question of revising the French Constitution, 1851.

GENTLEMEN, let us come at the pith of this debate. It is not our side of the House, but you, the monarchists, who have provoked it. The question, a republic or a monarchy, is before us. No one has any longer the power or the right to elude it. For more than two years this question, secretly and audaciously agitated, has harassed the country. It weighs upon the Present. It clouds the Future. The moment has come for our deliverance from it. Yes, the moment has come for us to regard it face to face—to see what it is made of. Now, then, let us show our cards! No more concealment !

VICTOR HUGO.

I affirm, then, in the name of the eternal laws of human morality, that monarchy is an historical fact and nothing more.

Now, when the fact is extinct, nothing survives, and all is told. It is otherwise with *right*. Right, even when it no longer has *fact* to sustain it, even when it no longer exerts a material authority, preserves still its moral authority, and is always right. Hence is it that in an overthrown republic there remains a right, while in a fallen monarchy there remains only a ruin.

Cease, then, ye legitimists, to appeal to us from a position of right! Before the right of the people, which is sovereignty, there is no other right but the right of the individual, which is liberty. Beyond that all is a chimera. To talk of the kingly right in this great age of ours, and at this great tribune, is to pronounce a word void of meaning.

But if you cannot speak in the name of right, will you speak in the name of fact? Will you say that political stability is the offspring of hereditary royalty, and that royalty is better than democracy for a state? What! You would have those scenes renewed, those experiences recommenced, which overwhelmed kings and princes—the feeble, like Louis the Sixteenth; the able and strong, like Louis Philippe; whole families of royal lineage, high-born women, saintly widows, innocent children! And of those lamentable experiences you have not had enough? You would have yet more?

But you are without pity, royalists, or without memory! We ask your mercy on these unfortunate royal families. Good Heavens! These streets which you traverse daily on your way to this House—they, then, teach you nothing—when, if you but stamped on the pavement two paces from those deadly Tuileries, which you covet still—but stamped on that fatal pavement—you could conjure up at will the scaffold from which the old monarchy was plunged into the tomb, or the cab in which the new royalty escaped into exile.

Ah, men of ancient parties! you will learn ere long that at this present time—in this nineteenth century—after the scaffold of Louis the Sixteenth, after the downfall of Napoleon, after the exile of Charles the Tenth, after the flight of Louis Philippe, after the French Revolution in a word—that is to

27

say, after this renewal, complete, absolute, prodigious, of prin-
ciples, convictions, opinions, situations, influences and facts—it
is the republic which is solid ground, and the monarchy which
is the perilous quicksand.

VICTOR HUGÒ (*original translation from the French*).

161.—REPLY TO MR. FLOOD, 1783.

IT is not the slander of an evil tongue that can defame me.
I maintain my reputation in public and in private life. No
man who has not a bad character can ever say that I deceived.

GRATTAN.

No country can call me
a cheat. But I will
suppose such a public
character. I will sup-
pose such a man to have
existence. I will begin
with his character in his
political cradle, and I
will follow him to the
last stage of political
dissolution.

I will suppose him, in
the first stage of his
life, to have been intemperate; in the second, to have been
corrupt; and in the last, seditious; that after an envenomed
attack on the persons and measures of a succession of vice-
roys, and after much declamation against their illegalities and
their profusion, he took office and became a supporter of gov-
ernment, when the profusion of ministers had greatly increased
and their crimes multiplied beyond example.

With regard to the liberties of America, which were insep-
arable from ours, I will suppose this gentleman to have been
an enemy decided and unreserved; that he voted against her
liberty, and voted, moreover, for an address to send four
thousand Irish troops to cut the throats of the Americans; that

he called these butchers "armed negotiators," and stood with a metaphor in his mouth and a bribe in his pocket, a champion against the rights of America—of America, the only hope of Ireland and the only refuge of the liberties of mankind.

Thus defective in every relationship, whether to constitution, commerce, or toleration, I will suppose this man to have added much private improbity to public crimes; that his probity was like his patriotism, and his honor on a level with his oath. He loves to deliver panegyrics on himself. I will interrupt him, and say:

Sir, you are much mistaken if you think that your talents have been as great as your life has been reprehensible. You began your parliamentary career with an acrimony and personality which could have been justified only by a supposition of virtue; after a rank and clamorous opposition you became, on a sudden, *silent;* you were silent for seven years; you were silent on the greatest questions, and you were silent—for money!

You supported the unparalleled profusion and jobbing of Lord Harcourt's scandalous ministry. You, sir, who manufacture stage-thunder against Mr. Eden for his anti-American principles, you, sir, whom it pleases to chant a hymn to the immortal Hampden, you, sir, approved of the tyranny exercised against America, and you, sir, voted four thousand Irish troops to cut the throats of the Americans fighting for their freedom, fighting for your freedom, fighting for the great principle, *liberty!*

But you found at last that the court had bought but would not trust you. Mortified at the discovery, you try the sorry game of a trimmer in your progress to the acts of an incendiary; and observing with regard to prince and people the most impartial treachery and desertion, you justify the suspicion of your sovereign by betraying the government, as you had sold the people. Such has been your conduct, and at such conduct every order of your fellow-subjects have a right to exclaim! The merchant may say to you, the constitutionalist may say to you, the American may say to you, and I,

I now say, and say it to your beard, Sir, you are not an honest man ! *

HENRY GRATTAN, 1746–1820.

162.—INAUGURAL ADDRESS.

Delivered before the Senate, March 4, 1801.

JEFFERSON.

LET us reflect, fellow-citizens, that, having banished from our land that religious intolerance under which mankind so long bled and suffered, we have yet gained little, if we countenance a political intolerance as despotic, as wicked and as capable of as bitter and bloody persecutions. During the throes and convulsions of the ancient world—during the agonizing spasms of infuriated man, seeking, through blood and slaughter, his long-lost liberty—it is not wonderful that the agitation of the billows should reach even this distant and peaceful shore, that this should be more felt and feared by

---

* At the time of this speech in the Irish Parliament, Flood and Grattan, although previously friends, stood before the British public as rival leaders. A bitter animosity had risen between them, and Grattan having unfortunately led the way in personality by speaking of his opponent's "affectation of infirmity," Flood replied with great asperity, denouncing Grattan as "a mendicant patriot," who, "bought by his country for a sum of money, then sold his country for prompt payment." He also sneered at Grattan's "aping the style of Lord Chatham." To these taunts Grattan replied in a speech, an abridgment of which we here give. An arrangement for a hostile meeting between the parties was the consequence of this speech; but Flood was arrested, and the crime of a duel was not added to the offense of vindictive personality, of which both had been guilty. Grattan lived to regret his harshness and speak in generous terms of his rival.

some and less by others, and should divide opinions as to measures of safety; but every difference of opinion is not a difference of principle. We are all republicans; we are all federalists.

If there be any among us who would wish to dissolve this Union or to change its republican form, let them stand undisturbed, as monuments of the safety with which error of opinion may be tolerated, where reason is left free to combat it. I know, indeed, that some honest men fear that a republican government cannot be strong; but would the honest patriot, in the full tide of successful experiment, abandon a government which has so far kept us free and firm, on the theoretic and visionary fear that this government, the world's best hope, may by possibility want energy to preserve itself? I trust not.

I believe this, on the contrary, the strongest government on earth. I believe it the only one where every man, at the call of the law, would fly to the standard of the law, and would meet invasions of the public order as his own personal concern. Sometimes it is said that man cannot be trusted with the government of himself. Can he, then, be trusted with the government of others? Or have we found angels in the form of kings to govern him? Let history answer this question.

Let us, then, with courage and confidence pursue our own federal and republican principles. These principles form the bright constellation which has gone before us and guided our steps through an age of revolution and reformation. The wisdom of our sages, the blood of our heroes, has been devoted to their attainment; they should be the creed of our political faith, the text of civic instruction, the touchstone by which to try the services of those we trust; and should we wander from them in moments of error or of alarm, let us hasten to retrace our steps and to regain the road which alone leads to peace, liberty and safety.

THOMAS JEFFERSON, 1743–1826.

27 *

163.—THE BELLS OF SHANDON.

Sabbata pango,
Funera plango,
Solemnia clango.

INSCRIPTION ON AN OLD BELL

WITH deep affection
And recollection
I often think of
  Those Shandon bells,
Whose sounds so wild would,
In the days of childhood,
Fling round my cradle
  Their magic spells.

On this I ponder
Where'er I wander,
And thus grow fonder,
  Sweet Cork, of thee,
With thy bells of Shandon,
That sound so grand on
The pleasant waters
  Of the river Lee.

I've heard bells chiming
Full many a clime in,
Tolling sublime in
  Cathedral shrine;
While at a glib rate
Brass tongues would vibrate;
But all their music
  Spoke naught like thine.

For memory, dwelling
On each proud swelling
Of thy belfry knelling
  Its bold notes free,
Made the bells of Shandon
Sound far more grand on
The pleasant waters
  Of the river Lee.

I've heard bells tolling
Old Adrian's Mole in,
Their thunder rolling
  From the Vatican;
And cymbals glorious
Swinging uproarious
In the gorgeous turrets
  Of Notre Dame.

But thy sounds were sweeter
Than the dome of Peter
Flings o'er the Tiber,
  Pealing solemnly.
Oh! the bells of Shandon
Sound far more grand on
The pleasant waters
  Of the river Lee.

There's a bell in Moscow;
While on tower and kiosk O
In Saint Sophia
  The Turkman gets,
And loud in air
Calls men to prayer,
From the tapering summit
  Of tall minarets.

Such empty phantom
I freely grant them;
But there's an anthem
  More dear to me;
'Tis the bells of Shandon,
That sound so grand on
The pleasant waters
  Of the river Lee.

FRANCIS MAHONY (*Father Prout*).

164.—THE NATURE OF JUSTICE.

From the speech on the trial of Warren Hastings, June 6, 1788.

SHERIDAN.

LET me call the attention of the court to the magnificent paragraph in which Mr. Hastings concludes his communication. It will give you some idea of this man's notions of justice. "I hope," says Mr. Hastings, "it will not be a departure from official language to say that the *majesty of justice ought not to be approached without solicitation.* She ought not to descend to inflame or provoke, but withhold her judgment until called on to determine."

Justice ought not to be approached without solicitation! Justice ought not to descend! But, my lords, do you, the judges of this land and the expounders of its rightful laws—do you approve of this mockery and call it justice? No! *justice* is not this halt and miserable object; it is not the ineffective bauble of an Indian pagod; it is not the portentous phantom of despair; it is not like any fabled monster, formed in the eclipse of reason and found in some unhallowed grove of superstitious darkness and political dismay! No, my lords.

In the happy reverse of all these, I turn from this disgusting caricature to the real image! *Justice* I have now before me, *august* and *pure*—the abstract idea of all that would be perfect in the spirits and the aspirings of men; where the mind rises, where the heart expands; where the countenance is ever placid and benign; where her favorite attitude is to stoop to the unfortunate, to hear their cry and to help them; to rescue and relieve, to succor and save; majestic from its mercy, venerable from its utility; uplifted without pride, firm without obduracy; beneficent in each preference, lovely though in her frown!

On that justice I rely, deliberate and sure, abstracted from all party purpose and political speculation, not in words, but

in facts.   You, my lords, who hear me, I conjure, by those
rights it is your best privilege to preserve ; by that fame it is
your best pleasure to inherit ; by all those feelings which refer
to the first term in the series of existence, the *original compact*
of our nature, our controlling rank in the creation,—to vindi-
cate that justice.   This is the call on all, to administer to truth
and equity, as they would satisfy the laws, as they would sat-
isfy themselves with the most exalted bliss possible or conceiv-
able for our nature—the self-approving consciousness of virtue,
when the condemnation we look for will be one of the most
ample mercies accomplished for mankind since the creation
of the world!   My lords, I have done.

RICHARD BRINSLEY SHERIDAN, 1751–1816.

165.—SIR LUCIUS AND BOB ACRES.*

Acres. By my valor, then, Sir Lucius, forty yards is a good
distance.   Odds levels and aims! I say it is a good distance.

Sir Lucius. Is it for muskets or small field-pieces?   Upon
my conscience, Mr. Acres, you must leave those things to me.
Stay, now—I'll show you.   (*Measures paces along the floor.*)
There, now! that is a very pretty distance—a pretty gentle-
man's distance.

Acr. Zounds! we might as well fight in a sentry-box.   I
tell you, Sir Lucius, the farther he is off, the cooler I shall take
my aim.

Sir L. Faith! then I suppose you would aim at him best
of all if he was out of sight?

Acr. No, Sir Lucius; but I should think forty or eight and
thirty yards—

Sir L. Pooh, pooh, nonsense!   Three or four feet between
the mouths of your pistols is as good as a mile.

Acr. Odds bullets, no! by my valor! there is no merit in
killing him so near!   Do, my dear Sir Lucius, let me bring

* Sir Lucius O'Trigger, an Irish gentleman, after having encouraged
Acres to send a challenge for a fancied affront, consents to act as his
second. The two appear on the field, Sir Lucius carrying a pistol and
followed by Acres.

him down at a long shot—a long shot, Sir Lucius, if you love me!

Sir L. Well, the gentleman's friend and I must settle that. But tell me now, Mr. Acres, in case of an accident, is there any little will or commission I could execute for you?

Acr. I am much obliged to you, Sir Lucius, but I don't understand—

Sir L. Why, you may think, there's no being shot at without a little risk; and if an unlucky bullet should carry a quie'tus with it, I say it will be no time then to be bothering you about family matters.

Acr. A quietus!

Sir L. For instance, now, if that should be the case, would you choose to be pickled and sent home? or would it be the same to you to lie here in the Abbey? I'm told there is very snug lying in the Abbey.

Acr. Pickled! Snug lying in the Abbey! Odds tremors! Sir Lucius, don't talk so!

Sir L. I suppose, Mr. Acres, you never were engaged in an affair of this kind before?

Acr. No, Sir Lucius, never before.

Sir L. Ah! that's a pity! There's nothing like being used to a thing. Pray, now, how would you receive the gentleman's shot?

Acr. Odds files! I've practiced that. There, Sir Lucius—there! (*Puts himself in an attitude.*) A side front, hey? I'll make myself small enough; I'll stand edgeways.

Sir L. Now, you're quite out; for if you stand so when I take my aim— (*Leveling the pistol at him.*)

Acr. Zounds! Sir Lucius, are you sure it is not cocked?

Sir L. Never fear.

Acr. But—but—you don't know—it may go off of its own head!

Sir L. Pooh! be easy. Well, now, if I hit you in the body, my bullet has a double chance; for if it misses a vital part of your right side, 'twill be very hard if it don't succeed on the left.

v

Acr. A vital part!

Sir L. But there! fix yourself so. (*Placing him.*) Let him see the broadside of your full front; there, now, a ball or two may pass clean thro' your body, and never do any harm at all.

Acr. Can go through me—a ball or two clean through me!

Sir L. Ay, may they; and it is much the genteelest attitude in the bargain.

Acr. Look'ee, Sir Lucius! I'd just as lieve be shot in an awkward posture as a genteel one; so, by my valor! I will stand edgeways.

Sir L. (*Looking at his watch.*) Sure, they don't mean to disappoint us. Ha! no, I think I see them coming.

Acr. Hey? what? coming?

Sir L. Ay. Who are those yonder, getting over the stile?

Acr. There are two of them, indeed! Well, let them come —hey, Sir Lucius! we—we—we—we—won't run!

Sir L. Run!

Acr. No—I say—we won't run, by my valor!

Sir L. What's the matter with you?

Acr. Nothing—nothing—my dear friend—my dear Sir Lucius! but I—I—I don't feel quite so bold, somehow, as I did.

Sir L. Oh, fy! Consider your honor.

Acr. Ay—true—my honor. Do, Sir Lucius, edge in a word or two every now and then about my honor.

Sir L. Well, here they're coming.

Acr. Sir Lucius, if I wasn't with you, I should almost think I was afraid! If my valor should leave me! Valor will come and go.

Sir L. Then pray keep it fast while you have it.

Acr. Sir Lucius, I doubt it is going!—yes—my valor is certainly going!—it is sneaking off! I feel it oozing out as it were at the palms of my hands!

Sir L. Your honor! your honor! Here they are.

Acr. Oh, mercy!—now—that I was safe at Clod Hall! or could be shot before I was aware! (*Sir Lucius takes Acres by the arm and leads him reluctantly off.*)

RICHARD BRINSLEY SHERIDAN (see p. 319.)

166.—AN EXTENDED REPUBLIC.

HEARKEN not to the unnatural voice which tells you that the people of America, knit together as they are by so many cords of affection, can no longer live together as members of the same family; can no longer continue the mutual guardians of their mutual happiness; can no longer be fellow-citizens of one great, respectable and flourishing empire. Hearken not to the voice which petulantly tells you that the form of government recommended for your adoption is a novelty in the  political world; that it has never yet had a place in the theories of the wildest projectors; that it rashly attempts what it is impossible to accomplish.

MADISON.

No, my countrymen, shut your ears against this unhallowed language. Shut your hearts against the poison which it conveys. The kindred blood which flows in the veins of American citizens, the mingled blood which they have shed in defense of their sacred rights, consecrate their union, and excite horror at the idea of their becoming aliens, rivals, enemies. And if novelties are to be shunned, believe me, the most alarming of all novelties, the most wild of all projects, the most rash of all attempts, is that of rending us in pieces in order to preserve our liberties and promote our happiness.

But why is the experiment of an extended republic to be rejected merely because it may comprise what is new? Is it not the glory of the people of America that, whilst they have paid a decent regard to the opinions of former times and other nations, they have not suffered a blind veneration for antiquity, for custom or for names to overrule the suggestions of their own good sense, the knowledge of their own situation, and the lessons of their own experience? To this manly spirit posterity will be indebted for the possession, and the world for the example, of the numerous innovations displayed on the American theatre in favor of private rights and public happiness.

Had no important step been taken by the leaders of the Revolution for which a precedent could not be discovered—no government established of which an exact model did not present itself—the people of the United States might, at this moment, have been numbered among the melancholy victims of misguided councils—must, at best, have been laboring under the weight of some of those forms which have crushed the liberties of the rest of mankind. Happily for America—happily, we trust, for the whole human race—they pursued a new and a nobler course.

They accomplished a revolution which has no parallel in the annals of human society. They reared the fabrics of governments which have no model on the face of the globe. They formed the design of a great confederacy which it is incumbent on their successors to improve and perpetuate. If their works betray imperfections, we wonder at the fewness of them. If they erred most in the structure of the Union, this was the work most difficult to be executed; this is the work which has been new-modeled by the act of your convention, and it is that act on which you are now to deliberate and to decide.

JAMES MADISON, 1751–1836.

167.—ROCKS OF MY COUNTRY.

ROCKS of my country! let the cloud your crested heights array;
And rise ye, like a fortress proud, above the surge and spray!
My spirit greets you as ye stand breasting the billows' foam:
Oh, thus for ever guard the land, the sacred land of home!

I have left rich blue skies behind, lighting up classic shrines,
And music in the southern wind and sunshine on the vines;
The breathings of the myrtle-flowers have floated o'er my way;
The pilgrim's voice at vesper-hours hath soothed me with its lay:

The isles of Greece, the hills of Spain, the purple heavens of Rome,
Yes, all are glorious, yet again I bless thee, land of home!
For thine the Sabbath peace, my land! and thine the guarded hearth;
And thine the dead, the noble band that makes thee holy earth.

Their voices meet me in thy breeze, their steps are on thy plains;
Their names by old majestic trees are whispered round thy fanes;
Their blood hath mingled with the tide of thine exulting sea.;
Oh, be it still a joy, a pride, to live and die for thee!

FELICIA HEMANS, 1793–1835.

168.—THE SOUTH DURING THE WAR OF 1812.

I come now to the war of 1812—a war which, I well remember, was called in derision (while its event was doubtful) the Southern war, and sometimes the Carolina war, but which is now universally acknowledged to have done more for the honor and prosperity of the country than all other events in our history put together.

What, sir, were the objects of that war? "Free trade and sailors' rights!" It was for the protection of Northern shipping and New England seamen that the country flew to arms. What interest had the

ROBERT Y. HAYNE.

South in that contest? If they had sat down coldly to calculate the value of their interests involved in it, they would have found that they had everything to lose and nothing to gain. But, sir, with that generous devotion to country so characteristic of the South, they only asked if the rights of

28

any portion of their fellow-citizens had been invaded; and when told that Northern ships and New England seamen had been arrested on the common highway of nations, they felt that the honor of their country was assailed; and acting on that exalted sentiment "which feels a stain like a wound," they resolved to seek in open war for a redress of those injuries which it did not become freemen to endure.

Sir, the whole South, animated as by a common impulse, cordially united in declaring and promoting that war. South Carolina sent to your councils, as the advocates and supporters of that war, the noblest of her sons. How they fulfilled that trust let a grateful country tell. Not a measure was adopted, not a battle fought, not a victory won, which contributed in any degree to the success of that war, to which Southern councils and Southern valor did not largely contribute.

Sir, since South Carolina is assailed, I must be suffered to speak it to her praise, that, at the very moment when in one quarter we heard it solemnly proclaimed "that it did not become a moral and religious people to rejoice at the victories of our army or our navy," her legislature unanimously

"*Resolved*, That we will cordially support the government in the vigorous prosecution of the war, until a peace can be obtained on honorable terms; and we will cheerfully submit to every privation that may be required of us by our government for the accomplishment of this object."

South Carolina redeemed that pledge. She threw open her treasury to the government. She put at the absolute disposal of the officers of the United States all that she possessed—her men, her money and her arms. She appropriated half a million of dollars, on her own account, in defense of her maritime frontier; ordered a brigade of State troops to be raised; and when left to protect herself by her own means, never suffered the enemy to touch her soil without being instantly driven off or captured. Such, sir, was the conduct of the South— such the conduct of my own State—in that dark hour "which tried men's souls!"

ROBERT Y. HAYNE (see p. 192).

169.—WISDOM AND WEALTH.

I ONCE saw a poor fellow, keen and clever,
Witty and wise; he paid a man a visit,
And no one noticed him, and no one ever
Gave him a welcome. "Strange!" cried he, "whence is it?"
 He walked on this side, then on that,
 He tried to introduce a social chat;
Now here, now there, in vain he tried;
Some formally and freezingly replied,
And some said, by their silence, "Better stay at home."

 A rich man burst the door,
 As Crœsus rich; I'm sure
He could not pride himself upon his wit;
And as for wisdom, he had none of it;
He had what some think better—he had wealth.
 What a confusion! all stand up erect—
These crowd around to ask him of his health;
 These bow in honest duty and respect;
And these arrange a sofa or a chair;
And these conduct him there.
"Allow me, sir, the honor;" then a bow
Down to the earth—is 't possible to show
Meet gratitude for such kind condescension?

 The poor man hung his head,
 And to himself he said,
"This is indeed beyond my comprehension:"
 Then looking round, one friendly face he found,
 And said, "Pray tell me why is wealth preferred
To wisdom?" "That's a silly question, friend!"
Replied the other. "Have you never heard,
 A man may *lend* his store
 Of gold or silver ore,
But *wisdom* none can borrow, none can lend?"
Translated from the Russian of KHEMNITZER *by* BOWRING.

170.—WAR CONSEQUENT ON DISSOLUTION.

MR. PRESIDENT, I have said, what I solemnly believe, that the dissolution of the Union and war are identical and inseparable—that they are convertible terms. Such a war, too, as that would be! Sir, we may search the pages of history, and none so furious, so bloody, so implacable, so exterminating, from the wars of Greece down, including those of the Commonwealth of England, and the Revolution of France—none, none of them raged with such violence, none was ever conducted with such bloodshed and enormities, as must attend that war which shall follow the disastrous event—if that event ever happen—of the dissolution of the Union.

HENRY CLAY.

And what would be its termination? Standing armies and navies, to an extent draining the revenues of each portion of the dissevered empire, would be created; exterminating wars would follow—not wars of two or three years, but wars which would endure until some Philip or Alexander, some Cæsar or Napoleon, would rise to cut the Gordian knot, and solve the capacity of man for self-government, and crush the liberties of both the dissevered portions of this Union. Can you doubt it?

Look at history; consult the pages of all history, ancient or modern; look at human nature; look at the character of the contest in which you would be engaged in the event of a war following the dissolution of the Union, such as I have suggested; and I ask you if it is possible for you to doubt that the final but perhaps distant termination of the whole would be some despot treading down the liberties of the people?—that the final result would be the extinction of this last glorious light which is leading all mankind, who are gazing upon it, to cherish hope and anxious expectation that the liberty which prevails here will, sooner or later, be the lot of the rest of the civilized world? Can you lightly contemplate the consequences? Can you yield yourself to the tyranny of passion, amid the dangers which I have depicted in colors far too tame—far short of what would be the reality, if the event should ever happen?

I implore gentlemen, whether from the South or the North, by all they hold dear in the world, by all their love of liberty, by all their veneration for their ancestors, by all their regard for posterity, by all their gratitude to Him who has bestowed upon them such unnumbered blessings; by all the duties which they owe to mankind and all the duties which they owe to themselves,—by all these considerations I implore them to pause—solemnly to pause—at the edge of the precipice, before the fearful and disastrous leap is taken into the yawning abyss below, the abyss of certain and irretrievable destruction. And, finally, I implore, as the best blessing which heaven can bestow upon me on earth, that if the direful event of the dissolution of the Union shall happen, I may not survive to behold the sad, the heart-rending spectacle. CLAY.

171.—THE ANTIQUITY OF FREEDOM.

O FREEDOM! thou art not, as poets dream,
A fair young girl, with light and delicate limbs,
And wavy tresses gushing from the cap
With which the Roman master crowned his slave
When he took off the gyves. A bearded man,
Armed to the teeth, art thou; one mailèd hand
Grasps the broad shield, and one the sword; thy brow,
Glorious in beauty though it be, is scarred
With tokens of old wars; thy massive limbs
Are strong with struggling.

28 *

Power at thee has launched
His bolts, and with his lightnings smitten thee;
They could not quench the life thou hast from Heaven.
Merciless Power has dug thy dungeon deep,
And his swart armorers, by a thousand fires,
Have forged thy chain; yet while he deems thee bound,
The links are shivered, and the prison walls
Fall outward; terribly thou springest forth,
As springs the flame above a burning pile,
And shoutest to the nations, who return
Thy shoutings, while the pale oppressor flies.

Thy birthright was not given by human hands.
Thou wert twin-born with man.   In pleasant fields,
While yet our race was few, thou sat'st with him
To tend the quiet flock and watch the stars,
And teach the reed to utter simple airs.
Thou by his side, amid the tangled wood,
Didst war upon the panther and the wolf,
His only foes; and thou with him didst draw
The earliest furrows on the mountain side,
Soft with the deluge.   Tyranny himself,
Thy enemy, although of reverend look,
Hoary with many years, and far obeyed,
Is later born than thou; and as he meets
The grave defiance of thine elder eye,
The usurper trembles in his fastnesses.

Thou shalt wax stronger with the lapse of years,
But he shall fade into a feebler age—
Feebler, yet subtler.   He shall weave his snares,
And spring them on thy careless steps, and clap
His withered hands, and from their ambush call
His hordes to fall upon thee.   He shall send
Quaint maskers, wearing fair and gallant forms,
To catch thy gaze, and, uttering graceful words
To charm thy ear; while his sly imps, by stealth,

Twine round thee threads of steel, light thread on thread,
That grow to fetters; or bind down thy arms
With chains concealed in chaplets. Oh! not yet
May'st thou unbrace thy corslet, or lay by
Thy sword! nor yet, O Freedom! close thy lids
In slumber; for thine enemy never sleeps;
And thou must watch and combat, till the day
Of the new earth and heaven.

WILLIAM C. BRYANT.

172.—THE GREAT REPUBLIC.

HOLMES.

So surely as American society founds itself upon the rights of civilized man, there is no permanent safety for any nation but in the progressive recognition of the American principle. The right of governing a nation belongs to the *people* of the nation; and the urgent duty of those provisional governments which we call monarchies, empires, aristocracies, is to educate the people with a view to the final surrender of all power into their hands.

Just so far as the *people* of Europe understand the nature of our armed controversy they will understand that we are pleading *their* cause. Nay, if the mass of our Southern brethren did but know it (as they one day will), we are pleading their cause just as much. The emancipation of industry has never taken effect in the South, and never can until labor ceases to be degrading.

No deeper humiliation could be asked for our foreign enemies than the spectacle of our triumph. No Tartar hordes pouring from the depths of Asia, no northern barbarians swarming out of the hive of nations, no Saracens sweeping from their deserts to plant the crescent over the symbol of Christendom, were more terrible to the principalities and powers that stood in their way than the great Republic, *by the bare fact of its existence,* will become, to every government which does not hold its authority from the people.

The spirit of republican America is not that of a wild propagandism. It is not by war that we have sought or should ever seek to convert the Old World to our theories and practice in government. If this young nation is permitted, in the providence of God, to unfold all its possibilities into powers, the great lesson it will teach will be that of *peaceful* development. American civilization hates war as such. It values life because it honors humanity. It values property because property is for the comfort and good of all, and not merely plunder to be wasted by a few irresponsible lawgivers. It wants all the forces of its population to subdue Nature to its service. It demands all the intellect of its children for *con*struction, not for *de*struction.

Let us not, therefore, waste our strength in threats of vengeance against those misguided governments who mistook their true interest in the prospect of our calamity. We can conquer them by peace better than by war. When the Union emerges from the battle-smoke—her crest towering, her eyes flashing defiance to all her evil-wishers, her breast heaving under its corslet of iron, her arm wielding the mightiest enginery that was ever forged into the thunderbolts of war—her triumph will be grand enough, without her setting fire to the stubble with which the folly of the Old World has girt its thrones.

OLIVER WENDELL HOLMES.

173.—AGAINST MARK ANTONY.

THE SPEECH THAT COST CICERO HIS LIFE.

THE doings of this day—defend them, Antony, if you can. Why is the Forum hedged in with armed troops? Why stand your satellites listening to me sword in hand? Why are not the gates of the Temple of Peace flung open? Why have you marched into the city men of all nations—but barbarians chiefly—savages, armed with slings, from Ituræa?

You pretend that it is all to protect your person. Is it not better far to die a thousand deaths than not to be able to live in one's own country without guards of armed men? But, trust me, there is no safety in defenses like these. If we would be secure, we must be girt around with the love and the respect of our countrymen, and not with armed defenders.

Look back, Mark Antony, to that day when you abolished the dictator-

ROMAN EMBLEMS.

ship; recall the satisfaction of the Senate and people of Rome; contrast that act with the traffic in which you and your creatures are now engaged; realize, if you can, the vast difference between glory and gain. Yet as in some diseases men lose the sense of taste, and cannot distinguish the flavor of food, so do the profligate, the rapacious, the desperate, lose the relish of true fame.

But if glory cannot charm, cannot fear deter you? You have no uneasiness about criminal prosecutions. Be it so. If from conscious innocence springs your confidence, I commend it; but if from your reliance upon mere *force*, do you not perceive that he who thus defies the terrors of the law may himself become the victim of the lawless?

If, shielded by satellites, you have no fear of brave men and patriotic citizens, have a care lest your own partisans turn against you. And what a life is his whom fears of his own followers distract! Can you bind yours to *you* by obligations greater than those by which Cæsar bound to him some of the very men who put him to death? Can you, in any respect, be compared to *him*—to Cæsar?

In him there was genius, judgment, culture, zeal, and high resolve. His exploits in war, how mischievous soever to his country, were yet transcendent. Devoted for years to the attainment of supreme power, he accomplished his object with vast labor, through countless perils. By his munificence, his public works, his largesses, his hospitalities, he won over to his cause the dazzled multitude. His followers he attached by his generosity, his adversaries by his specious clemency. In a word, partly because he was feared, and partly because he was tolerated, he made a free state familiar with slavery.

That great man you may resemble in your lust of power, but in nothing else are you like him. And does it never occur to you what the Roman people have learnt? Do you not comprehend that brave men now recognize how beautiful the deed, how precious the service, how glorious the fame of extirpating a *tyrant?* The people who could not endure a Cæsar, will they now submit to an Antony?

Look to yourself, Mark Antony! What my principles are I will now freely proclaim. I defended the republic when I was young—I will not desert it now I am old! I have despised the sword of Catiline, and the sword of Antony shall not alarm me. Most willingly would I sacrifice this body, if by my death the liberty of Rome could be established. Did not I say twenty years ago, in this very Senate, that when a man perished who had reached the dignity of consul, he could not be said to have perished prematurely?

And do you think, now that old age is come upon me, I will retract or deny this doctrine? Conscript fathers, I wish for death; I have gained all that the republic can bestow; I have performed all that it can require! Let death come when it will, I am prepared to meet it. I have only two things to implore—first, that my country may deal out to all her children the punishment or reward they merit; next, that when I *do* die, I may leave Rome free. If the gods grant me this, there is no higher boon which they can bestow.*

MARCUS TULLIUS CICERO (see p. 106).

174.—THE PIBROCH.†

PIBROCH of Donuil Dhu, pibroch of Donuil,
Wake thy wild voice anew, summon Clan-Conuil.
Come away, come away, hark to the summons!
Come in your war array, gentles and commons.

Come from deep glen, and from mountain so rocky;
The war-pipe and pennon are at Inverlochy;
Come every hill-plaid, and true heart that wears one,
Come every steel-blade, and strong hand that bears one.

Leave untended the herd, the flock without shelter;
Leave the corpse uninterred, the bride at the altar;
Leave the deer, leave the steer, leave nets and barges,
Come with your fighting gear, broadswords and targes.

Come as the winds come when forests are rended;
Come as the waves come when navies are stranded:
Faster come, faster come, faster and faster,
Chief, vassal, page and groom, tenant and master.

Fast they come, fast they come; see how they gather!
Wide waves the eagle plume blended with heather.
Cast your plaids, draw your blades, forward each man set!
Pibroch of Donuil Dhu, knell for the onset!

SIR WALTER SCOTT.

---

* Stung by the philippics of Cicero, Antony insisted on his death, and Octavius basely consented to it. Cicero perished in the year 43 B. C. He was opposed to Cæsar, though not a party to his assassination. See note p. 107.

† A pibroch is among the Highlanders of Scotland a martial air played on the bag-pipe.

175.—HOTSPUR AND GLENDOWER.

SHAKSPEARE.

Glendower. Hail, good cousin Percy! hail, good cousin Hotspur!
For by that name, as oft as Lancaster
Doth speak of you, his cheeks look pale, and, with
A rising sigh, he wisheth you in heaven.

Hotspur. And you—in the other place, as often as he hears
Owen Glendower spoken of.

Glen. I cannot blame him. At my nativity
The front of heaven was full of fiery shapes,
Of burning cressets; and at my birth
The frame and huge foundation of the earth
Shaked like a coward.

Hot. Why, so it would have done
At the same season if your mother's cat
Had but kittened, though yourself had never been born.

Glen. I say the earth did shake when I was born.

Hot. And I say the earth was not of my mind,
If you suppose as fearing you it shook.

Glen. The heavens were all on fire; the earth did tremble.

Hot. Oh, then the earth shook to see the heavens on fire,
And not in fear of your nativity.
Diseasèd nature oftentimes breaks forth
In strange eruptions; oft the teeming earth
Is with a kind of colic pinched and vexed
By the imprisonment of unruly wind
Within her held, which, for enlargement striving,
Shakes the old beldamed earth, and topples down
Steeples and moss-grown towers. At your birth,
Our grandam earth, having this distemperature,
In passion shook.

Glen. Cousin, of many men
I do not bear these crossings. Give me leave
To tell you once again that at my birth
The front of heaven was full of fiery shapes;
The goats ran from the mountains, and the herds
Were strangely clamorous in the frighted fields.
These signs have marked me extraordinary,
And all the courses of my life do show
I am not in the roll of common men.

    Hot. I think there is no man speaks better Welsh.

    Glen. I can speak English, lord, as well as you;
For I was trained up in the English court,
Where, being but young, I framëd to the harp
Many an English ditty, lovely well,
And gave the tongue a helpful ornament—
A virtue that was never seen in you.

    Hot. Marry, and I'm glad of it, with all my heart.
I had rather be a kitten, and cry *mew!*
Than one of those same meter ballad-mongers;
I'd rather hear a brazen candlestick turned,
Or a dry wheel grate on an axle-tree;
And that would set my teeth nothing on edge,
Nothing so much as mincing poetry.
'Tis like the forced gait of a shuffling nag!

    Glen. I can call spirits from the vasty deep.

    Hot. Why, so can I, or so can any man;
But will they *come*, when you do *call* for them?

    Glen. I can teach you, cousin, to command the devil.

    Hot. And I can teach thee, coz, to shame the devil,
By telling truth: tell truth, and shame the devil.

    Glen. No more of this unprofitable chat!   (*Exit.*)

    Hot. No more, and welcome, Owen Glendower!
He can "call spirits from the vasty deep!"
And he can teach me to "command the devil!"
O, he's as tedious as is a tired horse, a railing wife;
Worse than a smoky house; I had rather live
With cheese and garlic, in a windmill, far,

29   W

Than feed on cates, and have him talk to me,
In any summer-house in Christendom!

SHAKSPEARE (altered).

176.—AGAINST WHIPPING IN THE NAVY.

THERE is one broad proposition, senators, upon which I
stand. It is this—that an American sailor is an American
citizen, and that no American citizen shall, with my con-
sent, be subjected to the infamous punishment of the lash.
Placing myself upon this proposition, I am prepared for any
consequences. I love the navy. When I speak of the navy,
I mean the sailor as well as the officer. They are all my fellow-
citizens and yours; and come what may, my voice will ever be
raised against a punishment which degrades my countrymen
to the level of a brute, and destroys all that is worth living
for—personal honor and self-respect.

In many a bloody conflict has the superiority of the Ameri-
can sailors decided the battle in our favor. I desire to secure
and preserve that superiority. But can nobleness of sentiment
or honorable pride of character dwell with one whose every
muscle has been made to quiver under the lash? Can he long
continue to love a country whose laws crush out all the dig-
nity of manhood and rouse all the exasperation of hate in his
breast?

Look to your history—that part of it which the world
knows by heart—and you will find on its brightest page the
glorious achievements of the American sailor. Whatever his
country has done to disgrace him and break his spirits, he has
never disgraced her. Man for man, he asks no odds, and he
cares for no odds, when the cause of humanity or the glory of
his country calls him to the fight. Who, in the darkest days
of our Revolution, carried your flag into the very chops of the
British Channel, bearded the lion in his den, and awoke the
echo of old Albion's hills by the thunder of his cannon and
the shouts of his triumph? It was the American sailor; and the

names of John Paul Jones and the Bon Homme Richard will go down the annals of time for ever.

Who struck the first blow that humbled the Barbary flag—which, for a hundred years, had been the terror of Christendom—drove it from the Mediterranean, and put an end to the infamous tribute it had been accustomed to exact? It was the American sailor; and the names of Decatur and his gallant companions will be as lasting as monumental brass.

In your war of 1812, when your arms on shore were covered by disaster—when Winchester had been defeated, when the army of the North-west had surrendered, and when the gloom of despondency hung like a cloud over the land—who first relit the fires of national glory, and made the welkin ring with the shouts of victory? It was the American sailor; and the names of Hull and the Constitution will be remembered as long as we have anything left worth remembering. That was no small event. The wand of British invincibility was broken when the flag of the Guerrière came down.

That one event was worth more to the republic than all the money which has ever been expended for the navy. Since that day the navy has had no stain upon its national escutcheon, but has been cherished as your pride and glory; and the American sailor has established a reputation throughout the world, in peace and in war, in storm and in battle, for a heroism and prowess unsurpassed.

The great climax of Cicero in his speech against Verres is that, though a Roman citizen, his client had been scourged. Will this more than Roman senate long debate whether an American citizen, sailor though he be, shall be robbed of his rights? whether, freeman as he is, he shall be scourged like a slave? Shall an American citizen be scourged? Forbid it, Heaven! Humanity forbid it! For myself, I would rather see the navy abolished, and the stars and the stripes buried, with their glory, in the depths of the ocean, than that those who won for it all its renown should be subjected to a punishment so brutal, to an ignominy so undeserved.

COMMODORE R. F. STOCKTON.

GRASMERE, THE RESIDENCE OF WORDSWORTH.

177.—ODE.

INTIMATIONS OF IMMORTALITY FROM RECOLLECTIONS OF EARLY CHILD-HOOD.

I.

THERE was a time when meadow, grove and stream,
The earth, and every common sight,

WORDSWORTH.

> To me did seem
> Appareled in celestial
> light,
> The glory and the
> freshness of a
> dream.
> It is not now as it hath
> been of yore;
> Turn wheresoe'er I
> may,
> By night or day,
> The things which I
> have seen I now
> can see no more.

II.

The rainbow comes and goes,
And lovely is the rose;
The moon doth with delight
Look round her when the heavens are bare;
Waters on a starry night
Are beautiful and fair;
The sunshine is a glorious birth;
But yet I know, where'er I go,
That there hath passed away a glory from the earth.

III.

Now, while the birds thus sing a joyous song,
And while the young lambs bound
As to the tabor's sound,
To me alone there came a thought of grief;
A timely utterance gave that thought relief;
And I again am strong.
The cataracts blow their trumpets from the steep—
No more shall grief of mine the season wrong:
I hear the echoes through the mountains throng;
The winds come to me from the fields of sleep;
. And all the earth is gay.
Land and sea
Give themselves up to jollity;
And with the heart of May
Doth every beast keep holiday;
Thou child of joy,
Shout round me, let me hear thy shouts, thou happy shepherd-
boy!

IV.

Ye blessèd creatures, I have heard the call
Ye to each other make; I see
The heavens laugh with you in your jubilee;
My heart is at your festival,
My head hath its coronal,

29 *

The fullness of your bliss I feel—I feel it all.
  Oh, evil day! if I were sullen,
  While Earth herself is adorning,
    This sweet May morning;
  And the children are culling,
    On every side,
  In a thousand valleys far and wide,
  Fresh flowers; while the sun shines warm,
And the babe leaps up on his mother's arm:—
  I hear, I hear, with joy I hear!
  —But there's a tree, of many one,
A single field which I have looked upon—
Both of them speak of something that is gone:
    The pansy at my feet
    Doth the same tale repeat:
Whither is fled the visionary gleam?
Where is it now, the glory and the dream?

                    v.

Our birth is but a sleep and a forgetting:
The soul that rises with us, our life's star,
    Hath had elsewhere its setting,
      And cometh from afar;
    Not in entire forgetfulness,
    And not in utter nakedness,
But trailing clouds of glory do we come
      From God, who is our home:
Heaven lies about us in our infancy!
Shades of the prison-house begin to close
      Upon the growing boy;
But he beholds the light and whence it flows,
      He sees it in his joy;
The youth, who daily farther from the east
    Must travel, still is Nature's priest,
      And by the vision splendid
      Is on his way attended;

At length the man perceives it die away,
And fade into the light of common day.

VI.

Earth fills her lap with pleasures of her own :
Yearnings she hath in her own natural kind ;
And even with something of a mother's mind,
    And no unworthy aim,
  The homely nurse doth all she can
To make her foster-child, her inmate man,
    Forget the glories he hath known
And that imperial palace whence he came.

VII.

Behold the child among his new-born blisses,
A six years' darling of a pigmy size !
See, where 'mid work of his own hand he lies,
Fretted by sallies of his mother's kisses,
With light upon him from his father's eyes !
See, at his feet, some little plan or chart,
Some fragment from his dream of human life,
Shaped by himself with newly-learnèd art ;
    A wedding or a festival,
    A mourning or a funeral ;
      And this hath now his heart ;
    And unto this he frames his song :
      Then will he fit his tongue
To dialogues of business, love or strife ;
    But it will not be long
    Ere this be thrown aside,
    And with new joy and pride
The little actor cons another part ;
Filling from time to time his " humorous stage "
With all the persons, down to palsied age,
That Life brings with her in her equipage ;
    As if his whole vocation
    Were endless imitation.

VIII.

Thou, whose exterior semblance doth belie
    Thy soul's immensity,
Thou best philosopher, who yet dost keep
Thy heritage, thou eye among the blind,
That, deaf and silent, read'st the eternal deep,
Haunted for ever by the eternal mind—
    Mighty prophet! seer blest!
    On whom those truths do rest,
Which we are toiling all our lives to find,
In darkness lost, the darkness of the grave; .
Thou, over whom thy immortality
Broods like the day, a master o'er a slave,
A presence which is not to be put by;
Thou little child, yet glorious in the might
Of heaven-born freedom on thy being's height,
Why with such earnest pains dost thou provoke
The years to bring the inevitable yoke,
Thus blindly with thy blessedness at strife?
Full soon thy soul shall have her earthly freight,
And custom lie upon thee with a weight
Heavy as frost, and deep almost as life!

IX.

    Oh, joy! that in our embers
    Is something that doth live!
    That nature yet remembers
    What was so fugitive!
The thought of our past years in me doth breed
Perpetual benediction: not indeed
For that which is most worthy to be blest;
Delight and liberty, the simple creed
Of childhood, whether busy or at rest,
With new-fledged hope still fluttering in his breast,—
    Not for these I raise
    The song of thanks and praise;

But for those obstinate questionings .
Of sense and outward things,
Fallings from us, vanishings ;
Blank misgivings of a creature
Moving about in worlds not realized,
High instincts, before which our mortal nature
Did tremble, like a guilty thing surprised :
But for those first affections,
Those shadowy recollections,
Which, be they what they may,
Are yet the fountain light of all our day,
Are yet a master light of all our seeing ;
Uphold us, cherish, and have power to make
Our noisy years seem moments in the being
Of the eternal silence : truths that wake
To perish never ;
Which neither listlessness nor mad endeavor,
Nor man nor boy,
Nor all that is at enmity with joy,
Can utterly abolish or destroy !
Hence, in a season of calm weather,
Though inland far we be,
Our souls have sight of that immortal sea
Which brought us hither ;
Can in a moment travel thither,
And see the children sport upon the shore,
And hear the mighty waters rolling evermore.

x.

Then sing, ye birds, sing, sing a joyous song !
And let the young lambs bound
As to the tabor's sound !
We, in thought, will join your throng,
Ye that pipe and ye that play,
Ye that through your hearts to-day
Feel the gladness of the May !

What though the radiance which was once so bright
Be now for ever taken from my sight,
    Though nothing can bring back the hour
Of splendor in the grass, of glory in the flower?
      We will grieve not, rather find
      Strength in what remains behind;
      In the primal sympathy
      Which having been must ever be;
      In the soothing thoughts that spring
      Out of human suffering;
      In the faith that looks through death,
In years that bring the philosophic mind.

XI.

And, O ye fountains, meadows, hills and groves,
Forebode not any severing of our loves!
Yet in my heart of hearts I feel your might;
I only have relinquished one delight,
To live beneath your more habitual sway.
I love the brooks, which down their channels fret,
Even more than when I tripped lightly as they;
The innocent brightness of a new-born day
      Is lovely yet;
The clouds that gather round the setting sun
Do take a sober coloring from an eye
That hath kept watch o'er man's mortality:
Another race hath been, and other palms are won.
Thanks to the human heart by which we live;
Thanks to its tenderness, its joys and fears;
To me the meanest flower that blows can give
Thoughts that do often lie too deep for tears.
        WILLIAM WORDSWORTH,* 1770–1850.

---

* Coleridge describes the higher efforts of Wordsworth's pen as being characterized by "an austere purity of language, both grammatically and logically." No English poet, who has dealt with lofty themes, is more thoroughly English in his style.

178.—ANCIENT ORATORS COMPARED.*

LUMINOUS truths, noble thoughts, expressions adequate and strong, mark the discourse of the true orator. He thinks, he feels, and language follows. "He does not depend on his words," says St. Augus-
tine, "but his words de-
pend upon *him*." A man
with force and grandeur
of soul, with some natural
facility in speaking and
sufficient practice, need
never fear that words
will fail him. His most
unconsidered discourse
will have original traits
which florid declaimers
can never imitate. He is
not a slave to words. He
goes straight to the truth.

FENELON.

He knows that earnestness is the very soul of speech.

Remounting to the first principle of the subject he has to unfold, he places that principle in its elementary point of view, and from it, as from a centre, radiates light over every part of his discourse; even as a painter distributes his light over the objects of his picture, in due proportion, from some common point. The whole speech is a unit. It is reduced to a single proposition, exhibited in its perfect simplicity by the aid of various forms of expression. From this unity of design it follows that the entire work is presented to us in a single glance, just as from the central public place in a city we may see all the streets and gates, when the lines are straight, equal and symmetrical. The discourse is the proposition developed; the proposition is the discourse abridged.

A rare quality is order like this; and when combined with justice in the sentiment, with vehemence and pith in the ex-

* Translated for Oxford's Senior Speaker.

pression, it contributes chiefly to the perfection of a discourse. But to know the precise place for every word, one must have seen, penetrated, and embraced his subject wholly; and this is what the unskillful declaimer, carried away by his imagination, fails to do.

Isoc'ra-tes is smooth, insinuating, and elegant, but can we compare him to Homer? Let us go farther. I do not hesitate to say that to me Demosthenes seems superior to Cicero. I yield to no one in my admiration of Cicero. He embellishes whatever he touches. He does honor to speech. He uses words as no one else can use them. His versatility is amazing. He is even concise and vehement when he wills to be so—as against Catiline, against Verres, against Antony. But we detect the embellishment in his discourses. The art is marvelous, but it is not concealed. The orator, in his concern for the republic, does not forget himself, nor does he allow himself to be forgotten.

Demosthenes, on the contrary, seems to go out of himself and to recognize only his country. He does not *seek* for the beautiful. All unconsciously, he *creates* it. He is superior to admiration. He uses language, as a modest man does his garment, for a covering. He thunders, he lightens; he is like a torrent hurrying all before it. We cannot criticise him, for we are in the sweep of his influence. We think on *what* he says, and not on *how* he says it. We lose sight of the speaker. We are occupied only with the all-invading, all-absorbing Philip.

To both of these matchless orators I yield my homage; but I confess that I am less touched by the infinite art and magnificent eloquence of Cicero than by the rapid simplicity of Demosthenes.

FENELON,* 1651–1715.

---

* Francis de Salignac de la Motte Fenelon, archbishop of Cambray in France, was one of the most distinguished persons who have adorned the religious profession in any age. As a man of letters he won high fame, but he was good as well as great, and his character is one of the noblest and most lovable in all history.

POPE'S VILLA AT TWICKENHAM.

179.—ORDER OF NATURE.

SEE through this air, this ocean and this earth,
All matter quick, and bursting into birth.
Above, how high progressive life may go !
Around, how wide! how deep extend below!
Vast chain of being, which from God began,
Natures ethereal, human, angel, man,
Beast, bird, fish, insect—what no eye can see,
No glass can reach—from infinite to thee—
From thee to nothing—on superior powers
Were we to press, inferior might on ours ;
Or in the full creation leave a void,
Where, one step broken, the great scale's destroyed :
From nature's chain whatever link you strike,
Tenth or ten thousandth, breaks the chain alike.

And if each system in gradation roll,
Alike essential to the amazing whole,

30

The least confusion but in one, not all
That system only, but the whole, must fall.
Let earth, unbalanced, from her orbit fly,
Planets and suns run lawless through the sky ;
Let ruling angels from their spheres be hurled,
Being on being wrecked, and world on world,
Heaven's whole foundations to their centre nod,
And nature trembles to the throne of God !
All this dread order break ? For whom? For thee,
Vile worm !—oh, madness ! pride ! impiety !

What if the foot, ordained the dust to tread,
Or hand to toil, aspired to be the head?
What if the head, the eye or ear repined
To serve mere engines to the ruling mind ?
Just as absurd for any part to claim
To be another in this general frame—
Just as absurd, to mourn the tasks or pains,
The great directing Mind of all ordains.

All are but parts of one stupendous whole,
Whose body Nature is, and God the soul ;
That, changed through all, and yet in all the same,
Great in the earth as in the ethereal frame,
Warms in the sun, refreshes in the breeze,
Glows in the stars, and blossoms in the trees,
Lives through all life, extends through all extent,
Spreads undivided, operates unspent,
Breathes in our soul, informs our mortal part,
As full, as perfect, in a hair as heart ;
As full, as perfect, in vile man that mourns,
As the rapt seraph that adores and burns :
To him, no high, no low, no great, no small;
He fills, he bounds, connects and equals all.

ALEXANDER POPE, 1688–1744.

180.—THE PLYMOUTH SETTLERS.

METHINKS I see it now, that one solitary, adventurous vessel, the Mayflower of a forlorn hope, freighted with the prospects of a future State and bound across the unknown sea. I behold it pursuing with a thousand misgivings the uncertain, the tedious voyage. Suns rise and set, and weeks and months pass, and winter surprises them on the deep, but brings them not the sight of the wished-for shore. I see them now scantily supplied with provisions, crowded almost to suffocation in their ill-stored prison, delayed by calms, pursuing a circuitous route, and now driven in fury before the raging tempest in their scarcely seaworthy vessel.

The awful voice of the storm howls through the rigging; the laboring masts seem straining from their base; the dismal sound of the pumps is heard; the ship leaps, as it were, madly, from billow to billow; the ocean breaks and settles with ingulfing floods over the floating deck, and beats with deadening weight against the staggered vessel.

I see them escaped from these perils, pursuing their all but desperate undertaking, and landed at last, after a five months' passage, on the ice-clad rocks of Plymouth, weak and exhausted from the voyage, poorly armed, scantily provisioned, without shelter, without means, surrounded by hostile tribes.

Shut now the volume of history, and tell me on any principle of human probability what shall be the fate of this handful of adventurers. Tell me, man of military science, in how many months were they all swept off by the thirty savage tribes enumerated within the boundaries of New England?

Tell me, politician, how long did this shadow of a colony, on which your conventions and treaties had not smiled, languish on the distant coast? Student of history, compare for me the baffled projects, the deserted settlements, the abandoned adventures of other times, and find the parallel of this.

Was it the winter's storm, beating upon the houseless heads of women and children? was it hard labor and spare meals? was it disease? the tomahawk? was it the deep malady of a blighted hope, a ruined enterprise and a broken heart, aching, in its last moments, at the recollections of the loved and left, beyond the sea?—was it some or all of these united that hurried this forsaken company to their melancholy fate?

And is it possible that no one of these causes, that not all combined, were able to blast this bud of hope? Is it possible that from a beginning so feeble, so frail, so worthy not so much of admiration as of pity, there have gone forth a progress so steady, a growth so wonderful, an expansion so ample, a reality so important, a promise, yet to be fulfilled, so glorious!

EDWARD EVERETT, 1794–1865.

181.—ON THE REFORM BILL, 1831.

My lords, I do not disguise the intense solicitude which I feel for the event of this debate, because I know full well that the peace of the country is involved in the issue. I cannot look without dismay at the rejection of the measure. But grievous as may be the consequences of a temporary defeat—temporary it can only be; for its ultimate and even speedy success is certain—nothing now can stop it. Do not suffer yourselves to be persuaded that even if the present ministers were driven from the helm, any one could steer you through the troubles that surround you without reform. But our successors would take up the task amid circumstances far less auspicious. Under them you would be fain to grant a bill compared with which the one we now proffer is moderate indeed.

Hear the parable of the Sibyl, for it conveys a wise and wholesome moral. She now appears at your gate, and offers you mildly the volumes—the precious volumes—of wisdom and peace. The price she asks is reasonable—to restore the franchise which, without any bargain, you ought voluntarily to give. You refuse her terms—her moderate terms—she darkens the porch no longer. But soon, for you cannot do without her wares, you call her back. Again she comes, but with diminished treasures; the leaves of the book are in part torn away by lawless hands—in part defaced with characters of blood. But the prophetic maid has risen in her demands : it is Parliament by the year, it is vote by the ballot, it is suffrage by the million! From this you turn away indignant, and for the second time she departs.

Beware of her third visit, for the treasure you must have, and what price she may next demand who shall tell? It may be even the mace which rests upon that woolsack. What may follow your course of obstinacy, if persisted in, I cannot take upon me to predict, nor do I wish to conjecture. But this I know full well—that as sure as man is mortal and to err is human, justice deferred enhances the price at which you must purchase safety and peace ; nor can you more expect to gather in another crop than they did who went before you, if you persevere in their utterly abominable husbandry of sowing injustice and reaping rebellion.

But among the awful considerations that now bow down my mind, there is one which stands pre-eminent above the rest. You are the highest judicature in the realm ; you sit here as judges, and decide all causes, civil and criminal, without appeal. It is a judge's first duty never to pronounce sentence, in the most trifling case, without hearing. Will you make this the exception? Are you really prepared to determine, but not to hear, the mighty cause upon which a nation's hopes and fears hang? You are! Then beware of your decision! Rouse not, I beseech you, a peace-loving but a resolute people —alienate not from your body the affections of a whole empire.

As your friend, as the friend of my order, as the friend of my country, as the faithful servant of my sovereign, I counsel you to assist with your utmost efforts in preserving the peace and upholding and perpetuating the constitution. Therefore I pray and I exhort you not to reject this measure. By all you hold most dear, by all the ties that bind every one of us to our common order and our common country, I solemnly adjure you —I warn you, I implore you—yea, on my bended knees, I supplicate you—reject not this bill! LORD BROUGHAM.

182.—THE HELMSMAN OF LAKE ERIE.

I.

EPES SARGENT.

BRAVE fellows in
　my day
Have I beheld,
Brave on the
　quarter-deck,
Brave in the hour
　of wreck,
Brave where no
　hope impelled
And death be-
　fore them lay.

II.

But if you ask
　of me
Who of them
　all
First to my
　thought ap-
　pears,

Bright through the mist of years,
　Foremost at memory's call,
This would my answer be:

III.

John Maynard, he's the first—
　Here's to his fame!
He of the Ocean Queen,
He of that fearful scene,
　Who out of smoke and flame
On us a saviour burst!

IV.

Crowded with passengers
　Was our good boat;

Crossing Lake Erie, we
Hardly the shore could see
   When came that dreadful note
   (Which most the heart-blood stirs),

V

"Fire!" and the captain cried,
   "See to it there!
Wheel, ho! Whose hand is on?"
"John Maynard's." "Steady, John!
   East-south-east let her tear!"
"Ay, ay, sir!" John replied.

VI.

John, a rough sailor lad,
   Why should he stay?
Thrust at by tongues of fire,
There at his post expire?
   "Fly, John, at once! Away
Where rescue may be had!

VII.

"True, all to God, in thee,
   Look now for aid;
Trembling in view of death,
Men, women, hold their breath;
   But shall they safe be made
Through thy deep agony?"

VIII.

Swathed round with flame and smoke,
   John still held on;
"Only five minutes more,
And we may jump ashore—
   Steady!" (the captain spoke).
"Steady it is," said John.

IX.

"One minute longer, John,
   Can you remain?"
"Ay, with God's help I can,"
Quoth the lad, grown to man
   In that extreme of pain,
   His crown celestial on!

X.

Up, on its wings of flame,
   Up drove the keel;
Up to the shelving beach,
Out of the billows' reach,
   Where men could leap, and kneel,
   All with a glad acclaim.

XI.

"Saved! All are saved!" one cries,
   "Three hundred saved!
John Maynard—where is he?
Bring him forth! Let us see
   Him who the fire-fiend braved!"
"Hush! There in death he lies!"

                         SARGENT.

183.—ON THE GREEK QUESTION, 1824.

PERHAPS one of the prettiest themes for declamation ever presented to a deliberative assembly is this proposition in behalf of Greece. But, sir, I look at the measure as one fraught with deep and deadly danger to the best interests of the American people. Liberty and religion are objects as dear to *my* heart as to that of any gentleman in this or any other assembly. But, in the name of these holy words, by this powerful spell, is this nation to be conjured and persuaded out of the highway of Heaven—out of its present comparatively happy state—into all the disastrous conflicts arising from the policy of European powers, with all the consequences which flow from them?

Sir, I am afraid that along with some most excellent attributes and qualities—the love of liberty, jury trial, the writ of habeas corpus, and all the blessings of free government which we have derived from our Anglo-Saxon ancestors—we have got not a little of their John Bull, or rather bull-dog, spirit— their readiness to fight for anybody and on any occasion. Sir, England has been for centuries the game-cock of Europe. It is impossible to specify the wars in which she has been engaged for contrary purposes, and she will, with great pleasure, see us take off her shoulders the labor of preserving the balance of power. We find her fighting now for the queen of Hungary; then, for her inveterate foe, the king of Prussia; now at war for the restoration of the Bourbons, and now on the eve of war with them for the liberties of Spain.

If we pursue the same policy, we must travel the same road and endure the same burdens under which England now groans. But, glorious as such a design might be, a President of the United States would, in my apprehension, occupy a prouder place in history, who, when he retires from office, can say to the people who elected him, "I leave you without a debt," than if he had fought as many pitched battles as Cæsar, or achieved as many naval victories as Nelson.

And what, sir, is debt? In an individual it is slavery—it is slavery of the worst sort, surpassing that of the West India Islands, for it enslaves the mind as well as the body; and the creature who can be abject enough to incur and to submit to it receives in that condition of his being an adequate punishment. Of course, I speak of debt with the exception of unavoidable misfortune. I speak of debt caused by mismanagement, by unwarrantable generosity, by being generous before being just. I know that this sentiment was ridiculed by Sheridan, whose lamentable end was the best commentary upon its truth.

No, sir; let us abandon these projects. Let us say to these seven millions of Greeks, "We defended ourselves when we were but three millions against a power in comparison to which the Turk is but as a lamb. Go, and do thou likewise."

JOHN RANDOLPH, 1773–1833.

184.—THE CONTEST IN AMERICA.

I CANNOT join with those who cry "Peace, peace!" I cannot wish that this war should not have been engaged in by the North, or that, being engaged in, it should be terminated on any conditions but such as would retain the whole of the territories as free soil. War in a good cause is not the greatest evil which a nation can suffer. War is an ugly thing, but not the ugliest of things: the decayed and degraded state of moral and patriotic feeling which thinks nothing *worth* a war is worse.

When a people are used as mere human instruments for firing cannon or thrusting bayonets, in the service and for the selfish purposes of a master, such war degrades a people. A war to protect other human beings against tyrannical injustice, a war to give victory to their own ideas of right and good, and which is their own war, carried on for an honest purpose by their free choice, is often the means of their regeneration.

A man who has nothing which he is willing to fight for, nothing which he cares more about than he does about his personal safety, is a miserable creature, who has no chance of being free, unless made and kept so by the exertions of better men than himself. As long as justice and injustice have not terminated *their* ever-renewing fight for ascendency in the affairs of mankind, human beings *must* be willing, when need is, to do battle for the one against the other.

I am far from saying that the present struggle on the part of the Northern Americans is wholly of this exalted character—that it has arrived at the stage of being altogether a war for justice, a war of principle. But there was from the beginning, and now is, a large infusion of that element in it; and this is increasing, will increase, and, if the war lasts, will in the end predominate. Should that time come, not only will the greatest enormity which still exists among mankind as an institution receive far earlier its *coup de grace* than there has ever, until now, appeared any probability of; but in effecting this, the free States will have raised themselves to that elevated position in the scale of morality and dignity which is derived from great sacrifices consciously made in a virtuous cause, and the sense of an inestimable benefit to all future ages brought about by their own voluntary efforts.

JOHN STUART MILL, 1806–1873.

185.—RELIGION OF REVOLUTIONARY MEN.

I KNOW, and I sigh when I think of it, that hitherto the French people have been the least religious of all the nations of Europe. The great men of other countries live and die on the stage of history, looking up to Heaven. *Our* great men live and die looking at the spectator, or, at most, at posterity!

Open the history of America, the history of England and the history of France. Washington fought, spoke and suffered always in

ALPHONSE DE LAMARTINE.

the name of God, for whom he acted; and the liberator of America died confiding to God his own soul and the liberty of the people. Sidney, the undaunted martyr of a patriotism guilty of nothing but impatience, and who died to expiate his country's dream of liberty, said to his jailer, "I rejoice that I die innocent toward the king, but a victim resigned to the King on high, to whom all life is due." The republicans of Cromwell sought only the way of God, even through the blood of battles.

But look at Mirabeau on the bed of death! "Crown me with flowers," said he, "intoxicate me with perfumes. Let me die to the sound of delicious music!" Not a word of God or of his own soul! Sensual philosopher, supreme sensualism was his last desire in his agony. Contemplate Madame Roland, the strong-hearted woman of the Revolution, on the cart that conveyed her to death. Not a glance toward Heaven! Only one word for the earth she was quitting: "O Liberty, what crimes in thy name are committed!" Approach the dungeon door of the Girondins. Their last night is a banquet, their only hymn the Marseillaise! Hear Danton on the platform of the scaffold: "I have had a good time of it; let me go to sleep." Then, to the executioner: "You will show my head to the people; it is worth the trouble!" His faith, annihilation; his last sigh, vanity!

Behold the Frenchman of this latter age! What must one think of the religious sentiment of a free people, whose great figures seem thus to march in procession to annihilation, and to whom death itself recalls neither the threatenings nor the promises of God! The republic of these men without a God was quickly stranded. The liberty, won by so much heroism and so much genius, did not find in France a conscience to shelter it, a God to avenge it, a people to defend it, against that atheism which was called glory. All ended in a soldier, and some apostate republicans travestied into courtiers.

An atheistic republicanism cannot be heroic. When you terrify it, it yields. When you would buy it, it becomes venal. It would be very foolish to immolate itself. Who would give it credit for the sacrifice—the people ungrateful, and God non-existent? So end atheistic revolutions!

ALPHONSE DE LAMARTINE, 1792–1869.

186.—THE SEVENTH PLAGUE OF EGYPT.

'Twas morn; the rising splendor rolled
On marble towers and roofs of gold;
Hall, court and gallery, below,
Were crowded with a living flow;
Egyptian, Arab, Nubian there,
The bearers of the bow and spear,
The hoary priest, the Chaldee sage,
The slave, the gemmed and glittering page—
Helm, turban and tiara shone,
A dazzling ring, round Pharaoh's throne.

There came a man; the human tide
Shrank backward from his stately stride;
His cheek with storm and time was tanned,
A shepherd's staff was in his hand.
A shudder of instinctive fear
Told the dark king what step was near;
On through the host the stranger came,
It parted round his form like flame.

He stooped not at the footstool stone,
He clasped not sandal, kissed not throne;
Erect he stood amid the ring,
His only words, "Be just, O king!"
On Pharaoh's cheek the blood flushed high,
A fire was in his sullen eye;
Yet on the chief of Israel
No arrow of his thousands fell:
All mute and moveless as the grave
Stood chilled the satrap and the slave.

"Thou'rt come," at length the monarch spoke;
Haughty and high the words outbroke:
"Is Israel weary of its lair,
The forehead peeled, the shoulder bare?
Take back the answer to your band:
Go, reap the wind; go, plow the sand;

31

Go, vilest of the living vile,
To build the never-ending pile,
Till, darkest of the nameless dead,
The vulture on their flesh is fed !
What better asks the howling slave
Than the base life our bounty gave?"

Shouted in pride the turbaned peers,
Upclashed to Heaven the golden spears.
" King, thou and thine are doomed!   Behold!"
The prophet spoke—the thunder rolled !
Along the pathway of the sun
Sailed vapory mountains, wild and dun.
" Yet there is time," the prophet said ;
He raised his staff—the storm was stayed.
" King ! be the.word of freedom given ;
What art thou, man, to war with Heaven?"

There came no word.   The thunder broke.
Like a huge city's final smoke,
Thick, lurid, stifling, mixed with flame,
Through court and hall the vapors came.
Loose as the stubble in the field,
Wide flew the men of spear and shield ;
Scattered like foam along the wave,
Flew the proud pageant, prince and slave ;
Or, in the chains of terror bound,
Lay, corpse-like, on the smouldering ground.
" Speak, king !—the wrath is but begun.
Still dumb?   Then, Heaven, thy will be done."

Echoed from earth a hollow roar,
Like ocean on the midnight shore ;
A sheet of lightning o'er them wheeled,
The solid ground beneath them reeled ;
In dust sank roof and battlement ;
Like webs the giant walls were rent ;

Red, broad, before his startled gaze,
The monarch saw his Egypt blaze.
Still swelled the plague—the flame grew pale;
Burst from the clouds the charge of hail;
With arrowy keenness, iron weight,
Down poured the ministers of fate;
Till man and cattle, crushed, congealed,
Covered with death the boundless field.

Still swelled the plague—uprose the blast,
The avenger, fit to be the last;
On ocean, river, forest, vale,
Thundered at once the mighty gale.
Before the whirlwind flew the tree,
Beneath the whirlwind roared the sea;
A thousand ships were on the wave:
Where are they? ask that foaming grave!
Down go the hope, the pride of years;
Down go the myriad mariners;
The riches of earth's richest zone,
Gone! like a flash of lightning, gone!

And, lo! that first fierce triumph o'er,
Swells ocean on the shrinking shore;
Still onward, onward, dark and wide,
Engulfs the land the furious tide.
Then bowed thy spirit, stubborn king,
Thou serpent, reft of fang and sting;
Humbled before the prophet's knee,
He groaned, "Be injured Israel free!"

To heaven the sage upraised his wand;
Back rolled the deluge from the land;
Back to its caverns sank the gale;
Fled from the noon the vapors pale;
Broad burned again the joyous sun:
The hour of wrath and death was done.

REV. GEORGE CROLY, 1780–1862.

187.—PEACE OUR POLICY.

OUR policy is peace. A kind Providence has cast our lot on a portion of the globe sufficiently vast to satisfy the most grasping ambition, and abounding beyond all others in resources which only require to be fully developed to make us the greatest and most prosperous people on earth. To the full development of these resources we have political institutions most happily adapted.

As a friend to human improvement, to civilization, to progress, I am opposed to war. Never in the history of the world has there occurred a period so remarkable as the present. The inventive genius of man has seized upon and subjugated two great agencies of the natural world which never before were made his servants—*steam* and *electricity*, under which I include magnetism in all its phenomena. We have been distinguished by Providence for a great and noble purpose, and I trust we shall fulfill our high destiny.

Again, I am opposed to war, because I hold that it is now to be determined whether two such nations as the United States and England shall exist for the future as friends or enemies. A declaration of war by one of them against the other would be pregnant with miseries, not only to themselves, but to the world. Mighty means are now put into the hands of both, to cement and secure a perpetual peace, by breaking down the barriers of commerce, and uniting the two nations more closely in an intercourse mutually beneficial. If this shall be accomplished, other nations will, one after another, follow the fair example, and a state of general prosperity heretofore unknown will gradually unite and bless the people of the world.

And, far more than all, an intercourse like this points to that inspiring day which philosophers have hoped for, which poets have seen in their bright dreams of fancy, and which prophecy has seen in holy vision—when men shall learn war no more. Who can contem'plate a state of the world like this, and not feel his heart exult at the prospect? And who can doubt that, in the hand of an omnipotent Providence, a 'free and unrestricted commerce shall prove one of the greatest agents in bringing it about ?

Finally, I am against war, because peace—peace is pre-eminently our policy. Our great mission as a people is to occupy this vast domain, there to level forests, and let in upon their solitude the light of day ; to clear swamps and morasses, and redeem them to the plow and the sickle ; to spread over hill and dale the echoes of human labor, and human happiness and contentment ; to fill the land with cities and towns ; to unite its opposite extremities by turnpikes and railroads ; to scoop out canals for the transmission of its products and open rivers for its internal trade.

War can only impede the fulfillment of this high mission of Heaven ; it absorbs the wealth and diverts the energy which might be so much better devoted to the improvement of our country. All we want is peace—established peace ; and then time, under the guidance of a wise and cautious policy, will soon effect for us all the rest. Yes, time—ever-laboring time —will effect everything for us. Our population is now increasing at the annual average of six hundred thousand. Let the next twenty-five years elapse, and our increase will have reached a million a year, and at the end of that period we shall count a population of forty-five millions. Before that day it will have spread from ocean to ocean. The coasts of the Pacific will then be as densely populated and as thickly settled with villages and towns as is now the coast of the Atlantic.

If we can preserve peace, who shall set bounds to our prosperity or to our success ? With one foot planted on the Atlantic and the other on the Pacific, we shall occupy a position between the two old continents of the world—a position eminently calculated to secure to us the commerce and the influence of both. If we abide by the counsels of common sense, if we succeed in preserving our constitutional liberty, we shall then exhibit a spectacle such as the world never saw.

I know that this one great mission is encompassed with dif-

31 *

ficulties; but such is the inherent energy of our political system, and such its expansive capability, that it may be made to govern the widest space. If by war we become great, we cannot be free; if we will be both great and free, our policy is peace.

JOHN C. CALHOUN (see p. 267).

188.—CATILINE TO THE GALLIC CONSPIRATORS.

MEN of Gaul!
What would you give for Freedom—
For Freedom, if it stood before
    your eyes;
For Freedom, if it rushed to
    your embrace;
For Freedom, if its sword were
    ready drawn
To hew your chains off?
Ye would give death or life!
    Then marvel not
That I am here—that Catiline would join you!
The great Patrician? Yes, an hour ago,
But *now* the rebel; Rome's eternal foe,
And *your* sworn friend! My desperate wrong's my pledge.
There's not in Rome—no, not upon the earth—
A man so wronged. The very ground I tread
Is grudged me. Chieftains! ere the moon be down
My land will be the Senate's spoil; my life
The mark of the first villain that will stab
For lucre. But there's a time at hand! Gaze on!
    If I had thought you cowards, I might have come
And told you lies. But you have now the thing
I am—Rome's enemy—and fixed as fate
To you and yours for ever!
The State is weak as dust.
Rome is broken, helpless, heart-sick. Vengeance sits

Above her, like a vulture o'er a corpse
Soon to be tasted. Time and dull decay
Have let the waters round her pillar's foot,
And it *must* fall. Her boasted strength's a ghost,
Fearful to dastards, yet to trenchant swords
Thin as the passing air! A single blow,
In this diseased and crumbling state of Rome,
Would break your chains like stubble.
    But " ye've no swords!"
Have you no plowshares, scythes?
When men are brave, the sickle is a spear!
Must Freedom pine till the slow armorer
Gilds her caparison and sends her out
To glitter and play antics in the sun?
Let hearts be what they ought, the naked earth
Will be their magazine ; the rocks, the trees—
Nay, there's no idle and unnoted thing
But in the hand of Valor will out-thrust
The spear, and make the mail a mockery !
GEORGE CROLY, 1780–1862.

189.—LABOR AND GENIUS.

WHILE I am descanting upon the conduct of the understand-
ing and the best modes of acquiring knowledge, some men
may be disposed to ask, " Why conduct my understanding with
such endless care? and what is the use of so much knowledge?"
What is the use of so much knowledge? What is the use of
so much life? what are we to do with the seventy years of
existence allotted to us? and how are we to live them out to
the last ?

I solemnly declare that, but for the love of knowledge, I
should consider the life of the meanest hedger and ditcher as
preferable to that of the greatest and richest man in existence ;
for the fire of our minds is like the fire which the Persians
burn in the mountains—it flames night and day, and is im-
mortal and not to be quenched ! Upon something it *must* act

and feed—upon the pure spirit of knowledge or upon the foul dregs of polluting passions.

Therefore, when I say, in conducting your understanding, love knowledge with a great love, with a vehement love, with a love coeval with life, what do I say, but love innocence; love virtue; love purity of conduct; love that which, if you are rich and great, will sanctify the blind fortune which has made you so, and make men call it justice; love that which, if you are poor, will render your poverty respectable, and make the proudest feel it unjust to laugh at the meanness of your fortune; love that which will comfort you, adorn you and never quit you—which will open to you the kingdom of thought, and all the boundless regions of conception, as an asylum against the cruelty, the injustice and the pain that may be your lot in the outer world—that which will make your motives habitually great and honorable, and light up in an instant a thousand noble disdains at the very thought of meanness and of fraud!

Therefore, if any young man here have embarked his life in pursuit of knowledge, let him go on without doubting or fearing the event; let him not be intimidated by the cheerless beginnings of knowledge, by the darkness from which she springs, by the difficulties which hover around her, by the wretched habitations in which she dwells, by the want and sorrow which sometimes journey in her train; but let him ever follow her as the angel that guards him, and as the genius of his life. She will bring him out at last into the light of day, and exhibit him to the world, comprehensive in acquirements, fertile in resources, rich in imagination, strong in reasoning, prudent and powerful above his fellows in all the relations and in all the offices of life.

> " What is a man,
> If his chief good and market of his time
> Be but to sleep and feed ? a beast, no more !
> Sure He that made us with such large discourse,
> Looking before and after, gave us not
> That capability and Godlike reason
> To rust in us unused !" SYDNEY SMITH (see p. 303).

190.—THE BRIDGE OF SIGHS.

HOOD.

One more unfortunate,
  Weary of breath,
Rashly importunate,
  Gone to her death!

Take her up tenderly,
  Lift her with care;
Fashioned so slenderly,
  Young, and so fair!

Look at her garments,
Clinging like cerements,
  Whilst the wave constantly
Drips from her clothing;
  Take her up instantly,
Loving, not loathing.

Touch her not scornfully,
Think of her mournfully,
  Gently and humanly;
Not of the stains of her:
All that remains of her
  Now is pure womanly.

Make no deep scrutiny
Into her mutiny

Rash and undutiful;
Past all dishonor,
Death has left on her
  Only the beautiful.

Still, for all slips of hers,
  One of Eve's family;
Wipe those poor lips of hers,
  Oozing so clammily.

Loop up her tresses
  Escaped from the comb—
Her fair auburn tresses;
Whilst wonderment guesses,
  Where was her home?

Who was her father?
Who was her mother?
Had she a sister?
Had she a brother?
  Or was there a dearer one
  Still, and a nearer one
Yet, than all other?

Alas! for the rarity
Of Christian charity
  Under the sun!
Oh, it was pitiful!
Near a whole city full,
  Home she had none.

Sisterly, brotherly,
Fatherly, motherly,
  Feelings were changed;
Love, by harsh evidence,
Thrown from its eminence
Even God's providence
  Seeming estranged.

Where the lamps quiver
So far in the river,

With many a light
From window and casement,
From garret to basement,
She stood, with amazement,
    Houseless by night.

The bleak winds of March
    Made her tremble and shiver;
But not the dark arch,
    Or the black flowing river;
Mad from life's history,
Glad to death's mystery
    Swift to be hurled—
Anywhere, anywhere
    Out of the world!

In she plunged boldly,
No matter how coldly
    The rough river ran;
Over the brink of it,
Picture it, think of it,
    Dissolute man!
Lave in it, drink of it,
    Then, if you can!

Take her up tenderly,
    Lift her with care;

Fashioned so slenderly,
    Young, and so fair!
Ere her limbs frigidly
Stiffen so rigidly,
    Decently, kindly,
Smooth and compose them;
And her eyes, close them,
    Staring so blindly!

Dreadfully staring
    Through muddy impurity,
As when with the daring
Last look of despairing
    Fixed on futurity.

Perishing gloomily,
Spurred by contumely,
Cold inhumanity,
Burning insanity,
    Into her rest!
Cross her hands humbly,
As if praying dumbly,
    Over her breast!
Owning her weakness,
    Her evil behavior,
And leaving with meekness
    Her sins to her Saviour.
        THOMAS HOOD, 1798–1845.

191.—STILL WATERS RUN DEEP.

Hawksley. A thousand pardons, my dear fellow; one gets so absorbed in these figures! Take a chair. You'll allow me to finish what I was about.

Mildmay. Don't mind me. I'm in no hurry.

Hawk. By the way, if you'll look on that table, you'll find a plan of our Inexplosive Galvanic Boat somewhere. Just glance your eye over it, while I knock off this calculation; it will give you an idea of the machinery. (*After a minute or*

two of pretended work, putting away his papers and rising.)
And now, my dear Mildmay, I am at your service. But before
we come to business, how are all at Brompton? The ladies
all well?

Mild. Mrs. Sternhold's a little out of sorts this morning.

Hawk. Ah! Had a bad night?

Mild. I should think so.

Hawk. Well, I had a note from Potter. He tells me you
had some thoughts of taking shares in our Galvanics. I've
mislaid his note, but he mentioned your wanting something
like two hundred shares—wasn't it?

Mild. I beg your pardon; not exactly, I think.

Hawk. Why, wasn't that the figure you put it at yourself
last night?

Mild. Last night—yes.

Hawk. You haven't changed your mind?

Mild. No.

Hawk. Then let us understand one another. Do you want
more than two hundred, or fewer?

Mild. Neither more nor fewer.

Hawk. What do you mean?

Mild. I mean I don't want any at all.

Hawk. Indeed! You surprise me. I suppose you've slept
upon it.

Mild. Exactly. I have slept upon it.

Hawk. Perhaps Mrs. Sternhold's advice may have had
something to do with your sudden change of intention?

Mild. Mrs. Sternhold knows nothing of my sudden change
of intention.

Hawk. Well, as you don't know your own mind for four
and twenty hours together, there's nothing more to be said.
But as you don't want these shares, may I ask what has pro-
cured me the pleasure of seeing you this morning?

Mild. Certainly. I had two objects in coming. In the
first place, about two months ago my father-in-law, Mr. Potter,
took twenty shares in your company. Those shares have come
into my hands this morning, by Mr. Potter's indorsement.

Now, as I don't care about them myself, and as there seems such a rush for them in the market, I suppose you'll have no objection to take them off my hands at par.

Hawk. Eh! Take them off your hands at par? Ha! ha! ha! Upon my word, that's rather too good! My dear Mr. Mildmay, I know you're the most amiable of men, but I had no idea how great you were at a practical joke.

Mild. Very well. We'll drop the shares for the present, and come to motive number two.

Hawk. Pray do; and if it's better fun than motive number one, I shall have to thank you for two of the heartiest laughs I've enjoyed for many a day.

Mild. We shall see. You have in your possession thirteen letters, addressed to you by Mrs. Sternhold. The second motive for my visit was to ask you to give up those letters. Do I make myself understood?

Hawk. (*Aside.*) So! the murder's out! She prefers war! She shall have it. (*Aloud.*) Mr. John Mildmay, your first demand was a good joke. I laughed at it accordingly. But your second you may find no joke, and I would recommend you to be careful how you persist in executing this commission of Mrs. Sternhold.

Mild. I beg your pardon. I have no commission from Mrs. Sternhold.

Hawk. It was not she who told you of those letters?

Mild. Certainly not.

Hawk. Who did?

Mild. You must excuse my answering this question.

Hawk. Then you are acting now on your own responsibility?

Mild. Entirely.

Hawk. Very well; then this is my answer: Though you have married Mrs. Sternhold's niece, I do not admit your right to interfere, without authority from Mrs. Sternhold herself, in an affair in which she alone is interested. I refuse to give up her letters. As to your first request, my business is to sell shares, not to buy them.

Mild. I was prepared for both refusals, so I have taken my measures for compelling you to grant both demands.

Hawk. Indeed! you have? Do let me hear what they are. I am all impatience to know how you propose to make Harry Hawksley say *yes*, when he has begun by saying *no.*

Mild. When you explained to me, a little while ago, the theory of your speculation, you thought you were speaking to a greenhorn in such matters. You were under a mistake. Some four years ago I was a partner in a house in the city which did a good deal in discounting paper—the house of Dalrymple Brothers, in Broad street. You may have heard of it. One day—it was the 30th of April, 1850—a bill was presented for payment at our counting-house, purporting to be drawn on us by our correspondents, Watson & Wright, of Buenos Ayres. Though we had no advices of it, it was paid at once, for it seemed all regular and right; but it turned out to be a forgery. Our correspondents' suspicions fell at once upon a clerk who had just been dismissed from their employment for some errors in his accounts. His name *then* was Burgess. The body of the bill was apparently in the same handwriting as the signature of the firm, but a careful examination showed it to be that of the discharged clerk, and in a blotting-book left accidentally behind him were found various tracings of the signature of the firm. The detectives were at once put on his track, but he had disappeared, and no trace of him could ever be discovered. Well, this money was repaid and the affair forgotten. It so happened that when the bill was presented for payment only one person was in the counting-house—the clerk who paid the money, and who is since dead. But in the private room of the firm, which was separated from the counting-house by a glazed door, was the junior partner, who, through the door, saw the bill presented and observed the face of the person who presented it. I was that junior partner. The person who presented the bill—Burgess, as he was then called—the forger, was *you.*

Hawk. It is an infamous calumny, an abominable lie! Your life shall answer for this insult.

32

Mild. I don't think that, quite. But allow me to conclude. How you have passed your time since that 30th of April, 1850, I have not the advantage of knowing; but I know that soon after my marriage and retirement from business I met you as a visitor at my father-in-law's house. I have a wonderful memory for faces; I remembered yours at once.

Hawk. It is a lie, I tell you.

Mild. No, it isn't. I resolved not to speak till I could back my words by proofs. I applied to my late partners for the forged bill. One of them was dead, the other absent in South America, so that for ten months I found myself obliged to receive as a guest at my own table, as the intimate and trusted friend of my wife's family, a person whom I knew to be a swindler and a forger. The letter I had been so long waiting for, containing the forged bill, arrived yesterday. That bill is in my pocket. If I do not deliver it into your hands before I leave the room, it goes at once into those of the nearest police magistrate.

Hawk. (*After a pause, gloomily.*) What are your terms?

Mild. The price of those shares at par, and Mrs. Sternhold's letters.

Hawk. Here's the money.

Mild. You'll excuse my counting. It is a mercantile habit I learned in the house of Dalrymple Brothers. Quite correct. Here are the scrip certificates. And now, if you please, the letters.

Hawk. Here they are.

Mild. You'll excuse my counting them, too. Thirteen, exactly! Here is the forged bill. And now, Captain Burgess— I mean Hawksley—I have the honor to wish you a very good morning.

TOM TAYLOR.

192.—THE BRITISH SLAVE-TRADE, 1792.

WHY ought the slave-trade to be abolished? Because it is incurable injustice. How much stronger, then, is the argument for immediate than gradual abolition! By allowing it to continue even for one hour, do not my right honorable friends weaken, do they not desert, their own argument of its injustice? If, on the ground of injustice, it ought to be abolished at last, why not now? Why is injustice to be suffered to remain a single hour?

WILLIAM PITT.

From what I hear without doors, it is evident that there is a general conviction entertained of its being far from just, and from that very conviction of its injustice some men have been led, I fear, to the supposition that the slave-trade never could have been permitted to begin but from some strong and irresistible necessity—a necessity, however, which, if it was fancied to exist at first, I have shown cannot be thought by any man whatever to exist now.

This plea of necessity thus presumed, and presumed, as I suspect, from the circumstance of injustice itself, has caused a sort of acquiescence in the continuance of this evil. Men have been led to place it among the rank of those necessary evils which are supposed to be the lot of human creatures, and to be permitted to fall upon some countries or individuals rather than upon others, by that Being whose ways are inscrutable to us, and whose dispensations, it is conceived, we ought not to look into.

The origin of evil is indeed a subject beyond the reach of the human understanding, and the permission of it by the supreme Being is a subject into which it belongs not to us at present to inquire. But where the evil in question is a moral evil, which a man can scrutinize, and where that evil has its origin with ourselves, let us not imagine that we can clear our consciences by this general, not to say irreligious and impious, way of laying aside the question.

If we reflect at all on the subject, we must see that every necessary evil supposes that some other and greater evil would be incurred were it removed; I, therefore, desire to ask, What can be a greater evil which can be stated to overbalance the one in question? I know of no evil that ever has existed, nor can imagine any evil to exist, worse than the tearing of seventy or eighty thousand persons annually from their native land by a combination of the most civilized nations, inhabiting the most enlightened quarter of the globe, but more especially under the sanction of the laws of that nation which calls herself the most free and the most happy of them all!

WILLIAM PITT (see p. 306).

193.—CARCASSONNE.*

" I'M growing old, I've sixty years ;
　　I've labored all my life in vain ;
In all that time of hopes and fears
　　I've failed my dearest wish to gain.
I see full well that here below
　　Bliss unalloyed there is for none.
My prayer would else fulfillment know—

---

* Carcassonne, an old manufacturing city of France, 53 miles S. of Toulouse, and having a population of 15,380. In the time of Cæsar it was a city of considerable note. It is the seat of a bishopric.

Never have I seen Carcassonne.
Never have I seen Carcassonne!

"You spy the city from the hill—
    It lies beyond the mountain blue;
And yet to reach it one must still
    Five long and weary leagues pursue,
And to return as many more!
    Had but the vintage plenteous grown!
But, ah! the grape withheld its store!
    I shall not look on Carcassonne.
    I shall not look on Carcassonne!

"They tell me every day is there
    Not more or less than Sunday gay;
In shining robes and garments fair
    The people walk upon their way.
One gazes there on castle walls
    As grand as those of Babylon,
A bishop and two generals!
    What joy to dwell in Carcassonne!
    Ah! might I but see Carcassonne!

"The vicar's right: he says that we
    Are ever wayward, weak and blind;
He tells us in his homily
    Ambition ruins all mankind;
Yet could I there two days have spent,
    While still the autumn sweetly shone,
Ah, me! I might have died content
    When I had looked on Carcassonne.
    When I had looked on Carcassonne!

"Thy pardon, Father, I beseech,
    In this my prayer if I offend;
One something sees beyond his reach
    From childhood to his journey's end.
My wife, our little boy Aignan,

32 *

Have traveled even to Narbonne;
My grandchild has seen Perpignan.
And I have not seen Carcassonne.
And I have not seen Carcassonne."

So crooned, one day, close by Limoux,
A peasant, double-bent with age.
" Rise up, my friend," said I ; " with you
I'll go upon this pilgrimage."
We left next morning his abode,
But (Heaven forgive him !) halfway on
The old man died upon the road ;
He never gazed on Carcassonne.
Each mortal has his Carcassonne!

GUSTAVE NADAUD (*translated by* JOHN R. THOMPSON).

194.—THE CONSTITUTION A PERMANENCY.

THE Constitution of the United States creates direct relations between this government and individuals. This government may punish individuals for treason and all other crimes in the code when committed against the United States. It has power also to tax individuals, in any mode and to any extent; and it possesses the further power of demanding from individuals military service. Nothing, certainly, can more clearly distinguish a government from a confederation of states than the possession of these powers. No closer relations can exist between individuals and any government.

The state constitutions are established by the people of the states. *This* Constitution is established by the people of *all* the states. How, then, can a state secede? How can a state undo what the whole people have done? How can she absolve her citizens from their obedience to the laws of the United States? How can she annul their obligations and oaths? How can the members of her legislature renounce their own oath ?*

Sir, secession, as a revolutionary right, is intelligible; as a right to be proclaimed in the midst of civil commotions and asserted at the head of armies, I can understand it. But as a practical right, existing under the Constitution, and in conformity with its provisions, it seems to me to be nothing but a plain absurdity; for it supposes resistance to government, under the authority of government itself; it supposes dismemberment, without violating the principles of union; it supposes opposition to law, without crime; it supposes the violation of oaths, without responsibility; it supposes the total overthrow of government, without revolution.

The Constitution regards itself as perpetual and immortal. It seeks to establish a union among the people of the states which shall last through all time. Or if the common fate of things human must be expected at some period to happen, yet that catastrophe is not anticipated. The instrument contains ample provisions for its amendment at all times; none for its abandonment at any time. It declares that new states may come into the Union, but it does not declare that old states may go out.

The Union is not a temporary partnership of states. It is the association of the people under a Constitution of government, uniting their power, joining together their highest interests, cementing their present enjoyments, and blending, in one indivisible mass, all their hopes for the future. Whatsoever is steadfast in just political principles, whatsoever is permanent in the structure of human society, whatsoever there is which can derive an enduring character from being founded on deep-laid principles of constitutional liberty and on the broad foundation of the public will,—all these unite to entitle this instrument to be regarded as A PERMANENT CONSTITUTION OF GOVERNMENT.

DANIEL WEBSTER (see p. 240).

*Their oath to support the Constitution of the United States.

LONGFELLOW.

195.—PAUL REVERE'S RIDE.

LISTEN, my children, and you shall hear
Of that midnight ride of Paul Revere,
On the eighteenth of April, in seventy-five.
Hardly a man is now alive
Who remembers that famous day and year.

He said to his friend, "If the British march
By land or sea from the town to-night,
Hang a lantern aloft in the belfry-arch
Of the North-Church tower, as a signal-light—
One if by land, and two if by sea;
And I on the opposite shore will be,
Ready to ride and spread the alarm
Through every Middlesex village and farm,
For the country-folk to be up and to arm."

Then he said good-night, and with muffled oar
Silently rowed to the Charlestown shore,
Just as the moon rose over the bay,
Where swinging wide at her moorings lay

The Somerset, British man-of-war;
A phantom ship, with each mast and spar
Across the moon like a prison-bar,
And a huge black hulk that was magnified
By its own reflection in the tide.

Meanwhile, his friend through alley and street
Wanders and watches with eager ears,
Till in the silence around him he hears
The muster of men at the barrack-door,
The sound of arms, and the tramp of feet,
And the measured tread of the grenadiers
Marching down to their boats on the shore.

Then he climbed the tower of the church,
Up the wooden stairs, with stealthy tread,
To the belfry-chamber overhead,
And startled the pigeons from their perch
On the sombre rafters, that round him made
Masses and moving shapes of shade—
Up the light ladder, slender and tall,
To the highest window in the wall,
Where he paused to listen and look down
A moment on the roofs of the quiet town,
And the moonlight flowing over all.

Meanwhile, impatient to mount and ride,
Booted and spurred, with a heavy stride,
On the opposite shore walked Paul Revere.
Now he patted his horse's side,
Now gazed on the landscape far and near,
Then impetuous stamped the earth,
And turned and tightened his saddle-girth;
But mostly he watched with eager search
The belfry tower of the old North Church,
As it rose above the graves on the hill,
Lonely, and spectral, and sombre, and still.

And, lo! as he looks, on the belfry's height,
A glimmer, and then a gleam of light!
He springs to the saddle, the bridle he turns,
But lingers and gazes, till full on his sight
A second lamp in the belfry burns!

A hurry of hoofs in a village street,
A shape in the moonlight, a bulk in the dark,
And beneath from the pebbles, in passing, a spark
Struck out by a steed that flies fearless and fleet:
That was all! And yet, through the gloom and the light,
The fate of a nation was riding that night;
And the spark struck out by that steed in his flight
Kindled the land into flame by its heat.

It was twelve by the village clock
When he crossed the bridge into Medford-town.
He heard the crowing of the cock,
And the barking of the farmer's dog,
And felt the damp of the river fog,
That rises after the sun goes down.

It was one by the village clock
When he rode into Lexington.
He saw the gilded weather-cock
Swim in the moonlight as he passed,
And the meeting-house windows, blank and bare,
Gaze at him with a spectral glare,
As if they already stood aghast
At the bloody work they would look upon.
It was two by the village clock
When he came to the bridge in Concord town.
He heard the bleating of the flock,
And the twitter of birds among the trees,
And felt the breath of the morning breeze
Blowing over the meadows brown.
And one was safe and asleep in his bed
Who at the bridge would be first to fall,

Who that day would be lying dead,
Pierced by a British musket-ball.

You know the rest. In the books you have read
How the British regulars fired and fled—
How the farmers gave them ball for ball
From behind each fence and farmyard wall,
Chasing the red-coats down the lane,
Then crossing the fields to emerge again
Under the trees at the turn of the road,
And only pausing to fire and load.

So through the night rode Paul Revere;
And so through the night went his cry of alarm
To every Middlesex village and farm—
A cry of defiance, and not of fear—
A voice in the darkness, a knock at the door,
And a word that shall echo for evermore!
For, borne on the night-wind of the Past,
Through all our history, to the last,
In the hour of darkness, and peril, and need,
The people will waken and listen to hear
The hurrying hoof-beat of that steed,
And the midnight message of Paul Revere.

HENRY W. LONGFELLOW.

196.—THE SPIRIT OF INTOLERANCE.

IT is very difficult to make the mass of mankind believe that the state of things is ever to be otherwise than they have been accustomed to see it. I have very often heard old persons describe the impossibility of making any one believe that the American Colonies could ever be separated from this country. It was always considered as an idle dream of discontented politicians, good enough to fill up the periods of a speech, but which no practical man, devoid of the spirit of party, considered to be within the limits of possibility.

There was a period when the slightest concession would

have satisfied the Americans; but all the world was in heroics. One set of gentlemen met at the Lamb and another at the Lion—blood and treasure men, breathing war, vengeance and contempt—and in eight years afterward an awkward-looking gentleman in plain clothes walked up to the drawing-room of St. James's, in the midst of the gentlemen of the Lion and the Lamb, and was introduced as the *ambassador from the United States of America!*

Mild and genteel people do not like the idea of persecution, and are advocates for toleration, but then they think it no act of intolerance to deprive Catholics of political power. The history of all this is that all men secretly like to punish others for not being of the same opinion with themselves, and that this sort of privation is the only species of persecution of which the improved feeling and advanced cultivation of the age will admit. Fire and fagot, chains and stone walls, have been clamored away; nothing remains but to mortify a man's pride, and to limit his resources, and to set a mark upon him by cutting him off from his fair share of political power. By this receipt insolence is gratified and humanity is not shocked.

The gentlest Protestant can see, with dry eyes, Lord Stourton excluded from Parliament, though he would abominate the most distant idea of personal cruelty to Mr. Petre. This is only to say that he lives in the nineteenth instead of the sixteenth century, and that he is as intolerant in religious matters as the state of manners existing in his age will permit.

Is it not the same spirit which wounds the pride of a fellow-creature on account of his faith, or which casts his body into the flames? Are they anything else but degrees and modifications of the same principle? The true spirit is to search after God and for another life with lowliness of heart; to fling down no man's altar, to punish no man's prayer; to heap no penalties and no pains on those solemn supplications which, in divers tongues, and in varied forms, and in temples of a thousand shapes, but with one deep sense of human dependence, men pour forth to God.

REV. SYDNEY SMITH (see p. 303).

197.—THE KING OF THULE.

In Thu'le dwelt a king, and he was leal even to the grave;
A cup to him of the red, red gold his true love dying gave:
He drained it to the dregs whene'er he drank amid his peers,
And ever as he quaffed from it his eyes would brim with tears.
And when his end drew nigh, he told his kingdom's cities up,
Gave all his wealth unto his heir, but with it not the cup.
He sat and feasted at the board; among his knights sat he,
Within the castle of his sires, the castle by the sea.
Then up he rose, one draught he took, a long last breath he drew,
And down the cup he loved so well into the ocean threw.
He watched it flashing, filling and sinking beneath the sea,
And then his eyes were darkened, and never again drank he.

GOETHE, 1749–1832.

33

198.—THE UNFORGOTTEN FOE.

CHARACTERS.—*Maro, a banished Roman ; Paulus, a Christian.*

Enter MARO.

Maro. Alone, in this impenetrable forest!
What ho! What ho! My voice is hoarse with shouting.
No answer comes, save from some startled bird.
[*Calls.*] Ho! Hear me! Hear me!
Hark! A crackling bough!
A human footstep! Yes; relief is nigh!

Enter PAULUS.

Oh, welcome, stranger, whosoe'er thou art!
For I am lost in these bewildering thickets.
Most timely is thy coming.
   Paulus. And who art thou?
   Maro. A Roman; once in power, now an exile,
A wretched outcast, plundered and forsaken.
   Paul. If thou art wretched and an exile, welcome!
I claim thee as a brother; and my heart
Throws open all its doors to take thee in.   [*Gives his hand,
   then starts and looks distrustfully at Maro.*]
   Maro. Thou shalt not find me poor in gratitude,
Though otherwise a beggar. Is there not
Some place of refuge near us?
   Paul. On the border
Of this thick wood, I, with my wife and children,
Have my poor hut. I will not call it house.
   Maro. How happens it a person of thy speech
Can in a wild like this content himself,
Far from the guardianship and pomp of Rome?
   Paul. The guardianship of Rome! The guardianship!
Man, to Rome's fatal guardianship I owe
The massacre of kindred and of friends;
Of father, mother, brothers, butchered—butchered
All in cold blood! And oh, for what?

Maro. How? Butchered?
When was it? Where?

Paul. Ten years ago, in Rome!
[*Aside.*] Oh, last of all shouldst thou be ignorant!
Yes, it is he,—none other.

Maro. Butchered by whom?

Paul. By thee! by thee! Thou art the man! thou, Maro!
The unjust judge, the craven magistrate,
Creature of Nero, agent of his fell,
His fiendish cruelties! Thou art the man!
For what—for what was all that wealth of blood,
Of pure and innocent blood, poured out like water?
Because it ran in Christian veins!

Maro. Thou ravest!
Thou hast mistaken me for some one else.
I will depart. [*Going.*]

Paul. Not yet. Thy cowering glance
And trembling knees belie thy faltering words.
Though *I* may be forgot, *thou*'rt not forgot.
Dost thou recall not that eventful day,
In the great amphitheatre, when first
Thou wert informed the famous Libyan lion,
The emperor's favorite, that dreadful beast
Which thou hadst ordered out to tear in pieces
A white-haired man, Serenus Claudianus
(My father!), had been slain?
Dost thou recall thy rage against the slayer?
Thou dost! *I* slew the beast! Vain all disguise.
Thy brows are knit, thy teeth gnaw at thy lip
In impotent renewal of thy anger.

Maro. Nay—how didst thou escape?

Paul. Ah ha! thy words,
Thy very words betray thee! I escaped:
I'll tell thee how. The man thou didst most trust
Became a Christian.

Maro. He! Servilius Dorso!
Betrayed by him? by him?

Paul. Dost thou regret, even in retrospection,
The relish of a disappointed vengeance?
Why do thy fingers work so? Ah! thou *wouldst,*
But durst not!

   Maro. Nay, I am not what I was.

   Paul. What canst *thou* do?
What are *thy* limbs and sinews
Compared with *these,* that have been trained and tested
In wrestling with wild nature for my food,
With the fierce bear for life, or with the gale
Upon the lake for safety?

   Maro. Do not abuse thy power! Forgive—forgive me!

   Paul. Forgive thee? Oh, have I not often reveled
In the anticipation of a moment
Like this one now, when I could have thee thus,
With no one by, when I could grasp thee thus—
Thus—thus by the throat, and shout into thy ear,
Remember old Serenus!

   Maro. Mercy!

   Paul. Mercy?
Ay! even such mercy as *thou* didst show, abhorred one!
Show to that gray-haired man, his kneeling wife,
And his imploring children!
The only answer to their prayer was *death!*
Not a swift, easy death, but one of torture,
Of horror—in the amphitheatre—
Torn by wild beasts! Dost *thou* dare plead for mercy?

   Maro [*on his knees*]. As thou'rt a man, be merciful!

   Paul. That plea
Will not avail.

   Maro. Ah, then, as thou'rt a Christian!

[*A pause, during which* PAULUS *gently and gradually releases his hold, and* MARO *rises.*]

   Paul. And dost thou venture to pronounce *that* name—
The sacred name, by thee so spurned and hated?
I thank thee for it, Maro! Ay, I thank thee.

The old, the heathen spirit, had possessed me,
And driven out the very grace of Christ!
Thou hast recalled me to my better self.
The pent-up vengeance all explodes in words.
Bloody oppressor, diligent murderer
And persecutor of all Christian men,
As thou hast been—
Still, do not fear! Thou'rt safe—
Thou'rt safe!

   Maro. Thanks! thanks! [*Going.*]

   Paul. Why, whither wouldst thou go?

   Maro. To find a shelter for the night.

   Paul. To perish!

Here! Come with *me*, and thou shalt have a bed
In my poor hut, with food, and warmth, and safety.
Wilt thou not trust me?

   Maro. Oh, thy wrongs have been
Too deadly for forgiveness!

   Paul. Knowest thou not,
The Christian, *if* a Christian, *must* forgive,
As he would be forgiven by the Father?

   Maro. But here forgiveness fails. I blame thee not;
For now, in this majestic solitude,
My crimes start up between me and all hope
In their true outline—hideous, grim, unearthly.
I know it is not in the heart of man,
Where such wrongs cry aloud, to cast out vengeance.

   Paul. "Vengeance is mine! I will repay, saith the Lord!"
I do forgive thee, Maro—I have said it.
The Christian's *act* shall tell thee what his *faith* is.
Not the dear child who hangs about my neck
And calls me *father* shall more tenderly
Be cared for and protected from all danger
Than thou, if thou wilt come and be my guest.
Dost thou believe me?

   Maro [*covering his face*]. Ay! I cannot help it.
The power *must* be divine that works a change

33 *

In thee, in me, like this!   My soul is flooded
With sudden light!   Celestial guards environ!
I see, as in a vision, coming down,
The beauty and the sanctity of mercy;
The truth of God and immortality;
The might and glory of that law of love,
That supreme law, eternal, absolute,
Which bade thee crush this proud and stony heart,
Melt and remould it, with forgiving words.
Oh that I could blot out the hateful past!
Oh that I might cast off that weight of sin!
    Paul. This is no fitful mood.
'Tis Christ's own hand has led thee here, my brother;
And from that hand, with awe, do I accept thee.
Do not despair!   There's balm for thee in Gilead.
Hereafter, should I waver in my kindness,
Utter again that plea: "As thou'rt a Christian!"   [*Exeunt.*
                                   SARGENT.

199.—A PLEA FOR DUNCES.

THACKERAY.

LET us people who are so uncommonly clever and learned have a great tenderness and pity for the poor folks who are not endowed with the prodigious talents which we possess. I have always had a regard for dunces; those of my own school-days were amongst the pleasantest of the fellows, and have turned out by no means the dullest in life; whereas many a youth who could turn off Latin hexameters by the yard, and construe Greek quite glibly, is no better than a feeble prig now, with not a pennyworth more brains than were in his head before his beard grew.

Master Hulker, at Dr. Birch's, is the most honest, kind, active, plucky creature. He can do many things better than most boys. He can go up a tree, jump, play at cricket, drive and swim perfectly, he can eat twice as much as almost any-body (as Miss Birch well knows), he has a pretty talent of carving figures with his hack-knife, he makes and paints little coaches, he can take a watch to pieces and put it together again. He can do everything but learn his lessons, and there he sticks at the bottom of the school, hopeless. As the little boys are drafted from Miss Raby's class (it is true she is one of the best instructresses in the world), they enter and hop over poor Hulker. He would be handed over to the governess, only he is too big.

. If you could see his grammar ! It is a perfect curiosity of dog's ears. The leaves and cover are all curled and ragged. Many of the pages are worn away with the rubbing of his elbows, as he sits poring over the hopeless volume, or with the blows of his fists as he thumps it madly, or with the poor fellow's tears. You see him wiping them away with the back of his hand as he tries and can't do it. The doctor has operated upon Hulker (between ourselves), but the boy was so little affected you would have thought he had taken chloro-form. Birch is weary of whipping now, and leaves the boy to go his own gait.

Prince, when he hears the lesson, adopts the sarcastic man-ner with Master Hulker, and says, " Mr. Hulker, may I take the liberty to inquire if your brilliant intellect has enabled you to perceive the difference between those words which gram-marians have defined as substantive and adjective nouns? If not, perhaps Mr. Ferdinand Timmins will instruct you." And Timmins easily hops over Hulker's head. I wish Prince would leave off girding at the poor lad. He's an only son, and his mother is a widow woman who loves him with all her might.

WILLIAM MAKEPEACE THACKERAY, 1811–1864.

200.—LAMENTATION FOR CELIN.*

AT the gate of old Granada, when all its bolts are barred,
At twilight, at the Vega-gate, there is a trampling heard;
There is a trampling heard, as of horses treading slow,
And a weeping voice of women and a heavy sound of woe.
" What tower is fallen? what star is set? what chief come
      these bewailing?"
" A tower is fallen! A star is set! Alas, alas for Celin!"

Three times they knock, three times they cry, and wide the
      doors they throw;
Dejectedly they enter and mournfully they go!
In gloomy lines they mustering stand beneath the hollow porch,
Each horseman grasping in his hand a black and flaming torch.
Wet is each eye as they go by, and all around is wailing,
For all have heard the misery—"Alas, alas for Celin!"

Him yesterday a Moor did slay of Bencerraje's blood:
'Twas at the solemn jousting; around the nobles stood;
The nobles of the land were by, and ladies bright and fair
Looked from their latticed windows, the haughty sight to share;
But now the nobles all lament, the ladies are bewailing,
For he was Granada's darling knight—"Alas, alas for Celin!"

Before him ride his vassals, in order two by two,
With ashes on their turbans spread, most pitiful to view;
Behind him his four sisters, each wrapped in sable veil,
Between the tambour's dismal strokes take up the doleful
      tale;
When stops the muffled drum, ye hear their brotherless be-
      wailing,
And all the people, far and near, cry, "Alas, alas for Celin!"

Oh! lovely lies he on his bier above the purple pall,
The flower of all Granada's youth, the loveliest of them all;
His dark, dark eye is closed, his rosy lip is pale,
The crust of blood lies black and dim upon his burnished mail;

* Pronounce *Say'lin.*

And evermore the hoarse tambour breaks in upon their wailing;
Its sound is like no earthly sound—" Alas, alas for Celin !"

The Moorish maid at her lattice stands, the Moor stands at
his door ;
One maid is wringing of her hands and one is weeping sore.
Down to the dust men bow their heads, and ashes black they
strew
Upon their broidered garments of crimson, green and blue ;
Before each gate the bier stands still, then bursts the loud
bewailing,
From door and lattice, high and low—" Alas, alas for Celin !"

An old, old woman cometh forth when she hears the people
cry ;
Her hair is white as silver, like horn her glazëd eye ;
'Twas she who nursed him at her breast, who nursed him
long ago ;
She knows not whom they all lament, but, ah ! she soon shall
know !
With one loud shriek, she through doth break, when her ears
receive their wailing—
" Let me kiss my Celin ere I die !   Alas, alas for Celin !"

JOHN GIBSON LOCKHART.

201.—ON COMPETITIVE EXAMINATIONS.

CERTAIN objections have been made to the system of com-
petitive examinations.   Some people say it leads to cramming.
It often happens that when mankind seize upon a word they
imagine that word to be an argument, and go about repeating
it, thinking they have arrived at some great and irresistible
conclusion.   So when they pronounce the word "cramming"
they think they have utterly discredited the system to which
that word is by them applied.   Some people seem to imagine
that the human mind is like a bottle, and that when you have
filled it with anything you pour it out again and it becomes

as empty as it was before. That is not the nature of the human mind.

The boy who has been crammed, to use the popular word, has, in point of fact, learned a great deal, and that learning has accomplished two objects. In the first place, the boy has exercised the faculties of his mind in being crammed ; and in the next place, there remains in his mind a great portion of the knowledge so acquired, and which probably forms the basis of future attainment in different branches of education. Depend upon it that the boy who is crammed, if he is crammed successfully, not only may succeed in the examination for which he is preparing, but is from that time forward more intellectual, better informed and more disposed to push forward the knowledge which by that cramming he has acquired.

It is also said that you are teaching young men a great variety of things which will be of no use to them in the career which they are destined to pursue, and that you are pandering to their vanity by making them believe they are wiser than they really are. These objections also are in my opinion utterly futile. As to vanity and conceit, those are most vain and conceited who know the least. The more a man knows, the more he acquires a conviction of the extent of that which he does not know. A man ought to know a great deal to acquire a knowledge of the immensity of his ignorance. If competitive examination is not liable to objection upon the score that it tends to raise undue notions of superiority on the part of those who go through it, so also it is a great mistake to imagine that a range of knowledge disqualifies a man for the particular career and profession to which he is destined.

Nothing can be more proper than that a young man, having selected a particular profession, should devote the utmost vigor of his mind to qualify himself for it by acquiring the knowledge which is necessary for distinction in that line of life ; but it would be a great mistake for him to confine himself to that study alone, and you may be sure that the more a young man knows of a great variety of subjects, and the more he exercises his faculties in acquiring a great range of knowledge, the better he will perform the duties of his particular profession. That sort of general knowledge may be likened to the gymnastic exercises to which soldiers are accustomed. It is not that it can be expected that these particular movements would be of any use to them on the day of battle, but these gymnastic exercises render their muscles flexible, strengthen their limbs, invigorate their health, and make them better able to undergo fatigue and to adapt themselves to all circumstances.

So with a wide range of study: it sharpens the wits; it infuses general knowledge into the mind; it sets a young man thinking; it strengthens the memory and stores it with facts, and in this way makes him a better and more able man in the particular profession which he is intending to pursue.

LORD PALMERSTON.

————

202.—THE GERMAN RHINE.

THEY never shall subdue it, the German Rhine's free stream!
Though fierce as vultures to it they flock with hungry scream:
While yet it calmly weareth its green and tranquil vest;
While yet the wanderer heareth one oar upon its breast!

They never shall o'ercome it, our glorious German Rhine!
While yet our hearts name from it the fresh and generous wine:
While proud its rocks are raising their iron brows of might;
While airy domes are gazing into its mirror bright.

They never shall subdue it, the German Rhine, the free!
While youths and maidens woo it, pledge of their vows to be:
While yet one fish below it sports gladsomely along,
Or on its shores one poet can breathe a deathless song.

They never shall subdue it, our German Rhine's free stream!
Though fierce as vultures to it they flock with hungry scream:
No! they shall win it never, our German Rhine's free wave,
Till it hath closed for ever o'er the last German's grave!

FROM THE GERMAN OF BECKER.

203.—THOUGHTS IN A GREAT LIBRARY.

THIS is the library. What a world of wit is here packed up together! I know not whether this sight doth more dismay or comfort me: it dismays me to think that here is so much that

I cannot know; it comforts me to think that this variety yields so good helps to know what I should. There is no truer word than that of Solomon: "There is no end of making many books." This sight verifies it; there is no end; indeed, it were pity there should be.

God hath given to man a busy soul, the agitation whereof cannot but through time and experience work out many hidden truths; to suppress these would be no other than injurious to mankind, whose minds, like unto so many candles, should be kindled by each other. The thoughts of our deliberation are the most accurate, and these we commit to paper.

What a happiness is it that without the offense of necromancy I may here call up any of the ancient worthies of learning, whether human or divine, and confer with them of all my doubts!—that I can at pleasure summon whole synods of reverend fathers and acute doctors, from all the coasts of the earth, to give their well-studied judgments on all points of questions which I propose! Neither can I cast my eye casually upon any of these silent masters, but I must learn somewhat

Blessëd be God that hath set up so many clear lamps in his church! Now none but the willfully blind can plead darkness; and blessëd be the memory of those his faithful servants that have left their blood, their spirits, their lives, in these precious papers, and have willingly wasted themselves into these enduring monuments to give light unto others!

BISHOP HALL, 1574–1656.

204.—LAMENT OF THE ERRING ONE.

How happy are they who can find in reflection
No act that cries "shame"—no abhorred recollection!
They whose thoughts shed the light of tranquillity round them
To cheer and support when the cold world hath bound them
In cankering chains!

But wretched is he whose career is in blindness,
Who joins hands with hatred and battles with kindness;
Who, keenly alive to a fine sense of pleasure,
Abandons the cup of delight for a measure
Of poison most foul.

And such have I been but too long, to my sorrow;
I've done that to-day which I've wept for to-morrow;
Still loving the right, and the wrong still pursuing,
Making vows to be wise, and yet madly renewing
Old follies again.

I have dreams—I have dreams—by these dull midnight embers,
Of things which my soul with reluctance remembers;
Of dear household scenes, where, at morn, drooping-hearted,
With eyes raining tears, in my boyhood I parted
From one now no more.

All empty his seat—it were vain to deplore him;
Yet I wish the deaf grave for an hour would restore him,
Until, from the erring lips prized far too dearly,
He heard his son's grief that he ever severely
A fond bosom pained.

The wish is opposed by the justice of Heaven:
'Tis right man should suffer before he's forgiven;
And oh, never dagger cut keener or deeper
Than useless regret o'er the poor silent sleeper
We've injured and loved.

I see through the lattice the stars dimly gleaming,
Blest beacons of hope o'er a troubled sea beaming;

34

I turn from their light to the Being who made them,
And pray that the beauty in which he arrayed them
                    May one day be mine.

Thou know'st, O Unknown, whom to scan dare we never,—
Who art that thou art—hast been still—shalt be ever,—
Thou knowest that thy creature, now humbled before thee,
With his weak human sense doth sincerely adore thee ;
                    Then hear him—oh, hear !

Oh ! hear him, this hour, while the hues of his spirit
Are undimmed by the stain all are born to inherit ;
And grant that, unmoved by life's joy or life's sorrow,
Man's smile or man's frown, he may act on the morrow
                    The thoughts of to-night.

I ask not for riches, for power I care not—
To win them, as most mortals win them, I dare not ;
And the fame which I covet, I'll never here know it :
I may not deserve it—ye cannot bestow it,
                    Blind brothers of clay !

But guide me, O God, in a course still improving,
As this orb round the sun, in thy light always moving ;
And let naught unholy arise to conceal thee
From him who, whenever he ceases to feel thee,
                    Contentment hath none.

May my life-time glide on, as these night sands are going,
To eternity's ocean, a quiet stream flowing ;
O my soul, be thy waters still pure as they now are—
Still blessed—lest they wander—O Lord, with thy power
                    To turn them to thee.

Then I'll grasp thy cold hand, mystic Death, as the hoary
High priest of a temple with clouds on its glory ;
And though in the portal the pilgrim may falter,
He'll forward with joy when he thinks of the altar
                    Bright burning within.
                        WILLIAM KENNEDY.

205.—THE FUTURE OF AMERICA.

FELLOW-CITIZENS, the hours of this day are rapidly flying, and this occasion* will soon be passed. Neither we nor our children can expect to behold its return. They are in the distant regions of futurity, they exist only in the all-creating power of God,—they who shall stand here a hundred years hence, to trace through us their descent from the Pilgrims, and to survey, as we have now surveyed, the progress of their country during the lapse of a century.

We would anticipate their concurrence with us in our sentiments of deep regard for our common ancestors. We would anticipate and partake the pleasure with which they will then recount the steps of New England's advancement. On the morning of that day, although it will not disturb us in our repose, the voice of acclamation and gratitude, commencing on the rock of Plymouth, shall be transmitted through millions of the sons of the Pilgrims, till it lose itself in the murmurs of the Pacific seas.

We would leave for the consideration of those who shall then occupy our places, some proof that we hold the blessings transmitted from our fathers in just estimation ; some proof of our attachment to the cause of good government, and of civil and religious liberty ; some proof of a sincere and ardent desire to promote everything which may enlarge the understandings and improve the hearts of men. And when, from the long distance of a hundred years, they shall look back upon us, they shall know at least that we possessed affections which, running backward and warming with gratitude for what our ancestors have done for our happiness, run forward also to our posterity, and meet them with cordial salutation ere yet they have arrived on the shore of being.

Advance, then, ye future generations! We would hail you as you rise in your long succession to fill the places which we now fill, and to taste the blessings of existence where we are

* The centennial celebration of the landing of the Pilgrims at Plymouth, Massachusetts, December 22, 1820.

passing, and soon shall have passed, our own human duration. We bid you welcome to this pleasant land of the fathers. We bid you welcome to the healthful skies and the verdant fields of New England. We greet your accession to the great inheritance which we have enjoyed. We welcome you to the blessings of good government and religious liberty. We welcome you to the treasures of science and the delights of learning. We welcome you to the transcendent sweets of domestic life—to the happiness of kindred, and parents, and children. We welcome you to the immeasurable blessings of rational existence, the immortal hope of Christianity, and the light of everlasting truth.

DANIEL WEBSTER (see p. 240).

206.—LIBERTY OF THE PRESS.

HAVING restricted universal suffrage and the right of public meetings, you would now wage war against the liberty of the Press. In the crisis through which France is passing, it is asked, " Who is making all this trouble ? Whom must we punish ? " The alarm party in Europe say, " It is France ! " In France they say, " It is Paris ! " In Paris they say, " It is the Press ! " The man of observation and reflection says, " The culprit is not the Press; it is not Paris; it is not France; it is the human mind ! "

Yes, it is the human mind which has made the nations what they are; which from the beginning has scrutinized, examined, discussed, debated, doubted, contradicted, probed, affirmed and pursued without ceasing the solution of the problem eternally placed before the creature by the Creator. It is the human mind which, since history began, has transformed societies and governments according to a law progressively acceptable to the reason; which has been theocracy, aristocracy, monarchy, and which is to-day democracy. It is the human mind which has been Babylon, Tyre, Jerusalem, Athens, and which to-day is Paris; which has been, turn by turn, and sometimes all at once, error, illusion, schism, protestation, truth. It is the human mind which is the great leader of the generations, and which, in short, has always marched toward the Just, the Beautiful and the True, enlightening multitudes, elevating life, raising more and more the head of the people toward the Right, and the head of the individual toward God.

And now I address myself to the alarm party—not in this chamber merely, but wherever they may be, throughout Europe—and I say to them : Consider well what you would do ; reflect on the task that you have undertaken, and measure it well before you commence. Suppose you should succeed : when you have destroyed the Press, there will remain something more to destroy—Paris! When you have destroyed Paris, there will remain France. When you have destroyed France, there will remain the human mind.

I repeat it, let this great European alarm party measure the immensity of the task which, in their heroism, they would attempt. Though they annihilate the Press to the last journal, Paris to the last pavement, France to the last hamlet, they will have done nothing. There will remain yet for them to destroy something always paramount, above the generations, and, as it were, between man and his Maker ; something that has written all the books, invented all the arts, discovered all the worlds, founded all the civilizations ; something which will always grasp, under the form of revolutions, what is not yielded under the form of progress ; something which is itself unseizable as the light and unapproachable as the sun, and which calls itself the human mind.

VICTOR HUGO (see p. 312).

207.—OUT, JOHN!

OUT, John! out, John! what are you about, John?
If you don't say, "Out," at once, you make the fellow doubt, John!
Say I'm out, whoever calls, and hide my hat and cane, John!
Say you've not the least idea when I shall come again, John.
Let the people leave their bills, but tell them not to call, John;
Say I'm courting Miss Rupee, and mean to pay them all, John.

34 *   2 A

Run, John! run, John! there's another dun, John;
If it's Prodger, bid him call to-morrow week at one, John;
If he says he saw me at the window as he knocked, John,
Make a face, and shake your head, and tell him you are shocked, John;
Take your pocket-handkerchief, and put it to your eye, John;
Say your master's not the man to bid you tell a lie, John.

Oh, John, go, John! there's Noodle's knock, I know, John;
Tell him that all yesterday you sought him high and low, John.
Tell him, just before he came you saw me mount the hill, John;
Say you think I'm only gone to pay his little bill, John;
Then, I think, you'd better add that if I miss to-day, John,
You're sure I mean to call when next I pass his way, John.

Hie, John! fly, John! I will tell you why, John—
If there is not Grimshaw at the corner, let me die, John.
He will hear of no excuse—I'm sure he'll search the house, John,
Peeping into corners hardly fit to hold a mouse, John;
Beg he'll take a chair and wait—I know he won't refuse, John—
And I'll pop through the little door that opens on the mews, John.

Thomas Haynes Bayly, 1797-1839.

208.—JUSTICE.

In this God's world, with its wild-whirling eddies and mad foaming oceans, where men and nations perish as if without law, and judgment for an unjust thing is sternly delayed, dost thou think that there is therefore no justice? It is what the fool hath said in his heart. It is what the wise in all times were wise because they denied and knew for ever not to be. I tell thee again there is nothing else but justice. One strong thing I find here below—the just thing, the true thing.

My friend, if thou hadst all the artillery of Woolwich trundling at thy back in support of an unjust thing, and infinite bonfires visibly waiting ahead of thee to blaze centuries long for thy victory on behalf of it, I would advise thee to call halt, to fling down thy baton, and say, "In God's name, No!" Thy "success!" Poor devil, what will thy success amount to? If the thing is unjust thou hast not succeeded—no, not though bonfires blazed from north to south, and bells rang, and editors wrote leading articles, and the just thing lay trampled out of sight, to all mortal eyes an abolished and an annihilated thing.

Success! In a few years thou wilt be dead and dark—all cold, eyeless, deaf; no blaze of bonfires, ding dong of bells, or leading articles visible or audible to thee again at all for ever! What kind of success is that?

THOMAS CARLYLE (see pp. 47, 404).

209.—THE DRUM.

YONDER is a little drum, hanging on the wall;
Dusty wreaths and tattered flags round about it fall.
A shepherd youth on Cheviot's hills watched the sheep whose skin
A cunning workman wrought, and gave the little drum its din;
And happy was the shepherd-boy whilst tending of his fold,
Nor thought he there was in the world a spot like Cheviot's wold.

And so it was for many a day; but change with time will come,
And he (alas for him the day!)—he heard the little drum.
"Follow," said the drummer-boy, "would you live in story!
For he who strikes a foeman down wins a wreath of glory."
"*Rub-a-dub! and rub-a-dub!*" the drummer beats away—
The shepherd lets his bleating flock on Cheviot wildly stray.

On Egypt's arid wastes of sand the shepherd now is lying;
Around him many a parching tongue for "water" faintly crying.
Oh that he were on Cheviot's hills, with velvet verdure spread,
Or lying 'mid the blooming heath where oft he made his bed;
Or could he drink of those sweet rills that trickle to its vales,
Or breathe once more the balminess of Cheviot's mountain gales.

At length upon his wearied eyes the mists of slumber come,
And he is in his home again, till wakened by the drum.
"To arms! to arms!" his leader cries; "the foe—the foe is nigh!"
Guns loudly roar, steel clanks on steel, and thousands fall to die.
The shepherd's blood makes red the sand: "O water—give me some!
My voice might meet a friendly ear but for that little drum!"

'Mid moaning men and dying men, the drummer kept his way,
And many a one by "glory" lured abhorred the drum that day.

"*Rub-a-dub!* and *rub-a-dub!*" the drummer beat aloud—
The shepherd died; and, ere the morn, the hot sand was his shroud.
And this is "glory"? Yes; and still will man the tempter follow,
Nor learn that glory, like its drum, is but a sound, and hollow.

DOUGLAS JERROLD, 1803–1857.

210.—HONOR TO LABOR.

CARLYLE.

Two men I honor, and no third. First, the toil-worn crafts-man that with earth-made implements laboriously conquers the earth and makes her man's. Venerable to me is the hand, hard and coarse, wherein notwithstanding lies a cunning virtue, indefeasibly royal, as of this planet. Venerable, too, is the rugged face all weather-tanned, besoiled with his rude intelligence, for it is the face of a man living man-like. Oh, but the more venerable for thy rudeness, and even because we must pity as well as love thee! Hardly entreated brother, for us was thy back so bent, for us were thy straight limbs and fingers so deformed; thou wert our conscript on whom the lot fell, and fighting our battles wert so marred. For in thee too lay a God-created form, but it was not to be unfolded; encrusted must it stand with the thick adhesions and defacements of labor; and thy body, like thy soul, was not to know freedom. Yet, toil on, toil on; *thou* art in thy duty, be out of it who may; thou toilest for the altogether indispensable daily bread.

A second man I honor, and still more highly—him who is seen toiling for the spiritually indispensable—not daily bread, but the bread of life. Is not he too in his duty, endeavoring toward inward harmony, revealing this by act or by word, through all his outward endeavors, be they high or low? Highest of all when his outward and his inward endeavors are one; when we can name him artist; not earthly craftsman only, but inspired thinker, who with heaven-made implement conquers heaven for us! If the poor and humble toil that we have food, must not the high and glorious toil for him in return that he may have light, guidance, freedom, immortality? These two in all their degrees I honor; all else is chaff and dust, which let the wind blow whither it listeth.

There is a perennial nobleness and even sacredness in work. Were he ever so benighted or forgetful of his high calling, there is always hope in a man that actually and earnestly works; in idleness alone there is perpetual despair. Consider how, even in the meanest sort of labor, the whole soul of man is composed into real harmony. He bends himself with free valor against his task; and doubt, desire, sorrow, remorse, indignation, despair itself, shrink murmuring far off into their caves. The glow of labor in him is a purifying fire, wherein all poison is burnt up; and of smoke itself there is made a bright and blessèd flame.

Blessed is he who has found his work; let him ask no other blessedness—he has a life purpose. Labor is life. From the heart of the worker rises the celestial force breathed into him by Almighty God, awakening him to all nobleness, to all knowledge. Hast thou valued patience, courage, openness to light or readiness to own thy mistakes? In wrestling with the dim brute powers of fact thou wilt continually learn. For every noble work the possibilities are diffused through immensity; undiscoverable, except to faith.

Man, son of heaven! is there not in thine inmost heart a spirit of active method, giving thee no rest till thou unfold it? Complain not. Look up, wearied brother. See thy fellow-workmen surviving through eternity, the sacred band of immortals!

THOMAS CARLYLE (see p. 47).

211.—THE VENGEANCE OF MUDARA.

To the chase goes Rodrigo, with hound and with hawk;
But what game he desires is revealed in his talk:
"Oh, in vain have I slaughtered the infants of Lara;
There's an heir in his hall, there's the stripling Mudara;
There's the son of the renegade—spawn of Mahoun;
If I meet with Mudara, my spear brings him down."

While Rodrigo rides on in the heat of his wrath,
A stripling armed cap-a-pie crosses his path:
"Good-morrow, young esquire." "Good-morrow, old knight."
"Will you ride with our party, and share our delight?"
"Speak your name, courteous stranger," the young man
          replied—
"Speak your name and your lineage, ere with you I ride."

"My name is Rodrigo," thus answered the knight;
"Of the line of old Lara, though barred from my right;
For the kinsman of Salas proclaims for the heir
Of our ancestor's castles and forestries fair,
A bastard, a renegade's offspring—Mudara—
Whom I'll send, if I can, to the infants of Lara."

"I behold thee, disgrace to thy lineage, with joy
I behold thee, thou murderer!" answered the boy;
"The bastard you curse, you behold him in me;
But his brothers' avenger that bastard shall be:
Draw! for I am the renegade's offspring—Mudara—
We shall see who inherits the life-blood of Lara!"

"I am armed for the forest chase, not for the fight;
Let me go for my shield and my sword," cries the knight.
"Now the mercy you dealt to my brothers of old,—
Be the hope of that mercy the comfort you hold!
Die, foeman to Sancha—die, traitor to Lara!"
As he spake, there was blood on the spear of Mudara.

                    JOHN GIBSON LOCKHART, 1794–1854.

212.—UNITY OF OUR COUNTRY.

Our country, with all its sectional diversity of views and feelings, is one. It is one in the rich, manly, vigorous, expressive language we speak, which is become the vernacular tongue, as it were, of parliamentary eloquence—the very oldest of constitutional freedom. It is one in the fame of our fathers, and in the historical reminiscences which belong to us as a nation. It is one in the political principles of republicanism; one in the substantial basis of our manners; one in the ties of friendship, affinity and blood, binding us together, throughout the whole extent of the land, in the associations of trade, of emigration and of marriage; one in that glorious constitution, the best inheritance transmitted to us by our fathers, the monument of their wisdom and their virtue, under whose shelter we live and flourish as a people.

To this great republic, union is peace, union is grandeur, union is power, union is honor, union is everything which a free-spirited and mighty nation should glory to possess. To us all, next to independence, next to liberty, next to honor, be we persuaded that a cordial and abiding confederacy of the American people is the greatest of earthly goods.

Here, in the eyes of our countrymen and of the world, with the Muse of History before us to record our deeds and our words, let us, like Hannibal at the altar of his gods, swear eternal faithfulness to our country, eternal hatred to its foes! Show we that we are wedded to the Union for weal or for woe, as the fondest lover would hug to his heart the bride bound to him in the first bright ardor of young possession. We have not purposed to embark in this venture only to sail on the smooth surface of a summer sea, with hope and pleasure to waft us joyously along, but with resolved spirits, ready to meet, like true men, whatever of danger may descend upon our voyage, and to stand up gallantly for the treasure of honor and faith intrusted to our charge.

Rally we, then, to the stripes and stars as the symbol of glory to us, and the harbinger of liberty to all the nations of the world! So long as a shred of that sacred standard remains to us, let us cling to it with such undying devotion as the Christian pilgrims of the Middle Age cherished for the last fragment of the Cross. Let us fly to its rescue when periled, whether by foreign or domestic assault, as they did to snatch the Holy Sepulchre from the desecration of the infidel!

CALEB CUSHING.

213.—THE GLOVE AND THE LIONS.

KING FRANCIS was a hearty king, and loved a royal sport,
And one day, as his lions strove, sat looking on the court;
The nobles filled the benches round, the ladies by their side,
And 'mongst them Count de Lorge, with one he hoped to make
    his bride;
And truly 'twas a gallant thing to see that crowning show,
Valor and love and a king above, and the royal beasts below.

Ramped and roared the lions, with horrid laughing jaws;
They bit, they glared, gave blows like beams, a wind went with
    their paws;
With wallowing might and stifled roar they rolled one on another,
Till all the pit, with sand and mane, was in a thund'rous smother;
The bloody foam above the bars came whizzing through the air;
Said Francis then, "Good gentlemen, we're better here than there!"

De Lorge's love o'erheard the king, a beauteous lively dame,
With smiling lips, and sharp bright eyes, which always seemed the
    same:
She thought, "The count, my lover, is as brave as brave can be;
He surely would do desperate things to show his love of me!
King, ladies, lovers, all look on; the chance is wondrous fine!
I'll drop my glove to prove his love; great glory will be mine!"

She dropped her glove to prove his love: then looked on him and
    smiled;
He bowed, and in a moment leaped among the lions wild!
The leap was quick; return was quick; he soon regained his place;
Then threw the glove, but not with love, right in the lady's face!
"Well done!" cried Francis, "bravely done!" and he rose from
    where he sat:
"No love," quoth he, "but vanity sets love a task like that!"

LEIGH HUNT, 1784–1859.

214.—OUR COMMON SCHOOLS.

SIR, it is our common schools which give the keys of knowledge tc the mass of the people. Our common schools are important in the same way as the common air, the common sunshine, the common rain, invaluable for their commonness. They are the corner-stone of that municipal organization which is the characteristic feature of our social system; they are the fountain of that widespread intelligence which, like a moral life, pervades the country.

EDWARD EVERETT.

From the humblest village school there may go forth a teacher who, like Newton, shall bind his temples with the stars of Orion's belt; with Herschel, light up his cell with the beams of before undiscovered planets; with Franklin, grasp the lightning. Columbus, fortified with a few sound geographical principles, was, on the deck of his crazy caravel, more truly the monarch of Castile and Aragon than Ferdinand and Isabella, enthroned beneath the golden vaults of the conquered Alhambra. And Robinson, with the simple training of a rural pastor in England, when he knelt on the shore of Delft Haven, and sent his little flock upon their gospel errantry beyond the world of waters, exercised an influence over the destinies of the civilized world which will last to the end of time.

35

Sir, it is a solemn, a tender and sacred duty, that of education. What, sir, feed a child's body, and let his soul hunger! pamper his limbs, and starve his faculties! Plant the earth, cover a thousand hills with your droves of cattle, pursue the fish to their hiding-places in the sea and spread out your wheat-fields across the plain, in order to supply the wants of that body which will soon be as cold and as senseless as the poorest clod, and let the pure spiritual essence within you, with all its glorious capacities for improvement, languish and pine!

What! build factories, turn in rivers upon the water-wheels, unchain the imprisoned spirits of steam to weave a garment for the body, and let the soul remain unadorned and naked! What! send out your vessels to the farthest ocean, and make battle with the monsters of the deep, in order to obtain the means of lighting up your dwellings and work-shops, and prolonging the hours of labor for the meat that perisheth, and permit that vital spark which God has kindled, which he has entrusted to our care, to be fanned into a bright and heavenly flame—permit it, I say, to languish and go out!

What considerate man can enter a school, and not reflect with awe that it is a seminary where immortal minds are training for eternity? What parent but is, at times, weighed down with the thought that *there* must be laid the foundations of a building which will stand when not merely temple and palace, but the perpetual hills and adamantine rocks on which they rest, have melted away; that a light may *there* be kindled which will shine not merely when every artificial beam is extinguished, but when the affrighted sun has fled away from the heavens! I can add nothing, sir, to this consideration. I will only say, in conclusion, *Education*, when we feed that lamp, we perform the highest social duty! If we quench it, I know not where—humanly speaking—for time or for eternity,—

"I know not where is that Promethean heat
That can its light relume!"

EDWARD EVERETT (see p. 351).

215.—FAITH.

YE who think the truth ye sow
Lost beneath the winter snow,
Doubt not, Time's unerring law
Yet shall bring the genial thaw.
　　God in nature ye can trust :
　　Is the God of mind less just ?

Read we not the mighty thought
Once by ancient sages taught ?
Though it withered in the blight
Of the mediæval night,
　　Now the harvest we behold ;
　　See ! it bears a thousand fold.

Workers on the barren soil,
Yours may seem a thankless toil ;
Sick at heart with hope deferred,
Listen to the cheering word :
　　Now the faithful sower grieves ;
　　Soon he'll bind his golden sheaves.

If great Wisdom have decreed
Man may labor, yet the seed
Never in this life shall grow,
Shall the sower cease to sow ?
　　The fairest fruit may yet be born
　　On the resurrection morn !

216.—THE SENSITIVE AUTHOR.

CHARACTERS.—*Dangle, Sneer, Sir Fretful Plagiary.*

Dan. Ah, my dear friend ! We were just speaking of your tragedy. Admirable, Sir Fretful, admirable !

Sneer. You never did anything beyond it, Sir Fretful— never in your life.

Sir F. Sincerely, then, you do like the piece ?

Sneer. Wonderfully !

Sir F. But come, now, there must be something that you think might be mended, hey ?   Mr. Dangle, has nothing struck you ?

Dan. Why, faith, it is but an ungracious thing, for the most part, to—

Sir F. With most authors it is just so indeed; they are in general strangely tenacious!   But, for my part, I am never so well pleased as when a judicious critic points out any defect in me; for what is the purpose of showing a work to a friend if you don't mean to profit by his opinion?

Sneer. Very true.   Why, then, though I seriously admire the piece upon the whole, yet there is one small objection, which, if you'll give me leave, I'll mention.

Sir F. Sir, you can't oblige me more.

Sneer. I think it wants incident.

Sir F. You surprise me!—wants incident?

Sneer. Yes; I own I think the incidents are too few.

Sir F. Believe me, Mr. Sneer, there is no person for whose judgment I have a more implicit deference.   But I protest to you, Mr. Sneer, I am only apprehensive that the incidents are too crowded.   My dear Dangle, how does it strike you?

Dan. Really, I can't agree with my friend Sneer.   I think the plot quite sufficient, and the first four acts by many degrees the best I ever read or saw in my life.   If I might venture to suggest anything, it is that the interest rather falls off in the fifth.

Sir F. Rises, I believe you mean, sir?

Dan. No; I don't, upon my word.

Sir F. Yes, yes, you do, upon my word—it certainly don't fall off, I assure you.   No, no, it don't fall off.

Dan. Well, Sir Fretful, I wish you may be able to get rid as easily of the newspaper criticisms as you do of ours.

Sir F. The newspapers!   Sir, they are the most villainous, licentious, abominable, infernal—   Not that I ever read them!   No! I make it a rule never to look into a newspaper.

Dan. You are quite right, for it certainly must hurt an author of delicate feelings to see the liberties they take.

Sir F. No! quite the contrary; their abuse is, in fact, the best panegyric; I like it of all things. An author's reputation is only in danger from their support.

Sneer. Why, that's true; and that attack now on you the other day—

Sir F. What? where?

Dan. Ay, you mean in a paper of Thursday; it was completely ill-natured, to be sure.

Sir F. Oh, so much the better! Ha! ha! ha! I wouldn't have it otherwise.

Dan. Certainly, it's only to be laughed at; for—

Sir F. You don't happen to recollect what the fellow said, do you?

Sneer. Pray, Dangle—Sir Fretful seems a little anxious—

Sir F. Oh, no! anxious—not I, not the least. I— But one may as well hear, you know.

Dan. Sneer, do you recollect? [*Aside to Sneer.*] Make out something.

Sneer. [*Aside to Dangle.*] I will. [*Aloud.*] Yes, sir, I remember perfectly.

Sir F. Well, and pray now—not that it signifies—what might the gentleman say?

Sneer. Why, he roundly asserts that you have not the slightest invention or original genius whatever, though you are the greatest traducer of all other authors living.

Sir F. Ha! ha! ha! Very good!

Sneer. That as to comedy you have not one idea of your own, he believes, even in your commonplace book, where stray jokes and pilfered witticisms are kept with as much method as the ledger of the Lost and Stolen Office.

Sir F. Ha! ha! ha! Very pleasant!

Sneer. Nay, that you are so unlucky as not to have the skill even to steal with taste, but that you glean from the refuse of obscure volumes, where more judicious plagiarists have been before you; so that the body of your work is a composition of dregs and sediments—like a bad tavern's worst wine.

Sir F. Ha! ha!

Sneer. In your more serious efforts, he says your bombast would be less intolerable if the thoughts were ever suited to the expression; but the homeliness of the sentiment stares through the fantastic incumbrance of its fine language like a clown in one of the new uniforms!

Sir F. Ha! ha!

Sneer. That your occasional tropes and flowers suit the general coarseness of your style as tambour sprigs would a ground of linsey-wolsey; while your imitations of Shakspeare resemble the mimicry of Falstaff's page, and are about as near the standard of the original.

Sir F. Ha!

Sneer. In short, that even the finest passages you steal are of no service to you; for the poverty of your own language prevents their assimilating, so that they lie on the surface like lumps of marl on a barren moor, encumbering what it is not in their power to fertilize.

Sir F. [*After great agitation.*] Now, another person would be vexed at this.

Sneer. Oh! but I wouldn't have told you, only to divert you.

Sir F. I know it—I am diverted. Ha! ha! ha!—not the least invention! Ha! ha! ha! very good! very good!

Sneer. Yes—no genius! Ha! ha! ha!

Dan. A severe rogue! ha! ha! ha! But you are quite right, Sir Fretful, never to read such nonsense. You are quite right.

Sir F. To be sure; for if there is anything to one's praise it is a foolish vanity to be gratified at it, and if it is abuse, why, one is always sure to hear of it from one good-natured friend or another!

R. B. SHERIDAN (see p. 319).

217.—FATHERLAND SONG.

IRON God gave us, so that man
should never be a slave ;
Therefore the sabre, sword and
spear to man's right hand He
gave.
Therefore He gave him fiery mood,
fierce speech and free-born
breath,
That he might fearlessly the feud
maintain through blood and
death.

And now God's gracious gift alway
we'll faithfully retain,
And never a fellow-creature slay a
tyrant's pay to gain !
By stroke of brand the wretch shall
fall who fighteth for sin and
shame,
And never inherit the German land
with the men of German name.

O Germany ! bright fatherland !   O German love so true !
Thou sacred land, thou beauteous land, we swear to thee anew !
Outlawed, each knave and coward shall the crow and raven feed,
But we will to the battle all, to serve our country's need.

Flash forth, flash forth, whatever can, to bright and flaming life !
Now, all ye Germans, man for man, forth to the holy strife !
Your hands lift upward to the sky, let every heart upsoar,
And, man for man, let each one cry, Our slavery is o'er !

Let sound, let sound, whatever can—trumpet, and fife, and drum :
This day our sabres, man for man, to stain with use we come ;
Hangman and tyrant to repel !   Oh, glorious day of ire,
That to all Germans soundeth good—day of our great desire !

Let wave, let wave, whatever can—banner and ensign wave !
Here do we purpose, man for man, to court a hero's grave.
Advance, ye brave ranks, hardily, your colors wave on high !
We'll gain us freedom's victory, or freedom's death we'll die.

From the German of E. M. ARNDT, 1769–1859.

218.—THE VOCATION OF THE SCHOOLMASTER.

SIR, there is nothing which the adversaries of improvement are more wont to make themselves merry with than what is termed the "*march of intellect;*" and here I will confess that I think, as far as the phrase goes, they are in the right. It is a very absurd, because a very incorrect, expression. It is little calculated to describe the operation in question. It does not picture an image at all resembling the proceeding of the true friends of mankind. It much more resembles the progress of the enemy to all improvement. The *conqueror* moves in a *march*. He stalks onward with the "pride, pomp and circumstance of war;" banners flying, shouts rending the air, guns thundering, and martial music pealing to drown the shrieks of the wounded and the lamentations for the slain.

Not thus the schoolmaster in his peaceful vocation. He meditates and purposes in secret the plans which are to bless mankind; he slowly gathers round him those who are to further their execution; he quietly though firmly advances in his humble path, laboring steadily but calmly, till he has opened to the light all the recesses of ignorance, and torn up by the roots all the weeds of vice. His is a progress not to be compared with anything like a *march*, but it leads to a far more brilliant triumph and to laurels more imperishable than the destroyer of his species, the scourge of the world, ever won.

Such men—men deserving the glorious title of Teachers of Mankind—I have found laboring conscientiously, though, perhaps, obscurely, in their blessed vocation, wherever I have gone. I have found them, and shared their fellowship, among the daring, the ambitious, the ardent, the indomitably active French; I have found them among the persevering, resolute, industrious Swiss; I have found them among the laborious, the warm-hearted, the enthusiastic Germans; I have found them among the high-minded but enslaved Italians; and in our own country, God be thanked, their numbers everywhere abound, and are every day increasing.

Their calling is high and holy; their fame is the property
of nations; their renown will fill the earth in after ages, in
proportion as it sounds not far off in their own times. Each
one of these great teachers of the world, possessing his soul in
peace, performs his appointed course, awaits in patience the
fulfillment of the promises, and resting from his labors, be-
queaths his memory to the generation whom his works have
blessed, and sleeps under the humble but not unglorious epi-
taph, commemorating " one in whom mankind lost a friend,
and no man got rid of an enemy."

LORD BROUGHAM (see p. 297).

219.—RANK AND WEALTH.

Is there, for honest poverty, that hangs his head, and a' that?*
The coward slave, we pass him by, we dare be poor for a' that!
For a' that, and a' that, our toil's obscure, and a' that,
The rank is but the guinea's stamp, the man's the gowd for a' that.

What though on hamely fare we dine, wear hoddin gray, and a'
    that?
Gie fools their silks, and knaves their wine, a man's a man for a'
    that!
For a' that, and a' that, their tinsel show, and a' that,
The honest man, though e'er sae poor, is king o' men for a' that!

Ye see yon birkie, ca'd a lord, who struts, and stares, and a' that;
Though hundreds worship at his word, he's but a coof for a' that!
For a' that, and a' that, his riband, star, and a' that,
The man o' independent mind, he looks and laughs at a' that!

A king can mak' a belted knight, a marquis, duke, and a' that;
But an honest man's aboon his might, guid faith he mauna fa' that!
For a' that, and a' that, their dignities and a' that,
The pith o' sense and pride o' worth are higher ranks than a' that!

Then let us pray that come it may, as come it will, for a' that,
That sense and worth, o'er a' the earth, may bear the gree, and a' that!
For a' that, and a' that, it's comin' yet, for a' that!
That man to man, the world o'er, shall brothers be for a' that!

ROBERT BURNS, 1758–1796.

* " Is there for honest poverty," etc., is an elliptical expression for " Is
there any one that hangs his head for honest poverty ?"

2 B

220.—ON BEING CALLED AN ARISTOCRAT.

You have called me an aristocrat. Listen to my reply. My only aristocracy is the superiority which industry, frugality, perseverance and intelligence will always assure to every man in a free state of society. I belong only to those privileged classes to which you may all belong in your turn. The privileges are not created *for* us, but created *by* us. Our wealth is our own; we have made it. Our ease is our own; we have gained it by the sweat of our brows, or by the labor of our minds.

Our position in society is not conferred upon us, but purchased by ourselves—with our own intellect, application, zeal, patience and industry. If you remain inferior to us, it is because you have not the intellect or the industry, the zeal or the sobriety, the patience or the application, necessary to your advancement. This is not our fault, but your own.

You wish to become rich, as some men do to become wise; but there is no royal road to wealth any more than there is to knowledge. You sigh for the ease and repose of wealth, but you are not willing to do that which is necessary to procure them. The husbandman who will not till his ground shall reap nothing but thistles and briers.

You think that there must be something wrong in human society if you do not become wealthy and powerful; but what right have you to expect—you idlers and drones in the hive— you shall always be fed on the honey and sweets of life? What right have you, who do nothing for yourselves, your families, your country or your kind, to imagine that you will be selected for public favor, confidence and reward?

I am not an aristocrat in that sense of the term in which it may be applied in absolute governments, or under imperial rule; but if by an aristocrat you mean a man who has earned his promotion by his labor, his honors by his toils, and his wealth by his industry, oh, then indeed I am an aristocrat; and, please God, I will always remain so.

The distinctions in human society displease you, because you have not the talent or the industry to amend your own position. You are too idle to labor, and too proud to beg; but I will endeavor to take care that you shall not rob me. I throw back, then, with indignation and resentment, the charge which is made. I belong to the middling classes of society. I have been selected by my fellow-citizens as one of their representatives; and, by the blessing of Heaven, I *will* represent them.

CASIMIR PERIER.

221.—PATRIA VICTRIX.

NOT in anger, not in pride,
The strain should close that consecrates our brave.
 Lift the heart and lift the head!
Lofty be its mood and grave.
 Boom, cannon, boom to all the winds and waves!
Clash out, glad bells, from every rocking steeple!
 Banners, advance with triumph, bend your staves!
 And from every mountain peak
 Let beacon-fire to answering beacon speak,
 Katahdin tell Monadnock, Whiteface he,
 And so leap on in light from sea to sea,
 Till the glad news be sent
 Across a kindling continent,
 Making earth feel more firm and air breathe braver;
" Be proud! for she is saved, and all have helped to save
  her!
 She that lifts up the manhood of the poor,
 She of the open soul and open door,
With room about her hearth for all mankind!
 The fire is dreadful in her eyes no more;
From her bold front the helm she doth unbind,
 Sends all her handmaid armies back to spin,
And bids her navies, that so lately hurled
 Their crashing battle, hold their thunders in,
Swimming like birds of calm along the unharmful shore.
No challenge sends she to the elder world,

That looked askance and hated; a light scorn
Plays o'er her mouth, as round her mighty knees
   She calls her children back, and waits the morn
Of nobler day, enthroned between her subject seas."

Bow down, dear land, for thou hast found release!
   Thy God, in these distempered days,
   Hath taught thee the sure wisdom of his ways,
And through thy enemies hath wrought thy peace!
   Bow down in prayer and praise!
  No poorest in thy borders but may now
  Lift to the juster skies a man's enfranchised brow.
O Beautiful! my country! ours once more!
Smoothing thy gold of war-disheveled hair
  O'er such sweet brows as never others wore,
   And letting thy set lips,
   Freed from wrath's pale eclipse,
The rosy edges of their smile lay bare,
  What word divine of lover or of poet
  Could tell our love and make thee know it,
Among the nations bright beyond compare?
  What were our lives without thee?
  What all our lives to save thee?
  We reck not what we gave thee;
  We will not dare to doubt thee,
But ask whatever else, and we will dare!

                   JAMES RUSSELL LOWELL.

222.—CORONACH.

HE is gone to the mountain, he is lost to the forest,
Like a summer-dried fountain, when our need was the sorest;
The fount, reappearing, from the rain-drops shall borrow,
But to us comes no cheering, to Duncan no morrow!
The hand of the reaper takes the ears that are hoary,
But the voice of the weeper wails manhood in glory;

The autumn winds rushing waft the leaves that are serest,
But our flower was in flushing when blighting was nearest.
Fleet foot on the correi, sage counsel in cumber,*
Red hand in the foray, how sound is thy slumber!—
Like the dew on the mountain, like the foam on the river,
Like the bubble on the fountain, thou art gone, and for ever!

SIR WALTER SCOTT.

BRET HARTE.

223.—CALDWELL OF SPRINGFIELD.

HERE'S the spot. Look around you. Above, on the height,
Lay the Hessians encamped. By that church on the right
Stood the gaunt Jersey farmers. And here ran a wall—
You may dig anywhere and you'll turn up a ball.
Nothing more. Grasses spring, waters run, flowers blow,
Pretty much as they did ninety-three years ago.

---

* A *coronach* is a wild expression of lamentation among the Scotch
Highlanders. The *correi* is the hollow side of the hill where game usu-
ally lies. By *cumber* the poet means *perplexity, distress.*

Nothing more, did I say?   Stay, one moment; you've heard
Of Caldwell, the parson, who once preached the word
Down at Springfield?   What! no?   Come—that's bad; why
    he had
All the Jerseys aflame!   And they gave him the name
Of the "rebel high priest."   He stuck in their gorge,
For he loved the Lord God, and he hated King George!

He had cause, you might say!   When the Hessians that day
Marched up with Knyphausen, they stopped on their way
At the "Farms," where his wife, with a child in her arms,
Sat alone in the house.   How it happened, none knew
But God, and that one of the hireling crew
Who fired the shot.   Enough! there she lay,
And Caldwell, the chaplain, her husband, away!

Did he preach—did he pray?   Think of him, as you stand
By the old church, to-day ; think of him, and that band
Of militant plowboys!   See the smoke and the heat
Of that reckless advance—of that straggling retreat!
Keep the ghost of that wife, foully slain, in your view—
And what could you, what should you, what would you do?

Why, just what he did!   They were left in the lurch
For the want of more wadding.   He ran to the church,
Broke the door, stripped the pews, and dashed out in the road
With his arms full of hymn-books, and threw down his load
At their feet!   Then, above all the shouting and shots,
Rang his voice—"Put Watts into 'em, boys! give 'em Watts!"

And they did.   That is all.   Grasses spring, flowers blow,
Pretty much as they did ninety-three years ago.
You may dig anywhere and you'll turn up a ball,
But not always a hero like this—and that's all.

                          BRET HARTE.

224.—THE INDEPENDENT VOTERS.

Samuel Weller. Election day, this, sir. Great doings down at the Town Arms.

Mr. Pickwick. All alive, I suppose, eh, Sam?

Sam. Reg'lar game, sir. Our people's a-collectin' and hollerin' themselves hoarse already. Some are roarin' out "Slunkey for ever!" Then comes the cry, "Firkin for ever! Firkin's the man!" Then another roarin', like that of a whole menagerie when the elephant has rung the bell for the cold meat.

Mr. P. Ah! Each man seems devoted to his party, eh, Sam?

Sam. Never see such devotion in my life, sir.

Mr. P. Energetic, eh?

Sam. Uncommon. I never see men eat and drink so much afore. I wonder they a'n't afeerd o' bustin'.

Mr. P. That's the mistaken kindness of the gentry here.

Sam. Werry likely.

Mr. P. Fine, fresh, hearty fellows they seem.

Sam. Werry fresh; me and the two waiters at the Peacock has been a-pumpin' over the independent woters as supped there last night.

Mr. P. Pumping over independent voters! What do you mean, Sam?

Sam. I mean that every man slept where he fell down; we dragged 'em out one by one this mornin' and put 'em under the pump, and they're in reg'lar fine order now. Shillin' a head the committee paid for that 'ere job.

Mr. P. Can such things be? *Can* such things be?

Sam. Lord bless your heart, sir, why, where were you half baptized? That's nothin'—that ain't.

Mr. P. Nothing! To treat independent voters in that fashion is nothing!

Sam. Nothin' at all, sir. Why, the night afore the last day of the last election here, the opposite party bribed the bar-maid at the Town Arms to hocus the brandy and water of fourteen unpolled electors as was a-stoppin' in the house.

Mr. P. What do you mean by *hocusing* brandy and water?

Sam. Puttin' laudanum in it, sir. Bless'd if she didn't send 'em all to sleep till twelve hours arter the election was over. They took one man up to the booth in a truck, fast asleep, by way of experiment, but it was no go—the judges wouldn't take his vote; so he was brought back and put to bed again.

Mr. P. Strange practices, these! Strange indeed in a civilized, enlightened country!

Sam. Not half so strange, sir, as a miraculous circumstance as happened to my own father at an election time in this werry place, sir.

Mr. P. What was that, Sam?

Sam. Why, sir, he drove a coach down here once. 'Lection time came on, and he was engaged by our party to bring down woters from London. Night afore he was going to drive up, committee on t'other side send for him quietly, and away he goes with the messenger, who shows him in. Large room—lots of gen'l'm'n—heaps of papers, pens and ink, and all that 'ere. "Ah, Mr. Weller," says the gen'l'm'n in the chair, "glad to see you, sir; how are you?" "Werry well, thank'ee, sir," says my father; "I hope *you're* pretty middlin'," says he. "Pretty well, thank'ee, sir," says the gen'l'm'n; "sit down, Mr. Weller."

Mr. P. Well, what did they want of him, Sam? No bribery, no corruption, I hope?

Sam. My father sits down, and he and the gen'l'm'n looks werry hard at each other. "You don't remember me?" says the gen'l'm'n. "Can't say I do," says my father. "Oh, I know *you*," says the gen'l'm'n; "know'd you ven you was a boy," says he. "Well, I don't remember you," says my father. "That's werry odd," says the gen'l'm'n. "Werry," says my father. "You must have a bad memory, Mr. Weller," says the gen'l'm'n. "Well, it *is* a werry bad 'un," says my father. "I thought so," says the gen'l'm'n.

Mr. P. Come to the point, Sam. What was his drift?

Sam. Then they pours him out a glass o' wine, and gammons him about his drivin', and gets him into a reg'lar good humor, and at last shoves a twenty-pound note into his hand.

Mr. P. A twenty-pound note! What for?

Sam. "It's a werry bad road between this and London," says the gen'l'm'n. "Here and there it is a *werry* heavy road," says my father. "Specially near the canal, I think," says the gen'l'm'n. "Nasty bit, that 'ere," says my father. "Well, Mr. Weller," says the gen'l'm'n, "you're a werry good whip, and can do what you like with your horses, we know. We're all werry fond of you, Mr. Weller; so in case you *should* have a haccident when you're a bringin' these here woters down, and *should* tip 'em over into the canal without hurtin' em, this is for yourself," says he.

Mr. P. But, Sam, Sam, that looks like a direct attempt to bribe your father to upset the coach. Did he denounce them?

Sam. "Gen'l'm'n, you're werry kind," says my father; "and I'll drink your health in another glass of wine," says he; vich he did, and then buttons up the money, and bows himself out.

Mr. P. Well, Sam, what came of it?

Sam. You wouldn't believe, sir, that on the werry day as he came down with them woters his coach *was* upset on that 'ere werry spot, and ev'ry man on 'em was turned into the canal.

Mr. P. But they got out again, Sam? They all got out again, safe and sound, eh?

Sam. Why, sir, I rather think that one old gen'l'm'n was missin'. I know his hat was found, but I ain't quite certain whether his head was in it or not.

Mr. P. Is it possible?

Sam. But what I look at, sir, is the hextraordinary and wonderful coincidence that arter what that gen'l'm'n said my father's coach *should* be upset, and upset in that werry place, and on that werry day!

Mr. P. Yes, the coincidence was extraordinary, very, seeing it was all an accident, Sam.

Sam. Ay, sir, as you say—seeing 'twas all a haccident!

Dramatized from CHARLES DICKENS.

36*

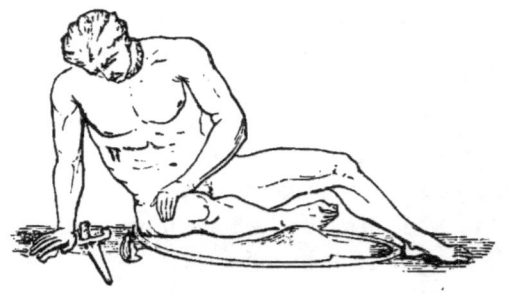

225.—THE GLADIATOR.

I SEE before me the gladiator lie:
　　He leans upon his hand; his manly brow
Consents to death, but conquers agony;
　　And his drooped head sinks gradually low;
　　And through his side the last drops, ebbing slow
From the red gash, fall heavy, one by one,
　　Like the first of a thunder-shower; and now
The arena swims around him—he is gone,
Ere ceased the inhuman shout which hailed the wretch
　　　　who won.

He heard it, but he heeded not; his eyes
　　Were with his heart, and that was far away;
He recked not of the life he lost, nor prize,
　　But where his rude hut by the Danube lay,
　　There were his young barbarians all at play,
There was their Dacian mother—he, their sire,
　　Butchered to make a Roman holiday!
All this rushed with his blood. Shall he expire,
And unavenged? Arise! ye Goths, and glut your ire!
　　　　　　　　LORD BYRON (see p. 176).

226.—THE QUALITY OF MERCY.

THE quality of mercy is not strained;
It droppeth as the gentle rain from heaven
Upon the place beneath.   It is twice blessed:
It blesseth him that gives and him that takes.
'Tis mightiest in the mightiest; it becomes
The thronëd monarch better than his crown.
His scepter shows the force of temporal power,
The attribute to awe and majesty,
Wherein doth sit the dread and fear of kings:
But mercy is above his sceptered sway,
It is enthronëd in the *hearts* of kings,
It is an attribute to God himself;
And earthly power doth then show likest God's
When mercy seasons justice.

SHAKSPEARE.

227.—THE SWISS AT FRASTENZ.

WHERE the swift Reuss foams and dashes through Uri's rocky glen,
Bearing aloft a banner, behold a crowd of men;
A black ox on a field of gold—lo! Uri's arms appear!
No yoke has ever pressed the neck of that unbroken steer.

There's a wooden house in the valley, on a little plot of green,
Where carved about the cornice in a rude scroll is seen,—
"I'm a free-born son of Switzerland, and Harry Wohlleb * hight,
This little house and its tenant stand only in God's might."

Before the threshold sits a man of venerable years,
Like a stripped field in autumn his hoary head appears;
A blooming little daughter sits smiling by his side,
As a rosebud decks a ruin with its beauty and its pride.

The earnest crowd approaching, the leader steps before,
And proffers the patriot standard to the veteran at the door:
The old man takes the banner, and he holds the strong shaft high,
While words in wingëd cadence from his lips like eagles fly;

* Pronounced *vole'eb*.

"Oh, keep, good Lord, thy people and thy servant in thy sight,
Who boldly raise their weapons for freedom and the right;
If thou will'st it, then as firmly as a tower upon a rock
This arm shall bear the standard thro' the battle's stormy shock.

"Out now, out of thy scabbard! be true to me, my brand—
True as the good scythe proves itself in the skillful reaper's hand;
Twice only thine appointed days of labor thou hast mown,
Yet as Morat and Grandson the well-reaped fields are known!

"Holy banner, float for ever round the forehead of the free!
And from our flashing glaciers wave in sign of Victory!
Oh, awake in all our valleys—Freedom, heavenly maid, arise,
Thou hast made thy couch already where the Alps blend with the
      skies!"

So speaks the white-hair'd Wohlleb; his heart feels youthful now,
And the flutter of the banner cools the fever of his brow;
Thereon how sweetly bloweth the gentle evening air!
Or does Tell's shade approving lay his hand in blessing there?

On the field in front of Frastenz, drawn up in battle array,
Stretched spear on spear in a crescent, the German army lay;
Behind a wall of bucklers stood bosoms steeled with pride,
And a stiff wood of lances that all assaults defied.

Oh, why, ye men of Switzerland, from your Alpine summits sally,
And armed with clubs and axes descend into the valley?
"The wood just grown at Frastenz with our axes we would fell,
To build homesteads from its branches where Liberty may dwell."

The Swiss on the German lances rush with impetuous shock;
It is spear on spear in all quarters—they are dashed like waves from
      a rock.
His teeth then gnashed the Switzer, and the mocking German cried,
"See how the snout of the greyhound is pierced by the hedgehog's hide!"

Like a song of resurrection, then sounded from the ranks:
"Illustrious shade, Von Winkelried! to thee I render thanks.
Thou beckonest. I obey thee! Up, Swiss, and follow me!"
Thus the voice of Henry Wohlleb from the ranks rang loud and free.

From its shaft he tore the banner, and twined it round his breast,
And hot with the lust of death on the serried lances pressed;

His red eyes from their sockets like gleaming torches glare,
And in front, in place of the banner, wave the locks of his snow-white
    hair!

The spears of six knights together—in his hand he seizes all—
And thereon thrusts his bosom—there's a breach in the lances' wall.
With vengeance fired, the Switzers storm the battle's perilous ridge,
And the corpse of Henry Wohlleb to their vengeance is the bridge.

ANASTASIUS GRÜN (translated by JOHN O. SARGENT).

228.—OTHELLO'S FAREWELL.

OH, now for ever
Farewell the tranquil mind! farewell content!
Farewell the plumëd troop, and the big wars,
That make ambition virtue!   Oh, farewell!
Farewell the neighing steed, and the shrill trump,
The spirit-stirring drum, the ear-piercing fife,
The royal banner, and all quality,
Pride, pomp and circumstance, of glorious war!
And oh, ye mortal engines, whose rude throats
The immortal Jove's dread clamors counterfeit,
Farewell!   Othello's occupation's gone!

SHAKSPEARE.

229.—THE END OF THE PLAY.

THE play is done—the curtain drops,
    Slow falling to the prompter's bell;
A moment yet the actor stops,
    And looks around, to say farewell.
It is an irksome word and task;
    And when he's laughed and said his say
He shows, as he removes the mask,
    A face that's anything but gay.

One word ere yet the evening ends—
    Let's close it with a parting rhyme,
And pledge a hand to all young friends,
    As fits the merry Christmas-time;
On life's wide scene you, too, have parts
    That fate ere long shall bid you play;
Good night!—with honest gentle hearts
    A kindly greeting go alway!

Good night!—I'd say, the griefs, the joys,
    Just hinted in this mimic page,
The triumphs and defeats of boys,
    Are but repeated in our age;
I'd say your woes were not less keen,
    Your hopes more vain, than those of men—
Your pangs or pleasures of fifteen
    At forty-five played o'er again.

I'd say we suffer and we strive
    Not less, nor more, as men than boys—
With grizzled beards at forty-five
    As erst at twelve in corduroys;
And if, in time of sacred youth,
    We learned at home to love and pray,
Pray Heaven that early love and truth
    May never wholly pass away.

And in the world, as in the school,
    I'd say how fate may change and shift—
The prize be sometimes with the fool,
    The race not always to the swift;
The strong may yield, the good may fall,
    The great man be a vulgar clown,
The knave be lifted over all,
    The kind cast pitilessly down.

Who knows the inscrutable design?
    Blessed be He who took and gave!

Why should your mother, Charles, not mine,
    Be weeping at her darling's grave?
We bow to Heaven that willed it so,
    That darkly rules the fate of all,
That sends the respite or the blow,
    That's free to give or to recall.

This crowns his feast with wine and wit—
    Who brought him to that mirth and state?
His betters, see, below him sit,
    Or hunger hopeless at the gate;
Who bade the mud from Di'ves' wheel
    To spurn the rags of Lazarus?
Come, brother, in that dust we'll kneel,
    Confessing Heaven that ruled it thus.

So each shall mourn, in life's advance,
    Dear hopes, dear friends, untimely killed—
Shall grieve for many a forfeit chance,
    And longing passion unfulfilled;
Amen!—whatever fate be sent,
    Pray God the heart may kindly glow,
Although the head with cares be bent,
    And whitened with the winter snow.

Come wealth or want, come good or ill,
    Let young and old accept their part,
And bow before the awful will,
    And bear it with an honest heart;
Who misses, or who wins, the prize,
    Go, lose or conquer as you can;
But if you fail, or if you rise,
    Be each, pray God, a gentleman.

A gentleman, or old or young,
    (Bear kindly with my humble lays);
The sacred chorus first was sung
    Upon the first of Christmas days;

The shepherds heard it overhead—
  The joyful angels raised it then:
Glory to Heaven on high, it said,
  And peace on earth to gentle men.

My song, save this, is little worth;
  I lay the weary pen aside,
And wish you health, and love, and mirth,
  As fits the solemn Christmas tide;
As fits the holy Christmas birth,
  Be this, good friends, our carol still—
Be peace on earth, be peace on earth,
  To men of gentle will.

Wm. M. Thackeray (see p. 390).